Mary Owens Wyckoff spent close to five years researching, compiling, and writing *The World of Cooking*. She has a long-time interest in the culinary arts and is a food historian. She teaches cooking professionally and is also on the staff of Bergen Community College, Paramus, New Jersey on a part-time basis.

THE WORLD OF COOKING

Recipes, Techniques, & Secrets of the Kitchen

MARY OWENS WYCKOFF

A SPECTRUM BOOK

PRENTICE-HALL, INC., Englewood Cliffs, New Jersey 07632

Library of Congress Cataloging in Publication Data

Wyckoff, Mary Owens.
  The world of cooking.

  (The Creative Cooking Series/Spectrum Reference shelf) (A Spectrum Book)
  Includes index.
  1. Cookery. I. Title.
TX651.W93   641.5   78-5802
ISBN 0-13-967687-2
ISBN 0-13-967679-1(PBK)

Dedicated to my son and daughter
James Lee and Maura Anne

A SPECTRUM BOOK

Printed in the United States of America

10 9 8 7 6 5 4 3 2 1

PRENTICE-HALL INTERNATIONAL, INC., *London*
PRENTICE-HALL OF AUSTRALIA PTY. LIMITED, *Sydney*
PRENTICE-HALL OF CANADA, LTD., *Toronto*
PRENTICE-HALL OF INDIA PRIVATE LIMITED, *New Delhi*
PRENTICE-HALL OF JAPAN, INC., *Tokyo*
PRENTICE-HALL OF SOUTHEAST ASIA PTE. LTD., *Singapore*
WHITEHALL BOOKS LIMITED, *Wellington, New Zealand*

PREFACE

WHAT IT'S ALL ABOUT

The word *nutrition* stems from the Latin, *nutritus*, meaning to nurture or to suckle. Like the ancient symbol, the tree of life, the science of nutrition has roots that go deep, even into the shadowy time before the dawn of history. Extending from its trunk are many branches whose soundness and beauty are affected by how carefully the whole tree has been sustained. Thus the delight one experiences in eating a finely prepared dish ultimately depends on the satisfaction of *many requirements*. Not the least of these is successful cooking, both in terms of nutritional benefit and sheer eating pleasure. *The World of Cooking* attempts to deal with the various facets that comprise the nutritional tree by examining various categories of foods in a systematic way. Each chapter begins with a short historical sketch relating in some way to that particular food category. The next two sections deal with consumer purchasing and nutrition planning. These are followed by guidelines to preparing food for cooking, the theory behind cooking a specific food, and actual cooking procedures. Finally, each chapter closes with a wide variety of recipes from the fundamental to those for special as well as festive occasions. This last section also includes *basic formulas*,—key recipes whose application can lead to a more scientific approach to cooking.

Miscellaneous items such as storing, freezing, cooking tests, temperature readings, and charts have been covered under each category. Interspersed throughout are do's, don'ts, and helpful hints.

Emphasis has been placed on the overall quality of food and cooking rather than on any particular cuisine. American cuisine, with its abundant borrowings and adaptations, has come to embody most of the world's great cuisines. It enjoys a unique place in the history of food and cooking in terms of abundance, diversity, and technology. Furthermore, the cook who can boast a sound basis in theory, techniques, and practice will be able to tackle almost any recipe, however exotic it may seem, with considerable skill and aplomb, for vegetables will react to heat pretty much the same whether they are to be used in a Creole dish, a Chinese preparation, or an Irish stew. The same holds for meats and other categories.

The following is a synopsis of the material dealt with under the various sections of each chapter.

HISTORICAL BACKGROUND

Just as history can be traced through technological developments, cultural achievements, or political ideology, so too can it be viewed in terms of satisfying human needs for food and drink. Ancient peoples pretty much ate what was available in any given area, and, aside from the relatively simple methods used as a means of preservation, consumed their foods in an unadulterated state. Our patterns of eating and drinking in the Western hemisphere developed more or less within the past two or three centuries, largely as a by-product of economic developments that often masqueraded under the guise of good nutrition. Although a people's economic status has always in some measure determined their eating patterns, at no time has society had the technological expertise to bring about the far-reaching results we take for granted today. Certain of the history sections trace these developments and attempt to bring them into focus. Some of the social changes which came about with industrialization have been related through stories of the things and people most affected. The contributions of such renowned French chefs as Soyer and Charpentier and the reflections of America's great naturalist and philospher Henry David Thoreau (on his daily bread) come in for their share of attention. Certain of the background, happenings, and trivia have been included simply as points of interest.

All in all, the history sections are included as important links to a better understanding of the complex subject of how we nourish ourselves and how we got where we are, nutritionally speaking.

CONSUMER INFORMATION AND PURCHASING

Today's consumer is more or less left to his or her own devices. There are few shopkeepers with the time to point out the many pitfalls in buying meats or how to choose one head of lettuce over another. Top professional chefs are fully aware of the extent to which the quality of ingredients will figure in the completed dish. Before the days of reliable inspection and grading services, the chefs of the great hotels and restaurants considered the quality of their raw materials so crucial to success or failure that they trusted the selection to no one but themselves, even though this frequently meant arriving at the markets at the crack of dawn.

Why professionals avoid certain grades and cuts of meat generally referred to as "gravy cuts," what can be done about processed grains and grain foods, and what to look for in produce are typical of the material covered. Included is a description of how certain cheeses are made primarily to establish guidelines for the selection of all cheeses.

This section throws some light on the increasingly important areas of the grading, inspection, and classification of all food categories.

NUTRITION PLANNING

The purpose of this section is to help in the planning and selection of the various food groups. The nutritive value of each of the food categories is included in turn. The Appendix contains a list of foods that are important sources of nutrients. The cholesterol content of foods is found in a table at the end of Chapter 14, and a short chapter on meal planning precedes it.

Certain of the historical background sections also serve to place in somewhat broader perspective many of the foods that form an important part of the overall diet of Western man.

THE KITCHEN LABORATORY

A separate chapter has been included to cover the problems associated with food preservation and the maintenance of safe and sanitary conditions, as important in the home as in the professional kitchen.

PREPARATION

In many instances the preparation of foods is almost as important as the actual cooking. This step may not always be as challenging as certain other areas of cooking but it can make the difference between success and failure. It is to cooking what clean brushes and good light are to the artist.

COOKING THEORY

While some of the chemical changes that take place when certain foods are exposed to heat have been outlined (in order to give the reader a basis for making qualified judgments), in reality cooking theory involves many aspects. These are interspersed throughout the book in numerous specific instructions as well as in the basic formulas and recipes.

Two of the important concepts that have been covered are (1) the need for a gradual and even penetration of heat in the cooking of all foods and how this affects the success or failure of the different methods and procedures; and (2) the retention of a certain amount of heat upon removing a preparation from the source. The following is a sampling of other areas which have been covered—What happens if whole eggs are used instead of yolks or vice versa in certain preparations, what constituent in meat is more or less responsible for "browning" and how valuable or invaluable is the practice, and how does the nature of foods regulate the choice of a cooking method or procedure.

This area makes possible a more professional approach to cooking by a better understanding of the how's and why's.

BASIC FORMULAS

Many of the formulas the great chefs of the late nineteenth and early twentieth centuries relied on in the preparation of old and new creations were very often closely guarded. Nonetheless home cooks of a generation or two ago had access to many of them, possibly through word of mouth from one generation to the next, and this treasury of knowledge generally resulted in good instincts and a feeling for what they were doing.

Basic formulas are recipes that call for a limited range of ingredients and follow a few simple steps and procedures—in brief, how to make different kinds of bread, cakes, soups, sauces, and desserts following a basic formula. While they are the starting point from which any number of dishes can be created, they can also stand on their own.

Besides allowing for creativity and individual taste, they are particularly helpful to the busy person whose time in the kitchen has to be limited out of necessity, but who wishes to partake of first-hand fare.

PROCEDURES

Since no two food categories are exactly alike, each requires different cooking methods and procedures, temperatures, and cooking tests. However, there are certain criteria that are applicable to all. For instance, all tender cuts of meat can be roasted following the same steps, be it beef, pork, or lamb, although there will be differences in cooking temperatures and cooked temperature readings. Fish, on the other hand, owing to its nature, requires somewhat different procedures.

How to roast any cut of meat, poach any kind of fish, stir-fry, steam, or boil vegetables, all aspects of bread making, and how to use alcoholic beverages in cooking is a broad description of the topics covered under this section. In a sense, it is the "how to cook" section.

Precise instructions intended for both the experienced and inexperienced cook have been carefully outlined. Both Oriental and Western procedures have been included, with the latter predominating. There are 65 procedures in all.

RECIPES

All ingredients have been listed in order of use. Most recipes will serve six to eight and, for the most part, have been given self-explanatory titles, with the exception of the classic and more familiar ones. Temperature control and cooking tests have been specified.

CONVERTING RECIPES FOR QUANTITY COOKING To serve larger groups, multiply measurements (where specified) by the appropriate number in order to arrive at the required number of servings. For example,

$$\left. \text{Ingredients as listed (6 to 8 servings)} \right\} \begin{array}{l} \times\ 5 = 30 \text{ to } 40 \text{ servings} \\ \times\ 6 = 36 \text{ to } 48 \text{ servings} \\ \times\ 8 = 48 \text{ to } 64 \text{ servings} \end{array}$$

To serve 12 to 16, double recipes.

Particular care should be taken when adding unspecified amounts of seasonings, as the tendency when preparing larger quantities is to add more rather than less.

LIQUIDS For the most part, regular milk, skim milk, light or heavy cream may be used interchangeably. The consistency will not be affected to any great degree, but there will be a difference in flavor.

SEASONING Precise measurements for salt and pepper have not been given, as these can only be determined by personal taste. With few exceptions, both may be omitted entirely as their use is largely determined by conditioning.

SUGAR Because sugar is a flavoring or condiment and not an ingredient per se, minimum amounts have been stressed throughout, or a choice as to quantity has been specified. (In most preparations it can be eliminated entirely, or at least drastically reduced, without any discernible effects on consistency. The only difference would be in the degree of "sweet" flavoring, which is also a matter of conditioning.)

COOKING FATS Whenever butter or oil is listed, an equal quantity of any type of fat may be substituted—sesame, safflower, peanut, corn, or olive oil, or margarine. Combinations may also be used. Consideration should, however, be given to the flavor of the fat, as this will affect the taste of certain products, particularly baked goods. In pan-frying or sautéing a good rule of thumb is one teaspoon to one tablespoon each of butter and oil (olive, peanut, sesame)—according to nature and quantity of ingredients being fried. In any case a minimum amount should be used.

INGREDIENTS   Whenever possible, the use of fresh, wholesome ingredients is recommended from the point of good nutrition as well as taste and enjoyment.

COOKING EQUIPMENT

Since about the beginning of the First World War there has been a tremendous reduction in the number of trained persons available to assist in food preparation, and this has affected both the professional and the home manager. In large measure, the place of this personnel has been filled by a wide array of readily available cooking equipment. As there is an almost infinite variety on the market and a great deal depends on the type of cooking as well as the space and funds available, the choice has been left up to the reader. It is advisable, however, to purchase from a vendor who also services the professional and is in a position to give qualified advice.

As for metals, copper is the best diffuser of heat. Aluminum is a satisfactory cooking metal but certain foods discolor when exposed to it. Iron is slow to heat, but once heated retains the heat well; it is also porous and is less likely to burn. Stainless steel is nonporous and burns more readily but is easier to clean. Copper pots must be lined, preferably with tin, but stainless steel, which is not as satisfactory, is used occasionally. Thin metals heat quickly and must be watched carefully. Thicker metals result in more even cooking. Tin, which is sometimes coated to prevent rust from forming, makes an excellent baking metal.

CHEMISTRY IN THE KITCHEN

Upon entering the laboratory the scientist has committed certain formulas to memory and has some understanding of the properties of the raw material to be put to the test, as well as having proven and well-documented data readily available. Top professional chefs come similarly equipped. They have at their fingertips a general knowledge of foods and cooking theory plus a stock of basic formulas and procedures that work when exposing foods to heat. These comprise a veritable storehouse from which any number of preparations and creations can be turned out. They also make for a high degree of foolproof cooking.

Auguste Escoffier and the six of his colleagues who were responsible for the compilation of *The Guide Culinaire*, all took a keen interest in knowing what they were doing and why. The brilliant Escoffier devoted 75 of the 89 years of his life to cooking, working as many as 18 hours a day. While he and the other chefs of his time had an almost unlimited retinue of garçons and cooks at their disposal, they lacked temperature-controlled heat, grading and inspection services, as well as modern day refrigeration and transport. Such advice as ". . . book-rules can only be understood when the light of practical knowledge is focussed upon them" was included in *The Guide* and referred specifically to roasting meats properly, and to determining whether a cut was from a mature or immature animal, whether it was tender or tough, fresh or over-aged. In Escoffier's day, experience alone would provide the answers. Today graded meats, thermostatically controlled heat, and an accurate thermometer go a long way toward making this operation fairly scientific, particularly when coupled with a general knowledge of cooking theory and practice. This applies equally to most other areas of food and cooking.

COOKING AND NUTRITION

Since Escoffier's time many changes have come about—changes in flour texture; amounts of sugar, butter, and cream used in any one preparation; the availability of fresh produce all year long; and the deluge of highly processed, packaged, and frozen foods. One of the outstanding changes has been a sharpened interest in the overall diet. While the kind of nutrition that would ultimately result in sound health has always been of concern to mankind, at no time has the average person been as aware and well-informed.

Nutritional data have frequently led the horse to water but haven't always made him drink. Oddly enough, the majority of nutrition research is done on uncooked foods, frequently before it even leaves the fields.

Dr. Margaret Mead captured the essence of Americans' rather ambivalent attitudes toward good eating versus good nutrition when she wrote,

> Why do we go on talking about food *and* nutrition, unless we are indicating that nutrition is the least attractive aspect of food—which we did in this country out of our own particular Puritan tradition?
>
> . . . we have steadily gone on treating the need for nutrition as an unfortunate aspect of the delights of food. The formula that "if you eat enough that isn't good but is good for you, you can eat a little that tastes good but is not good for you," became a basic element in our thinking and has affected a great many things in the world.

Foods cooked for maximum nutritional benefit will also give the most pleasure and satisfaction, because flavor, texture, color, and aroma *are* directly related to nutrition content and may act as the most reliable guides. This also applies to produce and other foods eaten in their fresh state.

COOKING AS AN ART

The creative aspect of cooking has often led to its being categorized as an art rather than as a science. This has undoubtedly contributed to the tendency to surround cooking with an air of mystery involving closely guarded secrets, certain flourishes, and recipes with long and sometimes undiscernible titles.

One area where artistry becomes quite apparent is of course in the arrangement and service of food. Both food and the entire ritual surrounding eating are intricately enmeshed with the human senses:

◇ Sight: the appearance of food, and of those serving it
◇ Hearing: the atmosphere in which we eat as well as the accompanying sounds
◇ Smell: the aroma given off
◇ Touch: the texture of the foods
◇ Taste: perhaps usually thought of as the primary sense in eating, but actually, according to Brillat-Savarin, only coming into play *after* swallowing.

Cooking involves both chemistry and creativity. It is both a scientific and an artistic endeavor. And therein lies its challenge.

CONTENTS

chapter one
SEASONINGS & BEVERAGES 1

chapter two
STOCK, SOUPS, & SAUCES 19

chapter three
THE MEAT MYSTIQUE 53

chapter four
GROUND MEATS, FISH, AND SHELLFISH 137

chapter five
DAIRY PRODUCTS 151

chapter six
FISH & SHELLFISH 201

chapter seven
PRODUCE OF THE LAND 241

chapter eight
FRUITS FOR ALL SEASONS 321

chapter nine
GRAINS: BROWN IS BEAUTIFUL 337

chapter ten
COOKING WITH SPIRITS   403

chapter eleven
MEAL PLANNING   417

chapter twelve
FATS & OILS   423

The proof of the pudding is in the eating.

Cervantes, *Don Quixote de la Mancha*

A land of wheat, and barley, and vines, and fig trees,
and pomegrantes; a land of oil olive, and honey;
A land wherein thou shalt eat bread without scarceness,
thou shalt not lack any thing in it . . .

Deuteronomy 8:8-9

Fingers were made before forks, and hands before knives.

Jonathan Swift, *Polite Conversation*, dialogue I

The stay and the staff, the whole stay of bread,
and the whole stay of water.

Isaiah 3:1

When the well's dry, we know the worth of water.

Benjamin Franklin, *Poor Richard's Almanac*

An animal swallows its food; a man eats it,
but only a man of intellect knows how to dine.

Brillat-Savarin

And ye shall eat the fat of the land.

Genesis 45:18

I ate umble pie with an appetite.

Charles Dickens, *David Copperfield*

Bad men live that they may eat and drink,
whereas good men eat and drink that they may live.

Socrates, from Plutarch, *How a Young Man Ought to Hear Poems*

Things sweet to taste prove in digestion sour.

William Shakespeare, *King Richard II*

At length I recollected the thoughtless saying of a great princess,
who, on being informed that the country people had no bread,
replied "Let them eat cake."

Jean Jacques Rousseau, *The Confessions*

A man has no better thing under the sun, than to eat,
and to drink, and to be merry.

Ecclesiastes 8:15

SEASONINGS & BEVERAGES

chapter one

SUGAR AND SPICE

The leaves, pods, bark, roots, and berries of a diversified number of plants have been put to many uses during their long and ancient history. One of their major roles has been as a flavoring for food and drink. A number have been used in both old and new medicines. Some have been associated with mild forms of addiction. Unfortunately, many of the uses to which the Indians put them have been lost along with other remnants of their past. The tales of conquest as well as the atrocities committed in order to gain possession of treasured herbs and spices have been recorded time and again in the annals of world history. Their role in today's world market may take a different guise, but basically the same underlying power tactics are at play.

The word *season* comes from a Latin word meaning "seed" or "to sow." It is the seeds from the pod of a member of the orchid family that are used as vanilla. The Aztecs of Mexico used the seeds of the cocoa pod to make a drink which they called "chocolath": the "choco" meant cocoa and "lath" meant water. The crushed seeds (usually referred to as beans) of the coffee plant grew in Arabia for centuries and were used to flavor a drink called "kaffa," after the Province of Kaffa where the plant grew wild. Kaffa was considered an intoxicating drink and was prohibited by the Koran. Severe penalties would be the fate of those who became addicted. The kaffa plants found their way to Africa, to the West Indies, and from there to Europe and the New World. Coffee houses became the center of all sorts of intrigue. London's first coffee house, located in St. Michael's Alley, was opened in 1652. The dried leaves of the tea bush, which is thought to have originated in ancient China, were first shipped to Europe from India by the Dutch in the early 1700s. Prior to the introduction of the new brews, beer and wine had been staple drinks.

The most extensively used flavoring—in fact it is commonly thought of as an ingredient—is cane sugar. Saccharum, botanically speaking, is a member of the grass family whose succulent stems are the source of cane sugar.

Sugar is thought to have originated in India and Cochin-China where it was cultivated from ancient times. In writings, it has been referred to as "the Indian honey-bearing reed"; "the sweet sap of the Indian reed"; and "the granulated salt-like product imported from India." The names of sugar in the modern Western languages are derived from the Persian *shakar*. It is described as a tall, perennial grass, giving off numerous erect stems ten to fifteen feet high and of a thick, solid, jointed root stock. The plant is propagated by means of cuttings rather than seeds. The tall, tough nature of the cane and the problems surrounding its plantings and harvesting might have caused it to lie fallow, were it not for certain actions taken by early explorers.

Portuguese, exploring the West Coast of Africa in 1442, exchanged captured Moors for ten African Negroes and a quantity of gold. This act led to the resurgence of slavery in the Western world after it had been laid to rest for hundreds of years. Following this most unfortunate incident, that promised its discoverers quick and easy profits, forts were established along the African Coast and ships were fitted out for the transportation of Africans to Spain and elsewhere to be sold as slaves.

The Spanish and Portuguese continued their explorations and the islands off the Caribbean were discovered one by one. Sugar cane cuttings were planted on each in quick succession. Columbus brought sugar cuttings to Haiti and San Domingo on his second voyage in 1493. On his trip back, in 1494, he carried, among his other prisoners, 500 native Indians to be sold as slaves in Seville. However "their docile and gentle nature" led to their plight being brought to the attention of Queen Isabella, who, in the light of certain legal interpretations, ordered that those who had withstood the trip be sent back.

By the early 1500s sugar production had been extended to Haiti, Cuba, Jamaica, Puerto Rico, Mexico, Martinique, Guadeloupe, and the Canary Islands. The job of harvesting the cane grown tall and tough under the tropical sun proved to be too much for many of the frail island natives, however, and many succumbed to its demands. Partly in answer to this problem, the descendants of those African slaves who had been brought to Spain beginning in 1442 were dispatched to the islands to carry on the work.

In 1516, the Spanish granted exclusive rights for the annual supply of several thousand African Negroes to be used to meet the labor problems, as and where they arose. Africans had long enjoyed an abundant and diversified agriculture, and given the extent of their outdoor life in a tropical climate, they were for the most part extremely healthy and rugged individuals and withstood the rigors to which they were exposed much better than the native Indians.

Toward the end of the fifteenth century the art of making loaf sugar had been invented by a Venetian, and eventually Venice became the European center of the sugar trade. Later developments in the sugar trade led to the creation of Viennese pastries—their artistry made them famous around the world.

Although the sweet juice extracted from reeds goes back to ancient times, it was crystallization that led to the change in its general use. Until well into the 1700s "a teaspoon of sugar to make the medicine go down" was more fact than fancy. With the exception of those who were in a position to afford the luxury of its use, sugar was primarily the domain of apothecaries—those persons who made and sold drugs and medical preparations.

In 1812, E. C. Howard took out an English patent for an improved method of crystallization, and another the following year for the closed vacuum pan used in the process. It was this and the age of machinery that led to the extraordinary use to which sugar is put today.

Brillat-Savarin wrote in his *Physiology of Taste*, published after his death in 1825, "The culture of the sugar-cane has become an object of the highest importance, for it is a source of riches both for those who cultivate it, for those who deal in its produce, for those who retail it, and, finally, for the governments who tax it." Charles V is said to have built his castles in Spain from the duties levied on imported sugar. Britain used it as a ploy in the struggle with Napoleon by cutting off France's raw sugar supply from the West Indies. (Sugar had been introduced into Barbados in 1641.) Napoleon, aware of the German Andreas Marggraf's discovery in 1747 of producing sugar from beets (a process which had never been put to practical use) had the French chemist, Jean Chaptal, work out the technical refinements that led to the establishment of the first sugar beet factory. Monsieur Chaptal was later created a count for his accomplishment. Beet sugar now accounts for half the world's supply of sugar. The name of another Frenchman, Benjamin Delessert (1773-1847), a highly successful sugar manufacturer in Paris, became synonymous with all the "sweets" and "goodies" served at the end of a meal.

For many years controversy flared as to whether or not sugar was a desirable item in the diet, but for the most part it was extolled as being extremely beneficial—recommended diets included large doses. Chocolate, sweetened with sugar, became the fashionable beverage to serve. In fact, when the first Delmonico arrived in New York in the early 1800s he opened up a small shop serving pastries and chocolate. Among its other virtues, chocolate was certain to ensure a sound sleep, which well it might have done, as at the time unadulterated cocoa seeds were crushed using a mortar and pestle or were ground by the user, resulting in a strength and purity far removed from what goes for cocoa on today's supermarket shelves. In the late 1700s, when coffee and tea began replacing cocoa as popular drinks, they too were combined with the sweet syrup of the tall grass.

Although sugar had been brought to what is now the United States of America somewhat earlier, it was not until around 1770 that it was grown successfully. Coinciding with the success of the sugar plantations (and with the rumblings of the American Revolution) was a decision handed down in 1772 in the English courts in the case of a Negro named Somerset to the effect that once a slave set foot on the soil of the British Isles proper he became free. Although this action did not abolish the slave trade in British possessions, it was, however, something of a harbinger. Meanwhile the predominant system of agriculture in the southern section of America patterned itself on the great agricultural estates of Great Britain and the Continent.

In the two centuries that followed, sugar became of such major importance that an international agreement was drafted to control the market. From time to time quotas were assigned, depending on the price of sugar, but they had little to do with supply and demand. U.S. domestic prices were controlled through the quota system established by the Sugar Act of 1934, under the direction of the Department of Agriculture. Tariff restrictions, government established quotas, bounties, and taxes all contributed to regulating and controlling sugar prices.

At the beginning of the 1970s, America was the world's largest sugar consumer, accounting for an average of 102 pounds per capita annually—more sugar on a dry basis than vegetables, fruits, and eggs combined. (The Chinese averaged less than three pounds per capita and were the world's smallest consumers).

Most of Americans' sugar intake is as a "hidden ingredient" in such items as processed foods, cereals, and soft drinks. It is widely used as a preservative. The flour used in many commercial mixes has been processed so as to combine with a maximum amount of sugar, with the result that many contain more sugar than anything else.

In 1974, the well-entrenched sugar industry was subjected to some startling and far-reaching developments, not the least of these being the termination of the Sugar Act. The ink on the official papers was barely dry when rumors began to circulate that world sugar supplies were extremely limited. As a result, between January and November the price of raw sugar on world and U.S. markets rose more than 300 percent. Rampant speculation (on all levels) quickly followed. Before long, unsuspected stores of sugar began "pouring from the rafters" and it became apparent that there had been no real shortage. Sugar prices then plummeted as sharply as they had risen.

In the meantime, the high prices had sent buyers representing big business scurrying to look for sugar substitutes (all told, manufacturers use about two-thirds of the sugar sold with the remaining one-third—termed "grocery sugar"—going to supermarket shelves). In the early 1960s, the Japanese had developed an enzyme with the potential to convert corn, as well as other starches, into syrups high in *fructose*—a sugar considerably sweeter than an equal amount of cane sugar, which is pure *sucrose*. This process was then further developed by American business interests, which eventually produced a corn syrup with an even higher percentage of fructose. Its production cost at the time of the soaring sugar prices was considerably lower than that of sugar, and manufacturers began to turn to it as a supplemental source. When sugar prices again fell to a lower level, however, the high-fructose syrup could not compete and industry returned to its old, familiar source for the bulk of its sweetener requirements. However, the high-fructose syrups continue to capture a small percentage of the market.

The development which may prove to have the greatest effect over the long run was that, faced with exorbitant prices, consumers began to think in terms of doing with less and they no longer bought sweets with the same reckless abandon. The high prices further gave pause to reconsider the whole subject of sugar—the possible harmful effects resulting from a high intake as well as the fact that refined sugar adds nothing but calories. For the first time in history, the per capita consumption of sugar began registering a downward trend. By the end of 1976, raw sugar prices were below production costs.

Sugar, a flavoring agent extracted from the sweet innards of a grass, has within the short span of approximately 150 years brought about vast changes in eating patterns, particularly in our Western hemisphere. The degree to which sugar was still being used at the beginning of the last quarter of the twentieth century has frequently been said to border on addiction. However, while it had a long way to go, the signs pointed in the direction that the use and misuse of refined sugar was well on its way to being curtailed.

THE HIDDEN SOUL OF COOKING

When used with imagination, almost every area of cooking can benefit from the discriminating use of seasoning. In this area, experience is one of the best teachers. Initially, it is advisable to be on the side of restraint, and to bear in mind that ingredients should always taste of what they are. Underseasoning can always be remedied, whereas overseasoning can prove disastrous. Seasoning should be used to enhance the good natural flavor of the food.

A new and different seasoning can be used to dispel the boredom of an old and tired preparation.

In times past, seasonings were used as a buffer against many things, including lack of refrigeration and a less sophisticated knowledge of the ways of preserving foods. Poor cooking facilities and hit and miss cooking methods, as well as the shortage of some foods and the ready availability of others, played a part. A pinch of this and a pinch of that was thought a certain cure, but overzealousness not infrequently led to poor digestion and fitful sleep. This was especially true in the use of dried seasonings, particularly if they had seen better days.

"The best is none too good" is a motto worth bearing in mind when it comes to the selection of seasonings, as quality is as important here as it is in all other food categories.

NUTRITIVE VALUE

Most spices and seasonings have no significant food value, particularly in the amounts generally used. Parsley has generous amounts of both ascorbic acid and vitamin A. It also contains calcium, phosphorus, and potassium as well as traces of other minerals and vitamins.

Salt (known chemically as sodium chloride) is the most common source of sodium in the diet. For some time now emphasis has been placed on decreasing salt consumption as nutritionists and medical personnel become aware of the harmful effects of excessive amounts, both in cooking and as an added taste enhancer. A great many of today's processed foods contain a high percentage of salt. The question of more or less salt in food and cooking is largely a matter of conditioning. (Fresh lemon juice makes a good salt substitute as a taste enhancer.)

As iodine is an important nutrient, federal standards require that iodized salt contain .01 percent of potassium iodide as a preventative for simple goiter caused by lack of iodine in the diet.

Refined sugar does nothing more than add calories to the diet.

PURCHASING—FRESH vs. DRIED

Fresh herbs are for the most part hard to come by, with the possible exception of parsley, dill, chives, and basil. Most have a short-lived season. When home-grown they should be cut, hung to dry, and stored in airtight containers before they go to seed, otherwise they will lose all their fragrance.

Once a person is familiar with herbs, it is not difficult to determine whether a dried herb has had an extended shelf life; that is, whether it has been around for too long. Rub the herb or spice between the palms of the hands and check the quality of the aroma.

It is preferable to omit a seasoning rather than use a stale one, and to select fresh over dried.

A PINCH OF THIS
AND A PINCH OF THAT

Before seasoning foods, hold a little of the herb or spice under your nose and take a whiff to see if it is to your liking. Add a little at a time and sample the mixture. Do not season foods just for the sake of seasoning.

Herbs are plants with distinctly flavored leaves which are used in very small amounts to season foods. As a general rule ¼ to ½ teaspoon dried herb is used in place of 1 tablespoon fresh. The equivalent in a powdered herb would be ⅛ teaspoon or a mere pinch.

Classes of Herbs

Herbs can be divided into two classes: the fine herbs and the robust herbs, both names being self-descriptive.

Among the fine herbs most often used are:

◇ Basil
◇ Chervil
◇ Oregano
◇ Thyme
◇ Rosemary
◇ Tarragon
◇ Chives

Robust herbs:

◇ Wild marjoram
◇ Mint
◇ Sage
◇ Savoury
◇ Bay leaves (Laurel)
◇ Caraway
◇ Dill
◇ Horseradish
◇ Parsley

Although herbs cannot be tied to any one set of rules, certain of them are known to combine well:

◇ oregano and thyme
◇ rosemary and thyme
◇ rosemary and tarragon
◇ chervil and basil
◇ savoury and sage

All seven of the fine herbs are sometimes used in combination and are especially effective if used in the fresh state. Freshly chopped parsley can be added to almost any preparation. The robust herbs stand up well on their own merits.

SPICES AND FLAVORINGS

The reputation of the spices goes back to ancient times. *Salt*, one of the earliest substances to be used as a spice, is also the world's oldest preservative.

◇ *Black* and *white pepper* differ only in their strength. White pepper is the milder and is recommended in certain dishes so as not to detract from appearance.

◇ *Cayenne* is an extremely strong red pepper. It should be used in mere pinches.

◇ *Pepperoni* is stronger than cayenne and should be used with even greater caution.

◇ *Paprika* is a mild red pepper that imparts a warm taste and coloring.

◇ *Cinnamon*, an often used spice, is the inner bark of the laurel.

◇ *Ginger* technically belongs to the herb family but is generally classified with the spices. It is basically a sweet spice and an American and Oriental favorite.

◇ *Curry* is a combination of several spices.

◇ *Nutmeg* and *mace* derive from the same plant. These extremely effective spices should be used in mere pinches and are best when combined with other spices.

◇ *Cloves* is the dominant spice in the allspice or five spices mixture. One or two dried whole cloves or a pinch of ground cloves can impart a strong accent.

◇ Next to salt, *mustard* is the most widely used of all the spices. The dark mustard seed variety is used in French mustard and the pale yellow seed in English mustard.

◇ *Saffron* imparts an exotic flavor and yellow coloring but is exorbitant in price.

◇ *Vanilla* seeds from the dried pod add immeasurably to almost any dessert.

◇ *Orange* and *lemon peel*, when finely chopped or grated, add zest to many different preparations.

◇ *Horseradish* is hot and can be used fresh or from a bottled sauce.

◇ *Tabasco* and *chili* are both hot and should be used sparingly. These are made using aged Red peppers as a base.

SUGAR AS A FLAVORING

Caution should be taken to treat sugar as a type of spice, that is, as a flavoring and not an ingredient. Amounts specified in recipes can be totally ignored for the most part and as little as desired may be substituted or it may be omitted altogether. For instance, if a recipe calls for 1 cup sugar, whether it be a cake, pudding, custard, or sauce, the amount may be reduced to as little as ⅛ or ¼ cup without affecting the consistency to any appreciable degree. Sugar does, however, have a certain tenderizing effect. Other sweeteners such as honey, corn syrup, or molasses may be used as a flavoring in place of sugar.

BEVERAGES

A beverage is defined as a liquid for drinking, especially one that is not water; however, the greater percentage of the liquid in most drinks is water. Coffee, tea, and cocoa are high on the list of the most popular beverages consumed by Americans, although consumption has gone down in recent years due to the drastic increase in prices, as well as a greater emphasis being placed on their possible harmful effects.

COFFEE

Experts rate most highly those varieties of coffee and tea which are grown in mountain areas rather than in the lowlands—the superior flavor is said to result from the richness and mineral content of the soil. The largest share of U.S. imports are in the form of "green" coffee. After roasting, the green beans become driea and brown in color, their oils water soluble. The flavor and aroma of coffee are derived from caffeol, and to a lesser degree from tannins. Caffeine, which gives coffee its stimulating quality, is extracted mainly during the first few minutes of preparation.

Coffee Preparation

The aim in preparing coffee is to extract the maximum amount of flavoring substances (caffeol) and the minimum amount of tannin (as well as the maximum amount of caffeine for those who drink coffee for its stimulating effect). Coffee may be made using a drip coffee maker or a pot designed for this purpose, or it may be perked using a coffee percolator. In percolating, there is the possibility that the coffee infusion will be brought up to boiling, thus giving it a bitter flavor. The drip method is generally more satisfactory as the caffeol extracts are immediately dissolved and the tannins kept to a minimum. The grind of coffee should be suited to its preparation method—very fine for drip, coarser for percolators. The quality of the water (hard or soft) will also affect the flavor. Keep the coffee pot clean or the odor of stale coffee will impair the flavor as well. Remove coffee grounds as soon as coffee is made. Any particles of coffee remaining will give it a cloudy appearance. Paper filters have contributed to both flavor and ease in coffee preparation.

Instant coffee, which is finely ground roasted coffee, has been improved and is convenient. Decaffeinated coffee, which comes in both regular grind and instant forms, is manufactured by first removing the caffeine and then roasting and grinding the beans.

The following are recommended measurements for making drip and percolated coffee ("one for the pot" is totally unnecessary):

◇ 2 tablespoons coffee to 6 fluid ounces of water (¾ cup)
◇ 20 cups coffee: ½ pound coffee to 4 quarts water (1 gallon)
◇ 40 cups coffee: 1 pound coffee to 2 gallons water

TEA

All three "kinds" of tea—green, black, and oolong—can be derived from the same tea plant. The difference lies in the processing. Green tea is fermented after the fresh leaves have been steamed and dried. In black tea, however, the fresh leaves are fermented and then dried, a process that causes them to turn dark brown. Essentially, the oxidation of the tannin in the leaf is carried further in black tea than in green tea. (The fermentation of tea results from the activity of enzymes in the leaves rather than from microbial action.)

Both green and black teas are classified according to the size of the leaves, as well as their relative position on the plants. Thus, orange pekoe has the longest leaves, followed by pekoe and then souchong. Orange pekoe has a delicate flavor and pekoe has a stronger, full-bodied flavor. Black tea is generally a blend of the two. Oolong teas have some of the characteristics of both black and green teas.

Tender orange pekoe leaves are sometimes scented with blossoms of other plants and are flavored with spices—these teas are considerably higher in price than regular teas.

The stimulant in tea is referred to as theine, a chemical identical to caffeine in coffee. Tannins, which dissolve slowly in hot water and impart a bitter, unpleasant taste, are found in large amounts in tea. The amount of tannin extracted depends on the length of time the tea is steeped. As tannins are more soluble at boiling temperature, tea should be steeped under the simmering point and for no longer than 3 or 4 minutes.

Tea Preparation

In making tea, the aim is to develop the flavor and to extract as little tannin as possible. The quality of the water (hard or soft) will also affect the flavor. In addition, earthenware pottery makes better tea than does china or glass. Needless to say, the teapot should be kept scrupulously clean.

To prepare, bring fresh cold water to a boil and pour over teabags or loose tea, using one teabag or one teaspoon loose tea per cup. A tea diffuser or ball may be used to hold loose tea. Water should be added as soon as it has boiled, otherwise loss of minerals will cause the tea to become flat tasting. Set teapot over low heat (using some type of heat diffuser) and steep for no longer than 3 or 4 minutes. If making tea in a cup, set a saucer over the cup for a half minute or so, or until the tea is of desired strength. In either case, remove teabags or ball containing loose tea as soon as it has steeped.

One other cautionary note: Boiling and not merely hot water is necessary for the proper infusion. It is also advisable to preheat the pot or cup by rinsing with boiling water beforehand.

Iced Tea

Prepare a double strength tea (2 teabags per cup) and remove teabags as soon as tea has developed full flavor. Cool at room temperature—do not refrigerate. If tea appears cloudy, add a small amount of boiling water. Pour tea over a generous amount of ice cubes. Add fresh lemon juice prior to serving or serve lemon wedges on the side. To sweeten or not to sweeten, using finely granulated sugar, is a matter of taste.

Substitute for Strong Tea or Coffee

Add fresh lemon or orange juice to very weak tea (merely colored) or to plain boiling water. For a more pronounced flavor, add lemon or orange zest (thin strips of peel).

STORAGE OF COFFEE AND TEA

Tea will retain its flavor for a slightly longer period of storage than coffee. However, both tea and coffee should be kept in airtight containers. Store opened cans of coffee in refrigerator.

NUTRITIVE VALUE OF COFFEE AND TEA

In recent years, many Americans have "kicked" the coffee habit, or have cut down on the number of cups they drink. Younger Americans (between the ages of 18 and 30) did not generally take to coffee drinking, but turned to soft drinks instead. (Incidentally the caffeine removed from coffee goes into some of the more popular soft drinks, many of which are also relatively high in sugar content.)

Emphasis has been placed on the undesirability of the excessive consumption of either tea or coffee, mainly because of their tannin, theine, and caffeine content.

Neither coffee nor tea has any nutritive value unless served with milk or lemon.

COCOA

Like coffee and tea, cocoa is a stimulant. It contains theobromine, which is similar to caffeine in composition. Tannins are also present in a soluble form. It is made from the beans or seeds of the cacao tree, as is chocolate. Cocoa differs from chocolate in that the greater part of the fat of the bean is removed. Standards for both cocoa and chocolate have been set by the Food and Drug Administration: High-fat cocoa, called breakfast cocoa, must contain not less than 22 percent fat; medium-fat cocoa not less than 10 percent; and low-fat cocoa can contain less than 10 percent. This information, however, does not have to appear on retail packaging.

HOT COCOA

To prepare hot cocoa, combine, 1 tablespoon cocoa per cup, 1 to 2 tablespoons sugar (according to desired degree of sweetness), a pinch of salt, and 1 tablespoon boiling water. Set over low heat, stirring until dissolved. Gradually add 1 cup milk and cook, stirring until just under boiling point. Do not allow to boil. For a foamy cocoa, place in blender for about ten seconds, beat with a rotary beater, or use a wire whisk. Garnish with 1 tablespoon whipped cream (optional).

STORAGE OF COCOA

Due to its fat content, cocoa (as well as chocolate) should be stored in a cool, dry place in an air-tight container.

NUTRITIVE VALUE OF COCOA

Unlike coffee and tea, cocoa and chocolate have some food value. One ounce of chocolate contains 143 calories and one ounce of cocoa contains 98. Both contain calcium, phosphorus, and potassium, as well as traces of other minerals.

STOCK,
SOUPS, & SAUCES

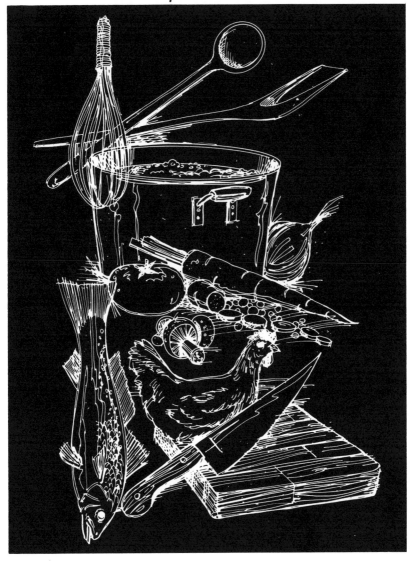

chapter two

ALEXIS SOYER

Alexis Soyer, born in France in the year 1809, arrived in London at the age of 21 during one of the most challenging periods in England's long history and a short time after the revolutionaries overthrew the Bourbon monarchy in France . . . already a full-fledged chef, having served a four-year apprenticeship at which he had toiled and applied himself from dawn to dusk, as was more or less the custom. It was the prelude to a career that was to prove one of the most fulfilled and varied of any chef of modern times.

After working for several English dukes, he became head chef for Mr. Lloyd of Aston Hall, staying for four years and earning himself great esteem. Less than six years after his arrival in London he was offered and accepted the coveted post of head chef at the exclusive Reform Club, the home away from home for the gentlemen-elite of London's high society. He was also charged with organizing and designing the kitchens for the club which when completed were considered to be the most up-to-date in all of England. He served the Reform Club for many years, retiring only after a section of it was opened to the general public, detracting in Monsieur Soyer's opinion from the intimate and personal nature of his position. This transition from private to public was characteristic of what was to take place during the latter half of the nineteenth and early twentieth century. Its effects were felt by all those serving in a similar capacity, many of whom reacted in kind, depending on the degree of independence they were in a position to exercise.

During his lifetime, Monsieur Soyer invented pots, pans, tea and coffee pots, strainers, and innumerable gadgets, many of which are still in use today. These he patented but, soon tiring of them, sold for a pittance as new ones came to mind. He did the same with sauces, relishes, and at least one exotic and effervescent drink which he dubbed "Soyer's Nectar." One such recipe was obtained by Crosse & Blackwell who produced it for nearly three-quarters of a century, featuring Monsieur Soyer donned in his red cap on the label.

He devised a means to improve the method of canning and preserving then in use, as well as a method of extracting meat juices, which both he and Monsieur Brillat-Savarin before him had referred to as "Ozmazone." (Monsieur Brillat-Savarin, however, was more concerned with solving the chemical problem of what specific constituent in meats was responsible for the flavor element, a task that was to further challenge food chemists in the second half of the twentieth century.)*

Monsieur Soyer left an account of his intense research and its practical applications in such works as *Gastronomic Regenerator*, *The Modern Housewife*, and *Shilling Cookery*. He was one of the first chefs to write for both the struggling home cook and the professional. His books were written in a practical and useful vein, an approach frequently ignored by Careme and others before him. In 1853, five years before his death at the age of 44, he produced a book entitled *The Pantropheon*, or *A History of Food and its Preparation from Earliest Ages of the World*, an intensely researched volume of over 450 pages. *A Culinary Campaign*, written on his experiences in the Crimean War, was used as a basis of instruction for military cooks.

His books sold quickly. The concept of professional secrets was foreign to his nature—he shared his knowledge and recipes and was always happy to divulge the ingredients of his success.

Monsieur Soyer's concern was not all for soufflés, barons of beef, and sensational entremets to cater to the lavish and competitive tastes of the upper gentry. His awareness went out to the needs of London's poor, particularly during depressed periods, culminating in his invention of the soup boiler and the setting up of soup kitchens, often at his own expense. His boiler made it possible for him personally to oversee the daily feeding of upwards of 8,000 Irish souls during the potato famine of 1845.

His belief in soup as a mainstay was put to the test on more than one occasion. In 1854, during the Crimean War, London's *The Times* made history by reporting "firsthand" conditions at the front. Monsieur Soyer, reading of the shortages, the kind of food being eaten, the soldiers' inability to cook, and the conditions under which they coped, rallied to the cause and volunteered not only his services but assumed all travel expenses.

---

*In the early 1960s, it became possible to isolate meat flavors and freeze dry the extract in powder form, which, when subjected to heat, produces the aroma of meat or poultry. These flavors are used extensively by the processed food industry in canned soups, broths, and in an unlimited variety of dried soup mixes, the latter of which are used in vast quantities, particulary by those cooking for the general public. They usually have a high percentage of seasonings, salt, and sugar.

The soup bones which one could usually count on from the butcher are now hard to come by, even for a price. The "bone man" collects such bones, selling at least half for bonemeal to be used for fertilizer and supplemental feed for animals.

His motto had always been "Cleanliness is the soul of the kitchen." On his arrival in the Crimea, he found the kitchens, under the superintendence of Ms. Florence Nightingale, in a deplorable state with the exception of one small unit. Soldiers doing the cooking, untrained for the most part, preferring conditions at the front to those of providing fodder, were lumping meat rations together, using string and a less than clean piece of rag to identify them, throwing them into rapidly boiling liquid and indiscriminately removing them, resulting in some being raw in the center and others a stringy lump of fiber. Most startling of all to Monsieur Soyer was that the liquid in which the meats were cooked was more or less ignored. Upon cleaning up the kitchens, he proceeded to adjust the heat, lowering the temperature to allow meats and liquid to simmer. He added seasoning and vegetables to the stock, removed and reserved the fat for frying, and cut up the now properly cooked meat into edible bite-size pieces, pouring the hot soup over it.

Prior to leaving England, M. Soyer had ordered a number of his recently patented portable stoves to be shipped to him at the front. Called Soyer's Magic Lamp, this device was light in weight, conserved fuel, and was the forerunner of gas ranges which were soon to make the fireplace obsolete.*

M. Soyer and Ms. Nightingale worked side by side throughout the war, organizing and battling against all odds, both at the fronts and in the hospitals. They both contracted crimean fever, a form of cholera, the aftermath of which was to lead to M. Soyer's death. After his bout with the fever, and against the advice of his doctors, he went back to the front, where he worked and lived in dirty, cold, and infested quarters. At the close of the war he returned to England, thin, sad, and disillusioned. He was never well again and died less than two years later, in the midst of organizing a dinner party for his many friends.

Monsieur Soyer's Magic Lamp, later referred to as a brazier, was to show up in eating places around the world, enthralling patrons with the intimacy and delight of watching their food

---

*When the gas range came into use it was considered by most to be inferior for cooking, but was widely promoted, as not only was it a fuel saver, but the industrial age was gaining momentum and smoke abatement was becoming of great concern, particularly in England. However, the use of the kitchen range was much more prevalent in America than in England, because of the British reluctance to give up the traditional fireplace. At the turn of the century, Monsieur August Escoffier, organizer of the kitchens of the first of the Ritz Hotels in Paris, insisted that gas-fired ranges would not give his meats the same flavor; consequently he made use of the traditional fuels, coal and charcoal with which he had cooked during his long and esteemed career.

being cooked and tossed about over an open fire. In the latter part of the nineteenth century, New York's incomparable Delmonico's was featuring its now famous Lobster Newburg—the little stove and recipe having been introduced to them by a travelling Sea Captain named Wenburg.

Two years after Monsieur Soyer's death, the well-remembered Ms. Nightingale wrote in her *Notes on Nursing*: "Every careful observer of the sick will agree in this that thousands of patients are annually starved in the midst of plenty, from want of attention to the ways which alone make it possible for them to take food." Earlier on, M. Soyer had written, "War is the evil genius of a time, but good food for all is a daily and paramount necessity."

Alexis Soyer's soup kitchens, which came to the rescue of many during America's deep depression of the 1930s, were born of his vast knowledge of culinary science, his inventive genius, and his strong feelings to succor the hungry in a way he knew to be nourishing, satisfying, and at a cost of tuppence.

THE STOCK POT

Stock is produced by simmering bones, carcasses, meats, vegetables, herbs, and seasonings in liquid over low heat in a covered pot for a long period of time. It serves as the basis for soups, sauces, and the liquid used in moist heat cooking procedures, such as braisings and pot roasts.

Theory

The protein matter of bone is similar to the collagen of connective tissue in that it can be converted into gelatin when freed from the mineral matter. The cartilage masses and sheath on bones can also be converted into gelatin. Most of the calcium content of the animal is in the bones. These constituents contribute to a good, rich gelatinous stock. As bone and its constituents are not readily parted, 10 to 12 hours of simmering over low heat is generally required. (Three or four hours has little effect insofar as extraction is concerned.) Bones may be given a head start and softened somewhat by being heated in a 350° F. (177° C.) oven for about half an hour. When bones have given their all to stock, they will appear dull and rough and be on the verge of falling apart. However, overexposure to heat is as possible in cooking bones as in any other phase of cooking. If stock is cooked for too long, it will acquire a bitter taste and take on a slightly muddy appearance.

Veal bones, by nature of their immaturity, result in a higher gelatin content than beef bones. Poultry carcasses are also used as a basis for stock; since they are softer, they cook in a shorter time than either beef or veal bones, but acquire the same dull, rough appearance when totally spent.

Meats

Cuts of meat from the more exercised muscles of older animals will give the most flavor to stock. Shin of beef is an excellent cut to use. Beef chuck is also very good. Fowl will impart a much more pronounced flavor than will chicken. The quantity of meats used in a stock preparation is more or less dependent on the degree and richness of flavor desired.

Vegetables

Aromatic vegetables—carrots, celery, onions, leeks—will add flavoring to stock. Do not use starchy vegetables such as potatoes or turnips. Vegetables should be cut up as fine as possible—an electric chopper, mixer attachment, or food processor will do the job in a few minutes once the vegetables have been peeled. Keep quantities to amounts that will add flavor but will not dominate. Take the freshness and flavor quality of the vegetables into consideration. For example, fresh carrots, purchased with their tops intact, are quite possibly twice as flavorful as plastic-wrapped carrots which have been subjected to a long period of cold storage. The tops and leaves of a head of celery offer more flavor than the stalks. Large, firm red onions produce a stronger flavor than small ordinary white onions. Leeks are an excellent flavoring agent for stock but must be firm and fresh; if soft and wilted, they will have little to offer.

Herbs and Spices

Most herbs, especially parsley, thyme, dill, bay leaf, and chervil, are effective. They should, however, be used with discretion, as an overabundance particularly of dried herbs can ruin stock. One or two fresh herbs will give better results than five or six dried. Add salt and pepper at the beginning but do so with caution, because the salty flavor will intensify as the stock is reduced. As with the seasoning of all foods, it is much simpler to correct than to undo.

Liquid

As the aim is to draw out the constituents of the contents of the stock pot into the liquid, cold water, rather than hot, is added at the beginning. (Hot water would set or coagulate the surface juices, thereby holding them in.) All ingredients with the exception of any meats being used are placed in the pot with enough cold water to cover. A small proportion of dry wine may be added to act as a tenderizer, as well as for flavoring.

NUTRITIVE VALUE OF STOCK

The cartilage masses and sheath on bones (the ends of muscle attachments to bones) contain the protein collagen—a tender and transparent tissue which can be converted into gelatin. The protein matter of bone is similar to collagen in that it, too, can be converted into gelatin when freed from the mineral matter. It is the gelatin content that gives stock its smooth appearance. Gelatin is high in protein—100 grams of dry gelatin contain 85.6 grams of protein. The marrow running through the center of the bone also contains protein, and the bone tissue itself contains good quantities of calcium.

All the water-soluble nutrients from bones and carcasses, as well as those from any meats and vegetables used, are extracted through long, slow cooking, resulting in a solution with high nutritive value.

ALL-PURPOSE STOCK

All measurements are approximate and are stipulated to give a general idea as to proportions and quantities. The overall amounts, particularly as to bones and meats, will largely depend on the desired degree of richness.

Bones

4 pounds (approx. 1.8 kg) veal bones

2 pounds (900 g) beef bones

1 poultry carcass (fowl, chicken, or turkey)

poultry parts (necks, wings, giblets)

Meats

3 pounds (1350 g) shin of beef or beef chuck

1 fowl

Vegetables

3 medium-size carrots, peeled and finely chopped

celery, tops and leaves of 1 head, coarsely chopped

2 large onions, peeled and finely chopped

2 leeks (white part only), cut through center, washed, and sliced

Herbs and Spices

3 or 4 sprigs fresh parsley, coarsely chopped

3 or 4 sprigs fresh dill, coarsely chopped

1 bay leaf, fresh or dried

1 tablespoon fresh or ½ teaspoon dried thyme

salt and freshly ground pepper

Liquid

1 cup (240 ml) dry white wine

sufficient cold water to fully cover ingredients

Place all ingredients, with the exception of meats, in stock pot with enough cold water to cover, and bring to a slow simmer over low heat. Keep lid on pot throughout cooking period. (Bones may be softened slightly by placing in a 350° F. (177° C.) oven for about half an hour before adding.)

Add meats and maintain a slow simmering temperature. Meats may be removed as soon as fully cooked and put to any desired use, or they may be left in the pot to give their all to the stock.

Simmer stock for approximately 10 hours, or until bones appear dull and rough. When done, remove, strain, and discard contents. Cool as quickly as possible and refrigerate. When stock has jelled, remove congealed fat from surface. (Fat does not have good keeping qualities and may impart an off-flavor to stock.)

BROWN STOCK AND BROWN SAUCE

The ingredients in Brown Stock are essentially the same as for All-Purpose Stock with the exception that only beef or veal and beef bones are used.

To impart the rich amber color associated with this stock, as well as to add flavor, place one large unpeeled onion per quart of stock in a 350° F. (177° C.) oven for about 30 minutes or until skin turns slightly brown and syrup begins to ooze from stem. Remove and add to stock, skins and all, along with other ingredients (veal and beef bones, vegetables, herbs, spices, and liquid). Bring to a slow simmer and add whatever quantity of beef is being used. Proceed as with All-Purpose Stock.

Upon completion, the strained and de-fatted stock may be further enhanced with a tomato product such as tomato paste and is then known as Brown Sauce.

To make Brown Sauce, spoon the contents of a 4-ounce can of tomato paste (one can per 2 to 3 quarts of stock) into a heat-proof dish and set in a 300° F. (149° C.) oven, stirring occasionally, until paste is reduced somewhat and has taken on a slightly brown tinge. Add tomato paste to strained and de-fatted stock and simmer over low heat, uncovered, for about an hour, or until sauce is reduced by about a quarter of its original volume. The finished product should be slightly thick with a smooth, velvety appearance and a rich reddish brown color.

WHITE STOCK

White Stock is prepared and cooked using essentially the same ingredients as All-Purpose Stock with the exception that only veal bones and poultry carcasses and parts are used, and the meats are confined to poultry. (Vegetables, herbs, spices, and liquid remain the same). Simmer for approximately six or seven hours.

FISH STOCK

Fish Stock differs from All-Purpose Stock in that fish heads, bones, and trimmings (flounder, salmon, cod, snapper) replace meat and poultry bones. Portions of the flesh of fish may be added to enrich the stock. Due to the nature and softness of fish bones, the stock is simmered for a much shorter period, generally about 1½ to 3 hours. The addition of 1½ cups (360 ml) of dry white wine or vermouth to 2 quarts (960 ml) of water, will act as a tenderizer and shorten the cooking period somewhat as well as add flavoring—or substitute ¼ cup (60 ml) of vinegar to 2 quarts (1.9 l) of water. A small slice of fresh ginger root will serve to neutralize odors.

STORING

Strained and de-fatted stock will keep in the refrigerator for up to 5 or 6 days, after which it may be brought to a full rolling boil, cooled and re-stored. Stock will keep almost indefinitely following this regimen.

Stock may also be stored in heat-sealed boilable plastic pouches in the refrigerator or freezer and used as needed for soups, sauces, pot roasts, braisings, and other moist heat cooking procedures. The plastic pouches can be defrosted and heated by placing in an uncovered pot of boiling water for about 5 to 6 minutes.

NOURISHING AND FLAVORFUL SOUPS

THE BASIS OF SOUP MAKING   The success of both soups and sauces depends to a great extent on the quality of the stock used. A thin, nongelatinous, flavorless stock will produce a soup or sauce of equal stature.

Essentially, soups are preparations in which any one vegetable or combination of vegetables is cooked in one of the following liquids:

◇ All-Purpose Stock
◇ White, Brown, or Fish Stock
◇ White Stock combined with milk or cream
◇ A combination of Fish Stock and White Stock

Bring the stock to a full boil and add the peeled and uniformly chopped vegetables. These should be cooked, uncovered, over high heat to the slightly crisp stage. (The natural coloring of vegetables should be enhanced after proper cooking.) Coarser vegetables are cooked first. Members of the onion family are added last and are cooked over low heat in barely simmering liquid.

THICKENING   Soups may be lightly thickened if desired, using potato starch, cornstarch, or flour moistened with liquid. Use approximately one tablespoon starch and two tablespoons flour for every 2 quarts (1.9 l) liquid. For thicker soups, double the amount. Soups made from vegetables with a high starch content such as potatoes do not require thickening.

SEASONINGS   Finely chopped fresh herbs or dried herbs (parsley, dill, chervil, tarragon, oregano) may be added to enhance the flavor of soups. Such spices as salt, pepper, garlic powder, soy sauce, Tabasco, cayenne, paprika, saffron may also be used with discretion. A proportionate amount of dry sherry or wine imparts additional flavor to soups. These are added to accentuate the flavor or to give a more distinctive flavor to the soup.

Purees

Purees are soups in which the cooked preparation is pureed or strained, and thickened if necessary. While these soups were once pureed by pressing them through a wire strainer or handmill, this may now be quickly accomplished using an electric blender or food processor. Potato, bean, and pea soup are examples of soups that do not require further thickening, whereas carrot, mixed vegetable, and celery preparations would need some thickening.

Chowders or Bisques

Chowders or bisques are soups with a fish base, whose stock—Fish Stock or White and Fish Stock—is generally combined with milk or cream. Because of the natural tenderness of fish, these soups are simmered very slowly over low heat until both fish and vegetables are done. To ensure a shorter cooking period, vegetables should first be blanched. If potatoes form the main vegetable component of a chowder or bisque, no thickening is necessary, whereas a mixed vegetable preparation such as Manhattan Clam Chowder requires a slight thickening.

Broths and Consommés

Broths and consommés are clear, rich soups prepared by adding approximately one pound (.45 kg) of ground raw beef or poultry to every two quarts (1.9 l) of stock—All-Purpose, Brown, or White Stock—along with finely minced flavoring vegetables (carrots, celery, leeks). Dry wine or sherry in proportionate amounts (approximately ¼ cup (59 ml) wine or sherry to 1 quart (one liter) stock) may be added for additional flavoring. It is cooked, covered, over low heat for about an hour after it reaches the slow simmering stage. Stock is then removed, strained, and set aside to cool. When cool, remove all fat from surface.

Consommés and broths are served clear and must be clarified (see below). They may be served plain or with garnishes, such as strips of cooked vegetables or meats, croutons, rice, noodles, or poached ground meats molded into miniature shapes in the manner of quenelles (referred to as Royales when served with Broths and Consommés).

Clarifying Broths and Consommés

For every two quarts of broth, beat two egg whites to soft peaks and add to cold Consommé or Broth. Set over medium heat and stir using a wire whisk until liquid reaches a full boil. Turn off heat and let stand for about half an hour before straining through a paper filter or fine wire strainer. Reheat before serving. Consommés and Broths keep for a considerable period—up to 7 or 8 days—when stored in the refrigerator.

Aspics

Rich Consommés and Broths, when clarified, may be chilled and used as Aspics. If the broth has not sufficiently gelled, add approximately one envelope of unflavored gelatine to one quart (1 liter) of Consommé, depending on desired consistency, by first softening the gelatine in a small amount of stock, wine, or water over low heat. When the mixture is cool, it may be used to make molds of cold vegetables, meats, or fish, or to spoon over and coat pâtés and cold meats.

STORING

When completely cool, store soups in heat-sealed boilable plastic pouches or airtight containers and refrigerate or freeze. When ready to use, plastic pouches may be placed in boiling water for 10 or 15 minutes or until heated through.

REHEATING

Large quantities of soup may be reheated in an earthenware dish, such as a bean crock, in a preheated 325° F. (163° C.) oven until it just barely simmers. Small amounts may be reheated in an uncovered pot on top of the stove over low heat.

THICKENING AGENTS

To lightly thicken gravy, soups, sauces, and other liquids stir in any one of the following and maintain a low heat setting until the mixture thickens. To one pint of liquid (480 ml) add:

2 tablespoons flour ⎫ 1 tablespoon butter ⎬	Blend flour and butter and stir in. (This is known as beurre manié; see p. 40.)
2 tablespoons flour ⎫ 2 tablespoons cold water ⎬ 2 tablespoons hot liquid ⎭	Blend flour and water, forming a smooth paste and add hot liquid before stirring in.

1 tablespoon cornstarch	}	Blend cornstarch and water and add
2 tablespoons cold water	}	hot liquid before stirring in.
2 tablespoons hot liquid	}	

1 tablespoon potato starch	}	Blend potato starch and water and add
2 tablespoons cold water	}	hot liquid before stirring in.
2 tablespoons hot liquid	}	

If a moderately thick liquid (sauces, soups, gravies, etc.) is preferred, as opposed to a lightly thickened one, increase the above amounts accordingly.

Thickening with Egg Yolks

Egg yolks add flavor as well as a pale yellow coloring to any liquid. To lightly thicken a pint of sauce, soup, or gravy, blend 1 egg yolk with 2 tablespoons light cream or milk. Mix in a small amount of the hot liquid before adding. Care must be taken not to allow liquid to simmer once egg yolk mixture has been added, otherwise it will curdle. If the dish will not be served immediately, keep it warm in the top of a double boiler over hot (not boiling) water. (To avoid bacterial growth, keep it warm for relatively short periods or, to be on the safe side, add egg yolk immediately before serving.) Additional yolks may be added for a thicker preparation.

SOUP RECIPES

BASIC VEGETABLE SOUP

1. Bring the desired quantity of All-Purpose Stock to a full boil in an uncovered pot, over high heat. Add any or all of the following vegetables in the desired quantities* (peeled and uniformly sliced or chopped), as well as any *fresh* herbs being used:

carrots	*tomatoes, peeled, seeded, and*
celery	*chopped*
green beans	*fresh herbs (parsley, dill, tar-*
wax beans	*ragon, summer savoury,*
turnips (white or yellow)	*chervil, or oregano), finely*
	chopped

*In preparing vegetable soup, the proportion of vegetables to stock depends on individual preference for a thick or thin soup.

2. When above vegetables are still fairly crisp, add any or all of the following in the desired quantities, and cook for about 3 to 4 minutes, or until fairly tender:

greens (spinach, collards, swisschard), thoroughly washed and chopped medium fine

cabbage, red or white, washed and chopped medium fine
mushrooms, peeled and sliced

3. When this group of vegetables is tender, add any or all of the following cooked dried and grain vegetables in the desired quantities and cook over low heat just long enough to heat through and blend flavors (approximately 5 or 6 minutes):

beans (regular white beans, lima beans, navy beans, black beans, red beans, yellow-eyed beans)

fully cooked long-grained brown or white rice
barley
corn kernels
pasta (noodles, macaroni)

4. Finally, add any of the following members of the onion family, along with any *dried* herbs being used, in the desired quantities and cook for 2 or 3 minutes over low heat:

red onions, white onions, leeks, chives, shallots, scallions, all peeled and uniformly sliced

parsley, dill, tarragon, summer savoury, chervil, or oregano

5. Lightly thicken, if desired, using 1 tablespoon potato starch or 2 tablespoons finely sifted flour, moistened in 1 or 2 tablespoons of liquid, for every 2 quarts (1.9 l) of soup. Mix in using a wire whisk and cook over low heat until lightly thickened. Double the amount of starch or flour for a thicker soup.

6. Check seasoning (salt and pepper) and adjust if necessary.

LEEK AND POTATO SOUP

2 large leeks
1 large onion, Bermuda or
  regular
2 tablespoons butter
3 or 4 medium-size baking
  potatoes
2 cups (480 ml) boiling water

1 teaspoon salt
1 cup (240 ml) hot milk
salt and white pepper to taste
1 cup (240 ml) milk
1 cup (240 ml) light cream
1 tablespoon fresh dill, finely
  chopped

Cut green tops and roots from leeks. Slice through center and wash under cold running water to remove grime. Dry thoroughly and cut into dice-size pieces. Peel onion and finely chop. Melt butter over low heat in a 3½ quart saucepan and add leeks and onion. Cook, covered, until soft and translucent, stirring occasionally. Peel potatoes, uniformly slice, and add along with 2 cups (480 ml) boiling water and 1 teaspoon salt. Cover saucepan and simmer over low heat until potatoes are fork tender. Add 1 cup (240 ml) hot milk and seasoning (salt and white pepper) to taste. (Potatoes will have absorbed most of the salt previously added.) Puree in blender, food processor or handmill.

Return to heat and add 1 cup (240 ml) each of milk and light cream plus 1 tablespoon of finely chopped dill. Cook over low heat, stirring occasionally, until soup begins to simmer. Remove from heat and serve hot or chilled.

BEET SOUP (BORSCH)

1 pound (450 g) lean ground
  pork
5 medium-size beets, peeled
2 quarts (1.9 l) All-Purpose
  Stock
½ medium-size white cabbage,
  finely shredded

1 teaspoon vinegar
salt and pepper as desired
1 tablespoon fresh dill, finely
  chopped
sour cream

Remove any outside layers of fat on pork and put through meat grinder.

Cut up 3 of the peeled beets into thin, uniform size slices.

Bring stock to a full boil and add ground pork and thinly sliced beets. Turn heat to low and simmer, covered, until both pork and beets have given their all to the stock, that is, until very tender.

In the meantime, mince the 2 remaining peeled beets using an electric food processor or hand grater. Strain minced beets, reserving juice.

Add shredded cabbage to soup and simmer, uncovered, until tender.

Remove soup from heat and strain. Return strained soup to heat and add vinegar and beet juice. Simmer for about 1 minute. Add seasoning, taste, and adjust if necessary.

Sprinkle with chopped dill and serve sour cream on the side.

CARROT SOUP

2 quarts (1.9 l) All-Purpose
    Stock
5 or 6 carrots, peeled and
    thinly sliced

2 onions, finely chopped
1 cup (240 ml) milk or light
    cream
salt and white pepper to taste

Bring stock to a full boil in an uncovered pot over high heat and add thinly sliced carrots. Cook until carrots have reached the slightly crisp stage. Reduce heat to low and add finely chopped onions. Simmer, uncovered, for about 10 minutes. Gradually add milk or light cream and bring back to the simmering point. Season to taste with salt and white pepper.

For a thicker soup, prepare a beurre manié by blending 2 tablespoons flour with 1 tablespoon butter and gradually add to soup, stirring with a wire whisk.

Soup may be garnished with a light sprinkling of finely chopped fresh parsley.

CELERY SOUP

2 quarts (1.9 l) All-Purpose
  Stock
1 head of celery (lower stalks
  only), peeled and finely
  chopped

2 onions, finely chopped
1 cup (240 ml) milk or light
  cream
salt and white pepper to taste

Proceed as with Carrot Soup, substituting celery for carrots.

CREAM OF SPINACH SOUP

2 quarts (1.9 l) All-Purpose
  Stock
1 pound (450 g) fresh spinach,
  washed and finely chopped

1 cup (240 ml) milk or cream
salt and pepper to taste
4 tablespoons flour
2 tablespoons butter

Bring stock to a full boil in an uncovered pot over high heat and add spinach. Cook for about two minutes after liquid returns to a boil. (Do not overcook as spinach should remain green and retain its full flavor.)

Turn heat to low and gradually add milk or cream. Bring to a slow simmer and season to taste with salt and pepper. Blend flour and butter and gradually add to soup, stirring with a wire whisk. Simmer until lightly thickened.

CREAM OF MUSHROOM SOUP

1 pound (450 g) mushroom
  stems and tops, peeled and
  sliced
butter and oil for frying
2 quarts (1.9 l) All-Purpose
  Stock

1 onion, finely chopped
1 cup (240 ml) light cream
salt and white pepper to taste
4 tablespoons flour
1 tablespoon butter

Sauté peeled and sliced mushrooms in butter and oil until golden brown. Fry minced onion until translucent.

Bring stock to a slow simmer in an uncovered pot and gradually add light cream. Add mushrooms and onions and gently simmer for about 20 minutes. Season to taste with salt and white pepper. Blend flour and butter and gradually add to soup, stirring with a wire whisk. Simmer until lightly thickened.

BEAN SOUP

½ pound (225 g) dried beans
water or All-Purpose Stock
1 teaspoon dry mustard

¼ pound (115 g) lean salt pork,
  diced
2 onions, finely chopped
salt and pepper to taste

Wash and sort dried beans, discarding any that are blemished. Place in a saucepan with sufficient cold water to fully cover, or replace half of the water with an equal amount of All-Purpose Stock. Saucepan must be at least double the capacity of beans and liquid to allow for swelling. Cover and soak for several hours or overnight.

After soaking, set over low heat and bring to a slow simmer, adding additional liquid as necessary to cover beans throughout the cooking process. Dissolve mustard in a tablespoon of water and add along with diced pork and chopped onions. Add seasoning to taste, bearing in mind that the pork contains a quantity of salt. Cover and regulate heat so that liquid barely simmers throughout the cooking period. Cook for about 5 to 6 hours or until beans are tender. Taste and adjust seasoning if necessary.

Dried beans may be replaced with dried peas, lentils, or limas. Because of their size and nature, all three require a shorter cooking period.

ONION SOUP

3 onions, peeled and sliced
2 tablespoons butter
3 tablespoons finely sifted
    flour
2 quarts (1.9 l) Brown Stock

1 cup (240 ml) dry red wine
French bread, sliced
cheese slices, Gruyère or Swiss

Fry onions in butter over medium heat until lightly brown. Do not overcrowd pan. Add flour and stir over low heat for about 1 minute, adding additional butter if necessary.

Bring Brown Stock and wine to a full boil over high heat in an uncovered saucepan and cook for about 1 minute. Reduce heat to low and add onion-flour mixture. Simmer very gently for about 10 minutes. Pepper may be used as a seasoning but avoid salt because the cheese is already highly salted.

Ladle soup into individual ovenproof bowls. Spread French bread slices with butter and lay a slice of cheese on top of each. Add one each to bowls containing soup and place under broiler or in a 500° F. (260° C.) oven until cheese has melted. Serve at once.

SAUCES FOR GOOD NUTRITION

Basically, sauces are nothing more than stocks or combinations of stocks with milk or cream, lightly thickened. Sauces may also be prepared from a pure milk or cream base.

As with soup, the excellence of the sauce depends almost entirely on the quality of the stock. Sauces prepared with a rich, gelatinous stock—defatted and lightly thickened—are almost as nutritious as a clear broth or consommé. In the past, sauces were served heavily thickened with the fat content only partially removed, if at all. Also, flours were not as finely milled and took considerable time to form an emulsion. Today, the opposite is true and care must be taken not to expose the flour to too high a temperature or for too long, otherwise the cells will break down and the sauce will not thicken.

There are various ways of thickening liquids (see Thickening Agents, p. 32) but the following are the most commonly used for sauces.

Beurre Manié

To thicken a pint (480 ml) of sauce, prepare a beurre manié by blending 2 tablespoons finely sifted flour with 1 tablespoon butter. This mixture is added to barely simmering liquid over low heat, using a wire whisk, and takes but a few minutes to cook and thicken.

Roux

To thicken a pint (480 ml) of sauce by using a Roux, melt 1 tablespoon of butter over low heat and stir in two tablespoons finely sifted flour. Cook for about 1 minute, stirring, before gradually adding basis for sauce (stock, milk, or cream). Bring liquid to a slow simmer and cook, stirring, until lightly thickened (this should take no more than a minute or so once liquid reaches the simmering point). In a Beurre Manié the solid ingredients are gradually stirred into the liquid, whereas the liquid is gradually added to the cooked Roux.

Cornstarch Thickener

To thicken a pint (480 ml) of sauce, blend 1 tablespoon cornstarch with 2 tablespoons stock or water and mix into barely simmering liquid, using a wire whisk. Cook over medium low heat, stirring, until lightly thickened.

VARIATIONS OF SAUCES

Frequently, stocks are further enhanced to give sauces their distinctive flavor. For instance, fresh lemon juice is added to lightly thickened All-Purpose or White Stock to produce Lemon Sauce. It may be further enhanced with tarragon, along with a dash of garlic powder, to produce Lemon-Tarragon Sauce. This is a basic type of sauce which can be served with almost any food category—poultry, fish, shellfish, veal, pork, and vegetable dishes. Another variation is achieved by adding capers to the basic Lemon Sauce to produce Caper Sauce, a piquant-type sauce to add zest to fish, veal, and other mild-flavored preparations.

A weak stock can be improved by the addition of nonstarchy vegetables such as carrots, onions, leeks, celery, or shallots; or by lemon, tomato, or other juices, as well as sherry or wine. Herbs and seasonings may also be used. *A stock, however, must have some gelatinous content to give it a smooth, velvety quality.*

Canned Broths

Canned broths may be used as a stock base in the preparation of sauces. They are, however, not a true stock, since, for the most part, they have no gelatin content. One exception is canned beef broth to which unflavored gelatin is frequently added; nonetheless this is a poor substitute for the natural, gelatinous qualities of a good stock, in terms of both flavor and nutrition. Canned broths are usually prepared with a mixture of flavor compounds, and their preservative and spice strength (salt, sugar) is relatively high. They should be exposed to heat just long enough to bring to a full boil, otherwise the salt flavor is intensified as the liquid is reduced.

Hollandaise Sauces

The Hollandaise Sauces are based on fat (butter or oil), eggyolks, and vinegar or citrus juice, and are more of a dressing than a sauce, except that they are served warm and not cold.

USES FOR SAUCES

Sauces are served as accompaniments to meats, poultry, fish, shellfish, vegetables, pasta, and other grain products as well binders for casserole-type dishes, meat-vegetable pies, and similar preparations. Brown Sauce is frequently used for moist heat cooking procedures, as well as a flavor enhancer for meat dishes.

SAUCE RECIPES

LEMON SAUCE

1 pint (480 ml) All-Purpose
   Stock
dash of garlic powder

juice of one whole lemon
salt and pepper to taste

Bring stock to a slow simmer over medium low heat. Turn heat to low and add garlic powder, lemon juice, and seasoning to taste. Lightly thicken using a beurre manié.

LEMON-TARRAGON SAUCE

1 pint (480 ml) All-Purpose
   Stock
dash of garlic powder
2 teaspoons finely chopped
   fresh tarragon; or ½
   teaspoon dried tarragon

juice of one whole lemon
salt and pepper to taste

Bring stock to a slow simmer over medium low heat. Turn heat to low and add garlic powder, tarragon, lemon juice, and seasoning to taste. Cook long enough to blend and lightly thicken using a beurre manié.

MUSHROOM SAUCE

½ pound (225 g) mushrooms,
   peeled and sliced
butter for frying

1 pint (480 ml) All-Purpose
   Stock
salt and pepper to taste

Sauté peeled and sliced mushrooms in butter until golden brown and set aside. Bring stock to a slow simmer over medium low heat and add mushrooms and seasoning to taste. Cook long enough to blend and lightly thicken using a beurre manié.

MILDLY FLAVORED TOMATO SAUCE

*1 pint (480 ml) All-Purpose
Stock
1 8-ounce (225 g) can tomato
sauce*

*dash of garlic powder
juice of ½ lemon
salt and pepper to taste*

Bring stock and tomato sauce to a slow simmer over medium low heat. Reduce heat to low and add garlic powder, lemon juice, and seasoning to taste. Cook long enough to blend and lightly thicken using a beurre manié.

STRONGLY FLAVORED TOMATO SAUCE

*1 pint (480 ml) All-Purpose
Stock
1 8-ounce (225 g) can tomato
sauce
dash of garlic powder*

*1 tablespoon catsup
dash of Tabasco
juice of ½ lemon
salt and paper to taste*

Bring stock and tomato sauce to a slow simmer over medium low heat. Reduce heat to low and add garlic powder, catsup, Tabasco, lemon juice, and seasoning to taste. Cook long enough to blend and lightly thicken using a beurre manié.

CURRY SAUCE

*1 pint (480 ml) All-Purpose
Stock
1 onion, peeled and finely
chopped
butter for frying*

*1 tablespoon curry powder, or
to taste
½ cup (120 ml) cream (op-
tional)*

Bring stock to a slow simmer over medium low heat. In the meantime, fry onion in a small amount of butter until translucent. Remove and add to stock along with curry powder. Cook long enough to blend. Check seasoning and correct if necessary. Reduce heat to low and gradually add cream, stirring, until heated through. Lightly thicken using a beurre manié.

CAPER SAUCE

1 pint (480 ml) All-Purpose
    Stock
dash of garlic powder

juice of one whole lemon
salt and pepper to taste
2 tablespoons pickled capers

Bring stock to a slow simmer over medium low heat. Reduce heat to low and add garlic powder, lemon juice, and seasoning to taste. Cook long enough to blend, and add capers. Lightly thicken using a beurre manié.

ORANGE SAUCE NO. 1

1 cup (240 ml) orange juice
1 cup (240 ml) Chicken Broth
    or All-Purpose Stock

2 tablespoons dry sherry
1 tablespoon cornstarch, dissolved in 1 to 2 tablespoons of water

Bring orange juice, chicken broth or stock, and sherry to a slow simmer over low heat. Add dissolved starch, and cook, stirring with a wire whisk, until lightly thickened and sauce takes on a glossy appearance.

Serve with ham, pork, chicken, or duck.

Orange Sauce No. 2

Substitute 2 cups (480 ml) orange juice for 1 of orange juice and 1 of chicken broth or stock.

Cherry Orange Sauce

Add 2 tablespoons cherry or cherry-orange marmalade to Orange Sauce No. 1 or No. 2.

PARSLEY SAUCE

2 tablespoons fresh parsley, finely chopped and blanched

1 tablespoon fresh parsley, finely chopped

1 pint (480 ml) All-Purpose Stock

salt and pepper to taste

½ cup (120 ml) cream

Steep 2 tablespoons finely chopped fresh parsley in hot water over low heat for about 1 minute and drain, using a wire strainer.

Bring stock to a slow simmer over medium low heat and add blanched parsley along with remaining tablespoon of finely chopped fresh parsley. Cook long enough to blend over low heat and add seasoning to taste. Gradually add cream, stirring until heated through. Thicken lightly using a beurre manié.

ORIENTAL SAUCE

2 tablespoons soy sauce

¼ cup (60 ml) dry sherry

2 tablespoons granulated sugar

1 pint (480 ml) All-Purpose Stock

pinch of Oriental 5-spices or allspice

1 tablespoon cornstarch

2 tablespoons sherry

Add soy sauce, ¼ cup dry sherry, and sugar to stock and set over low heat, stirring until dissolved. Bring to a slow simmer and add spice. Dissolve cornstarch in 2 tablespoons sherry and mix in using a wire whisk, stirring until lightly thickened.

SPAGHETTI SAUCE

½ pound (225 g) sweet or hot
Italian sausage
½ pound (225 g) lean ground
beef
½ clove garlic, peeled and
finely diced
1 onion, peeled and finely
chopped
1 small green pepper, seeded
and coarsely chopped
¼ pound (115 g) mushrooms,
peeled and sliced

1 quart (960 ml) Brown Sauce
½ cup (120 ml) dry red wine
2 tablespoons tomato paste
1 tablespoon fresh parsley,
finely chopped
½ teaspoon dried oregano, or
to taste
olive oil for frying
salt and pepper to taste

Blanch sausage in enough cold water to cover and bring to a slow simmer over low heat. If you are using partially cooked sausage, cook for 3 or 4 minutes; if you are using uncooked sausage, cook for 10 to 15 minutes, or until both are fully cooked. (This also removes any excess fat). Drain and slice.

Sauté lean ground beef in a small amount of oil.

Fry garlic, onions, and pepper in oil over low heat until translucent. (They should be slightly crisp).

Sauté peeled and sliced mushrooms in oil until golden brown.

Bring Brown Sauce, wine, and tomato paste to a slow simmer over low heat and add sliced sausage, browned beef, cooked vegetables, finely chopped parsley and oregano. Cook just long enough to blend. Add salt and pepper to taste.

BORDELAISE SAUCE

2 tablespoons shallots, peeled
and finely chopped
butter and oil for frying

1 pint (480 ml) Brown Sauce
¾ cup (180 ml) dry red Bordeaux wine
salt and pepper to taste

Fry shallots in a small amount of butter and oil over low heat until translucent.

Add wine to Brown Sauce and bring to a slow simmer over medium low heat. Cook, uncovered, for 3 or 4 minutes, or, until slightly reduced. Stir in shallots and season to taste with salt and pepper. Lightly thicken using a beurre manié.

MADEIRA SAUCE

Follow recipe for Bordelaise Sauce, substituting ¾ cup (180 ml) Madeira wine or dry sherry for red Bordeaux wine.

BARBECUE SAUCE NO. 1

4 tablespoons vegetable oil
4 tablespoons flour (finely sifted)
2 cups (480 ml) All-Purpose Stock or Brown Stock
1 cup (240 ml) Tomato Sauce
2 tablespoons tomato paste
juice of 1 small lemon
4 tablespoons vinegar

1 tablespoon sugar
1 teaspoon dry mustard, dissolved in 1 to 2 teaspoons of water
1 tablespoon Worcestershire sauce
pinch of cayenne pepper
few grains garlic powder
1 tablespoon grated onion
salt and pepper to taste

Heat oil in saucepan, add flour and cook over low heat, stirring, for about 1 minute. Gradually add stock, tomato sauce, tomato paste, lemon juice, vinegar, sugar, dissolved mustard, Worcestershire sauce, pinch of cayenne pepper, garlic powder, and grated onion. Bring to a simmer over low heat and cook, uncovered, stirring with a wire whisk, until thickened. Continue to cook for another 5 to 10 minutes, or until slightly reduced and flavors are well blended. (For a thicker sauce, add 1 or 2 tablespoons additional flour.) Season to taste with salt and pepper.

Use with barbecued meats and poultry.

BARBECUE SAUCE NO. 2

½ cup (120 ml) vegetable oil   ½ cup (120 ml) soy sauce (light
½ cup (120 ml) honey   or dark)

Combine oil, honey, and soy sauce, stirring until well blended.

Use with barbecued meats and poultry.

CREOLE SAUCE

2 or 3 scallions (whites only), peeled and sliced
1 small green pepper, seeded and chopped
2 stalks celery, peeled and finely chopped
½ clove garlic
½ Spanish onion, peeled and finely chopped
butter and oil for frying
1 24-ounce (170 g) can tomatoes, pureed
2 cups (480 ml) All-Purpose Stock

2 tablespoons tomato paste
½ cup (120 ml) dry red wine
juice of 1 lemon
1 tablespoon fresh parsley, finely chopped
¼ teaspoon dried tarragon
½ teaspoon paprika
½ teaspoon chili powder, or to taste
pinch of cayenne pepper
salt and pepper to taste

Fry scallions, green pepper, celery, garlic, and onions in a small amount of butter and oil over low heat until translucent and slightly crisp.

Puree tomatoes in blender and remove seeds using a wire strainer. (Do not substitute canned tomato puree.)

Combine pureed and strained tomatoes, stock, tomato paste, wine, and lemon juice and bring to a slow simmer over low heat. Add parsley, tarragon, paprika, chili powder, and cayenne and simmer, uncovered, for about 10 minutes, or until slightly reduced. Add cooked vegetables and gently simmer just long enough to blend. (Vegetables should remain slightly crisp.)

Season to taste with salt and pepper.

WHITE SAUCE (BÉCHAMEL)

1 cup (240 ml) White Stock and 1 cup (240 ml) milk or light cream; or 2 cups (480 ml) milk or light cream

1 tablespoon butter
2 tablespoons finely sifted flour
salt and white pepper to taste

Bring 1 cup stock and 1 cup milk or light cream (or 2 cups milk or light cream) to a full boil over low heat. Remove and set aside. To prepare Roux, melt butter over low heat and stir in finely sifted flour. Cook for about 1 minute, stirring. Gradually add scalded liquid and cook, stirring with a wire whisk, until lightly thickened. (This should take but a minute or so.)

MUSTARD SAUCE

½ to 1 teaspoon dry English mustard

2 teaspoons butter

Blend mustard and butter and add to prepared White Sauce (Béchamel).

CHEESE SAUCE

½ to 1 cup (120 ml to 240 ml) grated cheese (Cheddar, Swiss, Parmesan), depending on desired degree of thickness.

Add grated cheese to prepared White Sauce (Béchamel) when hot. Set over very low heat, stirring until well blended. If necessary, keep warm over hot water (a double boiler may be used) but do not allow to simmer.

MUSTARD-CHEESE SAUCE

½ to 1 teaspoon dry English
  mustard

2 teaspoons butter
½ cup grated Cheddar cheese

Blend mustard and butter and add to White Sauce (Béchamel) when hot. Turn heat to very low and stir in grated cheese. Cook, stirring, just long enough to blend. Keep warm over hot water, but do not allow sauce to simmer.

SHELLFISH SAUCE

2 cups (480 ml) Fish Stock
  (clam juice may be
  substituted); or 1 cup Fish
  Stock (or canned clam
  juice) and 1 cup (240 ml)
  milk or light cream
1 tablespoon butter
2 tablespoons finely sifted
  flour

3 or 4 tablespoons cooked
  shellfish (shrimp, lobster),
  finely minced
pinch of cayenne pepper
1 teaspoon paprika
4 tablespoons dry white wine
salt and white pepper to taste

Bring Fish Stock, or combination of Fish Stock and milk or light cream, to a full boil over low heat.

Melt butter in saucepan over low heat and stir in finely sifted flour. Cook for about 1 minute. Gradually add scalded stock or combination of stock and milk or light cream. Add minced shellfish, cayenne pepper, paprika, and wine and gently simmer over low heat, uncovered, long enough to absorb shellfish flavor. Add salt and pepper to taste. Remove and strain before using.

SHRIMP OR LOBSTER SAUCE

8 to 10 small cooked shrimp;
or 4 or 5 tablespoons
cooked lobster meat, cut
into small chunks

Prepare a Shellfish Sauce, strain, and return to heat. Add shrimp or lobster and cook over low heat just long enough to heat through.

The following sauces are served with meats, fish, shellfish, and vegetables. Because of their rich nature, they are served in small quantities and are served warm, rather than hot.

HOLLANDAISE SAUCE

1½ sticks (or 170 g) butter (12   *3 large egg yolks*
   tablespoons)   *pinch of salt*
4 teaspoons lemon juice   *pinch of cayenne pepper*

Break butter into three pieces and place one in top of double boiler. Set over low heat. Add lemon juice and egg yolks, and whisk briskly until butter is melted. Add the second piece of butter and continue beating until mixture thickens. Check from time to time to make certain water in lower portion of double boiler is not boiling—it should be just under the simmering point throughout the cooking period. Add the last piece of butter and continue to beat. When sauce has thickened, remove from heat. Stir in salt and cayenne.

Sauce may be thinned out by the addition of hot water. For a thicker sauce, add an additional egg yolk.

Should sauce curdle, add about a tablespoon of boiling water and beat constantly to rebuild the emulsion.

Extra Light Hollandaise Sauce

Whip ⅓ cup (80 ml) heavy cream and fold in just before removing sauce from heat. Stir and cook about 30 seconds. Remove and stir in salt and cayenne as in regular Hollandaise Sauce.

Lemon Hollandaise Sauce

Add a teaspoon grated lemon rind to lemon juice.

Orange Hollandaise Sauce

Substitute orange juice for lemon and grated orange rind for grated lemon rind.

Mustard Hollandaise Sauce

Replace lemon juice with 1½ tablespoons tarragon vinegar. Mix 1½ teaspoons powdered mustard with 1 tablespoon water and let stand a few minutes for flavor to develop. Stir into finished sauce.

THE
MEAT MYSTIQUE

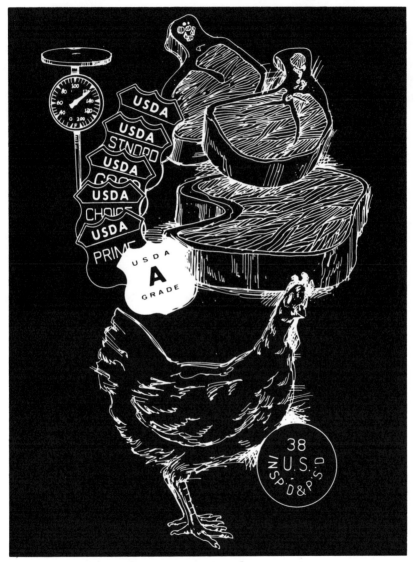

chapter three

THE STORY OF AMERICA'S
MEAT CONSUMPTION IN BRIEF

The cud-chewing process of ruminants makes it possible to convert low-cost grasses and grains into high-priced meat and milk. The stomachs of cattle, sheep, and goats differ from humans' in that they have four chambers. The "pig-headed" pig (so called because he refuses to be herded) also has but one stomach, and thus cannot use roughage to the same degree—but can convert grain into pork.

The meat industry has always been of prime importance in the overall scheme of the American economy. At times, it has done a greater volume of business than the combined output of the steel industry and one or two others. Up until the turn of the century, there had been little need for any high-pressure advertising. Prices had more or less risen over the years, and producers and processors remained satisfied. But the picture had begun to change. For one thing, England, known for the excellence of its beef, had reduced its share of imported meat from America. Some records indicate that the American beef did not compare favorably with that raised at home, and there seemed to be little demand for it. Careme has left us his impressions of English meat when he worked there in the nineteenth century: "The cattle are fat and of very good quality, as is the mutton, veal and lamb; the roast beef is succulent, much more so than ours in France." However, no doubt of greater significance to this development were the appearance of articles in British medical journals on the squalid conditions obtaining in American slaughter houses and meat-processing plants. During these same years, Upton Sinclair, now an honored and esteemed writer, but then a novice reporter for a New York weekly, was assigned to investigate these conditions. He aimed his sights at the Chicago stockyards, the largest and best known, although similar conditions were said to exist throughout the country. His exposure of grossly unsanitary conditions and the inhumane slaughtering of animals— by strangulation, by piercing the brain through the eye sockets with heated shears, or by dipping in vats of scalding water to facilitate the removal of their hides—not only aroused indignation but hit on a sensitive area, for aside from other considerations, puritans never wish to be reminded of the source of their food(!). Sinclair's intention in publishing *The Jungle* in 1906 was to arouse sympathy for the men who worked under such deplorable conditions in the meat-packing plants; instead, as he himself put it, "I aimed at the public's heart and by accident I hit it in the stomach."

The impact of these events led into the enactment of the National Meat Inspection Law, which mandated a system of rigid controls over animal health, before and after slaughter, and also provided for the inspection and supervision of meat-packing plants. Previous Acts of Congress had leaned in the direction of government inspection, but the appropriations were insufficient and so went unenforced. Since then, the consumer has been assured of clean, wholesome meat.

The meat industry had barely recovered from the above onslaught when food and health "experts" came up with some convincing arguments against the quantity of meat being consumed, claiming that it led to high blood pressure, heart disease, hardening of the arteries, and rheumatism, and that too much meat was definitely injurious to good health. As a result of these reports, which began gaining credence among the general public during those early years of the twentieth century, the meat industry suffered another relapse—of a rather persistent nature. Meat prices began to decline, based on decreasing demand. As it became more evident that some kind of drastic action would be required, representatives of every sector of the meat industry met and organized The National Livestock and Meat Board in 1922. Its main target was to research and publicize the overall nutritional value of meat. One widely publicized item was the importance of meat in weight-reducing diets, another was the discovery of the value of liver in the prevention and treatment of simple anemia. By-products were also developed, for example, margarine, which was originally made from beef fats known as oleos.

Meat cookery played a big part in the campaign. Recipe books were distributed in the millions. Charts showing photographs of various cuts of different grades and classes were made available.

Factual information for combating the anti-meat reaction stressed the high nutritional value of meat proteins and fats, such as the fact that meat fat has 2.25 times the energy value of carbohydrates. The meat diet of the hardy Eskimo was cited.

American consumers, always on the alert for some new need for adequate nutrition responded with more or less predictable behavior . . . if a little is good, more must be better. The pendulum swung back to higher meat consumption, with profits for the meat industry following suit.

Meat producers were ready to meet the increasing demands. Agriculture in the U.S. had more than kept step with the technological and industrial revolution—if anything, it was one or two paces ahead. Ultra-sophisticated farm machinery was already available, as were detoxification programs, pesticides, and insecticides, and methods had been developed for the artificial insemination of livestock.

In the meantime the number of births, worldwide, continued to outstrip the number of deaths. Heavily populated countries such as Japan and Russia began consuming increasing amounts of meat. The Chinese diet was no longer predominately vegetarian. These countries began to import large quantities of grain and corn from the U.S. and Canada to be converted into meat.

The American dream had also changed. No longer was it a "chicken in every pot" (one of Theodore Roosevelt's campaign promises) for Sunday dinner but rather a standing rib roast of top quality beef. Demand for those cuts requiring the least preparation time, and which might practically be considered meals in themselves, was on the increase. Commercially prepared hamburger meat—quick and easy for the home meal planner and profitable for the professional—became the biggest seller. By the 1970s meat consumption increased so much so that soybean proteins were introduced to "stretch" the consumer's meat dollar; ounce for ounce and dollar for dollar, however, these were deserving of some scrutiny.

As the demand for meat on the homefront and for feed grains abroad increased, prices went up while quality requirements for grading went down. The official U.S. grade standards were revised time and again: What was formerly "Good" was graded as "Choice" and what was formerly "Choice" was graded as "Prime" and so on. If a cut of meat did not appear to live up to the juicy Sunday roast served up in earlier times, it was more than mere fantasy.

By the beginning of the 1970s the consumption of meat per capita—and especially beef—had more than doubled since the days of the "Chicago Scandals." Later in the decade it began showing signs of a decline as prices became inflated and the effects of a high intake of meats on health and well-being were again being called into question. Producers of meat were quick to take heed, and in 1974 a committee to study the feasibility of initiating a new plan to "tell the industry's story" was formed. From this evolved the Beef Development Task Force representing beef and dairy producers as well as marketing organizations. This further led to the Beef Research and Information Act (signed into law on May 28, 1976), authorizing a nationally coordinated research and information program "to improve, maintain, and develop markets for cattle, beef, and beef products." The Act gave the Secretary of Agriculture responsibility for determining if an order should be issued permitting producers to establish, finance, and operate a program under the same rationale as existing programs for such products as wheat, potatoes, and eggs. Within a month, in June 1976, the U.S. Department of Agriculture published rules outlining the procedures to be followed in order to establish a Beef Board to collect and operate a research and information program in keeping with the Act. However, it was estimated that it would be some time before such a program would be developed to the point where even the first assessments could be made.

GRADING AND CLASSIFICATION

Perplexity and frustration are frequently registered on the faces of consumers standing over meat counters. It is the exceptional buyer who questions the contents of a meat package despite the fact that 35 to 40 percent of the American food dollar goes for meats. Experts confirm that less than nine percent of the meat produced can be placed in top grades. The distribution of the best of the top grades is usually restricted to those markets servicing wholesalers and professionals, sometimes referred to in the trade as those cooking for "paying guests."

In spite of the very real impact of meat purchases on a family's budget, few attempts have been made in recent years to educate the consumer, aside from charts distributed by the Livestock Board to retail outlets, who usually proceed to hang them on the far wall. "Choice Grade. Government Inspected" reads like choice fare but this label is only part of the story. Variations exist within each grade, sometimes referred to by those in the trade as heavy, average, or light. Officially, these classifications are known as yield grades, numbered 1 through 5 to indicate the amount of usable meat on a carcass after the waste fat has been trimmed off. Yield Grade 1 represents the highest yield of retail cuts and Yield Grade 5 the lowest. The two types of grades—quality and yield—are independent of each other. Choice, for example, can vary from Yield Grade 1 to Yield Grade 5. The yield designation does not, however, appear on retail cuts. Prior to 1939, this information was included along with the grade and inspection stamp on meats.

To recap, the top four grades of beef, out of an official eight, are Prime, Choice, Good, and Commercial. Within each grade are five yield grades. Taken together, the quality grade and the yield grade measure both the quality and quantity of lean meat. To further complicate the situation, the official standards for beef grading, first devised by the Department of Agriculture in 1928 (compliance still remains voluntary) are amended from time to time. The requiremetns for the Choice Grade have been changed most often, the last alteration having been proposed in 1975. After some opposition by consumer representative groups, the new standards for Choice became official in 1976.

Examples of Grade Descriptions

The official standard for Prime Grade beef reads in part: "The cut surface of the muscle must be firm, fine in texture, and bright in color. Slight abundant marbling must be evident in the rib eye muscles of carcasses with soft, red chine bones terminating in soft pearly white cartilages."

For Choice the description leaves considerable room for leeway: "The rib eye has a moderate amount of marbling and is usually slightly soft and fine in texture. Wholesale cuts are moderately blocky and compact and moderately thick-fleshed throughout. The color of the muscle usually ranges from a light red to slightly dark red. It is usually uniform and bright in color but may be slightly two-toned or slightly shady."

LAMB CHART

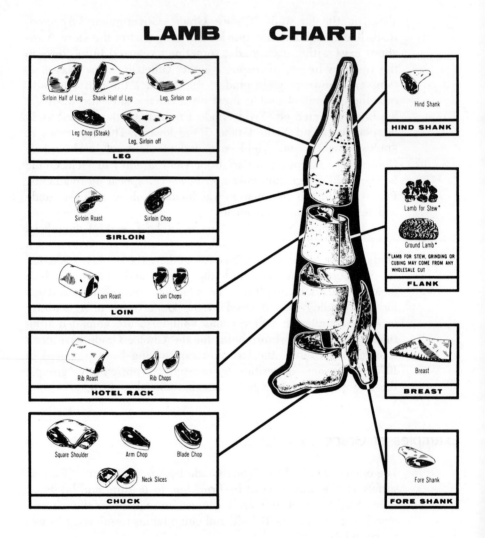

BEEF CHART

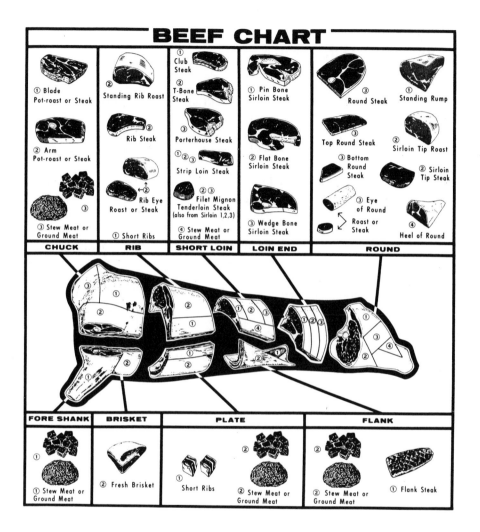

CHUCK
- ① Blade Pot-roast or Steak
- ② Arm Pot-roast or Steak
- ③ Stew Meat or Ground Meat

RIB
- Standing Rib Roast
- ② Rib Steak
- Rib Eye Roast or Steak
- ① Short Ribs

SHORT LOIN
- ① Club Steak
- ② T-Bone Steak
- ③ Porterhouse Steak
- ①②③ Strip Loin Steak
- ②③ Filet Mignon Tenderloin Steak (also from Sirloin 1,2,3)
- ④ Stew Meat or Ground Meat

LOIN END
- ① Pin Bone Sirloin Steak
- ② Flat Bone Sirloin Steak
- ③ Wedge Bone Sirloin Steak

ROUND
- ③ Round Steak
- ① Standing Rump
- ③ Top Round Steak
- ② Sirloin Tip Roast
- ③ Bottom Round Steak
- ② Sirloin Tip Steak
- ③ Eye of Round Roast or Steak
- ④ Heel of Round

FORE SHANK
- ① Stew Meat or Ground Meat

BRISKET
- ② Fresh Brisket

PLATE
- ① Short Ribs
- ② Stew Meat or Ground Meat

FLANK
- ② Stew Meat or Ground Meat
- ① Flank Steak

GUIDELINES
FOR SELECTING MEATS

The relative quality of meats will affect the degree of success in cooking more than any other food category. The following are guidelines for selecting quality meats on which much of the flavor and nutritional value will depend.

COLOR Muscle myoglobin and blood hemoglobin give meat its pink or red color, the degree of coloring being dependent upon the amount of both present. Usually, the older the animal, the darker the meat. Beef is always darker when first cut, but upon exposure to the air for half an hour changes to a bright shade of red. After a period of time, depending on favorable or unfavorable temperature and moisture conditions, the meat will again turn dark. Beef that has been aged for 6 to 8 weeks will show a very dark, even a moldy surface, but a thin slice will remove this discoloration and the newly cut surface will be bright and fresh.

The color of the lean is important in suggesting the age of the animal, because as the animal grows older the meat turns a darker shade.

◇ Beef ranges in color from a bright cherry red to a dark red.
◇ Veal is a very pale grey-pink.
◇ Pork is grey-pink to grey-red.
◇ Lamb is light pink, and mutton is brick red in color.

FAT The fat covering should be firm and dry; if it is soft and oily, the meat will reflect that softness in poor quality.

FIRMNESS A soft, soggy, watery meat is not a quality meat.

TEXTURE A fine texture gives meat a smooth, velvety appearance; a coarse textured meat appears globular because of the thicker cell walls.

MARBLING The intermingling of fat among the muscle cells is considered the most important factor in giving quality to meat, since it relates to all the other factors. The unmarbled cut falls into the category of a "gravy cut" because it has no protection. (It is given this label by professionals who are aware that most of the juices in poor quality meats end up in the pan.)

ALL THERE IN RED AND WHITE

To evaluate meat, take a good look at the marbling, the color, the firmness of the fat, and the texture. Compare the eye in a Prime rib roast and see how much larger it is than one in a Good Grade. The size of the rib eye may also serve as a guide to the overall quality of meat sold by any one particular retailer.

Trimming the fat has some distinct advantages for sellers of meat but presents somewhat of a problem for consumers. Most retailers have outlets to which the fat is sold to be put to different uses. Bared roasts without a generous fat covering, however, quickly lose their juices during cooking. Furthermore, while it is still possible to check the quality of meat based on factors other than fat, it is impossible to check the U.S. Government Grade Stamp if it has been trimmed off along with the fat. Coloring matter, sometimes added to meats to improve their natural color, also adds to the difficulty of making an accurate estimation of quality.

LIVESTOCK NUTRITION
AND TENDERNESS

Animal tissue has long served human beings as one of their most important food sources. In archaic speech the words *meal* and *meat* were synonymous. From ancient times, and even for lay persons today, no significant differences among various meats, either nutritionally or chemically, have been apparent. The precise diets of animals whose flesh is consumed by humans are rarely called into question; yet what is good or bad for animals (with the exception of certain grasses) generally corresponds very nearly to nutritious substances for humans.

Animal diets consist of grasses, grain, a combination of

grasses and grain, corn, soybeans, sunflower seeds, wild grasses, milk, and scraps. Meat from grass-fed cattle is leaner than that from grain-fed animals. Cattle fed a high percentage of grain supplements (germ and bran—the nutritious segments stripped from the greater percentage of grain used for human consumption) wind up with a blue chip grading certificate, for the higher the fat content, more or less, the higher the grade. These meats cook up juicy and tender. The following chart shows the composition of beef according to four different grades (the fat content decreases as the grade goes down):

	Choice Grade	Good Grade	Commercial Grade	Utility Grade
Percent Fat	31%	25%	20%	15%
Percent Lean	53%	57%	60%	64%
Percent Bone	16%	18%	20%	21%
	100%	100%	100%	100%

In February 1976, revisions in grade standards, allowing a slightly larger percentage of lean than shown in the above figures, became effective.

A look at the various diets of animals will also give some inkling as to the flavor of the respective meats. The flesh of a milk-fed calf is almost white and is mildly flavored. It is interesting to note that pigs, which have served for so long as scavengers and garbage collectors of a sort, and whose skin is similar to that of humans, were used as research subjects by such early medical practitioners as Galen. A further look at animals' exercise patterns will tell something about the relative tenderness of their various muscles. At opposite ends of the pole would be the capon roosting about the barnyard all day feeding on corn and the game animal running free and feeding on wild grasses. The former would be sweet and tender, the latter relatively tough and strong flavored.

The animal flesh consumed by humans consists largely of muscle tissue, the principal nutrients of which are protein (albumin and myosin), fat, extractives, some minerals and vitamins, and traces of carbohydrates. The fat is deposited around, between, and within the muscles and lends cooked meat the larger part of its juiciness and flavor. The calcium content is chiefly in the bones.

The term *cut* applies to a piece of muscle tissue with the accompanying fat and bone. The large wholesale cuts are subdivided into retail cuts, and divisions are made in such a way as to separate tender from less tender parts.

Tender cuts come from those parts of an animal which receive the least exercise, and tough cuts derive from the more exercised muscles. Age (mature or immature) is another determining factor. However, all cuts from immature animals are not necessarily tender, as certain cuts of veal, for instance, have a high proportion of connective tissue and are considered tough cuts.

White Meats and Red Meats

Meats may be further distinguished as white meats or red meats. White meats are from immature animals and are so called because there is no heavy concentration of juices—they are present in the form of albumin only. There are no tough fibers or muscle tissue, and they generally contain a low percentage of fat and a high water content. (The leaner the meat, the more water it contains.) The percentage of connective tissue in young animals also runs high.

Red meats are from mature animals and are so called because there is a heavy concentration of juices. The fibers and connective tissue are tougher. They also have a higher fat content and a lower percentage of water than do most white meats.

NUTRITIVE VALUE

Meat is a valuable source of protein. Protein (from the Greek *prōteios* meaning first or primary), discovered over a hundred years ago, was the first substance recognized as a vital part of living tissue. Proteins may be classified according to their source (animal or plant) or they may be classified in terms of their amino acid composition: Naturally occurring proteins contain 23 amino acids. While most of these can be synthesized by the human organism and by animals, eight cannot and so must be furnished by foods consumed. These eight are known as essential amino acids. Animal proteins, as well as those of most dried legumes (beans, peas, lentils) contain amino acids in proportions approximating human needs. These types of protein are said to have a high biological value. Plant proteins are classified as of low biological value and must be consumed in greater quantity in order to meet the minimum amino acid requirements. On the other hand, a comparatively small amount of animal protein will supply one's daily amino acid requirement. (One cup of cooked lean ground beef (chuck) supplies 70 percent of the U.S. Recommended Daily Allowance.) Protein that exceeds one's needs is either immediately metabolized (from the Greek word meaning to change or exchange) or it is converted and stored as body fat.

The caloric content of a cut of meat depends on the amount of protein and fat it contains. Fat has approximately 2.25 times the energy value of other nutrients. Proteins and carbohydrates have the same caloric value, weight for weight.

Cholesterol is found in all meat and meat products. Organ meats (liver, kidney, heart) are high in cholesterol, and the meat from a young animal has a higher concentration of cholesterol than that from a more mature animal—veal has more than beef and lamb has more than mutton. Chicken and turkey have somewhat less cholesterol than beef.

All lean meats contain some niacin, riboflavin, and thiamine. Vitamin A can be found in the organ meats. Pork is valued as a source of thiamine. The nutritive value of poultry is similar to that of other meats. The proteins supplied are complete and contain all the amino acids essential to building and repairing body tissues.

THE AGE-OLD PRACTICE
OF AGEING MEATS

Since fresh meat is usually tough, it is often held or aged for a period, during which time a tenderizing action transpires. This action of protein enzymes on the connective tissues in the meat to reduce them to a gelatinous consistency is also known under the names of *hanging, ripening, holding,* and *seasoning.* As a result of ageing, a clear, syrupy acid, known as sarcolactic acid, is formed within the muscle cells. Similar reactions occur during the process of digestion, as well as when wine, vinegar, or fruit juice (that is, acetic acid) is used as a marinade.

At one time (in the not too distant past) meat was aged for a period of from four to six weeks. Today, only top graded meats are exposed to ageing, and most of these are distributed to hotels, restaurants, and other such establishments. The lower grades of meat (generally distributed to retail outlets—particularly supermarkets) are aged for 1 to 2 days before being shipped, which means that by the time the meat has reached the retail counters, a period of no more than approximately 6 to 10 days has elapsed.

Aside from the consideration of time, facilities, and labor, there is the question of shrinkage. Hung meat may shrink 3 percent in 1 week, as compared to 15 percent in 3 weeks, making it a question of profit and loss as much as anything.

Fortunately, present-day models of home refrigerators make it possible to expose meats to some ageing. Simply wrap meat lightly in a porous-type paper, such as wax paper or butcher's wrapping, and place it on a rack, for example, a cake rack (to provide for some air circulation) in the meat tender or other cold area of refrigerator. If your refrigerator has a meat compartment with a controlled temperature setting, adjust it to about 45° F. (7° C.). (Any type thermometer may be used to take a reading.) Most red meats, particularly the tough cuts, improve after being aged in this manner for 3 or 4 days. As always, much depends on the quality of the meat. Care must be taken, however, not to over-age the meat, which can result in an off-flavor and odor, as ascertained by a nose test.

Ageing affects both the tenderness and the flavor. Well-seasoned meats are juicier, and brown better in cooking.

MARINATING: AN ALTERNATE TO AGEING

The acetic acid found in wines, vinegar, and fruit juices is sometimes used as a substitute for the acid formed in the muscle cells during the natural ageing process. As a tenderizer, a marinade also contributes to the flavor of meats. It is considered beneficial in tougher cuts and lower grades of meat.

In times past marinating was partially used as a substitute for refrigeration and also to tenderize tough cuts of wild game. The Chinese continue to make extensive use of soy sauce as a marinade in their cooking procedures. Salt, the age-old preservative, was traditionally added to prevent retardation. In light of the fact that salt draws out meat's juices, particularly raw meats, and with present day refrigeration, it is not recommended for marinades.

In marinating, sufficient liquid—wines, vinegar, fruit juices—should be used to fully cover meat and a certain amount of oil is added to retard dehydration. Additional oil rubbed on the surfaces of the meat will help prevent drying. Any of the following may be used as flavoring enhancers:

⋄ *Herbs:* Parsley, rosemary, thyme, dill, bay leaf. When using dried herbs, rub between the palms of the hands to release the oils. Fresh herbs should be finely chopped.

⋄ *Spices:* Ginger, pepper, cloves, Chinese five-spices or allspice.

⋄ *Vegetables:* Onions, celery, carrots must be lightly fried in order to contribute to the flavor of the marinade.

⋄ *Garlic cloves:* Peeled and crushed.

A special plastic water-proof bag, generally sold as a roasting bag, makes an excellent receptacle for marinating. Tied with its own twister, it can be laid on a refrigerator shelf and turned from time to time to give meat even exposure to the marinade.

FREEZING MEATS:
TO FREEZE OR NOT TO FREEZE

The purpose of freezing meats is to inactivate the enzymes and bacteria. The lower the temperature, the longer the period of satisfactory storage.

Lean meat has a high percentage of water, which expands at both high (cooking) and low (freezing) temperatures. The actual point at which meat juices freeze is 28° F. (−2° C.), not 32° F. (−0° C.). Slow freezing causes the water content to separate from the rest of the cell and to collect in pools, which in turn stretches and ruptures some of the cell walls. This loss of juices is referred to as *drip loss.* Juices collected in the bottom of plastic wrapped meat containers are drip losses, and they affect both the flavor and nutrient content of the meat.

Freezer burn (the dry area that sometimes appears on the surface of frozen foods) is caused by loss of moisture resulting from exposure to heat and light. This too is an indication of loss of nutrients and flavor. Incorrect storage temperatures, inadequate wrapping, fluctuating temperatures, opening and closing the freezer door all contribute to deterioration of frozen meat.

In view of the fact that most fresh meats will keep under normal refrigerator conditions for at least several days, it is not necessary to freeze several days' or even a week's supply of meat—particularly the large cuts that require considerable thawing time. It is advisable to restrict the supply of frozen meats to a quantity necessary for emergency use only.

Ground meat should not be frozen unless one is certain of its freshness and quality. However, when meat is of good quality and has been freshly ground, it can be made into patties or meatballs and frozen. Such meat will keep in freezer for up to 2 to 3 weeks with little deterioration, if properly wrapped.

For easy separation, pack ground meat patties between layers of wax paper. Thin patties and miniature meatballs thaw in about an hour at refrigerator or cool-room temperature.

Before freezing meats, wrap in opaque (freezer) paper, or in aluminum foil, and place in heavy plastic bags, pressing out as much air as possible. (An electric heating appliance especially designed for sealing plastic bags can be used for this purpose.) List contents and date of freezing on outside of package, using a crayon-type pencil.

EXPOSING MEATS TO HEAT

THE PURPOSE   The purpose in exposing meat to heat, thereby changing its constituents, is mainly threefold:

1. To develop flavor
2. To tenderize for chewability, as well as for assimilation by the body
3. To kill microorganisms

THE CHANGES The following are some of the changes that take place when meat is exposed to heat:

1. The proteins in the muscle fibers are coagulated. As they draw together, there is a progressive firmness and some shrinkage.
2. Pigments in the meat are decomposed, causing a gradual change in color.
3. A small percentage of the liquefied fat (about 3 percent) penetrates the interior and encapsulates the cells, forming a protective coating for the juices. Since fat can withstand higher temperatures than muscle fibers without breaking down, any outside layer of fat will be beneficial in protecting the meat as it melts. The fat is also largely responsible for browning.
4. The connective tissue is changed to a gelatinous substance, also resulting in some firmness and shrinkage.
5. The juices expand and vaporize, throwing off the excess water that is present in all lean meat. The minerals and extractives that are thrown off will collect on the surface, adding flavor to that area of the meat.

Under the Influence of Heat

The preceding changes take place as part of a gradual process. Under the influence of heat, whatever its nature (gas, charcoal, electricity), cooking begins on the surface or surfaces exposed thereto, and the changes occur slowly as the heat travels toward the center. When the heat has fully penetrated a tender cut of meat, it is considered fully cooked. Tough cuts of white meats (immature animals) are also cooked when the heat reaches the center, but require moist heat, such as in stewing or braising, as opposed to the dry heat of oven roasting or pan frying.

On the other hand, tough cuts of red meats (mature animals), because of tough fibers and connective tissue, are not fully tenderized when the heat reaches the center, and the cooking process must continue. The heat then travels in the opposite direction, that is, from the center to the outside surface. Furthermore, in such cuts, moist heat procedures such as pot roasting are required to effect the necessary changes.

The length of cooking time is based on the measurement of

the thickest area, that is, the longest distance the heat has to travel to get to the center, and, if necessary, as in tough cuts of red meats, back to the outside surface. Uniformity of size, as in pieces of stew meat or individual steak servings, will allow for even heat exposure, and is a major contributing factor to the successful cooking of meats.

Meats retain a certain amount of heat upon removal from the heat source, and this results in further cooking. (The degree to which a meat continues cooking depends on length and temperature of heat exposure.) Therefore, the desired degree of doneness should be incomplete upon removal. For instance, if a 5-pound roast is to be cooked to a temperature reading of 160° F. (71° C.), it should be removed when the thermometer registers approximately 150° F. (65° C.) (Or, the oven may be turned off and the meat left in for another 15 or 20 minutes.) Temperature will have reached 160° F. (71° C.) by the time meat has stood and is ready to be sliced.

COOKING PROCEDURES

To bring about the necessary changes in the constituents of meat, various cooking procedures are necessary and depend, basically, on whether the meat is categorized as tough or tender. However, regardless of the cooking procedure, working with low-grade, poor quality meat is akin to "making a silk purse from a sow's ear."

The three main procedures are: 1. dry heat, 2. moist heat, and 3. dry-moist heat combination.

1. Dry heat procedures are twofold: (1) those in which the meat cooks dry, that is, surrounded by hot air (roasting, broiling, rotisserie); or (2) those in which it cooks solely by means of a fatty substance (stir-frying, pan frying, sautéing, deep-frying).

2. Moist heat procedures are those which use some form of liquid in the cooking process: stewing, pot roasting, braising.

3. Dry-moist is that procedure in which meats are first exposed to dry heat and the completion of their cooking is done with moist heat: Meats are first pan fried, stir-

fried, or sautéed until partially cooked. They are then removed and some form of liquid (stock, wine, sherry) is added to the pan and heated. The partially cooked meat is returned to the pan, covered, and the cooking is completed using moist heat.

Determining the Correct Procedure

To determine the cooking procedure, know something about the nature of the cut on the basis of whether it is categorized as tough or tender, and whether it is from a mature or immature animal—beef or veal, lamb or mutton, chicken or fowl. The following tests can act as a quick and easy guide:

◊ *Color:* Light, dark, or medium? (Check with butcher as to whether or not some form of coloring has been added.)

◊ *Texture:* Fine and velvety, or heavy and globular?

◊ *Relative proportion of connective tissue:* Inspect cut with "no strings attached"—unwrapped and untied.

◊ *Fat content:* Well marbled or not?

◊ *Texture of surface fat:* Dry and firm, or soft and greasy?

◊ *Water content:* The leaner the meat, the higher the percentage of water.

◊ *Grade and Class:* Last but not least, look for the Grade Stamp and, whenever possible, inquire into which class of the Grade the cut falls (top, middle, or low—sometimes referred to as heavy, medium, and light).

◊ *See Meat Identification and Recommended Cooking Procedure Chart.*

COOKING TESTS FOR MEATS

Whatever procedure is used, once the cooking period begins to come to a close, one of the following tests should be made to determine degree of doneness:

1. Meat will have a plumped-up appearance, feel spongy, and have little resistance when tested with the fingers.

MEAT IDENTIFICATION AND RECOMMENDED COOKING PROCEDURE

Larger Wholesale Cuts	Bone	Smaller Retail Cuts	Beef	Veal	Pork	Lamb
*Tender Cuts**						
Rib cuts	Rib bone	Rib or hotel rack	Dry	Dry	Dry	Dry
Loin cuts	Backbone and T-bone	Loin or shortloin	Dry	Dry	Dry or Moist	Dry
Sirloin cuts	Hip bone	Sirloin or hip	Dry	Dry	Dry	Dry
Tough Cuts						
Blade cuts	Blade bone	Chuck	Moist	—	—	Moist (Neck)
		Shoulder	Moist	—	Dry or Moist	Moist
		Arm	Moist	—		—
Arm cuts		Shoulder	Moist	Dry or Moist	—	Dry
		Arm cuts	Moist	Dry or Moist	—	
Shank, brisket	Rib bones	Brisket	Moist	Moist	—	Moist
	Breast bone		Moist	Dry or Moist	—	Dry or Moist
Short plate	Rib bones	Short plate	Moist	Moist	Dry	—
Breast		Breast	Moist	Dry or Moist	—	Dry or Moist
Flank		Flank steak	Dry (top grade)	—	—	—
Leg, or Round or ham	Leg bone	round and ham cuts	Moist	Dry or Moist	Dry or Moist	Dry

*The location of the cut will be an indication of its relative tenderness in determining cooking procedure. The least used muscles, such as those found in the loin and rib cuts, are more tender than the fully developed muscles of the neck and round cuts.

2. Red meats are done when tested with a fork and no blood is drawn; white meats are done when the juice extracted is of a colorless nature.
3. Insert a fork or a sharp knife to test for resistance—if there is little or none, meat is cooked.
4. If the leg moves freely, the bird is cooked.

Such tests can be a hit or miss proposition. After long years of experience one will develop a "trained eye"; professionals whose only job is to "tend the meat" and who have the added advantage of working with top quality meats are, of course, in a position to develop such expertise. By and large, taking a temperature reading with an accurate meat thermometer is far and away the most reliable test.

Bear in mind, the poorer the quality of meat, the closer it needs watching, and that all meats retain heat to some degree and will continue to cook for a limited period after removal from source of heat.

TEMPERATURE CHART

	Doneness	° F	° C
Beef	Rare	135° to 140° F.	55° to 60° C.
	Medium	145° to 158° F.	62° to 70° C.
	Well Done	160° to 165° F.	71° to 75° C.
Veal	Well Done	165° to 170° F.	75° to 77° C.
Lamb	Medium	155° to 158° F.	68° to 70° C.
	Well Done	165° to 175° F.	75° to 80° C.
Cured Pork	Well Done	165° to 170° F.	75° to 77° C.
Fresh Pork	Well Done	170° to 185° F.	77° to 85° C.
Poultry	Well Done	170° to 185° F.	77° to 85° C.

COOKING PROCEDURES: DRY HEAT

> Roasting proper is almost unknown in these days of stoves and ranges—baking, a much inferior process, having taken its place. In roasting the joint is placed close to a brisk fire, turned so as to expose every part to the heat, and then moved back to finish in a moderate heat. The roast should be basted frequently with the drippings, and, when half cooked, with salt and water which has a tendency to keep the meat moist.
>
> *Cook Book*, published about 1860

Oven Roasting

PREPARATION Remove meat from refrigerator in sufficient time to bring it to cool room temperature.

Preheat oven, setting at required temperature.

If necessary, wipe meat clean with a damp cloth; *do not* wash under running water.

If roast's own fat has been removed, substitute by wrapping in a thin layer of fat. Fat, as well as lean, has its own distinctive flavor and should be given some consideration. For instance, use beef fat with beef, and pork fat with pork. Keep in mind that fat varies in quality, much the same as the lean portion of meats.

Do not salt meat, as this should be done only near the completion of the cooking period, and *do not* add liquid of any kind (water, wine, or stock) to roasting pan.

ROASTING PAN Many roasting pans are too deep, and their accompanying cover is not only unnecessary but detrimental. A pan of a depth of 3 to 4 inches, particularly when used with a cover, traps the heat and creates steam, thereby drawing out the meat's juices.

Do not lay meat directly on the bottom of the pan. Use a roasting rack, otherwise the meat will stew in its own juices. A shallow, broiler-type pan, having an insert with perforated openings, and made from a material heavy enough to prevent juices and fat from burning, makes an excellent roaster. The roasting rack is placed on top of the broiler pan cover and the meat laid on it. This allows the hot air to circulate around the meat, giving it even heat exposure; it also keeps to a minimum any contact with the steam created by the drippings in the bottom of the pan, which would tend to draw out the meat's juices. This type of roasting pan also acts as a preventative against splattered oven interiors.

OVEN TEMPERATURE   Maintain a constant heat setting throughout. Adjust to the lower rather than the higher end of the temperature range. For instance, when roasting cuts of meat from immature animals (veal, poultry, lamb), a 325° F. (163° C.) setting will give better results than a 350° F. (177° C.) to 375° F. (190° C.) setting. As a general rule, tender cuts of red meats retain their juices best at 325° F. Pork, on the other hand, requires a 350° F. (177° C.) setting. Roasts should be rotated during cooking to allow for a more even heat exposure.

BROWNING   Browning roasts by exposure to high temperatures—either at the commencement or closing of the cooking period—is generally detrimental. Roasts, for the most part, will brown of their own accord without increased temperature settings. The degree of browning will largely depend on the internal fat content, as well as on the outer layer of fat. The degree of exposure to ageing also has an effect on the browning of meats.

BASTING   Basting with any of the juices that have escaped into the pan should be confined, literally, to the last few minutes of cooking, if at all.

COOKING TEST   During the latter stages of cooking, check the internal temperature of the meat, using a thin-bulbed, professional-type meat thermometer. As cooking is speeded up during the latter period of cooking, meat should be watched very carefully to avoid overcooking. It should be removed at precisely the right temperature. Of course, one must consider the rise in temperature that results from the retained heat once it is removed from the oven. It is best to remove a roast when the temperature is approximately ten degrees under the desired reading, depending, of course, on the size and nature of the meat.

CARVING Allow meat to stand long enough for the cooking process to stop, which, as a general rule, is about 15 to 20 minutes, depending on the size of the roast and the length of heat exposure.

KEEPING WARM Roasts may be kept warm by placing in an oven set at 160° F. (71° C.).

The Rotisserie

For a long time, the unpleasant chore of turning the spit frequently fell to the lot of such unfortunate beings as slaves and indentured servants. Later, a very cruel contraption was devised in which dogs were trapped in a treadmill that was used to turn the spit. The expression "being treated like a dog" came in part from this practice. Today, the work is done effortlessly and efficiently with the flick of a switch.

Use of the rotisserie is a very satisfactory way of roasting meats, as it allows for an even penetration of heat and the cooking is done in a dry atmosphere.

The same basic rules listed for oven roasting are also applicable to this procedure.

Gravy from Roasts

Set pan containing drippings over medium high heat and add stock, wine, or water; or a combination thereof. Bring to a full boil. Using a rubber spatula or wooden spoon, scrape bottom of pan to release juices which have jelled and cooked to the bottom—in other words, de-glaze.

Remove all fat from liquid using a separator designed for this purpose, or pour liquid into a container and place in the freezer for a short period. Exposure to the low temperature will congeal the fat rather quickly so that it may be easily and totally removed. Liquid may also be placed in the refrigerator where it will take a comparatively longer period to congeal. Unless the fat is totally removed it is best not to serve gravy at all as it will only detract from the roast. In such cases, a sauce made from prepared stock or canned broth makes a satisfactory substitute.

Return de-fatted liquid to pan and season. Taste and adjust if necessary. Reduce heat and lightly thicken.

To thicken a pint (approx. ½ l) of gravy blend 3 or 4 tablespoons water with 2 tablespoons flour, forming a smooth paste. Stir in 2 tablespoons of the hot liquid and gradually add to pan using a wire whisk. At this point liquid should barely simmer; a high heat setting would break down the flour cells and prevent thickening.

If necessary, strain before serving.

Deep-Frying

Electrical, thermostatically controlled deep fryers have made this procedure one of the fastest, easiest, and most satisfactory. There is no comparison with the open kettle of hot fat on the coal range. In those days it took great expertise to learn to judge and control the correct temperature for frying foods, even with the use of a deep fat thermometer. However, most home cooks had to depend on "the crust of bread" or some other equally unreliable test. Old cookbooks are replete with the hazards of cooking with hot fat, in terms of both physical danger and the results of laborious culinary efforts. One author describes the "white gloves test": "If properly fried, the cooked food should leave no sign of fat when picked up with gloved hands."

As a general rule, deep-fried foods are coated beforehand. The coating acts as a buffer, holding in the juices, as well as a heat conductor. A breadcrumb coating or batter are the two most often used. (See section on Coatings).

Vegetable oils (corn, peanut, sesame), shortening, or a mixture of lard and shortening may be used. The fat should be preheated 5 to 10 degrees higher than the required temperature to allow for a drop when food is added. However, if food is cool room temperature as opposed to refrigerator temperature, thermostat may be set at the exact temperature requirement. The quantity of fat should be such as to allow the ingredients to swim around, rise to the surface, and float when done. Overcrowding should be avoided, since it also results in a severe drop of temperature when foods are added. When heated fat shows signs of bubbling, this is an indication it contains water as fat does not "boil."

The foods best suited to deep-frying are small and medium-size pieces of vegetables; tender cuts of meat; fish and shellfish; ground meat, cheese, and other coated morsels.

Deep-frying is done in two stages with the exception of those foods which take but a minute or so, such as cheese puffs and tender chunks of vegetables. The first step is done at a lower setting—as a general rule at about 360° F. (182° C.). The food is cooked until it is a light brown in color and placed on paper towels to absorb any excess fat. The temperature is then adjusted to 375° F. (190° C.) and given time to reheat. The period between the first and second frying gives the heat time to travel to the center of the food. When the thermostat registers the correct temperature, foods are fried for a second time until a deep golden brown. If not overcrowded, they will float to the surface when done. The second frying takes a much shorter time than the first. If properly cooked, the outside will be crisp and dry and the inside will be moist and tender.

Fried foods may be placed in a 160° F. (71° C.) oven to keep warm until ready to serve. One important rule is not to cover them, as the trapped heat would create steam resulting in overcooking and loss of crispness.

If desired, the frying may be done in two stages. The first frying may be done hours in advance of the second.

CLARIFYING FAT Fats should be clarified from time to time by straining through a paper filter or very fine strainer. Or, they may also be clarified by adding water to fat after it has *completely cooled* (adding water to hot fat could prove dangerous) and then reheated. After fat has been reheated, turn off heat and allow to cool before refrigerating. The clear fat will rise to the top and the residue will remain on the bottom with the water. Carefully remove fat, scraping off any residue from the underside, and dispose of water.

USE AND STORAGE All fats have a breaking point if exposed to too high temperature settings or after considerable usage. (see table, Smoke Points of Fats and Oils, Chapter 12). However, a good rich oil can be used repeatedly, particularly if clarified after each use.

While fats keep for a very long time, they will not keep indefinitely. After a protracted period, they may become rancid. They should be tightly capped, or otherwise covered, and stored in a cool, dry place.

COATINGS FOR DEEP FRYING

BREADCRUMB COATING

2 whole eggs   ¼ cup milk
1 tablespoon oil

Roll material to be coated in finely sifted flour and shake off excess. Lightly beat together the eggs, oil, and milk, and dip the floured material in this mixture. Now roll pieces in breadcrumbs, either flavored or plain.

BATTER COATING

½ teaspoon salt   ⅓ cup milk
¼ teaspoon white pepper   ¼ cup flat beer (room tempera-
1 cup flour   ture)
2 tablespoons fat, oil, or   2 egg whites
  melted butter   3 tablespoons sugar, finely
3 whole eggs   granulated

Combine seasonings and flour and cut in oil or melted butter, using a pastry cutter. Add eggs one at a time, using a wire whisk, until thoroughly blended. Combine milk and beer and gradually add to mixture. Consistency should be fairly thick. Refrigerate for several hours or overnight.

When ready to use, beat egg whites to soft peaks and fold into batter.

For sweet batters only

To prepare a sweet batter, gradually add the 3 tablespoons of sugar to the egg whites as they are being beaten.

Sautéing, Stir-Frying, and Pan Frying

All three procedures are best suited to tender cuts of meat.

Sautéing, the literal translation of which is *to jump*, and stir-frying are almost identical in principle. The former requires a pan with a long handle and straight sides of medium height, while stir-frying requires a pan (*wok*) with high sloping sides and short handles. In sautéing, the handle is used to toss and move the foods from one hot spot to another and a spatula is used for this purpose in stir-frying. Both are done over high heat.

The frying pan is similar to the wok in shape, but with comparatively low sloped sides and a long handle. Pan-fried foods, however, are cooked over medium to low heat, are not moved about, and are turned using a spatula.

In all three procedures, care should be taken not to over-crowd the pan. Crowding traps heat and creates steam, which in turn breaks down the constituents in the foods, drawing out the juices.

COOKING FAT   All three procedures—sautéing, stir-frying, and pan frying—require some type of cooking fat, which should always be kept to a minimum. Aside from other considerations, all fats contain a certain amount of moisture. Sweet butter contains less moisture than salted butter and makes a better frying medium. Its use, however, is confined to pan frying. As both stir-frying and sautéing are done over high heat, a vegetable oil (peanut, sesame, olive) is required.

PROCEDURES   In sautéing and stir-frying, small uniform-size pieces of meat are tossed and cooked quickly over high heat in a small amount of fat.

For pan frying the degree of heat should allow for an even penetration of heat to the center, depending on thickness. Thinner pieces of meat are cooked over medium to high heat and are cooked and browned at the same time. Thicker pieces of meat require a medium to low setting.

In all three procedures, meats are cooked when moisture begins to appear on the surface and should be removed at once to a warm platter.

Broiling

For successful broiling, it is important that meats contain a certain amount of fat marbling and be of top grade. While broilers and grills in most restaurants allow for much higher temperatures and are on the whole more satisfactory than home models, the quality of steaks and chops available to restaurateurs contributes almost as much to their measure of success as does their skill.

Broiling is not recommended for veal and other meats from immature animals which are low in fat.

Meats cut to a thickness of less than ¾" should be pan fried rather than broiled.

When broiling meats, turn from time to time to allow for even heat exposure.

The thicker the meat, the farther it should be from the source of heat.

Melted butter or oil may be brushed over meat both before and during broiling. However, if sufficient in fat marbling, this will not be necessary.

Check the degree of doneness by watching for a plumped-up appearance or test with fingers for a nonresistant spongy feeling. Check the color of the meat from time to time as it cooks.

If meat is thick enough, the most reliable test is to check the internal temperature using a thin-bulbed, professional-type thermometer.

MOIST HEAT COOKING PROCEDURES: POT ROASTING, STEWING, BRAISING

Restaurateurs, generally speaking, consider tough cuts of meat and those of poor quality to be uneconomical and impractical owing to the time-labor factor, as well as the skill required to make them tender and flavorful.

Originally, a *stew* was a bath or a hothouse, and *to stew* was to bathe. Later, the term came to mean "to boil slowly." Braising means essentially the same thing. In France, the term was originally used to designate cooking at a slow simmer over glowing coals. In American cooking, braising is generally conceded to mean long slow cooking in an oven, as opposed to pot roasting which is done on top of the stove over low heat.

Guidelines for Pot Roasting, Stewing, and Braising

RECEPTACLE   The receptacle used in moist heat procedures should be heavy enough to give even heat distribution and be just large enough to more or less hold the meat and whatever vegetables, if any, are to form part of the completed dish. The size of the pot is particularly important if the stock is not of the desired degree of richness.

BROWNING   Meats subjected to moist cooking may be browned slightly if desired; however, this will contribute neither to holding in the meat's juices nor to the flavor, but it may be helpful in giving it a more appetizing appearance. Meat should be browned in the same receptacle used for cooking so any juices that escape during this operation will go into the pan and form part of the liquid used for cooking.

LIQUID   In any type of moist cooking procedure, the nature of the liquid is of the utmost importance. The meat should have a natural attraction for the liquid and vice versa. A rich mellow stock made from bones, along with meat from the shin or plate, will give good results.

A small proportion of wine, sherry, or tomato sauce may be added to act as a tenderizer, as well as for added flavoring, but apart from that it should not be used as a substitute for mellow stock. Or, if water or a weak canned broth is substituted for a stock rich in gelatin and nutrients, the final result will be a tasteless lump of fiber rather than a succulent pot roast or stew. Using such substitutes, the liquid itself, upon completion of cooking, will more or less be the most valuable, both from the point of nutrition as well as flavor.

All liquids used in moist procedures should be brought to a

boil before adding meat, as cold liquids toughen meats. Once meat and flavorings are added, the heat should be adjusted to a very low temperature—barely simmering—and the receptacle tightly covered. During cooking, the meat must be kept moist, either through basting or turning. This operation is particularly important during the final stages of cooking.

FLAVORINGS If a good rich stock is used, there will be little need for further flavor additives. If the stock leaves something to be desired, however, the following may be used:

Onions cooked in a small amount of butter and oil until medium brown will give the liquid that deep amber color associated with pot roasts and braisings. They will also add flavor.

Vegetables such as carrots, celery, and green peppers will contribute flavor, providing they are lightly fried before adding.

HERBS AND SEASONINGS Parsley, bay leaf, thyme, garlic, dill, pepper, and ginger root are most commonly used. Caution should be taken when adding any of these, particularly if they are dried and not fresh.

VEGETABLES Those vegetables that frequently serve as an accompaniment to pot roast (such as, carrots, small potatoes, celery, and pearl onions) are best when blanched before being added. This will result in better texture and color, as it avoids overcooking but allows enough time for vegetables to absorb the sauce and contribute to the overall flavor. They should not be added, however, until after the sauce has been strained and de-fatted.

If the vegetables cook before the meat, or vice versa, remove to a warm platter and spoon over some of the sauce to protect surfaces from drying and set in a 160° F. (71° C.) oven to keep warm.

SAUCE Whenever fried vegetables, herbs, and seasonings have been added as flavorings, the sauce should be strained prior to the final stage of cooking. By this time they will have given their all and can only serve to give sauce a lumpy, unattractive appearance, and, if overcooked, an undesirable taste. Remove all fat at the same time. This operation is completed before adding any blanched vegetables that are to form part of the completed dish. Once the liquid has been strained and de-fatted, the sauce may be lightly thickened using two tablespoons flour to a pint (½ l) of sauce. Tomato paste may also be used.

COOKING TESTS   Tenderness may be determined by the insertion of a fork or sharp knife—if there is little or no resistance, meat is done. A temperature reading may also be taken using a meat thermometer. The length of cooking time will depend on the size, relative toughness, and overall quality of the meat. However, as a general rule, 2 to 3 hours would be the maximum time allowed for moist heat procedures. Smaller cuts would require much less time.

DO's, DON'Ts, AND HELPFUL HINTS FOR MEAT COOKERY

1. One of the most fundamental points in meat cookery is to know the nature of the cut and the proper procedure to use in cooking.

2. Because of its water-soluble constituents, meat should not be dipped in cold water. When it is necessary to wipe the surface, use a clean damp cloth.

3. Bone acts as a heat conductor and can result in shorter cooking periods; however, it adds little, if any, flavor to cooked meats. It might, however, be instrumental in a more even penetration of heat, giving better results.

4. Cold liquids added to meats will toughen them.

5. As a rule, meats should be exposed to lower temperatures than are generally recommended. High temperatures increase protein (juice) loss from meats.

6. Constant temperature settings, rather than switching from high to low, will result in an even penetration of heat and more satisfactory results.

7. Most cuts of beef—with the exception of commercially ground meat—can be kept in the refrigerator for up to 5 or 6 days if properly wrapped and stored. The period of storage for meat with more cut surfaces, such as stew meat, would be considerably shorter. In all types of meat, a great deal depends on the quality and freshness.

8. Meats should remain uncut for a time before carving because the meat's retention of heat further activates the cooking process for a time. The waiting period will depend on the size of the cut of meat, cooking temperature, and length of cooking period. A 4-pound roast cooked at a 325° F. (163° C.) temperature

should stand about 15 or 20 minutes before being carved. Steaks and chops on the other hand need only wait about a minute or so.

9. If meats are placed on a roasting rack or rotisserie surrounded by a layer of fat (preferably the meat's own fat), it will flow down over the surface of the lean and some (about 2 percent) will penetrate the interior and will aid considerably in retarding juice losses.

10. Salt does not penetrate a roast to a depth greater than about ½". It will, however, retard the browning of meats. It is best applied toward the end of the cooking period. Salting raw or slightly cooked meats draws out juices. Adding salt to marinades becomes a questionable practice, unless, of course, the marinade is going to be put to some useful cooking purpose. Heavy salting of meats is the equivalent of making a meat extract.

11. Meats roasted at high oven temperatures may shrink twice as much as meats roasted at lower temperatures. Tests may be made by weighing meats before and after cooking.

12. A kitchen scale makes a good short weight detective.

13. Better grades of meat are, unquestionably, better from the standpoint of flavor. They also result in better retention of the meat's juices.

14. Meats should be cooked so they retain their form and carve well.

15. Cooking by "minutes per pound" is not very accurate because cuts of meat vary in shape, thickness, and in proportion of meat to bone. The time required for cooking meats also depends upon the initial temperature, that is, whether the meat is cool-room or refrigerator temperature, as well as on its composition. Time-weight tables can, however, be useful guides in scheduling meal preparation.

16. Differences in procedures when cooking meats from different animals, as well as in recommended temperatures for various degrees of doneness, stem from the characteristics of the various meats.

17. Meats may be kept warm in an oven set at approximately 160° F. (71° C.) to 170° F. (77° C.) until ready to carve and serve. (Restrict holding period to half an hour or 45 minutes to prevent microbial growth.)

18. Open pan roasting—that is, in an uncovered pan—reduces juice losses. The meat should be placed on a rack at such a height that it will not come in contact with the steam that rises from the deposited fat and juices.

19. The rotisserie is superior to the oven for roasting insofar as there is no accumulation of steam; the meat cooks in a dry atmosphere.

20. It is not necessary to trim off Government Stamps (Grading and Inspection Stamps).

21. When meats are cooked in water, all water solubles (extractives and albumin) tend to be lost, unless, of course, the purpose is to produce stock.

22. The use of *preliminary high temperatures* to "seal in" juices has been found to increase rather than decrease cooking losses. It toughens the outer layer by draining off its juices. The aroma that is given off is a result of the lost juices coming in contact with the melted fat in the pan. There is, in fact, little flavor left in the hard surface crust. It is the extractives which collect on the surface of the meat, as a result of the expansion of the juices during cooking, that contribute flavor to the outside surface. The flavor is going to be considerably lessened if the juices have been depleted by browning. Higher heat temperature settings during the *final stages of cooking* will also increase the depletion of the meat's juices.

23. Browning will come about toward the end of cooking even when meat is exposed to lower temperatures, since the constituents of melting fat are essentially responsible for the "browning" of meats.

24. Meats should be removed from their wrappings before being stored in the refrigerator. To avoid drying of the surface, they should be lightly wrapped with wax paper or butcher's paper, and placed in the meat compartment or other area of the refrigerator where the temperature is, ideally, about 45° F. (7° C.). Any type of thermometer may be used to take a temperature reading.

25. Well-seasoned (aged) meats require comparatively shorter cooking periods and have considerably more flavor. They also brown more readily. In general practice, beef is the only kind of meat exposed to the ageing process, and even here, the wholesale shipper usually ages only Prime Grade cuts. Choice Grades are aged for 1 or 2 days at most before shipping. Including the transportation period, this amounts to a total of about 9 days. Generally speaking, meat should be aged for about four to six weeks—but only under ideal conditions, that is, correct temperature and humidity control.

26. Contrary to what most butchers advise, cuts of meat will benefit from some ageing in a home refrigerator: They should be

lightly wrapped and placed in the coldest area on a rack, so they will receive a certain amount of ventilation. Lamb, particularly when a deep red color, which indicates it is from a more mature animal (young lamb is a very light red in color), will benefit from three or four days ageing, as will tough cuts of beef. Veal, on the other hand, will dry out if it is stored for too long. Pork is high in fat, which has a tendency to develop rancidity during ageing; as a general rule, it should be exposed to little if any ageing.

27. If meat is too cold at the beginning of the cooking procedure, its juices will be lost rather quickly. Meat should be removed from the refrigerator in advance—the length of time depending on the nature and size of the cut. It should be close to cool-room temperature when cooking begins, as opposed to refrigerator temperature. One exception to this is commercially ground meat, which should be removed but a few minutes prior to cooking. However, if one is certain of its freshness and quality, ground meat, too, can benefit from being at cool room temperature when cooking begins.

28. When handling meats during cooking, particularly with dry heat procedures, do not stab or pierce with a fork. Use tongs or any other method that will prevent the loss of juices.

29. To glaze meats, dissolve a little honey or sugar in melted butter over low heat, and brush on cooked meats to give them a more attractive appearance. Glazes may be used with such meats as ham, poultry, or pork.

30. In gravy making, it is important to remove all fat either before or after de-glazing. To de-glaze, set pan over high heat and add water, sherry, wine, stock, cream, tomato juice, or canned broth. Boil rapidly, and using a wooden spoon or rubber spatula, stir and scrape pan bottom. (The juices that have escaped from the meat during cooking will be in the pan, some of which will have cooked and adhered to the bottom.) Liquid may be lightly thickened, if desired, using flour (2 tablespoons to a pint of liquid). Strain, if necessary, before serving.

31. A heavy pan is desirable for roasting to keep fat and drippings from burning.

32. Have oven thermostat checked periodically by utility company. This is generally a free service.

33. Purchasing large roasts which cannot be consumed in one or even two meals frequently proves to be undesirable, as well as uneconomical. Leftovers, unless very carefully wrapped, lose much of their flavor when stored. They also dry out when

reheated and lose a measure of their texture. Small roasts, of course, tax a butcher's patience as well as his pocketbook, but they have the added benefit for the consumer of requiring much shorter cooking periods.

34. Meats that have been thawed should not be refrozen. Aside from the risk of bacterial contamination and growth, every time meats are frozen and thawed there is a change in texture and some of the juices are lost.

35. When the outer layer of meat is a dark color—often seen in aged meat—this does not necessarily mean it is spoiled. When this layer is trimmed off, the remaining meat will frequently be bright in color, indicating its quality.

36. Frozen steaks and chops should be thawed prior to broiling, otherwise the outside portion will be cooked and the center will be raw.

37. There is considerable controversy over the effects of freezing on meats, particularly as to whether or not it results in a tenderizing action. It has generally been conceded that freezing has little or no effect in this regard.

38. Whenever possible, carving or cutting of meats should be done across the grain.

39. Dates of plastic wrapped meats should always be checked before purchasing. Occasionally meats are left in their original plastic wrappings, re-wrapped, and stamped with another date.

40. Meats do not "breathe" in plastic wrappings and are subjected to moisture accumulation. However, some meats are now being shipped in airtight, heavy plastic pouches, which has a notable effect on the length of time they can be stored.

41. Wood surfaces on which raw meats are cut should always be scrubbed clean with boiling water and baking soda. Do not use liquid ammonia.

42. Information as to date meats were slaughtered, whether or not they have been previously frozen, and the number of days or weeks they have been exposed to ageing would be extremely helpful to consumers.

43. It is important to check both grade and class of meat before purchasing.

44. Cuts of meat are generally packaged best side up but frequently leave a different impression when they are unwrapped. It is advisable to purchase meats "with no strings attached" whenever possible.

MEAT RECIPES

ROAST SIRLOIN OF BEEF

boneless sirloin of beef
salt and pepper to taste

stock, dry sherry, or water (or
combination thereof)
flour

When meat has been refrigerated, remove half an hour or so before roasting and place in an area where cool-room temperature is maintained (45° F. or 7° C.).

If meat does not have its own fat intact, wrap in a thin layer of beef fat and tie securely using butcher string, or brush surface of meat with vegetable oil. Set on a roasting rack and arrange rack in a roasting pan or on top of a broiler pan. Roast in a preheated 325° F. (163° C.) oven. Insert thermometer halfway into meat (at thickest portion) at the beginning, or check internal temperature at close of cooking period, using an instant reading thermometer. Season surface of meat with salt and pepper sometime during the latter half of cooking period. (To season or not to season is a matter of taste.)

Remove roast when it is 10 degrees F. (5 degrees C.) under desired reading. (See temperature chart on p. 74 for degree of doneness.) Let stand in a warm place for about 20 minutes before carving; cooking action will have stopped and temperature will have climbed the additional points. Trim off all fat before carving into slices of desired thickness.

In the meantime, skim all fat from pan drippings. Set pan over medium-high heat and de-glaze using stock, dry sherry, or water, or a combination thereof. Season to taste. Strain and serve over sliced meat, or return to pan and prepare a gravy in the following manner: Blend 3 or 4 tablespoons cold liquid with 2 tablespoons flour (per 1 pint [480 ml] of gravy) to form a smooth paste. Stir in 2 tablespoons of the hot liquid and gradually add to pan, stirring with a wire whisk. Turn heat to low, as liquid should just barely simmer at this point. When lightly thickened, remove and serve.

ROAST RIBS OF BEEF

ribs of beef
salt and pepper to taste

stock, dry sherry, or water (or combination thereof)
flour

Follow recipe for Roast Sirloin of Beef, placing fat side up.

TENDERLOIN OF BEEF

Follow recipe for Roast Sirloin of Beef. Tenderloin of Beef is generally served rare or medium rare rather than well done; however, this is a matter of preference.

STEAK WITH MUSHROOMS

mushrooms (3 or 4 per steak)
boneless steaks (tenderloin or sirloin)
vegetable oil
salt and pepper to taste

¼ cup (60 ml) brandy
¼ cup (60 ml) dry sherry
1½ cups (360 ml) tomato sauce
1 tablespoon butter
fresh parsley, finely chopped

Peel and slice mushrooms and sauté in oil over medium high heat until golden brown. Remove and keep warm.

Brush steaks with oil and season with salt and pepper. Fry steaks on either side until done and remove to a warm platter or individual serving plates.

Turn heat to high and add brandy and sherry. Ignite, using a match or by tilting pan toward flame. When flame has subsided, de-glaze pan using a rubber spatula or wooden spoon. Turn heat to low and add tomato sauce. Simmer gently for about five minutes before adding tablespoon of butter (to give sauce a smoother consistency). Strain sauce, if necessary.

Spoon a tablespoon or so of mushrooms over each steak. Serve sauce on the side or pour a little over or around each steak. Garnish with finely chopped fresh parsely.

STEAK WITH SHALLOTS

Follow recipe for Steak with Mushrooms, substituting 7 or 8 shallots (peeled and chopped) for mushrooms.

STEAK BORDELAISE

beef steaks   *salt and pepper to taste*
vegetable oil   *Bordelaise Sauce*

Brush steaks with oil and season with salt and pepper. Broil or fry steaks on either side until done to desired degree. Follow recipe for Bordelaise Sauce (under Sauce section) and spoon over steaks or serve on the side.

STEAK MADEIRA

Follow recipe for Steak Bordelaise, substituting Madeira Sauce (under Sauce section) for Bordelaise Sauce.

STEAKS WITH MUSHROOM SAUCE

Follow recipe for Steak Bordelaise, substituting Mushroom Sauce (under Sauce section) for Bordelaise Sauce.

BEEF SUKIYAKI

3 cups (720 ml) Brown Stock
or All-Purpose Stock
2 tablespoons soy sauce
½ cup (120 ml) dry sherry
2 tablespoons sugar
pinch of Oriental five-spices
or allspice
4 large carrots, peeled and
sliced (using fluted cutter)
6 celery stalks, peeled and
sliced diagonally
butter and oil for frying
1 green pepper, seeded and
sliced (julienne strips or
cubes)
1 large onion, peeled and
chopped

6 scallions, sliced (white
portions only)
1 6-ounce (170 g) can water
chestnuts, drained and
sliced
1 3-ounce (85 g) can Chinese
noodles
2 pounds (900 g) beef (sirloin
steak or beef tenderloin),
cut against grain into thin
1½" strips
½ cup (120 ml) dry sherry for
de-glazing
2 tablespoons cornstarch,
dissolved in sherry or
water

Prepare vegetables and meat as indicated and arrange near cooking area.

Combine stock, soy sauce, ½ cup (120 ml) dry sherry, sugar, and a pinch of five-spices or allspice, stirring to dissolve. Set aside.

Bring a 2½ quart (2.36 liters) pot of lightly salted water to a full boil and add peeled and sliced carrots and celery. Blanch, uncovered, over high heat for two or three minutes after water returns to a boil, or until vegetables are still fairly crisp. (Vegetables should be bright and retain their full color.) Remove and drain.

Heat butter and oil in a straight-sided frying pan and sauté carrots and celery over medium high heat. Do not overcook as vegetables should be crisp. Transfer vegetables, as they are cooked, to a heated dish and keep warm in a 160° F. (71° C.) oven. Turn heat to low and fry pepper, onion, and scallions until they take on a translucent appearance. Add water chestnuts and cook just long enough to heat through. Place Chinese noodles in a bowl and set in oven to warm.

Add additional butter and oil to frying pan and sauté meat, a small amount at a time, over medium high heat. Do not overcook, as meat should be crispy brown on the outside and the interior should be medium rare. Transfer meat to a warm platter and set in oven, uncovered, to keep warm.

De-glaze pan with ½ cup sherry over high heat and reduce to about ¼ cup. Strain, if necessary, and return to pan along with stock, soy sauce, sherry, sugar, and spice mixture. Bring to a slow simmer and add dissolved cornstarch, stirring until thickened. (For a thicker sauce, add additional cornstarch.)

Add cooked vegetables and meat to pan, stirring until heated through. (Do not cover as trapped heat and steam would overcook vegetables.) Serve on a bed of rice, surrounded by warm noodles.

CHICKEN SUKIYAKI

2 pounds (900 g) chicken
  breasts, skinned, boned,
  and sliced into 1½" strips,
  using poultry shears

Follow recipe for Beef Sukiyaki, substituting chicken for beef. However, chicken should be cooked all the way through and not left rare in the center. Sauté in the same manner as beef.

BUDDY-O MEAT BALLS
(Deep-Fried Miniature Meat Balls
of Beef, Chicken, or Ham)

2 pounds (900 g) uncooked
   beef, raw chicken breasts,
   or ham
2 egg whites, unbeaten
1 teaspoon salt
½ teaspoon pepper
½ cup wheat germ or
   breadcrumbs (optional)

¼ cup (60 ml) light cream
   (optional)
finely sifted flour
2 whole eggs ⎫ Lightly
1 tablespoon oil ⎬ beaten
¼ (60 ml) milk ⎭
flavored breadcrumbs
vegetable oil for frying

Put beef, skinned and boned chicken breasts, or ham through meat grinder or food processor.

Using electric mixer, add egg whites, one at a time, to ground beef, chicken, or ham, along with salt and pepper, and beat until well blended. (When using ham that has a high salt content, omit 1 teaspoon salt.)

Soak wheat germ or breadcrumbs in light cream until absorbed, and mix in. (Meat balls may be made without the addition of soaked wheat germ or breadcrumbs, as they simply more or less act as a filler; in this case, omit and proceed with remainder of recipe.) Using a miniature ice cream scoop, shape mixture into balls. Roll balls in flour, then in eggs, oil and milk mixture, and finally in breadcrumbs.

Preheat vegetable oil to 375° F. (190° C.) in an electric thermostatically controlled deep-fryer, and fry no more than 5 or 6 meat balls at a time. They will take but a few minutes to cook, and will float to the surface when done. They will be crisp and brown on the surface, and moist and juicy on the inside. Keep warm in a 160° F. (71° C.) oven but do not cover (otherwise they will lose their crispness, as well as overcook). Serve with or without a sauce (Tomato Sauce, Lemon Sauce, or Barbecue Sauce under Sauce section) with rice, noodles, french fries, or riced potatoes.

Balls may be frozen, uncooked, in heat-sealed plastic pouches or airtight containers. They are convenient as they defrost in a relatively short time. To defrost, remove from packaging, cover lightly with wax paper and set in refrigerator.

BRAISED OR POT ROASTED BEEF

butter and oil for frying
3 stalks celery, peeled and
  chopped
2 carrots, peeled and finely
  chopped
1 onion, peeled and chopped
1 cup (240 ml) dry red wine
4 cups (960 ml) Brown Stock
  or All-Purpose Stock
1 28-ounce (790 g) can
  tomatoes, blended and
  strained

½ bay leaf
¼ teaspoon dried thyme
1 tablespoon parsley, finely
  chopped
2½ to 3 pounds (900-1350 g)
  bottom round or rump of
  beef
2 tablespoons flour
1 tablespoon butter

Heat butter and oil in braising pot and cook celery and carrots over medium high heat until slightly crisp. Lower heat, add onions, and cook until translucent. Add wine, stock, strained tomatoes, bay leaf, thyme, and parsley and bring to a boil. (There should be sufficient liquid to fully cover meat.) Add meat and cook, covered, on top of stove over low heat, or in a 250° F. (121° C.) oven, for about 2 hours, or until meat is tender. Liquid should just barely simmer. Baste from time to time, as surface of meat should be kept moist. When done, meat should be fork tender, but not overcooked. The temperature may be checked, using a meat thermometer: 160° F. (71° C.) to 165° F. (74° C.).

Remove meat to a warm platter and ladle off all fat, or allow to cool slightly and refrigerate both meat and sauce for several hours, or until fat has congealed and can be readily removed. When fat has been removed, strain sauce, using a wire strainer. Return to pot and bring to a simmer. Mix flour and butter together, using a fork, and whisk into sauce over low heat, stirring until slightly thickened. Reheat meat in sauce, if necessary. Serve sauce over sliced meat, or on the side.

LONDON BROIL

2 pounds (900 g) London   vegetable oil
  broil steak

Place steak in a receptacle and pour oil over it, turning so as to cover all areas. Refrigerate for several hours or overnight. Remove and place on broiler rack. Broil for about 5 to 7 minutes on either side (depending on thickness), placing rack at closest point to flame. Meat should be brown and crisp on the outside and rare within. Cut across the grain in thin slices and serve. A Mushroom Sauce may be served on the side, if desired.

BEEF WITH SOUR CREAM (Stroganoff)

2 pounds (900 g) beef   1 tablespoon white vinegar
  tenderloin   2 cups (480 ml) Mushroom
butter and oil for frying   Sauce
½ cup (120 ml) dry white   salt and pepper to taste
  wine   1 cup (240 ml) sour cream

Slice meat into 1½″ strips about ⅛″ thick and sauté over medium high heat in butter and oil, until lightly browned (meat should be pink on the inside). Remove to a warm platter and keep warm. Cook white wine and vinegar over medium high heat until reduced by about a third. Add Mushroom Sauce, lower heat, and simmer gently for a few minutes. Add seasoning to taste. Gradually stir in sour cream, making certain sauce does not boil, otherwise it will curdle. Pour sauce over meat and serve with cooked rice or noodles.

MEAT LOAF NO. 1

½ cup (120 ml) whole wheat
breadcrumbs or wheat
germ
⅓ cup (80 ml) stock, milk, or
water
1 green pepper, seeded and
chopped
4 stalks celery, peeled and
finely chopped
1 onion, peeled and finely
chopped

salt and pepper to taste
2 tablespoons fresh parsely,
finely chopped
2 eggs, lightly beaten
1½ pounds (675 g) ground
beef (chuck, rump, or
bottom round)
vegetable oil

Place bread crumbs or wheat germ in a large mixing bowl and add stock, milk, or water. Set aside until absorbed.

Fry chopped green pepper, celery, and onion in a small amount of oil over low heat until they take on a slightly translucent appearance. Remove and add to moistened bread crumbs or wheat germ, along with seasoning to taste, chopped parsley, lightly beaten eggs, and ground beef. Mix thoroughly. Form into an oval-shaped loaf and place in a lightly greased or nonstick ovenproof pan. Brush top lightly with vegetable oil and bake in a preheated 325° F. (163° C.) oven. Remove when loaf begins to shrink from sides of pan, or when internal temperature is a few degrees under 160° F. (71° C.). (Do not overcook or loaf will become dry.) Remove and let stand for about 10 minutes before cutting into slices. Serve with or without a sauce.

MEAT LOAF NO. 2

1 green pepper, finely
chopped
1 onion, finely chopped
½ pound (225 g) mushrooms,
peeled and sliced
1 cup cooked brown rice or
white rice
salt and pepper to taste

2 tablespoons fresh parsley,
finely chopped
2 eggs, lightly beaten
1½ pounds (675 g) ground
beef
⅓ cup (80 ml) tomato sauce
1 tablespoon tomato catsup
vegetable oil

Fry chopped green pepper and onion in a small amount of oil until they take on a slightly translucent appearance and are fairly crisp when fork tested. Remove and set aside. Sauté peeled and sliced mushrooms over medium high heat, adding more oil if necessary.

Place cooked rice in a large mixing bowl and add green pepper, onion, and mushrooms, along with seasoning to taste, chopped parsley, lightly beaten eggs, ground beef, tomato sauce, and catsup. Mix thoroughly. Form into an oval-shaped loaf and place in a lightly greased or nonstick ovenproof pan. Brush top lightly with vegetable oil and bake in a 325° F. (163° C.) oven for about an hour (depending on thickness). Remove when loaf begins to shrink from sides of pan, or when internal temperature is a few degrees under 160° F. (71° C.). Do not overcook or loaf will become dry. Remove and let stand for about 10 minutes before cutting into slices. Serve with or without a sauce.

MEAT LOAF NO. 3

½ cup (120 ml) wheat germ
or flavored breadcrumbs
⅓ cup (80 ml) stock, milk, or
water
4 stalks celery, peeled and
finely chopped
1 green pepper, seeded and
finely chopped
2 tablespoons chives, finely
chopped
2 tablespoons chopped
pimiento
salt and pepper to taste

few grains garlic powder
2 tablespoons fresh parsley,
finely chopped
2 teaspoons Worcestershire
sauce
dash of Tabasco
2 eggs, lightly beaten
1½ pounds (675 g) ground
beef
½ cup (120 ml) tomato sauce
2 tablespoons tomato catsup
vegetable oil

Place wheat germ or breadcrumbs in a large mixing bowl and add stock, milk, or water. Set aside until absorbed.

Fry celery and green pepper in a small amount of oil over low heat until slightly crisp when fork tested, or until they take on a slightly translucent appearance. Add to moistened wheat germ or breadcrumbs along with chives, pimiento, salt and pepper to taste, few grains garlic powder, chopped parsley, Worcestershire sauce, dash of Tabasco, lightly beaten eggs, ground beef, tomato sauce, and catsup. Mix thoroughly. If too moist, add additional wheat germ or breadcrumbs; if too dry, add additional tomato sauce.

Form into an oval-shaped loaf and place in a lightly greased or nonstick ovenproof pan. Brush top lightly with vegetable oil and bake in a preheated 325° F. (163° C.) oven until loaf begins to shrink from sides of pan, or until internal temperature is a few degrees under 160° F. (71° C.). (Length of cooking period will largely depend upon thickness of loaf.) Remove and let stand for a few minutes before cutting into slices. Serve with or without a sauce.

HAMBURGERS

5 or 6½″ (1 cm)-thick slices
  bone marrow
1½ pounds (675 g) top quality
  lean ground beef

2 tablespoons minced onion
salt and pepper to taste
vegetable oil

Remove marrow from beef or veal bones and add to ground beef, along with minced onion and seasoning to taste. Mix thoroughly. Using a scoop, divide into six to eight equal portions and shape into patties, flattening slightly using a fork. Brush both sides lightly with oil, using a pastry brush. Set on rack and broil in a preheated broiler about 3 inches from flame, depending on thickness of patties (the thicker the patties, the farther from the flame), turning once. Cooking time depends on the desired degree of doneness. If patties are thick enough, a meat thermometer may be used (inserting halfway through) to determine exact degree of doneness. Do not overcook or patties will lose their juice and flavor.

CHEESEBURGERS

Follow recipe for Hamburgers and top with Cheddar or Swiss cheese slices (1 per patty) after turning and just prior to time meat is cooked to desired degree. Cheese will take but a minute or so to melt, depending on thickness.

SWISS STEAK

2 pounds (900 g) bottom
  round, cut into 8 4-ounce
  (110 g) steaks and trimmed
  of all fat
salt and pepper to taste
finely sifted flour
butter and oil for frying
2 celery stalks, peeled and
  finely chopped

1 onion, peeled and finely
  chopped
1 cup (240 ml) dry red wine
3 cups (720 ml) Brown Stock
¼ teaspoon dried thyme
½ small bay leaf

Season steaks with salt and pepper and dredge in flour, shaking off excess. Heat butter and oil in frying pan and brown over medium high heat on both sides. Transfer to brazier pan or ovenproof casserole. Fry celery until slightly crisp. Lower heat and cook onions until translucent. Add to pan containing steaks. De-glaze frying pan with red wine over high heat and pour over steaks. Heat Brown Stock and add to braising pan, along with thyme and bay leaf. Set in a 300° F. (150° C.) oven and cook, covered, for about an hour, or until meat is tender. Baste meat from time to time, as surfaces should be kept moist. Remove steaks to a warm platter, and strain sauce, using a wire strainer. Serve a small portion of sauce with each steak.

MEATBALLS

2 pounds (900 g) beef (rump,
  chuck, top, or bottom
  round)
1 egg (optional)
1 teaspoon salt

½ teaspoon pepper
2 tablespoons fresh parsley,
  finely chopped
vegetable oil

Remove any excess fat from meat, along with any tough connective tissue. Cut into strips and put through grinder or food processor. (If all fat has been removed and meat is very lean, add a proportionately small amount of beef fat. Fat content will largely depend on the grade and class of the cut.) Mix in egg, seasoning, and parsley. Shape into balls uniform in size, using a No. 12 or 20 scoop.* Fry meatballs in a small amount of oil over

*For scoop sizes, see the table in the Appendix.

medium to low heat (the thicker the ball the lower the heat), shaking pan from time to time so as to brown and cook evenly. Or, place meatballs in a greased shallow ovenproof pan and bake in a preheated 325° F. (163° C.) oven until cooked all the way through. (Length of cooking period will depend on thickness of balls.)

Meatballs with Sauce

Follow recipe for Meatballs and serve with Tomato Sauce (Mildly or Strongly Flavored), Mushroom Sauce, or Bordelaise Sauce, all listed in Chapter 3 under Sauces. Meatballs may be added to sauce and served over pasta or rice, or sauce may be simply spooned over meatballs and garnished with some chopped parsley.

BOILED BRISKET OF BEEF

2½ to 3 pounds (1125-1350 g) brisket of beef
stock or water
salt and pepper to taste
1 pound (450 g) carrots, peeled

7 or 8 celery stalks
3 or 4 onions, peeled and quartered
4 or 5 potatoes, peeled and quartered
fresh parsley, finely chopped

Using a receptacle just large enough to hold meat, bring stock or water to a boil and add beef (meat should be fully covered with liquid). Add seasoning and simmer, covered, over low heat until tender when fork-tested (there should be little resistance when fork is withdrawn). Turn off heat, remove cover, and let meat stand in liquid for about 20 minutes.

In the meantime, slice peeled carrots through center and cut into quarters. Peel and wash celery stalks and cut into 2″ (5 cm) lengths. Peel and quarter onions and potatoes. Cook vegetables separately in a large pot of lightly salted boiling water until fairly crisp when fork-tested. Remove and drain.

Remove meat and trim off any fat. Carve into ⅛″ (.3 cm) thick slices and arrange on heated platter or individual serving plates. Arrange vegetables to one side and garnish with finely chopped parsley. Skim all fat off broth and spoon a portion over meat. Serve remainder on the side.

BOILED CORNED BEEF

2½ to 3 pounds (1125-1350 g) corned beef

1 head of cabbage, cut into wedges

4 or 5 potatoes, peeled and quartered

1 pound (450 g) carrots, peeled and quartered

Follow recipe for Boiled Brisket of Beef, substituting the above meat and vegetables; the remainder of the recipe remains essentially the same.

BEEF ORIENTAL NO. 1

1 pound (900 g) beef, sirloin or tenderloin

¾ pound (340 g) snow peas

4 or 5 celery stalks, peeled

pimiento

vegetable oil

pinch of salt

soy sauce

dry sherry

All-Purpose Stock or beef broth

garlic clove, peeled

5 or 6 scallions, peeled and sliced

1 tablespoon cornstarch, moistened in sherry

pinch of Oriental five-spices or allspice (optional)

Prepare all ingredients and arrange near cooking area.

Cut beef against the grain into strips approximately 1½" long, ½" wide and ¼" (4 x 1 x .5 cm) thick. Wash snow peas and trim ends. Cut peeled and washed celery into strips about 1¼" (3 cm) in length, holding knife at an angle to give a more attractive appearance. Use enough pimiento to approximate 2 tablespoons and cut into strips 1" (2.5 cm) in length and ⅛" (.3 cm) in width.

Heat oil in wok over high heat until just under smoking stage. Stir-fry beef a small amount at a time until done to desired stage (rare, medium, or well-done); however, do not overcook, or meat will become dry and tasteless. Remove to a warm platter.

Add more oil to wok, along with a pinch of salt and a few drops of soy sauce. When oil is sufficiently hot (just under smoking stage), add 2 tablespoons dry sherry and 2 or 3 tablespoons stock or beef broth—pouring along inside rim of pan so it will be heated through before coming in contact with hot oil. Add garlic clove and stir-fry for a few seconds (or just long enough to extract flavor) and remove. Add snow peas and stir-fry until bright green in color and fairly tender. Remove to warm dish. Add celery and stir-fry until fairly crisp (do not overcook). Add peeled and sliced scallions to wok and stir-fry until they take on a slightly translucent appearance.

Add cooked meat to pan, along with snow peas and pimiento strips. Add approximately ½ cup (120 ml) stock or broth in a circular motion along inside rim of wok. Gradually add moistened cornstarch, stir-frying until sauce is slightly thick, smooth, and glossy. If desired, add a pinch of Oriental five-spices or allspice to sauce and cook just long enough to blend. Serve with cooked rice.

BEEF ORIENTAL NO. 2

Oriental Sauce
4 or 5 celery stalks, peeled
1 pound (450 g) beef, sirloin
or tenderloin
¾ pound (340 g) snow peas;
or 1 10-ounce package
frozen peas

1 teaspoon butter
vegetable oil
5 or 6 scallions, peeled and
sliced
¼ cup (60 ml) dry sherry
2 tablespoons pimiento, diced

To prepare sauce, follow recipe for Oriental Sauce (under Sauce section).

Cut peeled and washed celery into strips about 1¼" (3 cm) in length, holding knife at an angle to produce a more attractive appearance. Cut beef against the grain into strips approximately 1½" long, ½" wide, and ¼" (4 × 1 × 5 cm) thick. Wash snow peas and trim ends.

Cook celery and snow peas in a large pot of lightly salted boiling water until celery is fairly crisp and snow peas are bright green and fairly tender. Remove and drain. If using frozen peas, break up and cook in 1 teaspoon of butter over medium low heat in a covered saucepan until heated through. (Do not overcook vegetables.)

Heat oil in frying pan and sauté beef (a small amount at a time) until done to desired stage (rare, medium, or well-done). Remove to a warm dish. Add peeled and sliced scallions and fry over low heat until they take on a slightly translucent appearance. Remove to warm dish. Turn up heat and de-glaze pan with dry sherry. Strain, if necessary, and add to barely simmering Oriental Sauce, along with beef, celery, scallions, peas, and diced pimiento. Cook just long enough to heat through. Serve with cooked rice.

SWEDISH MEAT BALLS

½ cup (42.4 g) uncooked wheat germ or breadcrumbs
½ cup (120 ml) milk
butter for frying
1 onion, peeled and finely chopped
1 teaspoon salt
½ teaspoon pepper
pinch ground nutmeg
1 tablespoon fresh parsley, finely chopped

1 pound (450 g) lean beef, ground
½ pound (225 g) lean pork, ground
½ pound (225 g) veal, ground
2 egg whites, unbeaten
1 tablespoon butter
2 tablespoons flour
2 cups (480 ml) light cream or heavy cream
1 tablespoon fresh dill, finely chopped

Soak wheat germ or breadcrumbs in milk until thoroughly absorbed. Melt butter in frying pan and cook chopped onions over low heat, until translucent. Combine cooked onions, salt, pepper, nutmeg, parsley, ground beef, pork, and veal in bowl, and mix in egg whites with electric mixer, one at a time, until absorbed. Add soaked wheat germ or breadcrumbs and mix in. Remove and shape into balls, using a small scoop (No. 12) and round off using hands. Melt additional butter in a straight-sided frying pan and brown meatballs a few at a time over medium high heat, shaking pan now and then, using handle, to bounce meatballs about. Reduce heat to low and continue to cook until meatballs are well done (they must not be rare in the center). Transfer to a warm dish. Add one tablespoon butter to drippings in pan (if lean meat was used, there should not be an excess amount of fat). When melted, mix in 2 tablespoons flour to form a smooth paste. Gradually add cream and cook, stirring, until sauce begins to bubble. Add chopped, fresh dill and cook long enough to blend. Combine meatballs with sauce, or serve separately.

HAWAIIAN HAM STEAKS

2 pounds (900 g) fully cooked
  ham, cut into 8 4-ounce
  (110 g) steaks
vegetable oil

16 pineapple slices
4 tablespoons sugar
1 teaspoon cinnamon

Brush ham steaks with oil, and place under preheated broiler, close to flame. Cook two or three minutes on either side. Remove to a warm platter. Combine sugar and cinnamon and sprinkle over pineapple slices. Place under broiler, until glazed. Center over ham steaks and serve.

PORK CHOPS IN ORANGE SAUCE

8 center cut loin pork chops,
  trimmed of all fat
salt and white pepper to taste
finely sifted flour
butter and oil for frying
1 onion, peeled and chopped

2 cups (480 ml) fresh orange
  juice
2 tablespoons red currant jelly
1 tablespoon fresh parsley,
  finely chopped

Season pork chops with salt and pepper and dredge in flour, shaking off excess. Heat butter and oil in frying pan, and lightly brown chops on both sides. Transfer to an oven- and flame-proof dish. Fry onion until translucent and spread over chops. Heat orange juice and pour over chops. Bake in a 350° F. (177° C.) oven for about 50 minutes, or until tender and fully cooked. (Baste from time to time, as surface of chops should be kept moist.) Transfer chops to a warm platter. Place pan over low heat, and stir in red currant jelly to thicken sauce. Pour sauce over chops, and sprinkle a small amount of chopped parsley over center of each.

BAKED STUFFED PORK CHOPS

Potato Stuffing　　　　　　*vegetable oil*
loin pork chops　　　　　　*salt and pepper to taste*

Follow recipe for Potato Stuffing (under Produce of the Land, Vegetable section).

Using a sharp knife, make a pocket in each chop. Fill pocket with stuffing and press edges together, or, if necessary, fasten openings with toothpicks. Lay in shallow baking pan and brush tops of chops with vegetable oil, using a pastry brush. Season with salt and pepper and bake in a preheated 350° F. (177° C.) oven until fork tender and well done—185° F. (85° C.) reading on meat thermometer.

LAMB CURRY

Curry Sauce　　　　　　　*leftover leg of lamb*

Follow recipe for Curry Sauce (under Sauce section). Cut up leftover leg of lamb into cubes and add to simmering sauce. Cook just long enough to heat through; otherwise lamb will become soft and lose much of its flavor. Serve over a bed of cooked rice or noodles.

CHICKEN CURRY

Follow recipe for Lamb Curry, substituting strips of poached fowl or leftover roast chicken for leg of lamb.

BARBECUED SPARERIBS

3 to 4 pounds (1350-1800 g)
  spareribs
½ cup (120 ml) soy sauce
4 tablespoons All-Purpose
  Stock or Brown Stock
2 tablespoons dry sherry
¼ teaspoon garlic clove,
  minced

2 tablespoons catsup
1 teaspoon sugar
pinch of minced ginger root
  or powdered ginger
Barbecue Sauce No. 1 or
  No. 2

Trim excess fat from spareribs. Place in boiling water and gently simmer over low heat for approximately 20 to 30 minutes (depending on size and thickness of ribs). Remove and drain.

Prepare marinade by combining soy sauce, stock, dry sherry, garlic, catsup, sugar, and ginger. Place ribs in a receptacle just large enough to hold them and coat with marinade, using a pastry brush. Pour over remaining marinade and refrigerate for several hours or overnight—turning and basting with marinade from time to time. Remove from marinade and place ribs on a rack set in a shallow pan. Roast in a preheated 350° F. (177° C.) oven for approximately 1 hour, or until done—turning and basting with marinade during first half of cooking period. During latter half of cooking period, coat from time to time with Barbecue Sauce No. 1 or No. 2 (see recipe under Sauce section) using a pastry brush. Remove and cut ribs along the bone into single pieces, using a sharp knife or poultry shears.

BARBECUED CHICKEN

2 2½- to 3-pound (1125-1350 g)
  chickens, cut up
vegetable oil

salt and pepper to taste
Barbecue Sauce No. 1 or
  No. 2

Coat chicken with oil and season with salt and pepper. Lightly brown chicken on all sides using a barbecue grill; or, arrange chicken on a rack set in a shallow pan and roast in a preheated 325° F. (163° C.) oven. During latter half of cooking period, baste chicken from time to time with Barbecue Sauce No. 1 or No. 2 (see recipe under Sauce section) turning to expose all sides.

HAM STEAKS
WITH CHERRY ORANGE SAUCE

Cherry Orange Sauce   *vegetable oil*
cooked ham steaks, ¼"(.5 cm)
    thick

Prepare Cherry Orange Sauce (see recipe under Sauce section).

Lightly brush steaks with oil and place on broiler pan. Cook under preheated broiler 1 or 2 inches (2.5 to 5 cm) from the flame until heated through, turning once. Arrange steaks on a heated platter or individual serving plates and pour Cherry Orange Sauce over steaks.

CHICKEN WITH ORANGE SAUCE

Orange Sauce No. 1 or No. 2   *finely sifted flour*
3 to 4 whole chicken breasts,   *butter*
    skinned, boned and split   *cooked rice*
salt and white pepper

Prepare sauce according to recipe for Orange Sauce No. 1 or No. 2 (under Sauce section).

Season chicken with salt and pepper and dredge in flour, shaking off excess. Lightly dot with butter and place under preheated broiler 3 or 4 inches (7.5 to 10 cm) from the flame until lightly browned, turning once. (Do not overcook.)

Serve on a bed of cooked rice and pour over Orange Sauce No. 1 or No. 2.

ROAST LEG OF LAMB (Marinated)

Marinade
1 cup olive oil
juice of 1 small lemon
½ garlic clove, peeled and
  crushed
¼ teaspoon pepper
1 teaspoon dried rosemary

1 5- or 6-pound leg of spring
  lamb

Combine oil, lemon juice, garlic, and pepper. Rub dried rosemary between palms of hands to release oils, and add to mixture. Rub marinade over leg of lamb and place in a receptacle, or use a plastic bag designed for roasting. Add remaining marinade and, if using bag, tie securely. Place in refrigerator and reverse position from time to time. Lamb should be marinated for at least 24 hours, but will be more flavorful and tender if left for 2 or 3 days.

Roast in a 325° F. (163° C.) oven, turning from time to time. Check temperature reading toward end of cooking period: medium—155° to 158° F. (68° to 70° C.) and well-done, 165° to 175° F. (74° to 80° C.). Remove and allow to rest for about 20 minutes before carving into thin slices.

LAMB STEW

4 cups (960 ml) All-Purpose
  Stock
2 pounds (900 g) shoulder of
  lamb, cut into ¾" (2 cm)
  cubes
1 tablespoon butter

2 tablespoons flour
salt and pepper to taste
8 medium-size potatoes
8 large carrots, peeled and
  quartered
8 medium-size pearl onions

Bring stock to a full boil. Add lamb and lower heat. (There should be sufficient stock to fully cover meat.) Stock should just barely simmer throughout cooking.

Cook meat for approximately 1¼ hours, or until tender. Transfer meat to a warm platter and skim off all fat, or allow meat to cool in liquid and refrigerate for several hours, or long enough for fat to congeal on surface.

Blend butter and flour and whisk into de-fatted stock. Cook over low heat until lightly thickened. Add salt and pepper to taste.

Cook vegetables separately, and add to sauce along with lamb. Cook over low heat long enough to blend flavors.

CALF'S LIVER PATÉ

butter and oil for frying
2 onions, peeled and finely chopped
2 pounds (900 g) calf's liver, thinly sliced
2 sticks butter (½ pound or 225 g), softened
salt and freshly ground pepper

pinch of nutmeg
pinch of cayenne pepper
⅛ teaspoon ground cloves
1 teaspoon dry mustard
½ cup (120 ml) dry sherry, brandy, or port

Heat butter and oil in frying pan and fry onions over low heat until soft but not brown. Remove and set aside. Add liver, a few pieces at a time, and fry over medium high heat until lightly browned on both sides. Remove and grind liver and onions using meat grinder or food processor. Add softened butter to pulped liver and onion mixture and blend. Season to taste with salt and freshly ground pepper. Add nutmeg, cayenne pepper, cloves, and mustard and blend in. Use ¼ cup (60 ml) of sherry, brandy, or port to de-glaze frying pan. Strain and add to mixture along with remaining ¼ cup (65 ml), and mix in. Transfer to serving dish or individual molds, such as custard dishes, and cover with an airtight wrapping such as plastic wrap or sealed plastic bags. Chill in refrigerator for several hours or overnight. (Paté will keep refrigerated for several days to be used as needed.)

BREAST OF CHICKEN PATÉ

2 pounds (900 g) chicken breasts, skinned and boned

½ pound (225 g) fresh mushrooms, peeled

Follow recipe for Calf's Liver Paté, substituting chicken breasts for calf's liver. Pound skinned and boned chicken breasts between two layers of wax paper or plastic wrap using a cleaver, and fry until lightly browned on both sides before grinding along with onions.

Sauté peeled mushrooms in butter over medium high heat. Remove and chop into miniature dice. Blend into finished paté before transferring to serving dish(es). Refrigerate as with Calf's Liver Paté before serving.

CHICKEN LIVER PATÉ

2 pounds (900 g) chicken
    livers
1 onion, finely chopped
butter or oil for frying
2 sticks (½ pound or 225 g)
    butter; or, ½ cup rendered
    chicken fat
salt and freshly ground
    pepper

pinch cayenne pepper
¼ teaspoon allspice
1 teaspoon dry mustard
½ cup (120 ml) dry sherry or
    port
thin layers of fat or bacon
    slices

Blanch chicken livers in barely simmering water for about 10 minutes. Remove, drain, and set aside. Fry finely chopped onion in a small amount of butter or oil until soft but not brown. Grind chicken livers and onions using meat grinder or food processor. Add softened butter or rendered chicken fat to liver and onion mixture and blend. Mix in salt and pepper to taste, cayenne pepper, allspice, and dry mustard. Transfer to greased paté or baking dish and cover with thin layers of a good quality fat or thin bacon slices. Pour over ½ cup (120 ml) dry sherry or port. Bake in a 300° F. (149° C.) oven until paté has begun to shrink from sides of dish. Cool paté in baking dish. When thoroughly chilled, unmold onto serving platter.

SHEPHERD'S PIE

4 or 5 baking potatoes
2 ripe tomatoes
1 onion, peeled and chopped
1 green pepper, seeded and
 chopped
4 scallions, sliced
butter and oil for frying
2 pounds (900 g) lean ground
 beef

1 tablespoon fresh parsley,
 finely chopped
2 to 3 cups (480-720 ml)
 Brown Sauce or Tomato
 Sauce
butter

Peel potatoes, cut into quarters, and cook in boiling salted water until tender. Drain.

Blanch tomatoes, remove peel, squeeze out seeds, and chop.

Fry onion, green pepper, and scallions in a small amount of butter and oil until translucent and slightly crisp.

Brown lean ground beef in a small amount of oil.

Combine browned beef, onions, green pepper, scallions, and chopped tomatoes in an ovenproof dish, or use individual baking dishes. Add chopped parsley and pour Brown Sauce or Tomato Sauce (see Chapter 3, under Sauces) over mixture. Check seasoning.

Put cooked potatoes through a ricer directly on top of meat, vegetable, and sauce mixture. Potatoes should fully cover mixture and be light and fluffy. Dot with butter and set under broiler until lightly browned.

HAM AND POTATO PIE

5 or 6 baking potatoes, peeled
 and uniformly sliced
2 to 3 cups (480-720 ml)
 Mustard Sauce
1 onion, peeled and finely
 chopped

butter and oil for frying
1 tablespoon fresh dill or
 parsley, finely chopped
2 pounds (900 g) cooked ham
 (boiled or baked), cut into
 cubes

Cook peeled and uniformly sliced potatoes in boiling salted water until barely tender and drain.

Prepare Mustard Sauce according to recipe (see Chapter 3, under Sauces).

Cook onion in a small amount of butter and oil over low heat until translucent.

Combine potatoes, Mustard Sauce, fried onions, dill or parsley, and cubed ham in an ovenproof dish. Set in a pan containing hot water and bake in a 325° F. (163° C.) oven until heated through.

MINIATURE MEAT PIES (PIROZHKI)

Quick Enriched Pastry
1 onion, peeled and chopped
butter and oil for frying
½ pound (225 g) lean ground
  beef or ground raw chicken
  breasts
2 tablespoons parsley, finely
  chopped
salt and pepper to taste
2 tablespoons finely sifted
  flour
2 tablespoons water
2 hardboiled egg yolks, finely
  chopped

Prepare Quick Enriched Pastry (see Pastry section).

Fry onion in a small amount of butter and oil over low heat until translucent and slightly crisp. Add ground beef to pan and fry over medium high heat until lightly browned. If using ground chicken breasts, fry until fully cooked over medium low heat. Add salt and pepper to taste and stir in parsley. Remove from pan and set aside to cool.

Using same pan, add flour and cook over low heat, stirring and adding more butter if necessary. Add water and cook, continuing to stir, for about 1 minute. Stir flour paste into meat mixture, along with chopped egg yolk. Refrigerate until ready to use.

Roll out pastry and cut into rounds. Spoon 2 level teaspoons of meat mixture onto center of each. Bring both sides of pastry together and pinch edges, forming half-moon shapes. (A small seafood-type fork may be used to form attractive edges.) Refrigerate for at least an hour before baking. When ready to serve, bake in a preheated 425° F. (218° C.) oven until lightly browned. (Pies may be frozen and baked in frozen state. Egg whites must not be used as they turn rubbery when frozen.)

MEAT AND VEGETABLE PIE

½ pound (225 g) elbow
  macaroni or noodles
2 pounds (900 g) ground lean
  beef
4 carrots, peeled and
  uniformly sliced
1 pound (450 g) green beans,
  cut into ½" (1 cm) slices
4 stalks celery, peeled and
  sliced
1 onion, peeled and finely
  chopped
1 tablespoon fresh parsley,
  finely chopped
salt and pepper to taste
1½ pints (709 ml) brown
  sauce or tomato sauce
grated Parmesan cheese
butter

Cook macaroni or noodles in boiling salted water until tender and drain.

Brown ground beef in a small amount of oil.

Cook carrots, green beans, and celery in boiling salted water until slightly crisp and bright in color, and drain.

Fry onion over low heat in a small amount of butter and oil until translucent and slightly crisp.

Using a shallow ovenproof dish, spread browned beef over bottom. Top with mixture of cooked vegetables and onions. Sprinkle parsley over surface and pour over Brown Sauce or Tomato Sauce (see Sauces). Season to taste with salt and pepper.

Spread cooked macaroni or noodles over top layer and sprinkle with grated Parmesan cheese. Dot with butter and place under broiler until lightly browned. (If prepared in advance, set in a pan containing hot water and bake in a preheated 350° F. [177° C.] oven about 20 to 30 minutes or until heated through.)

BROWNED SCALLOPS OF VEAL (VEAL SCALOPPINE)

8 veal cutlets, thinly sliced   *finely sifted flour*
salt and white pepper to taste   *butter and oil for frying*

Place cutlets between two layers of wax paper or plastic wrap and pound, using a mallet or cleaver. Remove and season to taste with salt and white pepper. Dip in finely sifted flour and shake off excess. Heat butter and oil in frying pan. When hot, add cutlets and brown on both sides over medium to high heat. (Cooking and browning are done at the same time.) Remove and serve.

SCALLOPS OF VEAL WITH WINE

8 veal cutlets, thinly sliced   *juice of ½ lemon*
1 cup (240 ml) dry white wine

Cook veal as in Browned Scallops of Veal and transfer to a warm platter. Add wine and lemon juice to pan, and cook over high heat, scraping and stirring, using a wooden spoon or spatula, until wine is reduced by about a third. Pour over scallops and serve.

VEAL PIQUANTE (VEAL PICATTA)

8 veal cutlets, thinly sliced   *2 cups (480 ml) Lemon Sauce*
or Caper Sauce

Prepare cutlets as in Browned Scallops of Veal and transfer to a warm platter. Prepare Lemon Sauce or Caper Sauce (see Sauce section) and pour over cutlets.

SCALLOPS OF VEAL WITH MUSHROOMS

½ pound (225 g) mushrooms,
  peeled
olive oil
8 veal cutlets, thinly sliced
½ cup (120 ml) dry white
  wine

2 cups (480 ml) Tomato
  Sauce, Mildly Flavored
1 tablespoon parsley, finely
  chopped

Peel mushrooms and brush lightly with olive oil before slicing (this procedure contributes to browning). Set aside.

Prepare cutlets as in Browned Scallops of Veal and transfer to a warm platter. Add a small amount of olive oil to pan, and, when hot, sauté prepared mushroom slices over medium high heat until golden brown. Pour over browned veal. Combine wine with Tomato Sauce (Chapter 3, under Sauce section), and cook over high heat until slightly reduced. Pour over meat and mushrooms and garnish with finely chopped parsley.

BREADCRUMB-COATED VEAL CUTLETS

8 veal cutlets
salt and white pepper to taste
finely sifted flour
2 whole eggs
1 tablespoon olive
  oil   } lightly beaten
¼ cup (60 ml) milk

breadcrumbs, flavored or
  unflavored
butter and oil for frying

Place cutlets between two layers of wax paper or plastic wrap and pound, using a mallet or cleaver. Remove and season to taste with salt and white pepper. Dip in finely sifted flour and shake off excess. Dip in eggs, oil, and milk mixture, and then in breadcrumbs. Heat butter and oil in frying pan, add cutlets, and brown on both sides over medium heat. (Cooking and browning are done at same time.) Remove to a warm platter and serve.

VEAL CUTLETS WITH CHEESE

8 veal cutlets
8 ¼" (.5 cm) slices fresh
   tomato
8 ⅛" (.3 cm) slices Swiss or
   Gruyère cheese

1 tablespoon finely chopped
   parsley, as garnish

Prepare cutlets as in Breadcrumb-Coated Veal Cutlets and place on broiler pan or in a shallow ovenproof baking dish. Lay a fresh tomato slice over each, top with cheese slices, and dot lightly with butter, to prevent burning. Place under a preheated broiler until cheese has melted and is slightly brown. Transfer to a warm serving platter and garnish with finely chopped parsley.

BREADED VEAL CUTLETS, ITALIAN STYLE

8 veal cutlets
8 thin slices Mozzarella cheese
grated Parmesan cheese
butter and oil for frying
1 green pepper, seeded and
   chopped

1 onion, peeled and chopped
½ garlic clove, finely chopped
4 cups (960 ml) Tomato
   Sauce, mildly flavored
½ teaspoon dried oregano

Prepare cutlets as in Breadcrumb Coated Veal Cutlets and transfer to a shallow ovenproof dish. Lay a slice of Mozzarella cheese on top of each cutlet. Dust grated Parmesan cheese lightly over whole surface. Melt butter and oil in frying pan and cook chopped green pepper and onion until translucent. Add finely chopped garlic and cook, stirring, for about 30 seconds. Prepare Tomato Sauce, Mildly Flavored (see Sauce section) and add green pepper, onion, and garlic, and simmer for about 1 minute. Add oregano, and cook just long enough to blend. Remove sauce from heat and pour over cutlets and cheese. Place in a preheated 300° F. (149° C.) oven for about 20 minutes, or until cheese has melted. Serve with cooked rice or spaghetti.

BREADED VEAL CHOPS
WITH HAM AND CHEESE

8 veal chops
8 thin ham slices
8 thin slices Swiss or Gruyère
* cheese*
salt and white pepper to taste
finely sifted flour
2 whole eggs
1 tablespoon olive } *lightly*
* oil* } *beaten*
¼ cup (60 ml) milk

breadcrumbs, flavored or
* unflavored*
butter and oil for frying
2 cups (480 ml) Tomato
* Sauce, Mildly Flavored*
* (optional)*

Using a sharp knife with a fine blade, slice three-quarters of the way through center of chops. Open up and place between two layers of wax paper or plastic wrap and flatten slightly, using a mallet or cleaver. Remove and season to taste with salt and white pepper. Lay a slice of ham and cheese on each opened layer of chop, and fold over other layer, pressing edges together. Dip in finely sifted flour and shake off excess. Dip in eggs, oil, and milk mixture, and then in breadcrumbs. Heat butter and oil and brown chops lightly on both sides. Transfer chops to a shallow ovenproof dish and bake in a preheated 300° F. (149° C.) oven for about 30 minutes, or until meat is tender and registers 170° F. (77° C.) on meat thermometer. Serve on a bed of Tomato Sauce, Mildly Flavored (see Chapter 3, under Sauces), if desired.

VEAL OR BEEF SLICES WITH CREAM

2 pounds (900 g) veal or
* tenderloin of beef, sliced*
butter and oil for frying
1 onion, peeled and sliced
½ garlic clove, finely chopped

½ cup (120 ml) dry white
* wine (for veal)*
1 cup (240 ml) heavy cream
paprika

Cut veal or beef on the bias into 1¼" (3 cm) long strips, about ⅛" (.3 cm) thick. Heat butter and oil and sauté meat slices over medium high heat, until lightly browned. (Veal should be well done, but beef should be pink in the center.) Transfer to a warm platter. Fry onion over low heat until translucent. Add finely chopped garlic and cook, stirring for about 30 seconds. Add wine to pan and cook, scraping and stirring, using a spatula or wooden spoon, over high heat until reduced by about a third. Add cream and cook until slightly thickened. Pour sauce over meat. Dust lightly with paprika and serve over rice.

ROAST CHICKEN

1 5- to 6-pound (2.25-2.7 kg)   *olive oil and butter*
  roasting chicken   *salt and pepper*

When chicken has been refrigerated, remove half an hour or so before roasting and place in an area where cool-room temperature is maintained (45° F. or 7° C.). Cover with wax paper.

Melt oil and butter over low heat and brush over chicken using a pastry brush. Season with salt and white pepper to taste. Place chicken on side on a roasting rack and arrange rack in a shallow roasting pan or on top of a broiler pan. Place in a preheated 325° F. (163° C.) oven and roast for approximately 15 minutes on one side before changing to other side. Cook breast side up for the remainder of the roasting period. (If legs appear to be cooking before breast, or vice versa, cover that particular area with aluminum foil.)

When breast begins to feel spongy and there is little resistance when tested with the fingers, check temperature (using an instant reading thermometer) in thickest portion of breast located near leg, being careful not to touch bone. Remove when temperature reaches 165° F. (74° C.) and let stand in a warm place for about 20 minutes before carving. Cooking action will have stopped and temperature will have reached approximately 175° F. (80° C.).

Gravy

chicken stock   *3 or 4 tablespoons cold water*
2 tablespoons flour   *2 tablespoons hot water*

In the meantime, skim all fat from drippings in pan. Set pan over medium high heat and de-glaze using chicken stock or water, scraping pan bottom with a rubber spatula or wooden spoon. Turn heat to low. Blend 3 or 4 tablespoons cold liquid with 2 tablespoons flour (per pint [480 ml] gravy) to form a smooth paste. Stir in 2 tablespoons of the hot liquid and gradually add to pan, stirring with a wire whisk. Season to taste. Simmer gently until lightly thickened. Remove and strain, if necessary, before serving.

ROAST TURKEY

Follow recipe for Roast Chicken, substituting turkey for chicken.

ROAST CHICKEN OR TURKEY WITH STUFFING

Follow recipe for Potato Stuffing (under Produce of the Land, Vegetable section) and, when completely cool, insert in cavity of chicken or turkey. If the bird is not to be cooked at once, keep refrigerated.

Stuffing may also be cooked separately. Place in a greased, shallow heat-proof pan in the oven along with chicken or turkey during last half-hour of roasting period, or cook just long enough to heat through and crisp slightly on the surface. Stuffing may also be heated on top of the stove in a saucepan or frying pan over low heat.

CHICKEN KIEVS

4 whole chicken breasts,
skinned and boned
salt and white pepper to taste
garlic powder
4 tablespoons butter
dried tarragon
finely sifted flour

2 whole eggs
1 tablespoon olive ⎱ *lightly*
oil ⎰ *beaten*
¼ cup (60 ml) milk
flavored breadcrumbs
vegetable oil for frying

Split skinned and boned chicken breasts by cutting away remaining cartilage running through center (the thin line of matter connecting sides of breasts). Cut out tendons on underside of breasts. Separate fillets (small tender pieces of flesh on underside) from remainder of breasts and set aside.

Lay fillets and breasts between two sheets of parchment paper, wax paper, or plastic wrap, membrane side down (side from which outer skin has been removed). Using a wooden or metal mallet, pound carefully until thin but not broken. Remove top sheet and dust lightly with salt, white pepper, and a few grains of garlic powder. Place ½ tablespoon butter and a mere pinch of tarragon on center of each breast-half and lay flattened fillets on top and around butter. Bring up layers of breast-halves and fold over fillet-wrapped butter, leaving no gaps. The overall appearance is unimportant at this stage as the layers of flesh will adhere together when exposed to heat. Transfer to a plate and refrigerate.

In the meantime, prepare breadcrumb coating. Using 3 high-sided receptacles or bowls, place finely sifted flour in one, the lightly beaten combination of 2 eggs, 1 tablespoon olive oil, and ¼ cup (60 ml) milk in another, and flavored breadcrumbs in the third. Remove Kievs from refrigerator and secure edges by pressing together. Roll first in flour, then in the egg, oil, and milk mixture, and finally in the flavored breadcrumbs. If not frying immediately, arrange on plate, cover lightly with wax paper and refrigerate. (Do *not* use airtight plastic wrapping.)

To cook preheat oil to 360° F. (182° C.), using a thermostatically controlled deep-fryer. Fry Kievs until a pale golden brown. Do not overcrowd pan. This takes but a few minutes. Remove and lay on paper towels. Reheat fat to 375° F. (190° C.) and return Kievs, cooking until a deep golden brown. Kievs will float to the surface when done. Serve on a bed of rice.

Kievs may be kept warm, uncovered, in a 160° F. (71° C.) oven until ready to serve.

Uncooked Kievs may be frozen in heat-sealed plastic pouches or other airtight containers. Before cooking, remove and thaw, uncovered, in refrigerator.

DEEP-FRIED CHICKEN BREASTS

4 whole chicken breasts,   *flavored breadcrumbs*
  skinned and split in half   *vegetable oil for frying*
finely sifted flour
2 whole eggs
1 tablespoon olive   *lightly*
  oil   *beaten*
¼ cup (60 ml) milk

Remove skin from breast-halves and roll in finely sifted flour, shaking off excess. Combine eggs, oil, and milk, lightly beaten, and dip floured breast-halves in mixture, and then in the flavored breadcrumbs.

To cook, preheat oil to 360° F. (182° C.) using a thermostatically controlled deep-fryer. Fry until a light golden brown and drain on paper towels. (Do not overcrowd pan.) Reheat oil to 375° F. (190° C.) and return breasts, cooking until a deep golden brown. If not overcrowded, breasts will float to the surface when done. Chicken may be kept warm in a 160° F. (71° C.) oven, uncovered, until ready to serve.

Deep-fried Chicken Parts

Using whole cut-up chicken, proceed as in recipe for Deep-fried Chicken Breasts.

POACHED CHICKEN OR FOWL

1 5- to 6-pound (2.25 to 2.7 kg) fowl
finely sifted flour
vegetable oil
stock or water
celery, tops from 1 head
2 leeks
2 carrots, peeled and coarsely chopped
1 onion, peeled and coarsely chopped
sprigs of parsley
bay leaf (small)
salt and white pepper to taste

Dust fowl lightly with finely sifted flour and lightly brown on all sides in a small amount of oil over medium high heat (this removes some of the gamey flavor). Tie up fowl using butcher string. Place in a pot or receptacle just large enough to hold it and cover with stock or water.

Wash celery tops (including leaves) under cold running water and coarsely chop. Cut leek through center and remove grime under cold running water before cutting into ⅛″ (.3 cm) thick slices.

Add chopped celery, leek, carrots, and onions to pot, along with parsley, bay leaf and salt and white pepper. Cover and set over medium low heat. Gently simmer for approximately 1½ to 2 hours, or until tender. (Do not overcook or all the flavor from the chicken will go into the stock.) Turn off heat and let stand, uncovered, for about 15 minutes. Remove fowl and strain stock. Skim off all fat, or set in a cool place until fat congeals and can be readily and easily removed. Use stock as a basis for soup or sauce.

Remove skin from fowl while still warm. Carve meat off bones and cut into strips, using poultry shears. Add to soups, or use as a basis for pot pies, vegetable and meat pies, creamed chicken, Oriental dishes, or similar preparations requiring cooked chicken. (Poached meat is moist as well as flavorful, and lends itself to these preparations more readily than does roast chicken.)

CHICKEN TETRAZZINI

1 4- to 5-pound (1.8 to 2.25
   kg) poached chicken or
   fowl
1 pound (450 g) thin spaghetti
¾ pound (450 g) button-size
   mushrooms, peeled
olive oil
1 tablespoon butter
2 tablespoons finely sifted
   flour

2 cups White Stock or chicken
   broth (480 ml)
½ cup dry sherry or dry
   white wine (120 ml)
4 tablespoons light cream
salt and white pepper to taste
pinch of cayenne pepper
grated Parmesan cheese
butter

Follow recipe for Poached Chicken or Fowl. Remove skin, carve meat off bones, and cut into strips, using poultry shears. (Reserve 2 cups [480 ml] de-fatted stock for sauce.)

Cook spaghetti in a large pot of lightly salted boiling water until al dente (fairly firm when cut with a knife). Drain, using a colander, and rinse under cold running water if spaghetti contains excess starch.

Sauté peeled mushrooms in a small amount of oil over medium high heat until golden brown. Remove and set aside.

Melt 1 tablespoon butter in a saucepan over low heat, stir in flour and cook, stirring, for a few seconds before gradually adding stock. Turn heat to medium and cook, stirring, until sauce begins to simmer. Add dry sherry or wine and gently simmer for another few minutes, or until slightly reduced. Add light cream, cut-up chicken or fowl, mushrooms, salt and pepper to taste, and a pinch of cayenne pepper. Cook just long enough to heat through.

To reheat spaghetti, place 1 or 2 tablespoons olive oil in a saucepan and add water to a height of approximately ¼" (.5 cm) from pan bottom. Bring to a boil and add spaghetti, stirring long enough to coat. Cover pot, turn heat to low, and cook just long enough to heat through. Arrange spaghetti in a casserole dish or heat-proof serving bowls. Spoon over sauce containing chicken and mushrooms, piling slightly higher toward the center. Sprinkle with grated Parmesan cheese, dot lightly with butter, and place under a preheated broiler until lightly browned.

CHICKEN ORIENTAL NO. 1

1 pound (450 g) chicken breasts, skinned and boned
vegetable oil
soy sauce
pinch of salt
dry sherry
Chicken Stock or All-Purpose Stock
4 stalks celery, peeled and chopped
1 green pepper, seeded and chopped
4 or 5 scallions, peeled and sliced
1 16-ounce (450 g) can bean sprouts, drained
1 6-ounce (170 g) can water chestnuts, sliced
1 tablespoon cornstarch, dissolved in sherry

Prepare all ingredients and arrange near cooking area.

Cut skinned and boned raw chicken breasts into strips ½" wide and 1¼" long (1 cm x 3 cm).

Heat a small amount of oil in wok until just under smoking stage. Stir-fry chicken (do not overcrowd pan) over high heat, cooking and lightly browning at the same time. Remove to a heated platter. Before cooking vegetables, add additional oil, a few drops soy sauce, and a pinch of salt. When oil is hot but not smoking, add a proportionately small amount of dry sherry and stock (2 to 3 tablespoons or just enough to moisten), pouring along the inside rim of pan, so that it will be heated through before coming in contact with the hot oil. Stir-fry chopped celery, green pepper, and sliced scallions until fairly crisp. Add drained bean sprouts and sliced water chestnuts, and stir-fry long enough to heat through. Return cooked meat to pan and add approximately ⅓ cup (80 ml) stock in a circular motion along the inside rim. Gradually add prepared cornstarch paste, stirring until sauce is slightly thick and smooth. Serve at once with cooked rice.

CHICKEN ORIENTAL NO. 2

Oriental Sauce
1 pound (450 g) chicken
breasts, skinned and boned
vegetable oil (olive oil or
peanut oil)
4 stalks celery, peeled and
chopped
1 green pepper, seeded and
chopped

4 or 5 scallions, peeled and
sliced
1 16-ounce (450 g) can bean
sprouts, drained
1 6-ounce (170 g) can water
chestnuts, sliced

To prepare sauce, follow recipe for Oriental Sauce (under Sauce section), using light rather than dark soy sauce.

Cut skinned and boned raw chicken breasts into strips ½" wide and 1¼" long (1 cm x 3 cm). Heat a small amount of oil in frying pan and sauté chicken over medium high heat, cooking and lightly browning at the same time. (Do not overcrowd pan.) Remove to a warm platter. Add additional oil if necessary; reheat oil and fry chopped celery, green pepper, and sliced scallions until fairly crisp. Bring Oriental Sauce to a slow simmer and add cooked vegetables, drained bean sprouts, sliced chestnuts, and cooked chicken. Cook just long enough to heat through. Serve with cooked rice.

Chicken Oriental No. 3

Follow recipe for Chicken Oriental No. 2, substituting strips of Poached Chicken or Fowl for sautéed chicken breasts.

PORK ORIENTAL

Follow recipe for Chicken Oriental No. 1, substituting 1 pound (450 g) lean ground pork (pork shoulder) for chicken breasts. Stir-fry a small amount of pork at a time, making certain it is thoroughly cooked.

CREAMED CHICKEN

White Sauce (Béchamel)
poached fowl or chicken; or
   roasted chicken
   (approximately 2 cups)
½ pound (225 g) mushrooms,
   peeled and sliced

1 small green pepper, seeded
   and chopped
½ cup (120 ml) dry sherry or
   dry white wine (optional)
2 tablespoons chopped
   pimiento

To prepare sauce, follow recipe for White Sauce (Béchamel) under Sauce section.

When using poached fowl or chicken, remove skin, carve chicken, and cut into strips. When using roasted chicken, remove skin and dice.

Sauté peeled and sliced mushrooms in a small amount of oil over medium high heat until golden brown. Remove to a warm platter. Turn heat to low and fry chopped green peppers until they take on a slightly translucent appearance; then remove.

Bring White Sauce to a slow simmer and add ½ cup (120 ml) dry sherry or dry white wine. Cook over low heat, uncovered, until slightly reduced. Add mushrooms, green pepper, and chopped pimiento and cook just long enough to heat through. Carefully fold in chicken so as not to shred or break. Serve over a bed of cooked noodles or rice, in patty shells, or with toast points (slices of toast cut diagonally).

CREAMED CHICKEN CASSEROLE

Creamed Chicken
1 10-ounce (280 g) package
   frozen peas
butter

1 8-ounce (225 g) package
   noodles
pinch of salt
grated Parmesan cheese

Follow recipe for Creamed Chicken. Cook peas in a small amount of butter, covered, over low heat until defrosted and heated through. In the meantime, cook noodles in a large pot of lightly salted boiling water until tender. Remove and drain in colander. Arrange noodles in a greased casserole or ovenproof dish. Add cooked peas to Creamed Chicken and pour over noodles. Sprinkle Parmesan cheese over surface, dot with butter, and place under a preheated broiler until lightly browned.

HAM CASSEROLE

Follow recipe for Creamed Chicken Casserole, substituting diced cooked ham for chicken.

CHICKEN BREASTS WITH CHEESE

4 1-pound (450 g) chicken breasts, skinned, boned, and split
8 paper-thin slices Swiss or Gruyère cheese
salt and white pepper to taste

finely sifted flour
dried thyme
butter and oil for frying
3 tablespoons melted butter
fresh lemon juice
grated Parmesan cheese

Sauce

¾ cup (180 ml) dry sherry
1 cup (240 ml) light or heavy cream

1 tablespoon tomato paste

Using a sharp knife with a fine blade, cut open skinned and boned breast-halves three-quarters of the way through the center and insert a paper-thin slice of cheese in each between layers. Press edges together using fingers. Place between two layers of wax paper or plastic wrap and, using a mallet, flatten slightly. Remove paper and reshape into attractive uniform shapes. Using sharp knife, make diagonal slits about 1/16″ (2.5 mm) deep in membrane (skin) side so they will lie flat and not shrink during cooking. Season lightly with salt, white pepper, a mere pinch of dried thyme and press in. Dust both sides very lightly with finely sifted flour.

Heat butter and oil in frying pan and add breasts. Do not over-crowd pan. Fry over medium heat until golden brown on both sides. (Breasts will cook and brown at the same time.) Do not overcook or breasts will harden. Remove and place in an ovenproof dish or on broiler pan. Spread a teaspoon melted butter over each and add a few drops fresh lemon juice. Sprinkle grated Parmesan cheese over each and set under a preheated broiler (several inches from flame) until lightly browned.

To prepare Sauce, de-glaze frying pan with sherry over high heat. Boil rapidly and reduce by a half. Add light or heavy cream and continue to boil until slightly thick. Turn heat to low and stir in tomato paste. Serve Sauce on the side.

CHICKEN BREASTS WITH MUSHROOMS

4 chicken breasts, skinned, boned, and split
salt and white pepper to taste
finely sifted flour
butter and oil for frying
fresh lemon juice

1 pound (450 g) fresh mushrooms, peeled and sliced
¾ cup (180 ml) dry sherry
1 cup (240 ml) light or heavy cream

Remove tendons on underside of skinned and boned breast-halves. Place between two layers of wax paper or plastic wrap and pound lightly, using a mallet. Remove paper and shape into ovals. Using a sharp knife, make diagonal slits about 1/16" (2.5 mm) deep in membrane (skin) side so breasts will retain their shape during cooking. Season lightly with salt and white pepper. Dust both sides very lightly with finely sifted flour. Heat butter and oil in frying pan and fry breasts over medium heat until golden brown on both sides. Cook for 1 or 2 minutes longer over low heat and remove to a warm platter or serving dish. Squeeze a few drops of lemon juice over each breast-half. Keep warm in a 160° F. (71° C.) oven. Sauté peeled and sliced mushrooms in butter and oil until golden brown and spread over tops of browned chicken breasts.

De-glaze pan over high heat with dry sherry. Boil rapidly and reduce by a half. Add light or heavy cream and continue to boil until slightly thick. Serve sauce on the side.

CHICKEN BREASTS WITH SCALLIONS

Follow recipe for Chicken Breasts with Mushrooms, substituting 8 chopped scallions, including a portion of green tops, for mushrooms. Fry scallions in butter and oil for about 1 minute over low heat, or until translucent, being careful not to overcook. Spread over tops of browned chicken breasts.

BREAST OF CHICKEN CUTLETS

1½ pounds (675 g) raw
  chicken breasts, skinned
  and boned
2 tablespoons softened butter
2 egg whites, unbeaten
1 teaspoon salt
½ teaspoon white pepper

1 tablespoon fresh parsley,
  finely chopped
4 tablespoons breadcrumbs
¼ cup (60 ml) milk or light
  cream
finely sifted flour
butter and oil for frying

Remove tendons from underside of raw chicken breasts and put through meat grinder or food processor. (There should be approximately 3 cups ground meat.) Place in bowl and stir in softened butter with electric mixer at low speed. Add egg whites one at a time, along with salt and white pepper, beating until well blended. Mix in finely chopped parsley. Soak breadcrumbs in milk or light cream until absorbed and mix with ground chicken mixture. Chill for about an hour in refrigerator. Remove and divide into equal portions using a scoop and form into oval shapes. Dust lightly with flour, shaking off excess. Heat butter and oil in frying pan and fry cutlets over medium heat until lightly browned on both sides. (Cutlets will cook and brown at the same time.) Do not overcook or they will become dry and hard. Serve as is or with a sauce.

LAMB CUTLETS

Follow recipe for Breast of Chicken Cutlets, substituting raw lamb for breast of chicken.

BROILED BREAST OF CHICKEN

4 chicken breasts, skinned and   finely sifted flour
  split   softened butter
salt and white pepper to taste   paprika

Season skinned breast-halves with salt and white pepper and dust lightly with finely sifted flour, shaking off excess. Smear a little softened butter over both sides and cook under a preheated broiler, 3 or 4 inches (7.5 to 10 cm) from flame until lightly browned on both sides. Do not overcook, otherwise breasts will become dry and hard, rather than tender and juicy.

CHICKEN CACCIATORE

2 2½- to 3-pound (1125-1350   1 cup (240 ml) dry white wine
  kg) chickens, cut up   2 cups (480 ml) All-Purpose
finely sifted flour   Stock or Chicken Broth
olive oil   ½ teaspoon dried oregano
1 green pepper, seeded and   salt and pepper to taste
  chopped   1 tablespoon fresh parsley,
1 onion, peeled and chopped   finely chopped
1 small garlic clove, finely   1 tablespoon finely sifted flour
  chopped

Remove rib bones from underside of chicken breasts. Remove skin from breasts and legs. Dredge chicken in finely sifted flour, shaking off excess.

Fry green pepper, onion, and garlic in a small amount of olive oil over low heat. Remove and transfer to a braising pan or ovenproof casserole. Add additional oil, turn heat to medium high, and lightly brown chicken on both sides. Remove and add to casserole with other ingredients. Add white wine to pan, bring to a boil and de-glaze, scraping bottom using a rubber spatula or wooden spoon. Strain, if necessary, and return to pan. Add stock, oregano, salt and pepper to taste, and chopped parsley and bring to a slow simmer. Turn heat to low and lightly thicken by stirring in 1 tablespoon flour, using a wire whisk. Pour sauce over chicken and braise, covered, in a preheated 325° F. (163° C.) oven until tender. Keep chicken moist by basting from time to time. (Sauce should just barely simmer throughout.)

CHICKEN CREOLE

Creole Sauce
2 pounds (900 g) chicken
  breasts, skinned and boned

butter and olive oil

Follow recipe for Creole Sauce under Sauce section.

Cut chicken breasts into strips 1" wide and 1½" long (2.5 x 4 cm). Heat butter and oil in frying pan and sauté chicken over medium high heat until lightly browned; chicken will be cooked and browned at the same time. Bring Creole Sauce to a slow simmer, turn off heat, and add chicken. Serve at once over a bed of cooked rice.

LE COQ AU VIN

2 2½- to 3-pound (1125-
  1350 g) chickens, cut up
salt and white pepper
finely sifted flour
butter and olive oil
1 pound (450 g) button-size
  mushrooms, peeled
1 onion, peeled and chopped
1 small garlic clove, peeled
  and finely chopped
1 cup (240 ml) dry white wine
  or dry sherry

2 cups (480 ml) chicken broth
  or All-Purpose Stock
¼ cup (60 ml) brandy
  (optional)
¼ teaspoon dried thyme
¼ teaspoon dried tarragon
1 tablespoon fresh parsley,
  finely chopped
1 tablespoon finely sifted flour
½ pound (225 g) pearl onions,
  peeled

Remove rib bones from underside of chicken breasts. Remove skin from breasts and legs. Season chicken with salt and white pepper and dredge in finely sifted flour, shaking off excess.

Heat butter and oil in frying pan and sauté mushrooms until golden brown. Remove and place in braising pan or ovenproof pan with a cover. Fry onion and garlic over low heat and add to pan. Add additional oil, if necessary, turn heat to medium high, and lightly brown chicken on both sides. Remove and add to pan with other ingredients. Add wine or sherry to pan, bring to a boil and de-glaze, scraping bottom using a rubber spatula or wooden spoon. Strain, if necessary, and return to pan. Add stock, brandy, thyme, tarragon, parsley, and salt and pepper to taste. Bring to a slow simmer, uncovered, over low heat. Lightly thicken by stirring in 1 tablespoon of flour, using a wire whisk. Pour sauce over chicken and braise, covered, in a preheated 325° F. (163° C.) oven until tender. Keep chicken moist by basting from time to time. (Sauce should just barely simmer throughout.) In the meantime, bring a large pot of lightly salted water to a boil, add peeled onions and cook until fairly crisp when fork tested. Remove and drain. Add onions to braising pan during later stage of cooking period and baste with sauce.

TURBAN OF CHICKEN BREASTS WITH HAM*

1 pound (½ kg) cooked ham, ground
2 egg whites (unbeaten)
1 teaspoon French mustard
2 tablespoons fresh parsley, finely chopped

3 whole chicken breasts, skinned, boned, and split
salt and white pepper to taste

Grind end piece or thick slices of ham in food processor or grinder. (Use a good quality ham with a low water content.) Place in bowl and, with electric mixer, beat in egg whites one at a time until thoroughly blended. Add mustard and chopped parsley and mix in.

Remove tendons from underside of skinned and boned breast-halves and place between two layers of wax paper or plastic wrap. Pound lightly using a mallet until flattened somewhat. Grease a 1-quart circular mold and lay flattened chicken breasts in mold, membrane side down, with ends hanging over edges. Flattened breasts should overlap one another by about an ⅛" (.3 cm). Season lightly with salt and white pepper. Fill cavity with ground ham mixture and enclose by folding over ends of chicken breasts.

Set mold in a pan with enough hot (not boiling) water to come halfway up the sides and bake in a preheated 325° F. (163° C.)

*Turban of Chicken may also be made with ground tongue or ground raw chicken as a filling.

oven for about 30 to 40 minutes or until meat begins to shrink from sides of mold. Remove and let stand for about 20 minutes before unmolding. To unmold, center round serving platter or plate over mold and, holding securely, turn upside down. The dish will have an attractive rope-like appearance when unmolded. Serve with or without a sauce. Turban may also be served chilled and sliced.

GROUND MEATS, FISH, AND SHELLFISH

chapter four

THE AMERICAN HAMBURGER

Whenever the Earl of Sandwich, an enthusiastic card player and gambler, found himself facing a winning or losing streak, rather than break up the game, he had his servant bring cold meat placed between slices of buttered bread, thereby giving birth to the "sandwich"—or so the story goes.

"Get them hot" was the cry of vendors who first sold "hot dogs" to New York baseball fans.

The hamburger, however, is the food most often associated with America. In a sense, it developed along with the country, meeting each new challenge to its existence, to become symbolic of the inventiveness and ingenuity that are responsible for this country's remarkable growth.

At the time of America's beginnings, minced and cut-up meat had been around for hundreds of years. Sometimes it was pounded using an iron mortar, but for the most part it was cut up into bite-size pieces called collops. It was generally served in liquid, with pieces of bread being used to convey the meat to the mouth. This gave rise to the expression "to gob it all up."

It became the practice in America to cut the meat into much smaller pieces and to mold the pieces back into shape. Round steak and other tough cuts of beef were used. However, since the remolded steak was tender and juicy when cooked, it came to be known as "Hamburger Steak," inferring that it was some sort of choice fare. Monsieur Brillat-Savarin, the self-acclaimed gourmand of the period, had proclaimed "beef from Hamburg" to be the world's finest.

In the beginning, it was shaped into balls, fried, and served with gravy. It was not until late in the nineteenth century that the *Boston Cooking School Magazine* suggested flattening the balls before frying. One of America's earliest cookbooks gives the "receipt" for "Hamburger Steak"; yet for a good number of years thereafter it was widely known as "Hamburg Steak." Early English and European cookbooks make reference to "beef American style" and "beef a la American." It was not until more than halfway into the twentieth century that it reverted back to the original "Hamburger" and—given the tenor of the times—the "Steak" was left off.

From the beginning it was served with sauces and crisp fried potatoes. Catsup, a much used, highly spiced condiment,

played a role. There were "receipts" for tomato catsup, cucumber catsup, currant catsup, mushroom catsup, and grape catsup. However, tomato catsup usually headed the list.

It was not until the period following World War II, characterized by the upsurge of the fast food industry, that the "Hamburger" was placed between the layers of a bun, forming the perfect partnership. It was accompanied, quite naturally, by "ketchup" and "French Fries," a term that was now synonymous with crisp fried or deep-fried potatoes.

The following are some typical examples of the earlier versions of the "Hamburger," along with a "receipt" for catsup:

HAMBURGER STEAK

{From the American Cook Book, *published about 1860}*

Take of round steak as much as desired, chop until a perfect mince; it cannot be chopped too fine; season with salt and pepper and make into balls; fry in hot drippings; garnish the platter with celery tops. A brown gravy can be made and poured over the meat if desired. If you have an accommodating butcher he will chop this meat for you and will do it much cheaper and much better; see that no stringy bits go into it. This steak is preferred by many to the regular broiled.

RIPE TOMATO CATSUP (UNRIVALED)

{From the American Cook Book}*

One-half bushel tomatoes. Boil three hours. Strain out skins and seeds, and add 3 pints vinegar, one-half pound salt, one-fourth pound black pepper, 1 tablespoonful cayenne pepper, 2 tablespoonfuls ground cloves, 4 tablespoonfuls allspice, 2 pounds brown sugar. Boil one hour. Cannot be excelled. Two tablespoonfuls celery seed is an addition.

HAMBURG STEAK

{*From* 365 Breakfast Dishes—Selected from Mrs. Lincoln,*
Mrs. Lemcke, Table Talk, Boston Cooking School Magazine
and Others, *Copyright 1901*}

*Two lbs. of the round of beef chopped very fine; press it into
a flat steak, sprinkle with salt and pepper and a little onion juice;
flour it lightly and broil the same as beef steak. Make a brown
gravy with a little soup stock; thicken with flour.*

BASIC RULES FOR GROUND MEATS, GROUND FISH, AND SHELLFISH

The outstanding thing associated with ground meats, fish, and
shellfish is ease—in preparation, cooking, handling, and even in
eating. Not only are dishes based on them versatile and econom-
ical but they can be among the most delicious and appealing of all
meat and fish preparations. Elegant dishes such as salmon and
chicken quenelles, patés, and filled pastries can be made using
them as a base. Most can be prepared in advance (using only top
quality meats and fish) and take a relatively short time to cook.

Throughout history meats have been endlessly minced with
a pestle (mincemeat) or chopped with a knife (chopped meat).
Fish, too, was minced and chopped. The iron age of the industrial revolution brought the hand meat grinder, the exact replica
of which was later harnessed to electricity. Today, electric grind-
ers (they also come as separate attachments for mixers) and food
processors make it possible to grind meat and fish quickly and
easily.

It is a mistake to believe that only low grade, poor quality
meats justify being ground, for the flavor will still be dependent
on the overall quality and freshness. However, there is a definite
advantage in grinding tough cuts, allowing for simpler and
quicker cooking procedures, but here too, quality, freshness, and
fat content should be taken into consideration. (It is in this area

*Mrs. Lincoln organized one of America's earliest cooking schools of which
Fanny Farmer was a pupil.

that grinding one's own is a definite advantage.) It goes without saying that only the freshest fish should be ground.

COMMERCIALLY GROUND MEAT

While fish is generally ground as needed, great quantities of commercially ground meats (beef in particular) are used. It is important to know exactly what goes into ground meats—the cuts used, freshness, percentage of fat, filler content (cereals and/or water), possible addition of chemicals or other agents to temporarily give meat an improved color. However, this information is difficult, if not impossible, to come by, as commercially ground meats are generally prepared "in the back room." When using commercially ground meats, as opposed to grinding one's own, give it the old nose test both before and during cooking to determine whether or not its aroma leaves something to be desired. Check for excessive amounts of melted fat during cooking, as well as excess moisture. There shouldn't be the slightest hint of any off-flavor, when cooked. (Highly spiced condiments, pickles, and other extras are the saving grace for ground meats prepared from poor quality cuts, particularly when of questionable freshness.)

COOKING AND BROWNING
GROUND MEATS

Some consideration should be given to the nature of the meat (tender or tough), as well as its fat and moisture content.

When frying, do not overcrowd pan as this traps heat and creates steam, resulting in stewed rather than fried meat.

When browning ground beef that is to form part of another preparation, such as a spaghetti sauce or casserole, fry quickly over medium high heat and remove to a warm platter while portions of pink are showing. Do not pile portions of cooked meat on top of one another, as this results in further cooking, drawing out the juices. Overcooked ground meat will end up as dry, tasteless fiber. If properly cooked and of a good quality, it will be tender and juicy.

PREPARATION OF
GROUND FOODS*

Any kind of meat, poultry, fish, or shellfish may be put through a grinder. Its quality is as important as in other areas of cooking. Before grinding, remove any skin, bones, excess fat, or tough connective tissue.

The addition of fats such as beef or pork fat, marrow, butter or margarine will affect the flavor but not the consistency, and is determined largely by inner fat content, quality, kind, and nature of meat or fish.

Finely chopped herbs and seasonings add flavor to ground meats, poultry, and fish.

Since flesh adheres to itself when exposed to heat, binders such as eggs, egg whites, and moistened breadcrumbs are not, as a rule, absolutely necessary. They may or may not be used according to preference and depending on the nature of the preparation.† Egg whites or cream beaten in will, however, assist in making the preparation lighter. The addition of wheat germ or breadcrumbs made from whole wheat bread will supply added nutrition, as well as aid in stretching the preparation. Cooked brown rice may also be used.

When using ground meats or fish for stuffings, such as for flattened pieces of fish, poultry, or meat, toothpicks are unnecessary, as the meats will adhere one to another, upon cooking.

BASIC PROCEDURES FOR PREPARING
VARIOUS GROUND MEATS,
GROUND FISH, AND SHELLFISH

1. Remove any skin, bones, excess fat, tough connective tissue, and tendons using a sharp knife.

---

*Recipes for various ground meats, poultry, fish, and shellfish preparations are included in the corresponding chapter that deals with that food.
†See the section on Binders (p. 149), as well as the Basic Procedures section which follows.

2. Cut up into strips or cubes.

3. Put prepared meat, fish, or shellfish through grinder or food processor.

4. Add salt, pepper, and whatever herbs and other seasonings being used.

5. Mix in any binder, such as breadcrumbs or egg whites, that is to form part of the preparation.

6. Binders should be used according to the nature of the preparation, whether this be meatballs, fishballs, quenelles, mousses, patés, croquettes, and so on.

7. Cook following any one of the recommended procedures listed in the Ground Meats, Poultry, Fish, and Shellfish charts that follow.

GROUND MEATS, POULTRY, FISH, AND SHELLFISH (COOKED AND UNCOOKED)

Preparation	Uncooked Meat or Fish	Binders	Procedures
Meat or Fish Balls	Beef, poultry, ham, or veal and ham	None, egg whites, cereal	Simmer in sauces; or coat in breadcrumbs and deep-fry
	Shellfish, fillets of fish	Egg whites, egg whites extra light	Coat in breadcrumbs and deep-fry
Burgers	Beef	None, cereal, egg whites	Pan-fry or broil
	Chicken, turkey	None, cereal, egg whites	Pan-fry
Meat Loaves	Beef, poultry, beef-veal-pork, ham-chicken	Cereal, flour paste, egg whites	Bake in 325° F. (163° C.) oven until firm and slightly shrunken
Patés	Any one meat or combination: Pork, liver, chicken, duck	Additional fat plus an outer layer of fat	Bake in a 325° F. (163° C.) oven until firm and slightly shrunken; allow to set before removing from pan; serve cold
Sausage	Pork or pork and ham	Cereal, additional fat (highly seasoned)	Pan-fry or bake
Mousses	Breast of chicken or turkey, ham, veal and ham, chicken and ham	Egg whites, egg whites extra light	Place receptacle containing Mousse in a pan of hot water and poach in a 325° F. (163° C.) oven until firm and slightly shrunken
Kernels (Quenelles)	Shellfish, fillets of fish		
	Chicken breasts	Egg whites, egg whites extra light; additional fat (butter)	Shape into ovals and poach in sauce or stock until firm and slightly opaque in color

146

GROUND MEATS, POULTRY, FISH, AND SHELLFISH (continued)

Preparation	Uncooked Meat or Fish	Binders	Procedures
Kernels (Quenelles) (continued)	Fillets of fish (flounder, sole, salmon); shellfish, shrimp	Egg whites, egg whites extra light, additional fat (butter)	Shape into miniature ovals and poach in stock, sauce, wine, or water until firm and set
Stuffings	Roasts, chops (beef, pork, veal, lamb)	Cereal, flour paste	Stuff into cavity and roast
	Whole fish (trout, flounder, salmon)	Cereal	Insert in cavity of fish and bake or steam
Fillings for Kievs	Chicken, veal, ham	None, egg whites	Wrap flattened fillets of chicken or veal around ground ham or chicken; use a breadcrumb coating and deep-fry
	Shellfish, fillets of fish	Egg whites, additional fat (butter)	Wrap flattened fillets of fish or shrimp around ground shellfish or ground fish; coat with breadcrumbs and deep-fry (or poach, uncoated, in stock, sauce, wine, or water)
Medallions	Top quality beef: 1/3 flank steak, 1/3 sirloin, and 1/3 top round	Marrow from 3 or 4 two-inch beef bones for every 2 pounds of ground beef.	Shape into fairly thick patties and broil or fry.

GROUND MEATS, POULTRY, FISH, AND SHELLFISH (continued)

Preparation	Uncooked Meat or Fish	Binders	Procedures
Fillings: Pastry Pies	*COOKED MEAT OR FISH* Beef, chicken, ham, pork, turkey	Flour paste or flour egg paste	Wrap in a layer of pastry (miniature or regular size), or place in baking dish and top with pastry layer; bake in 425° F. (218° C.) oven until crust is lightly browned.
Basis for Meat Pies	Browned beef plus cooked ingredients: Beef, sauce, and vegetables; beef, sauce, and pasta topping; or beef, sauce, and potato topping	None; flour paste	Bake in ovenproof dish, set in a pan of hot water in a 375° F. (190° C.) oven until heated through
Croquettes	Chicken, turkey, ham, fish, shellfish	Egg whites; cereal	Coat with breadcrumbs and deep-fry

BINDERS

Any one of the following may be used as a binder or filler for ground meat and fish preparations. The amounts designated are based on 1 to 1½ pounds (450 to 675 g) of either meat or fish:

CEREAL BINDER

¼ to ½ cup (28.35 g to 56.70 g) cereal (plain or flavored breadcrumbs, wheat germ, soy meal, rice)

⅓ to ⅔ cup (80 to 160 ml) stock, water, milk, or light cream
pinch of salt

Add cereal to liquid, along with salt, and set aside until absorbed. More or less liquid may be added, as required.

EGG WHITE BINDER

1 whole egg white   ½ teaspoon salt

Add egg white and salt to ground meat or fish, and, using an electric mixer or food processor, beat in until completely absorbed. For a lighter mixture, add an additional egg white.

EGG WHITE EXTRA LIGHT BINDER

1 teaspoon salt
2 whole egg whites

½ to 1 cup (120 to 240 ml) heavy cream

Add salt to ground meat or fish and beat in egg whites one at a time, using an electric mixer or food processor. Add cream a little at a time, beating until well blended.

FLOUR PASTE BINDER

¼ *cup (60 ml) water, milk, or*   *pinch of salt*
   stock   ¼ *cup (28.35 g) finely sifted*
1 *tablespoon butter*   *flour*

Combine liquid, butter, and salt in a saucepan and set over medium heat. Bring to a full boil and add flour all at once. Stir briskly, using a wooden spoon. Continue to cook and stir until mixture no longer clings to sides of pan. Remove and set aside to cool.

DAIRY PRODUCTS

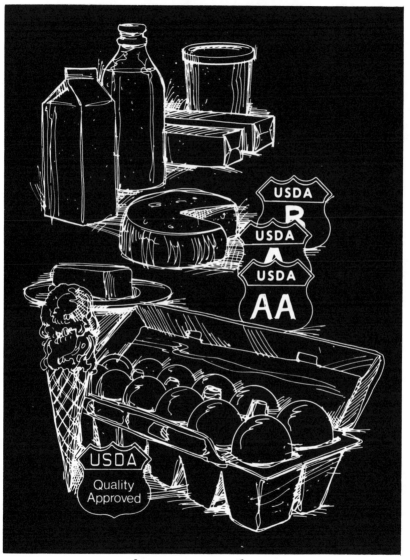

chapter five

BUTTER AND EGG BASKETS

"T'is the part of a wise man to keep himself today for tomorrow, and not venture all his eggs in one basket."

Miguel de Cervantes (1547-1616), Don Quixote de la Mancha

For close to three centuries, the womenfolk on the small farms across America handchurned the butter, milked the cows, and gathered the eggs. Cheese making, brought to America by the early settlers, was solely a domestic art.

Farmwives relied on their butter and egg baskets as a supplemental source of income. The nestegg in their sugarbowls provided a certain independence and served to relieve a somewhat frustrating way of life. The ready savings meant leafing through mailorder catalogues and spinning dreams by candlelight or served to pass the long hours on a sabbath afternoon. They also provided a satisfying trip to the village store.

As towns and cities grew, the demand for dairy foods increased, along with the prices. The sugarbowls began to bulge—but not for long. Jesse Williams, a farmer living in Rome, New York, was the first to take advantage of this situation. In 1851, he established what was to be known as the first "cheesery." Within a few years, in nearby Orange County, Alison Slaughter opened up a "creamery" for making butter. Their success was such that they not only used up their own excess supplies of milk to make cheese and butter, as had always been the custom, but they began to buy up milk from their neighbors as well. "Co-operatives" were soon popping up all over America. Dairymaids were relied on to do most of the work.

The partnership between husbands and wives, working side by side on farms all across the country, was on its way to becoming obsolete. Two years after the opening of Mr. Williams' cheesery, a state agricultural college was established in New York. Ten years later, in 1862, Abraham Lincoln signed the Morrill Act, establishing land-grant colleges and universities. These were intimately associated with the Department of Agriculture. By 1889 the Department had received full Cabinet rank.

The mechanization that followed drove the small farmer and

his partner off the land and into the towns and cities, creating bigger and bigger markets for agricultural products. At the beginning of the nineteenth century, nearly 90 percent of the American population was engaged in some type of farming. One hundred years later the number had decreased to less than a third—and continued to decline steadily with each passing year. At the same time, colleges and universities teaching agricultural research, land use and development, chemistry, pest control, economics, marketing, legal matters, food processing, insurance, storage, and every other aspect impinging on the provision of food continually expanded. Admissions to these colleges were almost totally limited to male students.

Professionalization of the food industry developed along other lines as well. The beginning of the twentieth century saw the development of Home Economics, Dietetics, and Domestic Science classes teaching basic food preparation, canning, home sewing, and other subjects designed to raise the quality of family life. Women were urged to enroll in these classes, and for many years representatives of such schools acted as the pipeline, directly and indirectly, to a growing number of housewives in America. *American Cookery,* formerly *The Boston Cooking-School Magazine,* advertised in succeeding issues during the 1920s, an 80-page handbook entitled *The Profession of Homemaking,* sent free on request. The ad read in part: "Homemaking is the greatest of all professions—the greatest in numbers and greatest in its influences on the individual and society. All industry is conducted for the home, directly or indirectly. . . . The growing industrial, manufacturing and agricultural industries found their greatest outlet in the homemaker." For the next 40 to 50 years the role of homemaker was accepted and motherhood was idealized. By the 1960s one representative of the manufacturing industry offered no less than 26 different household appliances. Woman's place seemed indeed to be in the home.

The late 1960s saw the beginning of new storm signals. The poor attendance, academic standing, and status of "Home Ec" courses came under question at a meeting of home economics representatives from various countries. Some colleges tried renaming their courses. One university changed its "College of Home Economics" to "College of Human Development" and appointed a male social scientist as its head. Others tried working "Ecology" into their new course offerings.

Automation and America's new life style were reflected in

changes in both the quality and content of the majority of foods appearing on grocery shelves. At the beginning of the 1970s, over half the consumer's food dollar was going for highly processed food in one form or another, and the percentage has increased with each consecutive year. The processed food industry had begun by taking over the supply of staples, fully prepared and ready for use, and progressed into complete meals: fish and meats, fruits, breads, and desserts. Concerned home economists, nutritionists, and some scientists found themselves in a position of little influence. The agriculturists, representatives of agri-business, and the advertising media had pulled the rug out from under them—production and promotion were largely in their hands.

Ads appearing in newspapers, magazines, and the television media stressed the nutritional necessity of the four basic food categories but placed little or no emphasis on the forms they took—fresh, frozen, packaged, canned, or dried. The important thing was to have all products reach the check-out counter.

Quality, safeness, and high health standards in food and eating, once an integral part of women's concerns, appeared to be in jeopardy. The powers that be had begun focusing on a new image which would exclude mother's own baked apple pie. The smart mother would rely on her friendly neighborhood supplier. As for the processed food industry and the women's liberation movement, it was a matter of viewpoint as to who was running with the hare and who was hunting with the hound.

The abdication of the traditional roles of women had come about one by one as the forces behind the industrial, technological, and agricultural revolutions gained influence. The womenfolk of the rural areas of America had come a long way.

NUTRITIVE VALUE

All dairy products are valued for their B_{12}, which is present in foods of animal origin only. Except for butter, they are also good sources of animal protein, calcium, and riboflavin.

Eggs contain generous amounts of protein, carbohydrates, fat, phosphorus, iron, sodium, potassium, vitamin A, thiamine, riboflavin, and traces of niacin. (However, the iron in egg yolks is not readily absorbed by the human body.) Vitamins D and E, as well as the fat substances, are concentrated in the yolk. The calcium content is mostly in the shell. There is a noticeable lack of fiber and ascorbic acid (vitamin C).

The proteins in milk are complete and need not be supplemented by any other protein. Milk and milk products are an important source of both calcium and vitamin A. In addition, milk is the only food in which lactose is found naturally. Because whole milk only contains traces of vitamin D, 400 U.S.P. units per quart are added. The amounts of vitamin D found naturally in milk depend on the amount of sunlight to which the cow is exposed.

Cheese contains protein, fat, calcium, phosphorus, vitamin A, riboflavin, niacin, thiamine, and traces of carbohydrates. It contains no ascorbic acid (vitamin C). As cheese is a highly concentrated form of milk, it is rich in nutrients—approximately five ounces of Cheddar cheese is equal in food value to one quart of milk. Cheeses made from whole milk are good sources of vitamin A and riboflavin. Some varieties, such as Cheddar, contain relatively high percentages of sodium (salt).

EGGS IN THE DIET

In both Eastern and Western cultures the egg is the symbol of life and is used in many rituals, especially those celebrating birth and death. The word *egg* comes from the Latin *ovum*. In ancient spring festivals, which in more modern times are celebrated as Passover and Easter, the egg was used to represent the renewal of all life.

In the past, the egg was always used sparingly and by no means with the sense of abandonment it is today. Throughout the first half of the century it brought relatively high prices. With the development of hybrid corn in 1955 by U.S. agriculturists and farmers came vast changes in all areas of the poultry industry. Eggs became much more plentiful and an inexpensive source of protein.

Eggs have always played an important part in cooking. Eggs are used in baking as binders and for all kinds of mixtures: omelets, sauces, soufflés, breakfast foods, custards and creams, as well as a number of other preparations.

PURCHASING FRESH EGGS

The Department of Agriculture grades for eggs are AA, A, B, and C. The size of an egg has nothing to do with the grade, that is, each size may come in any of the grades. The sizes are Jumbo, Extra Large, Large, Medium, Small, and Peewee. The Egg Product Inspection Act ensures the consumer of wholesome, unadulterated, and truthfully labeled eggs. The size and grade must appear somewhere on the carton; in some areas the date must appear as a reliable guide to freshness.

It is wise to inspect cartons for cracked or broken eggs before purchasing. Cracked eggs should never be put to use because of possible contamination from any number of sources.

The relative freshness of an egg may be judged by the yolk: The yolk of a fresh egg will stand up high in the center with the white surrounding it. The fresher the egg, the fuller the yolk. The freshness of an egg in its shell may be judged in one of two ways: (1) Hold the egg up vertically to a strong light and check to see if there is a void at the top end and, if so, how much. A small void area indicates freshness. (This original method for testing eggs was called candling.) (2) Lay the egg horizontally in sufficient cold water to cover: If it lies flat it is full and fresh, if it tilts slightly it is good enough to use, if it sits up it is not fit for consumption.

When a small blood clot appears on the surface of the yolk, an egg is usable; however, if there is a large blood clot which gives a pink appearance to the white, discard the egg. Likewise, if a small white mass has formed inside the egg, it can be removed and the egg may be used; however, a large globule means the egg should not be used.

It is always advisable to discard an egg if there is any doubt as to its freshness or quality.

STORING EGGS

Eggs keep best when stored in their carton in a closed area of the refrigerator, for example, a special egg drawer. They will deteriorate much more quickly when stored on the open egg shelves that are found in many refrigerators. Keep in mind that egg shells are porous and can absorb odors when not protected.

Eggs stay freshest when kept at a constant temperature, that is, when they are not taken out of the refrigerator and allowed to stand at room temperature and then put back.

Eggs should never be stored at room temperature.

Movement of the yolks is prevented when eggs are stored in their carton with the broader end up.

EGG COOKERY: THEORY AND OTHER CRITERIA

Egg Whites

Egg whites are frequently used as a binder for different foods because their high albumin content causes them to coagulate when exposed to heat and thus serves to hold the ingredients in a desired form.

Egg whites may be beaten directly into ingredients, but foods will be lighter if the whites are first beaten separately and then folded in.

While egg whites foam up faster at room temperature they will also collapse and drain more quickly. A copper bowl and a hand whip are no longer necessary to beat egg whites properly—the electric mixer makes the work of beating egg whites quick and simple. A pinch of cream of tartar also makes a satisfactory substitute for the copper in the bowl.

The addition of a small amount of sugar makes a smoother and more stable foam. However, sugar must be added very gradually so that it will be completely absorbed. Powdered or very fine granulated sugar is better than regular granulated for this operation.

The receptable or bowl used for beating egg whites must be completely free of any fat particles, as these will interfere with the foaming action. Egg yolk contains fat, and for this reason it must be totally separated from the white.

Egg whites are frequently overbeaten. They should be beaten until they form soft peaks and have a shiny, moist appearance and not until they are dry and stiff. However, when underbeaten they will not retain their rigidity.

Whole Eggs

Eggs are used as emulsifiers in many preparations, for example, cakes, custards, mayonnaise, hollandaise, mousses, and creams, to prevent separation of the ingredients. While both egg whites and yolks act to hold a mixture together, egg yolks contribute more to the consistency. Thus a thicker preparation results when the number of egg yolks is increased in proportion to the number of whole eggs or egg whites.

ADDITION OF STARCH   A starch may be added to egg-based preparations such as soufflés and creams to ensure against separation. Use 2 tablespoons flour or 1 tablespoon cornstarch to 1 pint (½ l) liquid. Add directly to the beaten eggs or moisten slightly and combine with the liquid.

DISHES, MOLDS, AND PANS   Receptacles used for custards, creams, mousses, and soufflés should be treated with some type of fat or oil to prevent sticking and for easy unmolding. A softened butter or other fat may be used to coat dish interior, but a canned liquid vegetable oil or similar type spray works best.

UNMOLDING   To unmold, center a serving plate over dish or mold. Hold securely in place and turn upside down. If necessary, carefully run a knife around sides before unmolding, or place dish in hot water for a few minutes. This step can generally be omitted if a canned spray has been used to grease interior.

ADDITION OF SUGAR   In most dairy preparations such as custards, puddings, and soufflés the amount of sugar used does not appreciably affect the consistency, only the degree of sweetness. Most of these dishes can be prepared with very little sugar and do not necessarily have to be "rich." For instance, anywhere from 2 tablespoons to 1 whole cup of sugar may be used in a custard containing 3 or 4 eggs and 2 cups (½ l) milk.

When sugar is added to dairy preparations it can be dissolved in the milk or beaten into the eggs. The latter, however, results in a smoother preparation.

LIQUID Milk may be used in place of light or heavy cream in dairy preparations without affecting the consistency to any degree, but there will be a slight difference in flavor.

BAIN MARIE Custards, creams, mousses, and such preparations are oven-baked in a bain marie. The dish or mold containing the preparation is placed in a shallow pan containing enough hot (not boiling) water to come halfway up the sides of the mold. The temperature should be regulated so the water remains hot but does not simmer. A temperature between 325° F. (163° C.) and 350° F. (177° C.) is recommended.

COOKING TEST Custard, creams, and custard puddings are cooked when a knife inserted part way into the preparation comes out clean. A one-quart (1 liter pan) size baking dish takes about 40 to 50 minutes to bake in a 325° F. (163° C.) oven.

COOKING PROCEDURES FOR EGGS

Boiled Eggs

Bring water to a full boil and add a pinch of salt. Using a needle or similar instrument puncture a hole in the top or bottom of the egg to prevent cracking when lowering into boiling water. Add egg and adjust heat so that water barely simmers during cooking. Do not cover. A large egg at refrigerator temperature takes 4 minutes to cook to the soft stage and 5 to 6 minutes for medium. A hardboiled egg requires 15 minutes.

Plunge hardboiled eggs into cold water as soon as cooked and remove shell under cold running water. Eggs will discolor when cooked at too high a temperature or for too long, or when left in their shells for more than 5 minutes or so.

Fried Eggs

For best results fry one egg at a time using a small frying pan. Preheat pan over high heat and add a small amount of butter or other fat. Add egg as soon as the fat foams and cover the pan. An egg fried in this manner will be fully cooked and the yolk will be soft and slightly enveloped by the white in about 1 minute. Remove cover and serve at once. Eggs should be watched carefully as they overcook very quickly.

Poached Eggs

Eggs must be very fresh to be satisfactorily poached. There are gadgets (egg poachers) especially made to hold an egg in the water during poaching, as well as for easy removal, but they are by no means necessary.

Use a straight-sided frying pan and bring water to a boil. Add a pinch of salt and a teaspoon of vinegar per quart (liter) of water. Carefully break eggs into a saucer or poacher before adding to water. Regulate heat so that water barely simmers. When the white has enveloped the yolk, the egg is done to the soft stage. This should take about 4 minutes. Remove, drain, and serve at once on toast or muffins.

Scrambled Eggs

Eggs will have a lighter texture if a tablespoon of water, milk, or cream is added for each egg. Using a fork or wire whisk, beat together, but do not overbeat as this toughens eggs.

Set a frying pan with sloping sides similar to an omelet pan over medium to high heat. Add a small amount of butter or other fat and add beaten eggs when it begins to foam. Shake pan and move eggs about in the manner of an omelet. It is important to neither overcook nor undercook them and to bear in mind they will continue to cook for a few seconds after removal from the heat. Scrambled eggs should be soft and creamy but fully cooked. Overcooked eggs are heavy and lumpy. Serve at once on a warm platter.

Fried Toast

This hearty and filling dish was originally referred to as American Toast but now generally goes under the name of French Toast. Lightly beat 2 whole eggs using a fork or wire whisk. Add 1 teaspoon to 2 tablespoons finely granulated sugar, depending on desired degree of sweetness. Whisk in ⅓ cup milk or cream. Add 2 to 3 slices (depending on texture and absorbency) of lightly buttered bread and soak until completely absorbed. Cook in a frying pan in a small amount of butter over medium heat until lightly browned on both sides. Or arrange in a nonstick or buttered ovenproof pan and brown under broiler.

Meringue

For each egg white use 1 to 3 tablespoons powdered or finely granulated sugar, according to taste.

Beat egg whites in an electric mixer until they begin to foam and add a pinch of cream of tartar. Beat for a few seconds and gradually add sugar. Continue to beat until meringue can be shaped into soft peaks and has a glossy appearance. Be careful not to overbeat, otherwise meringue will become stiff and dry.

Egg whites increase five to six times their original volume when beaten.

Bake in a preheated 450° F. (232° C.) oven. Meringue is cooked when light brown patches begin to form on surface. Remove at once. Meringue requires but a few minutes to bake and should be watched carefully. Do not, however, open oven door during earlier stages, or meringue will fall. Allow to cool at room temperature.

ALL ABOUT OMELETS

An individual omelet is made using two or three eggs. Larger omelets using five or six eggs will serve two or three persons. The size of the pan should be in accordance with the number of eggs used. It is possible to prepare a one-egg omelet if the pan is small enough.

Add 1 tablespoon of water, milk, or cream for each egg used and lightly beat together using a whisk or fork. Do not overbeat. Use a thin metal, nonstick-coated frying pan with sloping sides or a regular omelet pan made of medium-heavy cast iron or cast aluminum. The important thing is to control the heat according to the thickness and nature of the metal. For instance, a nonstick thin metal pan conducts heat much more rapidly than a heavy pan and thus requires a quicker hand and greater control, as well as a lower temperature setting.

Set pan over medium to high heat. Pan is ready when just under the smoking stage, or when a few drops of water bounce and boil away almost immediately. If pan smokes, remove from heat and shake around in the air. Judging temperature of pan will become instinctive after a little experience.

Add a *small* amount of butter to pan—be careful on the amount of butter as too much could ruin the omelet. The butter should sizzle and foam but not turn brown. If this should happen, remove browned butter using a paper towel and begin again. Shake pan to spread butter around sides and bottom and add egg mixture. Allow eggs to cook for a few seconds before stirring with a wooden fork or spoon. Make fast, circular motions bringing cooked portion in toward the center. Shake pan during cooking as this helps make omelet light and fluffy. Lift pan occasionally to prevent omelet from overcooking.

When eggs begin to set, spread the mixture evenly over pan bottom and reduce heat. If using filling, quickly spoon across center. Turn off heat. Roll the omelet over one-third, working from the handle side and tilting pan slightly. Fold the other edge over the first, forming an envelope. Grasp handle using left hand with fingers and palm up and, holding a warmed plate or platter in the right hand, turn omelet out on to it. Should omelet stick and not roll out easily melt a little butter under it. The whole operation takes but a minute or so.

Omelet Fillings and Garnishes

Prepare fillings in advance and place near working area. Fillings may be added to the egg mixture prior to cooking, folded into the cooked omelet, arranged across the finished omelet, or inserted into a slit made in the cooked omelet. When and how filling is added will depend on the nature of the filling. Some of the many possibilities follow.

◇ Grated Cheddar cheese
◇ Grated Swiss cheese
◇ Mushrooms, peeled, sliced, and sautéed in butter

◇ Cooked spinach or other greens, finely chopped and thoroughly drained
◇ Fresh herbs, finely chopped
◇ Cooked chicken livers, chopped
◇ Onions, sliced and fried to translucent stage
◇ Tomatoes, peeled, seeded, and chopped
◇ Green pepper, seeded, chopped, and fried to translucent stage
◇ Onion, tomato, and green pepper combination
◇ Chopped cooked ham
◇ Cooked potatoes, sliced or chopped and fried to brown stage
◇ Ham and potato combination
◇ Cooked diced bacon
◇ Cooked shellfish, chopped
◇ Cooked fish, shredded

Sauces such as Cheese or Tomato may be served with omelets.

Brush a small amount of softened butter over the surface of a cooked omelet to give it a more attractive appearance. A light dusting of paprika also adds to appearance.

Garnish with finely chopped parsley, a sprig of parsley or watercress, or julienne strips of pimiento.

BUTTER: PLANNING FOR NUTRITION AND PURCHASING

While the consumption of butter has decreased in recent years, its counterpart cheese has gone up in consumption. In a sense it is a little on the order of "robbing Peter to pay Paul."

Today butter is processed from the fat in cow's milk by means of sophisticated machinery. Less than a hundred years ago, however, much of it was still made by hand churning—that is, agitating the milk in order to solidfy the fat in it. Ordinarily the carotene (vitamin A) in the cow's diet made it pale yellow in color, but in the spring its hue reflected an excess amount of carotene in the new, succulent grasses. Today artificial coloring is added to give butter a much deeper color; its flavor, mild and faintly sweet, varies slightly depending on the cow's diet.

While sweet butter is available, salted butter is consumed in far greater quantities.

NUTRITIVE VALUE

Butter contains a certain percentage of water, the amount of which varies according to its preparation.

Nutritionally, butter is a high energy food which contains substantial amounts of vitamins A and D in their natural state.

Butter comes in Grades AA, A, and B. However, federal grading is not compulsory.

PROCEDURES

CLARIFIED BUTTER   Clarified butter can withstand higher temperatures than regular butter without burning. To prepare, melt butter over low heat in a receptacle designed for this purpose or in one of similar design. Remove from heat and carefully separate the top clear yellow portion from the bottom where the sediment will have collected.

FRYING WITH BUTTER   As a frying medium, butter should be exposed to temperatures of low to medium heat. Browned butter should not be disposed of as it has a pleasant nutty flavor; however, if butter is burned black it is of no use. One part butter to two parts oil (sesame, peanut, olive) makes an excellent frying fat, since both lend flavor to food and oil prevents butter from burning when exposed to higher temperatures.

FLAVORED BUTTERS   Butter combines well with finely chopped fresh herbs and spices such as dill, parsley, tarragon, garlic, and mustard. Onion juice may also be used. The butter is softened and blended with whatever flavoring base is used. It can be formed into rolls or blocks, refrigerated, and used as needed. Seasoned butters add flavoring to vegetables, meats, fish and sauces.

MOTHER'S MILK

Toward the end of the nineteenth century Dr. Brouzet, a Frenchman, implored his government to pass some sort of legislation that would disallow the breast feeding of infants. It was his belief that all forms of immorality and disease could be communicated through mother's milk. During the early part of the twentieth century, a famous chemist proposed as a substitute bread boiled in beer and honey—"Brute's Food" was the name he gave to his concoction.

Earlier, in the middle of the nineteenth century, Baron Justus von Liebig introduced "Foods for Infants," a formula that was to give rise to the patent baby food industry. During this same period, Newton received an English patent for his highly sweetened "condensed milk," and a few years later, in 1856, Gail Borden took out a United States patent for "evaporated milk." The latter two events followed close on the heels of the introduction of François Appert's method of canning foods. Pairing the two seemed like the perfect union. However, there were wrinkles to iron out before the wedding could take place, notably the problem of an unbreakable, cheap receptacle of light weight. Glass jars would not do.

The answer came in the tin can, but the fact that most foods contain acid, which causes the contents to be discolored when it comes in contact with tin, was overlooked. This problem was eventually solved by lacquering the interior of the can. However, as milk contains no acid, this did not directly affect its being canned successfully. The big wrinkle was the lack of control over canning temperatures, a complication that resulted in many reported cases of botulism.

The union of evaporated milk and the tin can was one on which industry was particularly anxious to have the public's blessing. The high costs of transporting whole milk had cut down considerably on the dairy industry's profits. This hope was short-lived, however. In spite of free recipe booklets, investments in advertising showing any number of uses, including candy making which was a popular diversion at the time, evaporated milk found little favor with the consumer, either as a substitute for fresh milk or as a back-up supply. The flavor of evaporated milk in no way resembled that of sweet, fresh milk and its color and texture were considerably changed. (Stabilizers such as sodium citrate and carageen are frequently used today to obtain a smooth product.)

During World War I, canned milk found an outlet for use in places where fresh milk was unattainable. After the war it was teamed up with vegetable fat under the brand name "hebe," and was advertised as a quick and handy aid for use in cooking vegetables, preparing sauces, and poaching eggs. But this too failed to catch on.

Evaporated milk was to come into its own, at long last, in an area that might be considered one of the most unlikely—that of replacing "the most wholesome food there is for infants," mother's own milk. It was to be supplemented by baby foods.

Doctors and hospitals gave out formulas consisting of evaporated milk with some form of sweetener as a substitute for the natural lactose found in mother's milk and also to make it more palatable to the baby. Breast feeding was discouraged for the most part and mothers were warned against possible complications.

The bottle–baby food diet gave birth to a new breed of nurse. In antiquity and until the nineteenth century, a "nurse" was one who suckled an infant not her own. In later times she was known for her care of the sick and wounded. In relatively modern times she became known as a wet nurse. Such a person served mothers whose position for one reason or another made breast feeding impractical or undesirable. Wet nurses also suckled the infants of those who were too ill to nurse, or of those who died in childbirth or from childbed fever.

The new "baby nurse" provided freedom for mothers who were busy with social commitments, dressmaker fittings, and trips abroad. The acceptance and prestige of this practice reflected itself in the long torsos and flat-chested styles of the roaring twenties. But for the vast majority of mothers, the purchasing, preparation, and procedure involved in the demanding bottle–babyfood routine tended to turn infant care into a somewhat less than enjoyable experience, while adding an unnecessary financial burden. (In the opinion of many, both mother and infant were deprived somewhat unwittingly of what might have been a satisfying emotional and nurturing experience.)

Toward the end of the 1960s, the relative merits of mother's own, ultra fresh milk as against cow's milk, which has been exposed to relatively long storage periods (and the quality of which is also dependent on the animal's diet and health), once again came under scrutiny. Many also questioned the soundness of allowing a multi-million dollar babyfood industry to dictate infant nutrition standards.

MILK FOR NUTRITION

Along with butter, eggs, and cheese, milk has always been consumed in large quantities. In recent years America's milk consumption has given way to a sharp increase in purchases of soft drinks. What does this mean nutritionally? Often called the complete food, milk contains protein of a high quality, readily digestible and quickly assimilated. It also contains phosphorus and is an important source of calcium. A twelve-ounce bottle of cola, on the other hand, contains approximately two heaping tablespoons of table sugar and the caffeine removed from the increasingly popular de-caffeinated coffee.

Milk is the only food in which the sugar lactose occurs naturally; it is this compound that is believed to contribute greatly to milk's digestibility. There are no data readily available to document what the relatively high temperatures used to process evaporated milk do to this natural sugar. When milk sours it has converted the lactose into lactic acid, the same chemical reaction that takes place when dough sours and meat ages.

Buttermilk

The rich flavorful buttermilk of the not too distant past was the liquid left after churning. It frequently was made more flavorful by the small particles of butter floating through it. Most of the buttermilk distributed today is made from skim milk which has been treated with a culture of lactic acid bacteria. Its low fat content makes it a good drink for those on restricted diets.

Yogurt

Yogurt comes from a Turkish word of the same spelling. Alternatively, it may be spelled "yoghurt." Either way it is nothing more than a fermented milk product, usually skim milk, to which cultures of two types of bacteria (one of these being lactic acid) are added. Milk solids may also be added. It is much higher in price than milk even without the addition of sweet fruit preserves, but its nutrient content does not differ essentially from that of the milk from which it is made.

THE ASSURANCE OF SAFE MILK

There are rigid sanitary controls surrounding the production and distribution of milk. In the late nineteenth century Louis Pasteur set the wheels in motion to ensure a safe product free of harmful bacteria. Today nearly all milk is pasteurized.

The United States Public Health Service has set up ordinances and codes that are generally adhered to in most areas. Modern refrigeration has contributed in no small way to fresh wholesome milk supplies and products.

HEAVY CREAM AT ITS BEST

Heavy cream gets thicker as it ages, up to a point of course, after which it turns sour. Very fresh cream is thin and thickens very slightly or not at all when whipped. Heavy cream is at its best after having been refrigerated for three or four days. It can also be thickened by allowing to stand at room temperature for several hours. This method is not as satisfactory as the former, however.

Whipped Cream

Cream whips best when very cold and a few days old. (It is also a good idea to chill the bowl beforehand.) A small amount of powdered sugar may be added to sweeten the cream and give it body.

Properly whipped cream to which powdered sugar has been added will keep in the refrigerator for several days without liquefying. It may also be piped onto a cookie sheet or aluminum foil into individual portions or rosettes, using a pastry bag, and frozen. Once frozen it can be stored in containers or plastic bags and used as needed. Frozen whipped cream thaws in a relatively short time at room temperature. It takes slightly longer when refrigerated.

Chantilly Cream is made by adding vanilla extract or vanilla seeds to whipped cream. Use 1 teaspoon extract or the seeds from a 2″ (5 cm) piece of vanilla pod to ½ pint (240 ml) of cream.

Caution should be taken not to overwhip cream, otherwise it will turn into whipped butter.

EARLY AMERICAN CHEESE MAKERS

Professor J. R. Campbell, brought to North America in 1889 as a consultant to the new cheese makers, found them confronted with many obstacles. Their equipment was crude—wooden and tin tubs, common teacups rather than graduated ones for measuring rennet (the substance used to curdle milk), and poor devices for heating the milk. Furthermore, they were working with hit or miss systems. One criticism was the high percentage of salt, which is still the practice today if to a somewhat lesser degree. In spite of everything, he found the cheese superior to English Cheddar. It had greater uniformity and "when toasted, the casein and butterfat did not separate."

Within a few short years, the Cheddar in parts of the United States and Canada was in the forefront and was being sought after in other parts of the world. The expanse and richness of the new land made no small contribution, because the flavor of good cheese and butter depends largely on the health and diet of the cow.

Cheddar became and remains the most popular cheese in both Canada and the United States

MEET THE FAVORITE AMERICAN-MADE CHEESES

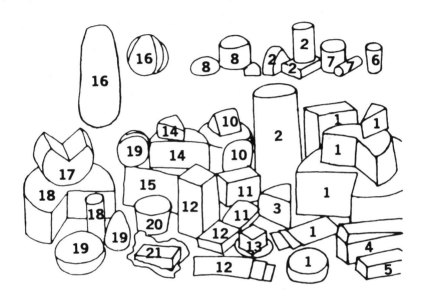

1. Cheddar	11. Brick
2. Colby	12. Swiss
3. Monterey or Jack	13. Limburger
4. Pasteurized Process Cheese	14. Blue
5. Cheese Foods	15. Gorgonzola
6. Cheese Spreads	16. Provolone
7. Cold Pack Cheese Food or	17. Romano
Club Cheese	18. Parmesan
8. Gouda and Edam	19. Mozzarella and Scamorze
9. Camembert	20. Cottage Cheese
10. Muenster	21. Cream Cheese

U.S. Department of Agriculture, *How to Buy Cheese*, Agriculture Marketing Service, Home and Garden Bulletin No. 193 (Washington, D.C.: Government Printing Office, 1971), pp. 12-13.

CHEESES

Cheeses are imported from almost every west European country, yet despite the plethora of overlapping names, there are really only about eighteen different varieties. As a general rule, cheeses are valued more for their flavor than for their nutritional value, neither of which has any bearing on the other. For instance, a cheese with a high food value can be much lower in price than a particular cheese with a distinctive flavor.

Basically, cheese is a concentrated form of milk. Although the percentages vary from one cheese to another, ripened cheese contains approximately one-quarter protein, one-third fat, and one-third water. Curd cheeses, such as cottage cheese, have acid-formed curds and retain only about 20 percent of their calcium, whereas cheeses with rennet-formed curds, such as Cheddar, retain about 80 percent. Cottage cheese has a low percentage of fat, contains only about 18 percent protein, and is about 75 percent water.

How Various Cheeses Are Made

The various labels under which cheeses are sold can be confusing without some understanding of their composition.

RIPENED CHEDDAR   This cheese is made by heating whole milk and adding sufficient rennet to coagulate the albumin (the substance that collects on the surface of milk when it is brought to a boil). Rennet derives from the lining membrane of the stomach of an unweaned animal, such as a calf, but is now in short supply, and the industry is looking for a substitute. Packaged rennet was purchased for a few pennies by early, rural Americans for use in making cheese on the farms.

Once the rennet is added, the mixture begins to curdle. Coloring and salt are added during the process. The cheese is then pressed and dried for several days before being coated with hot paraffin, to prevent moisture loss during ripening. At this stage, it is called green cheese.

It is then placed in a temperature-controlled room (around 50° F. or 10° C.) on shelves that allow for adequate ventilation.

The longer the cheese ages, the more flavor it develops; whether it be mild, medium, or sharp depends on the length of its ripening process. A package of "aged natural cheese" sometimes indicates the length of ageing, a useful bit of consumer information.

PROCESSED CHEESE This product is made by cutting up about 6 parts green cheese to 1 part ripened, and putting the whole through a grinder. It is then heated and mixed with water, salt, and an emulsifier, such as sodium citrate. The exposure to heat is necessary to retard spoilage, but at the same time, much of its original flavor is destroyed, and the product is prevented from further ripening. Processed cheese blends well, is smooth in texture, and is easily sliced.

In *processed cheese foods*, some form of milk product, such as dry powdered milk, is added to the processed cheese to attain a softer result with a somewhat milder taste.

PROCESSED CHEESE SPREADS Some form of milk product is also added to processed cheese to produce processed cheese spreads, but in such a quantity that processors are prohibited by law from labeling them as cheese and, therefore, they are given trade names.

COLDPACK CHEESE This mixture of green and ripened cheeses differs from processed cheese in that it is mixed and packed without being exposed to further heat treatment, making the flavor quite similar to natural cheese. It is soft, spreads easily, and blends beautifully with sauces. It comes in either Swiss or Cheddar.

PURCHASING:
WHAT TO LOOK FOR IN CHEESES

As it stands, there is no grading system available to consumers, while there is one for wholesale buyers. It is based on flavor, body, and texture. There are wide differences between the amount of water, protein, and fat in the various cheeses.

Cheddar is graded anywhere from AA to C and Swiss from A to D. These grades, as a general rule, are not indicated on the retail package. Top grades can sometimes be found in specialty stores, but are rarely sold in the average retail market.

Check packages of natural ripened cheeses for length of exposure, as for instance—"Aged – 90 days."

For grating purposes, it is best to purchase cheese in a solid piece and grate as needed. There are many inexpensive hand graters on the market, as well as grater attachments for electric mixers and food processors.

HOW TO COOK WITH CHEESE

The albumin contained in cheese causes it to coagulate when subjected to temperatures between 150° F. (65° C.) and 210° F. (99° C.). However, the composition of cheese is such that it does not exude water when subjected to too high a temperature, or for too long, but it does break down and separate.

As cheeses vary in composition, so then do some cheeses blend better than others. For instance, processed cheese is less prone to separation because of the way it is made. Cream cheese also blends easily with other ingredients.

Natural cheese imparts flavor and nutrition, but has more of a tendency to separate. However, when put through a grinder, or finely chopped, it blends reasonably well. Natural cheese combined with a coldpack cheese does even better, and imparts an excellent flavor.

When cheese is added to a tomato-based sauce, the tendency to separate is increased because of the acidity of the tomatoes. This may be modified by thickening the sauce with flour or some other starch (which acts as an emulsifier) before adding the cheese.

When cheese is used in any preparation cooked over direct heat, the temperature should be lowered and kept under the simmering point, otherwise the cheese will break down. Also, once cheese is added, the cooking period should be relatively short—or just long enough to blend.

To prepare foods (meat, fish, vegetables, casseroles) au gratin, spread grated cheese over surface, dot lightly with butter to prevent drying and burning, and place under a preheated broiler until lightly browned and crusty (or in a preheated 500° F. [260° C.] oven). Grated cheese may be combined with flavored or unflavored breadcrumbs.

CHARACTERISTICS OF SOME POPULAR VARIETIES OF NATURAL CHEESES

Kind or name Place of origin	Kind of milk used in manufacture	Ripening or curing time	Flavor	Body and texture	Color	Retail packaging	Uses
SOFT, UNRIPENED VARIETIES							
Cottage, plain or creamed. (Unknown)	Cow's milk skimmed; plain curd, or plain curd with cream added.	Unripened	Mild, acid	Soft, curd particles of varying size.	White to creamy white.	Cup-shaped containers, tumblers, dishes.	Salads, with fruits, vegetables, sandwiches, dips, cheese cake.
Cream, plain (U.S.A.)	Cream from cow's milk.	Unripened	Mild, acid	Soft and smooth	White	3- to 8-oz. packages	Salads, dips, sandwiches, snacks, cheese cake, desserts.
Neufchatel (Nū-shà-tel'). (France)	Cow's milk	Unripened	Mild, acid	Soft, smooth similar to cream cheese but lower in milkfat.	White	4- to 8-oz. packages.	Salads, dips, sandwiches, snacks. cheese cake, desserts.
Ricotta (Rĭ-cŏ'·ta) (Italy)	Cow's milk, whole or partly skimmed, or whey from cow's milk with whole or skim milk added. In Italy, whey from sheep's milk.	Unripened	Sweet, nut-like.	Soft, moist or dry	White	Pint and quart paper and plastic containers, 3 lb. metal cans.	Appetizers, salads, snacks, lasagne, ravioli, noodles and other cooked dishes, grating, desserts.
FIRM, UNRIPENED VARIETIES							
Gietost,[1] (Yĕt'ŏst). (Norway)	Whey from goat's milk or a mixture of whey from goat's and cow's milk.	Unripened	Sweetish, caramel.	Firm, buttery consistency.	Golden brown	Cubical and rectangular.	Snacks, desserts, served with dark breads, crackers, biscuits or muffins.
Mysost (Müs-ôst) also called Primost (Prēm'·ôst). (Norway)	Whey from cow's milk.	Unripened	Sweetish, caramel.	Firm, buttery consistency.	Light brown	Cubical, cylindrical, pie-shaped wedges.	Snacks, desserts, served with dark breads.
Mozzarella (Mŏ·tsa-rel'la) also called Scamorza. (Italy)	Whole or partly skimmed cow's milk. In Italy, originally made from buffalo's milk.	Unripened	Delicate, mild.	Slightly firm, plastic.	Creamy white	Small round or braided form, shredded, sliced.	Snacks, toasted sandwiches, cheeseburgers, cooking, as in meat loaf, or topping for lasagne, pizza, and casseroles.

1 Imported only.

Kind or name Place of origin	Kind of milk used in manufacture	Ripening or curing time	Flavor	Body and texture	Color	Retail packaging	Uses
SOFT, RIPENED VARIETIES							
Brie (Brē) (France)	Cow's milk..........	4 to 8 weeks.	Mild to pungent.	Soft, smooth when ripened.	Creamy yellow interior; edible thin brown and white crust.	Circular, pie-shaped wedges.	Appetizers, sandwiches, snacks, good with crackers and fruit, dessert.
Camembert (Kăm'ĕm-bâr). (France)	Cow's milk..........	4 to 8 weeks.	Mild to pungent.	Soft, smooth; very soft when fully ripened.	Creamy yellow interior; edible thin white, or gray-white crust.	Small circular cakes and pie-shaped portions.	Appetizers, sandwiches, snacks, good with crackers, and fruit such as pears and apples, dessert.
Limburger (Belgium)	Cow's milk..........	4 to 8 weeks.	Highly pungent, very strong.	Soft, smooth when ripened; usually contains small irregular openings.	Creamy white interior; reddish yellow surface.	Cubical, rectangular.	Appetizers, snacks, good with crackers, rye or other dark breads, dessert.
SEMISOFT, RIPENED VARIETIES							
Bel Paese [2] (Bĕl Pä-ā-zē). (Italy)	Cow's milk..........	6 to 8 weeks.	Mild to moderately robust.	Soft to medium firm, creamy.	Creamy yellow interior; slightly gray or brownish surface sometimes covered with yellow wax coating.	Small wheels, wedges, segments.	Appetizers, good with crackers, snacks, sandwiches, dessert.
(Brick) (U.S.A.)	Cow's milk..........	2 to 4 months.	Mild to moderately sharp.	Semisoft to medium firm, elastic, numerous small mechanical openings.	Creamy yellow....	Loaf, brick, slices, cut portions.	Appetizers, sandwiches, snacks, dessert.
Muenster (Mün' stēr). (Germany)	Cow's milk..........	1 to 8 weeks.	Mild to mellow.	Semisoft, numerous small mechanical openings. Contains more moisture than brick.	Creamy white interior; yellow tan surface.	Circular cake, blocks, wedges, segments, slices.	Appetizers, sandwiches, snacks, dessert.
Port du Salut (Por dü Sȧ-lü'r'). (France)	Cow's milk..........	6 to 8 weeks.	Mellow to robust.	Semisoft, smooth, buttery, small openings.	Creamy yellow....	Wheels and wedges.	Appetizers, snacks, served with raw fruit, dessert.

[2] Italian trademark—licensed for manufacture in U.S.A.; also imported.

Kind or name Place of origin	Kind of milk used in manufacture	Ripening or curing time	Flavor	Body and texture	Color	Retail packaging	Uses
			FIRM RIPENED VARIETIES				
Cheddar (England)	Cow's milk.........	1 to 12 months or more.	Mild to very sharp.	Firm, smooth, some mechanical openings.	White to medium-yellow-orange.	Circular, cylindrical loaf, pie-shaped wedges, oblongs, slices, cubes, shredded, grated.	Appetizers, sandwiches, sauces, on vegetables, in hot dishes, toasted sandwiches, grating, cheeseburgers, dessert.
Colby (U.S.A.)	Cow's milk..........	1 to 3 months.	Mild to mellow.	Softer and more open than Cheddar.	White to medium-yellow-orange.	Cylindrical, pie-shaped wedges.	Sandwiches, snacks cheeseburgers.
Caciocavallo (Kä'chô-kä-val'lõ). (Italy)	Cow's milk. In Italy, cow's milk or mixtures of sheep's, goat's, and cow's milk.	3 to 12 months.	Piquant, similar to Provolone but not smoked.	Firm, lower in milkfat and moisture than Provolone.	Light or white interior; clay or tan colored surface.	Spindle or ten-pin shaped, bound with cord, cut pieces.	Snacks, sandwiches, cooking, dessert; suitable for grating after prolonged curing.
Edam (Ē'däm) (Netherlands.)	Cow's milk, partly skimmed.	2 to 3 months.	Mellow, nut-like.	Semisoft to firm, smooth; small irregularly shaped or round holes; lower milkfat than Gouda.	Creamy yellow or medium yellow-orange interior; surface coated with red wax.	Cannon ball shaped loaf, cut pieces, oblongs.	Appetizers, snacks, salads, sandwiches, seafood sauces, dessert.
Gouda (Gou'·dá) (Netherlands)	Cow's milk, whole or partly skimmed.	2 to 6 months.	Mellow, nut-like.	Semisoft to firm, smooth; small irregularly shaped or round holes; higher milkfat than Edam.	Creamy yellow or medium yellow-orange interior; may or may not have red wax coating.	Ball shaped with flattened top and bottom.	Appetizers, snacks, salads, sandwiches, seafood sauces, dessert.
Provolone (Prô-vō-lõ'-ne) also smaller sizes and shapes called Provolette, Provoloncini. (Italy)	Cow's milk.........	2 to 12 months or more	Mellow to sharp, smoky, salty.	Firm, smooth........	Light creamy interior; light brown or golden yellow surface.	Pear shaped, sausage and salami shaped, wedges, slices.	Appetizers, sandwiches, snacks, souffle, macaroni and spaghetti dishes, pizza, suitable for grating when fully cured and dried.
Swiss, also called Emmentaler. (Switzerland)	Cow's milk.........	3 to 9 months.	Sweet, nut-like.	Firm, smooth with large round eyes.	Light yellow.......	Segments, pieces, slices.	Sandwiches, snacks, sauces, fondue, cheeseburgers.

Kind or name Place of origin	Kind of milk used in manufacture	Ripening or curing time	Flavor	Body and texture	Color	Retail packaging	Uses
VERY HARD RIPENED VARIETIES							
Parmesan (Pär´-mē-zän´) also called Reggiano. (Italy)	Partly skimmed cow's milk.	14 months to 2 years.	Sharp, piquant.	Very hard, granular, lower moisture and milkfat than Romano.	Creamy white.....	Cylindrical, wedges, shredded, grated.	Grated for seasoning in soups, or vegetables, spaghetti, ravioli, breads, popcorn, used extensively in pizza and lasagne.
Romano (Rō-mä´-nō) also called Sardo Romano Pecorino Romano. (Italy)	Cow's milk. In Italy, sheep's milk (Italian law).	5 to 12 months.	Sharp, piquant.	Very hard granular..	Yellowish-white interior, greenish-black surface.	Round with flat ends, wedges, shredded, grated.	Seasoning in soups, casserole dishes, ravioli, sauces, breads, suitable for grating when cured for about one year.
Sap Sago [1] (Säp´-sä-gō). (Switzerland)	Skimmed cow's milk.	5 months or more.	Sharp, pungent clover-like.	Very hard...........	Light green by addition of dried, powdered clover leaves.	Conical, shakers..	Grated to flavor soups, meats, macaroni, spaghetti, hot vegetables; mixed with butter makes a good spread on crackers or bread.
BLUE-VEIN MOLD RIPENED VARIETIES							
Blue, spelled Bleu on imported cheese. (France)	Cow's milk........	2 to 6 months.	Tangy, peppery.	Semisoft, pasty, sometimes crumbly.	White interior, marbled or streaked with blue veins of mold.	Cylindrical, wedges, oblongs, squares, cut portions.	Appetizers, salads, dips, salad dressing, sandwich spreads, good with crackers, dessert.
Gorgonzola (Gôr-gōn-zō´-lä). (Italy)	Cow's milk. In Italy, cow's milk or goat's milk or mixtures of these.	3 to 12 months.	Tangy, peppery.	Semisoft, pasty, sometimes crumbly, lower moisture than Blue.	Creamy white interior, mottled or streaked with blue-green veins of mold. Clay colored surface.	Cylindrical, wedges, oblongs.	Appetizers, snacks, salads, dips, sandwich spread, good with crackers, dessert.
Roquefort [1] (Rōk´-fêrt) or (Rôk-fôr´). (France).	Sheep's milk.......	2 to 5 months or more.	Sharp, slightly peppery.	Semisoft, pasty, sometimes crumbly.	White or creamy white interior, marbled or streaked with blue veins of mold.	Cylindrical, wedges.	Appetizers, snacks, salads, dips, sandwich spreads, good with crackers, dessert.
Stilton [1] (England).	Cow's milk........	2 to 6 months.	Piquant, milder than Gorgonzola or Roquefort.	Semisoft, flaky; slightly more crumbly than Blue.	Creamy white interior, marbled or streaked with blue-green veins of mold.	Circular, wedges, oblongs.	Appetizers, snacks, salads, dessert.

[1] Imported only.

CUSTARDS

Custard is a combination of milk and eggs, flavored and sweetened to taste. The number of eggs and the ratio of whole eggs to yolks depends on the consistency desired. For instance, a custard made with 2 whole eggs plus 3 yolks would be thicker than a custard made with 5 whole eggs. For a thicker custard, increase the number of egg yolks in proportion to the number of whole eggs, and decrease for a lighter custard.

The amount of sugar used will depend entirely on taste, and may be omitted altogether without affecting the consistency.

While vanilla is the most popular flavoring for custards, a liqueur or grated citrus peel may also be used. The seeds from a dried vanilla pod will give a more pronounced flavor than vanilla extract.

CUSTARD RECIPES

CUSTARD

2 cups (480 ml) liquid: milk, light cream, or heavy cream
⅛ to ¾ cup (24.8 g to 148.8 g) finely granulated sugar, according to taste

3 whole eggs plus 2 egg yolks, or 4 whole eggs
seeds from 2" (5 cm) piece vanilla pod, or 1 teaspoon vanilla extract

Scald liquid over medium to low heat, uncovered, and remove as soon as it reaches the boiling point. Add vanilla extract or other flavoring.

Using an electric mixer, gradually add sugar to eggs and egg yolks, beating until well blended. Add vanilla seeds and mix in (omit if extract has been used). Gradually add scalded liquid to mixture, beating at low speed, or use a wire whisk. To produce a smoother consistency, strain using a Chinese or other wire strainer. Pour into a greased ovenproof dish or individual dishes.

Set dish(es) in a bain marie and bake in a 325° F. (163° C.) oven for about 40 to 50 minutes. Insert a knife halfway through and if it comes out clean, custard is set. Serve warm or chilled.

Custard Puddings

Custard puddings are prepared by combining cooked rice, cooked noodles, bread pieces, or other filler with a custard base. The ratio is about 1 part filler to 2 parts liquid. In other words, use 1 cup cooked rice or other filler in a custard prepared with 2 cups milk or cream. Bake in the same manner as a custard. When custard begins to set, gently stir so that ingredients will be evenly distributed, otherwise filler will rest on the bottom and custard will rise to the top.

Moistened raisins or cooked fruit, such as lightly fried apple or pear slices, may be added to filler.

To produce a browner surface, lightly dot with butter.

CUSTARD SAUCE

2 cups (480 ml) liquid: milk
   or light cream
⅓ cup (65.24 g) finely
   granulated sugar

2 whole eggs plus 4 yolks
seeds from 2" (5 cm) piece
   vanilla pod
⅓ cup (37.24 g) flour

Scald liquid, uncovered, over medium to low heat and remove as soon as it reaches boiling point.

Using an electric mixer, gradually add sugar to eggs and egg yolks, beating until well blended. Add vanilla seeds and mix in. Gradually add flour and beat just long enough to blend. Gradually add scalded liquid, beating at low speed or using a hand whisk. Transfer to top of double boiler and cook, stirring, over low heat until mixture thickens. (Water in lower section of boiler should be kept just under simmering point.)

To produce a thinner sauce, stir in 1 or 2 tablespoons milk or light cream until of the desired consistency.

Serve warm or at room temperature with fruit, puddings, and other desserts.

CREAMS

A cream is a smooth, thick custard made virtually the same as custard with the exception that only the yolks of the eggs are used, as opposed to whole eggs or a combination of whole eggs and yolks. English Cream, La Crème, and Flan are all creams.

A cream may be cooked in the top of a double boiler or in a bain marie in the oven. They are served slightly warm, or chilled and unmolded.

UPSIDE-DOWN CREAM   This cream is made by coating the bottom of a greased, ovenproof dish or individual molds with caramel (melted sugar) over which the unbaked cream is poured. When baked and thoroughly chilled (to allow to set) it is turned upside-down (reversed) onto a serving plate. The French refer to this cream as La Crème Renversée and the Spanish as Flan.

BAVARIAN CREAM   To a regular cream preparation is added unflavored gelatin in the proportion 2 ounces (60 g) dissolved gelatin to a pint (½ l) of liquid. The cream is then enriched with whipped cream and served chilled and unmolded.

CREAM RECIPES

CREAM

2 cups (480 ml) liquid: milk, light cream, or heavy cream
¼ to ¾ cup (49.6 g to 148.6 g) finely granulated sugar, according to taste

6 egg yolks
2 tablespoons flour
seeds from 2" (5 cm) piece vanilla pod

Scald liquid, uncovered, over medium to low heat and remove as soon as boiling point is reached.

Using electric mixer, gradually add desired quantity of granulated sugar to egg yolks, beating until well blended. Add vanilla seeds and mix in. Gradually add flour and beat just long enough to blend. Gradually add scalded liquid, beating at low speed.

To produce a smooth consistency, strain Cream, using a Chinese or other wire strainer.

Cream may be cooked in one of two ways:

METHOD NO. 1. Pour into greased ovenproof dish, individual molds, or cream pots. Arrange dish(es) in a shallow pan with enough hot (not boiling) water to come halfway up the sides (a bain marie) and bake in a preheated 325° F. (163° C.) oven for about 40 minutes. Test by inserting a knife halfway through—if it comes out clean, Cream is set.

METHOD NO. 2. Transfer Cream to top of double boiler and cook, stirring, over low heat until mixture thickens and approaches the boiling point. Pour into greased mold, individual molds, or cream pots. Serve warm or chilled, or, refrigerate for 6 to 8 hours or overnight, and unmold.

Chocolate Cream

Add two 1-ounce packages (total of 60 g) chocolate (semi-sweet or unsweetened) dissolved in 2 tablespoons boiling water to cooked Cream, using Method No. 2 (double boiler method) and mix in. Cook for about 1 minute or just long enough to blend.

UPSIDE-DOWN CREAM
(LA CRÈME RENVERSÉE, FLAN)

Prepare an uncooked *Cream or Custard and make the following caramel:*

Caramel*

1 cup finely granulated sugar
¼ cup (60 ml) water
¼ teaspoon cream of tartar

Combine ingredients in a heavy saucepan and cook, stirring, over low heat until sugar is dissolved. Turn heat to high and bring to a boil. Shake pan during cooking (do not stir) until mixture turns a light amber color. Remove at once and pour into greased, ovenproof dish or individual molds. If mixture has cooked for too long and become too thick, add a few tablespoons hot water, very gradually, to prevent spattering.

Fill carmelized dish or molds with uncooked Cream or Custard and bake in a preheated 325° F. (163° C.) oven in a pan of hot (not boiling) water for about 40 minutes, or until knife comes out clean. In testing, be careful to insert knife no more than halfway, otherwise, there will be an opening in the top of the Cream, when unmolded. Refrigerate for 6 to 8 hours, or overnight, before unmolding.

ICE CREAM

Prepare recipe for Cream (vanilla or chocolate) and cook, using Method No. 2 (double boiler). (Double or triple recipe for larger amounts.) Set aside to cool, stirring occasionally to prevent crust from forming. When cool, combine with crushed or finely chopped fruit or berries, chopped nuts, or unsweetened shredded coconut. Use approximately 1 part fruit to 3 parts Cream, or 1 part nuts to 4 parts Cream. Freeze, using ice cream freezer, according to manufacturer's directions. Use 8 parts crushed ice to one part coarse salt, where indicated.

*For larger or smaller amounts, use 1 part water to 4 parts sugar.

BAVARIAN CREAM

Prepare recipe for Cream (vanilla or chocolate) and cook using Method No. 2 (double boiler). Transfer to a larger receptacle and set aside to cool, stirring from time to time to prevent crust from forming.

Sprinkle two ¼-ounce (total of 15 g) packages unflavored gelatin into ⅓ cup (80 ml) of water and set in a pan of hot (not boiling) water, over low heat, stirring until crystals are dissolved. To avoid lumps, stir 1 to 2 tablespoons of Cream into dissolved gelatin before combining with remaining Cream. When Cream has cooled sufficiently, set in refrigerator.

In the meantime, beat ½ pint (240 ml) of heavy cream, gradually adding 2 tablespoons powdered sugar, until it can be shaped into soft peaks. (Do not overbeat.) When thoroughly chilled and beginning to set, remove Cream from refrigerator and carefully fold in whipped cream. Turn into greased fancy mold or individual molds and refrigerate for 6 to 8 hours, or overnight, before unmolding.

BUTTER CREAM NO. 1

Prepare recipe for Cream (vanilla or chocolate) and cook using Method No. 2 (double boiler). Set aside to cool, stirring from time to time to prevent crust from forming. When completely cool, combine with ¾ to 1 pound (340 to 450 g) softened butter, depending on desired consistency. Use at cool room temperature to spread on cakes and pastries. Chill before serving.

BUTTER CREAM NO. 2

6 egg yolks
seeds from 2" (5 cm) piece
vanilla pod
1 cup (190 g) finely granulated
sugar

¼ cup (60 ml) water
¼ teaspoon cream of tartar
1 pound (450 g) butter,
softened

Using electric mixer, beat egg yolks until thick. Mix in seeds from vanilla pod and set aside. Combine sugar, water, and cream of tartar in a heavy saucepan and set over low heat, stirring until sugar is dissolved. Turn up heat and boil rapidly, shaking pan (do not stir) until syrup spins a thread, or registers 238° F. (114° C.) on candy thermometer. Watch carefully so as not to overcook. Gradually add syrup to yolks, beating until thick. Beat in softened butter a little at a time when mixture has reached room temperature. Use with cakes and pastries and chill before serving.

PASTRY CREAM

2 cups (½ l) liquid: milk or
   light cream
5 tablespoons finely
   granulated sugar
4 egg yolks plus 1 whole egg
Seeds from 2" (5 cm) piece
   vanilla pod

5 tablespoons flour, finely
   sifted
4 egg whites
2 tablespoons powdered sugar

Scald liquid over medium low heat, uncovered, and remove as soon as boiling point is reached.

Using electric mixer, gradually add granulated sugar to egg yolks and one whole egg, beating until creamy. Add vanilla seeds and mix in. Gradually add flour, beating just long enough to blend. Gradually add scalded liquid to mixture, beating at low speed or with a hand whisk.

Transfer to top of double boiler and cook, stirring, over low heat until mixture thickens. (Water in lower section of boiler must be kept just below simmering point.) Remove from heat.

Beat egg whites to a light foam, and gradually add powdered sugar, beating until they are glossy and can be shaped into soft peaks. Return mixture to low heat (keeping water in lower section of double boiler just below simmering point) and fold in beaten egg whites. Cook for about 1 minute longer.

Use for cake fillings and pastries.

SHERBETS

Sherbets may be flavored in a number of ways. The following measurements are approximate and are based on a 1-quart (1 l) sherbet recipe: Seeds from 2″ (5 cm) piece vanilla pod, 1 teaspoon lemon or other extract, 2 tablespoons fruit-base liqueur, or 1 tablespoon grated citrus peel.

Sugar may be added according to the amount of natural sugar in the fruit, and is a matter of personal preference. Slight variations will not affect the consistency.

SHERBET RECIPES

SHERBET FROM CITRUS FRUIT JUICES

⅓ to ⅔ cup (65.24 g to 130.48 g) powdered or finely granulated sugar, according to taste
1½ cups (360 ml) milk
flavoring
1 1-ounce (30 g) package unflavored gelatin

½ cup (120 ml) milk
⅓ cup (80 ml) strained fresh fruit juice (lemon, orange, lime, or combinations thereof)
2 tablespoons lemon juice
2 egg whites, unbeaten
pinch of salt

Combine sugar and 1½ cups (360 ml) milk in a saucepan and set over low heat, stirring until dissolved. Remove from heat as soon as mixture comes to a boil. Stir in liqueur, vanilla seeds, or whatever flavoring is being used. Set aside to cool.

Sprinkle gelatin into ½ cup (120 ml) of milk and set over hot (not boiling) water over low heat, stirring until dissolved. Remove from heat. Add fruit juice, along with 2 tablespoons lemon juice, to cooled milk mixture. Gradually stir in dissolved gelatin, or place the whole in a blender for a few seconds to ensure even and smooth distribution. Pour mixture into a freezer tray, or any other pan of equal volume, and set in freezer until almost firm.

This should take about half an hour. Turn into a bowl, add unbeaten egg whites and salt, and beat with electric mixer at low speed until fluffy. Do not overbeat, as mixture should not melt. Place in container or individual molds and freeze. When frozen, wrap securely to maintain full fresh flavor until ready to use. Serve using a scoop, or unmold. Decorate with cherries, angelique,* candied violets, or rosettes of whipped cream.

SHERBET FROM FRUIT PULP

2 ¼-ounce (total of 15 g)
   packages unflavored gelatin
4 tablespoons fresh lemon
   juice
⅓ to ⅔ cup (65.24 g to
   130.48 g) powdered or
   finely granulated sugar
1½ cups (360 ml) water

pinch of cream of tartar
2 tablespoons fruit-base
   liqueur
2 cups fully ripe fresh fruit
   pulp (strawberries, peaches
   or apricots)
pinch of salt
3 egg whites

Dissolve gelatin in lemon juice over hot (not boiling) water over low heat, stirring until dissolved. Remove from heat. Combine sugar, water, and cream of tartar in a saucepan and set over low heat, stirring until dissolved. Turn up heat and bring mixture to a slow simmer. Simmer for a few minutes without stirring. Add liqueur and remove from heat. Set aside until mixture cools slightly. Gradually stir in dissolved gelatin, or place in blender for a few seconds to ensure even and smooth distribution. Pour mixture into two freezer trays or receptacle of equal volume, and freeze until almost set.

In the meantime, clean and hull strawberries or peel and remove pits from whatever other fruit is being used. Puree fruit in blender, food processor, or foodmill. Turn almost-frozen mixture into bowl of electric mixer, along with egg whites and salt, and beat for a few seconds. Add fruit pulp and continue to beat until fluffy. Return to freezer trays, and freeze once again, until almost set. Remove, and using electric mixer, beat for about 1 minute at

*Angelique, as well as other decorative sweets, can be found in specialty stores.

low speed. Transfer to containers or molds, and return to freezer. Wrap securely to maintain full fresh flavor until ready to use.

Serve using a scoop, or unmold.

SOUFFLÉS

Basically, soufflés are eggs, separated and well beaten, and incorporated with a White Sauce. Fillings, such as cheese or ground meat, may be added.

Sugar is added to a dessert soufflé. The sugar content will not affect the consistency and may vary slightly according to taste. Dessert soufflés may be flavored using seeds from a vanilla pod, extracts, liqueurs, or grated citrus peel.

Soufflés may be baked in any type of ovenproof dish with high straight sides, or in a specially designated soufflé dish. Because a soufflé will rise above the rim of the dish when baked, a piece of parchment paper or aluminum foil, cut to size, should be wrapped around the exterior so that it extends about 2" (5 cm) above the rim. (It may be secured with a string if necessary.)

Any type of oil may be spread on interior of the dish and its collar to prevent sticking; a canned liquid spray is generally most satisfactory.

Do not open the oven door during the first 10 or 15 minutes of baking time, as any change in temperature could cause soufflé to fall.

To produce a higher dome in the center, make an indentation about ¾" (2 cm) deep around the top and about an inch (2½ cm) from the edge. This not only gives a more attractive appearance, but results in a more even rising.

A soufflé is baked when it is fully risen and has begun to shrink from the sides of the dish.

SOUFFLÉ RECIPES
(DESSERT & ENTREE)

DESSERT SOUFFLÉ

*4 tablespoons finely
granulated sugar
⅔ cup (160 ml) milk or light
cream
2 tablespoons finely sifted
flour
4 tablespoons milk*

*2 tablespoons butter
Seeds from 2" (5 cm) piece
vanilla pod
3 egg yolks
3 egg whites
2 tablespoons powdered sugar*

Combine 4 tablespoons granulated sugar and ⅔ cup (160 ml) milk or light cream in a saucepan. Set over low heat, stirring until dissolved. Turn heat to medium and stir until mixture begins to simmer. Blend 2 tablespoons flour and 4 tablespoons milk and add, stirring all the while. Turn heat to low and cook for about 1 minute. Remove from heat and stir in 2 tablespoons butter. Add seeds from vanilla pod and mix in.

Using electric mixer, gradually add 2 tablespoons powdered sugar to egg whites, beating until glossy and mixture can be shaped into soft peaks.

In a separate bowl, beat egg yolks for about 1 minute, using a hand whisk or electric beater. Fold into beaten whites, and gradually add hot mixture, folding in quickly and carefully. Turn into a greased and banded soufflé dish and bake in a 375° F. (190° C.) oven for about 30 minutes, or until soufflé has fully risen and has begun to shrink from sides of dish. Serve at once.

Chocolate Soufflé

Follow recipe for Dessert Soufflé, substituting two 1-ounce (total of 60 g) packages premelted chocolate for vanilla.

COOKED MEAT SOUFFLÉ

3 tablespoons finely sifted
flour
¾ cup (180 ml) milk or light
cream
2 tablespoons butter
salt and white pepper to taste
1 tablespoon fresh parsley,
finely chopped

dash of Tabasco
5 egg yolks
1 pound (450 g) cooked meat,
ground or finely chopped
(chicken, turkey, or ham)
pinch of cream of tartar
5 egg whites

Combine flour and milk or light cream in a saucepan and set over medium low heat. Cook, stirring with a wire whisk, until mixture begins to simmer and has lightly thickened. Remove from heat and stir in butter, seasoning to taste, parsley, and Tabasco. Set aside to cool slightly.

Beat egg yolks for about 1 minute and gradually add to warm mixture. Combine with ground or finely chopped meat. Add cream of tartar to egg whites, beating until they are glossy and begin to form soft peaks. Fold into mixture. Turn into a greased and banded 2-quart (2 l) soufflé dish and bake in a 375° F. (190° C.) oven for about 30 to 40 minutes, or until fully risen and mixture has begun to shrink from sides of dish. Do not overcook, or soufflé will become dry.

CHEESE SOUFFLÉ

1½ cups (170.09 g) finely
sifted flour
2½ cups (600 ml) milk or
light cream
3 tablespoons butter
Salt and white pepper to taste

8 ounces (225 g) grated cheese
(Parmesan, Cheddar, or
Swiss)
5 egg yolks
5 egg whites
pinch of cream of tartar

Combine flour and milk or light cream in a saucepan and set over medium low heat. Cook, stirring, using a wire whisk, until mixture begins to simmer and has lightly thickened. Remove from heat and stir in butter. Add salt and white pepper to taste and mix in grated cheese.

Beat egg yolks for about 1 minute and gradually add to cheese mixture.

Add cream of tartar to egg whites and beat until they are glossy and begin to form soft peaks. Fold into mixture.

Turn into a greased and banded 2-quart (2 l) soufflé dish and bake in a 375° F. (190° C.) oven for about 30 to 40 minutes, or until fully risen and mixture begins to leave sides of dish. Serve at once.

MOUSSE RECIPES
(DESSERT AND ENTREE)

FRESH FRUIT MOUSSE NO. 1

1 quart (1 l) fresh strawberries or 2 cups (480 ml) pureed fruit (peaches, apricots)
2 ¼-ounce packages (total of 15 g) unflavored gelatin
4 tablespoons water

2 tablespoons fresh lemon juice
1 pint (480 ml) heavy cream
4 tablespoons powdered sugar
2 whole eggs plus 4 egg yolks
¼ to ¾ cup (49.6 g to 157.8 g) finely granulated sugar*

Clean and hull strawberries or peel fruit and remove any stones or pits. Puree in blender, food processor, or food mill.

Dissolve gelatin in water and fresh lemon juice and set over hot (not boiling) water over low heat, stirring until dissolved. Remove from heat and set aside to cool.

Whip cream to soft peaks, gradually adding 4 tablespoons powdered sugar, and refrigerate.

Using electric mixer, beat whole eggs and egg yolks and gradually

*Amount of sugar will vary according to the desired degree of sweetness as well as the natural sugar content of the fruit.

add desired amount of sugar, beating until mixture is light and foamy.

Add dissolved gelatin to pureed fruit, stirring until well blended, or place in electric blender for about 10 seconds. Carefully fold into sugar and egg mixture. Remove whipped cream from refrigerator, reserving about one-fourth for decorating, and fold in remainder. Pour into greased 2-quart (2 l) mold, or individual molds, and refrigerate for 6 to 8 hours or overnight before unmolding. Decorate with rosettes of whipped cream, using pastry bag and star tube.

COFFEE MOUSSE

Follow recipe for Fresh Fruit Mousse No. 1, substituting 4 tablespoons double strength coffee for fruit. If using instant coffee, dissolve 2 tablespoons in 2 tablespoons boiling water. Two tablespoons rum or crème de cocoa may be added as additional flavoring. The amount of sugar will again vary according to the desired degree of sweetness.

CHOCOLATE MOUSSE

Follow recipe for Fresh Fruit Mousse No. 1, substituting 2 ounces (60 g) of melted unsweetened chocolate for fruit. Mix 2 or 3 tablespoons of beaten sugar and egg mixture with dissolved gelatin and blend with melted chocolate before combining with remaining sugar and egg mixture. A tablespoon of strong coffee may be added as additional flavoring. The amount of sugar will again vary according to the desired degree of sweetness.

FRESH FRUIT MOUSSE NO. 2

1 quart (1 l) fresh
strawberries or 2 cups (480
ml) pureed fruit (peaches,
apricots)
¼ to ¾ cup (49.6 g to 157.8
g) finely granulated sugar
2 ¼-ounce packages (total of
15 g) unflavored gelatin

4 tablespoons water
2 tablespoons fresh lemon
juice
1 pint (480 ml) heavy cream
4 tablespoons powdered sugar

Clean and hull strawberries or peel fruit and remove any stones
or pits. If using dried fruit, such as apricots, soak in water until
soft and of the desired consistency. Puree in blender, food processor, or food mill. Blend in desired amount of finely granulated
sugar.

Dissolve gelatin in water and lemon juice, and set over hot (not
boiling) water over low heat, stirring until dissolved. Remove
from heat and set aside to cool.

Whip cream to soft peaks, gradually adding 4 tablespoons
powdered sugar, and refrigerate until ready to use.

Add dissolved gelatin to fruit puree and blend for about 10 seconds, using electric blender. Set in refrigerator until mixture begins to thicken. When mixture has thickened slightly, remove
and carefully fold in whipped cream. Turn into greased mold or
individual molds and refrigerate for 6 to 8 hours or overnight before unmolding.

MOUSSE ENTREE (MEAT, FISH, OR SHELLFISH)

1 pound (450 g) ground ham, poultry, fish, or shellfish, uncooked
2 egg whites, unbeaten
1 teaspoon salt*

1 tablespoon fresh parsley or dill, finely chopped
½ pint (240 ml) heavy cream (optional)

Place ground meat or fish in bowl of electric mixer, along with salt, and beat in egg whites, one at a time. Mix in finely chopped parsley or dill. If using cream, add very gradually and beat until well blended. (The addition of cream will result in a lighter texture and richer flavor, but otherwise is not essential.) Chill in refrigerator for about an hour. Remove and turn into a greased, ovenproof 1-quart (1 l) dish or circular mold and set in a shallow pan containing enough hot (not boiling) water to come halfway up the sides. Bake in a preheated 325° F. (163° C.) oven until mousse begins to leave the sides of the pan and is set. Remove and let rest for about 20 minutes before unmolding.

Mousse may be prepared by alternating layers, such as ham and chicken or shrimp and flounder.

Fillet-Wrapped Mousse

To prepare filling, follow recipe for Mousse Entree. Flatten fillets between two sheets of wax paper or plastic wrap, using a mallet. (The number of fillets required, whether veal, poultry, or fish, would vary according to size.)

Lay flattened fillets across a greased circular mold, membrane (skin) side up, with ends hanging over the sides and one fillet slightly overlapping the other. Fill cavity with ground meat, fish, or shellfish. (Use ground ham mousse with flattened breast of chicken, or ground shrimp or salmon mousse with flattened flounder fillets.) Bring ends of fillets over to enclose meat or fish mousse filling, so as to completely cover it. As all flesh adheres to itself when exposed to heat, any gashes or holes in fillets resulting from pounding may be patched using remaining bits or pieces

*For ham, reduce to ¼ teaspoon.

of flesh. Brush softened or melted butter over surface to prevent drying. Refrigerate for about 1 hour before baking.

Set mold in a shallow pan containing enough hot (not boiling) water to come halfway up the sides. Bake in a preheated 325° F. (163° C.) oven until mousse begins to leave the sides of the pan and is slightly firm. Remove and let rest for about 20 minutes before unmolding.

Mousse may be served warm with or without a sauce; or chilled and sliced, if prepared using a meat base as opposed to fish.

When unmolded, mousse has an attractive rope-like appearance.

CHEESE RECIPES

CHEESE BALLS

½ cup (42.52 g) flavored breadcrumbs
¼ cup (60 ml) light cream or milk
1 cup (11.3.39 g) grated Cheddar cheese
1 cup (11.3.39 g) grated Swiss cheese
2 eggs, separated
1 teaspoon prepared mustard (Dijon)
dash of cayenne pepper
finely sifted flour
2 eggs
1 tablespoon oil } *lightly beaten*
¼ cup (60 ml) milk
breadcrumbs
fat for frying

Soak breadcrumbs in light cream or milk until liquid is absorbed. Combine with grated cheese, egg yolks, mustard, and cayenne pepper. Beat egg whites to the soft peak stage and fold in.

Mold into ¾" (2 cm) balls using hands or a miniature ice cream scoop. Roll in flour, then dip in egg, oil, and milk mixture, and finally in breadcrumbs.

Preheat fat to 360° F. (182° C.) and fry a few at a time until golden brown. This should take but a few seconds. Drain on paper towels.

Cheese Balls may be frozen uncooked and fried immediately after they are removed from the freezer.

CHEESE FONDUE

1 cup (240 ml) dry white wine
1 pound (450 g) grated cheese
  (Swiss, Gruyère, Cheddar)
1 ounce (30 g) kirsch

1 teaspoon potato starch or
  cornstarch
dash of Tabasco
bread, cut into squares

Add wine to fondue dish and gradually bring to a simmer over low heat. Add cheese a little at a time, stirring until smooth. Blend kirsch, potato or corn starch, and Tabasco and mix in. Dip squares of bread in fondue, using fondue forks.

CHEESE STICKS

2 cups (226.79 g) pastry flour
1 teaspoon baking powder
pinch of salt
3 sticks (340 g) sweet butter
1 egg, lightly beaten

¾ cup (180 ml) cold milk
½ pound (225 g) grated
  Cheddar or Parmesan
  cheese

Blend flour, baking powder, and salt. Cut in butter, using a pastry cutter or food processor. Combine lightly beaten egg and milk and mix in. (Do not overmix.) Shape into a ball and let stand in refrigerator for about an hour. Roll out dough on lightly floured board to about ¼" (.5 cm) thickness. Sprinkle half of the grated cheese over half the dough, and fold over the second half. Sprinkle remaining cheese over the top layer and fold again. Press layers together. Using a rolling pin, roll dough back to about its original size.

Cut dough into sticks of any desired length and place on a greased or nonstick baking sheet. Cover with wax paper and/or aluminum foil and refrigerate for several hours or overnight. Sticks may also be frozen and baked as needed.

When ready to serve, bake in a preheated 450° F. (232° C.) oven until lightly browned, or about 15 minutes.

CHEESE SPREAD

½ *pound (225 g) Gruyère or*
  Swiss cheese, grated
½ *pound (225 g) Cheddar*
  cheese, grated
1 *ounce (30 g) kirsch*

¼ *teaspoon cayenne pepper,*
  or to taste
1 *cup (225 g) sweet butter,*
  softened
paprika

Blend cheese, kirsch, and cayenne pepper, using flat or regular beater of electric mixer. Gradually add softened butter, beating until smooth. Fill one large serving dish or several small ones, such as individual custard dishes, making an attractive pattern over surface using a fork. Dust lightly with paprika. Cheese spread may be refrigerated and used as needed, or it may be frozen. (When frozen, defrost at room temperature before serving.)

CHEESE CANAPÉS

assorted cheeses at room
  temperature
cocktail crackers or thin
  bread squares or rounds
stuffed olives

Spread thin slices of cheeses such as Gourmandise, Roquefort, Camembert, Danish Havarti, Port Salut, Canadian Cheddar, Stilton, or Swiss on cocktail crackers or thin squares or rounds of bread. Top with slices of stuffed olives.

CHEESE AND SOUR CREAM DIP

1 pint (480 ml) sour cream
4 ounces (120 g) Blue or
  Roquefort cheese, crumbled

Mix sour cream with crumbled cheese and refrigerate until ready to serve. Serve with chips or crackers.

FISH & SHELLFISH

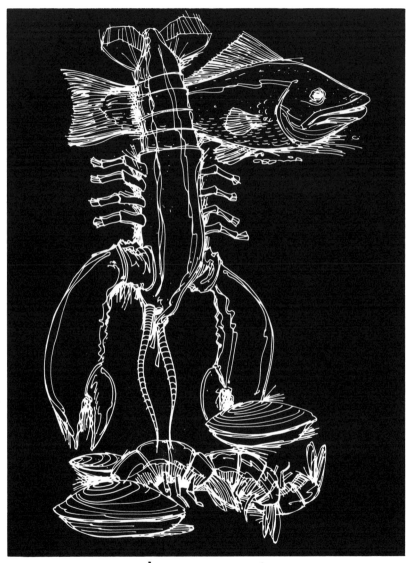

chapter six

THE AVAILABILITY OF FRESH FISH

Until recently, it had always been taken for granted that fish was an inexhaustible food source that would go on replenishing itself. And so it seemed. Fresh oysters, salmon, cod, flounder, bass, shad, perch, halibut, and smelts were in plentiful and cheap supply as late as the World War II period. In the early 1900s and just prior to the First World War, lobsters sold for 19 cents a pound. During this same period, the Bureau of Fisheries took steps to encourage home fish ponds to supply fresh fish for the table. In recent years, some Japanese families had their own fish tanks as close as their back doors.

The English Parliament passed an Act, in 1563, establishing Friday and Saturday as compulsory fish days. Queen Elizabeth I added Wednesday to the list ". . . that fleshe and fishe would both be more plentiful and beare less price than they doe." The consumption of meat throughout western Europe was already taboo on any of the 40 days of the Lenten season. All told, fish would replace beef and lamb for at least half of the 365 days. The intent, in part, of such laws was to encourage fishing and to discourage the use of land for grazing purposes.

Throughout history, fish has been associated with one taboo or another, some encouraging, others discouraging its consumption. Brainy people were said to originate from areas where fish was eaten often and regularly; a diet heavy in fish was also said to result in long life. On the other hand, there were religions which forbade its total consumption, regarding all flesh as holy.

Today, in the last quarter of the twentieth century, fish has been given an honored place in the role of good nutrition. However, the ready availability of fresh fish, even in coastal areas, runs short of the mark, and it is far from being a poor man's dish. In terms of America's past fishing history, the situation that presently confronts the consumer is unprecedented. In light of today's advanced technology, especially refrigerated transport, one would expect a surfeit of ultra fresh fish. Yet a number of apparently plausible reasons have been set forth to explain this relatively new phenomenon. Polluted waters, which was and remains a serious problem for humans and animals alike, were frequently reported as the single underlying cause for the short supply, as well as the reason why particular kinds of fish could no longer be had. The exorbitant prices demanded for fresh fish were also attributed to the waning interest in fishing as a liveli-hood. Furthermore, whatever limited supplies of top quality fresh fish were available went primarily to restaurants—with a small proportion going to a dwindling number of privately owned fish markets.

Many Americans had gotten out of the habit of eating fresh fish except when occasionally dining out. There was little aware-ness of this practice, as from about the turn of the century Ameri-cans had steadily been schooled into largely depending on meat as their main source of protein. Most supermarkets carried little if any fresh fish, and fish counters were at best but a fraction of the size of fresh meat departments.

However, a new nutrition consciousness was in the making. The dangers associated with an excessive intake of saturated fat, along with the problems of overweight, were in large part respon-sible for a marked trend toward a greater reliance on fish as a protein food. Conditions surrounding the preparation of meals in the home had also changed to a great degree, and fresh fish lent itself to quick cooking as well as to a variety of easy preparations. Demand increased and prices shot up even higher. Supermarkets began to take advantage by supplying more fresh fish on a regular basis; the overall quality, however, was not, as a general rule, on a par with that found in specialty stores. Consumers more or less accepted the apparent short supply of fresh fish and its accompa-nying unprecedented prices somewhat fatalistically, and went on the assumption that there was in fact a scarcity of fresh fish, for whatever reason.

In point of fact, the percentage of fish harvested, world-wide, had steadily increased. By the third quarter of the twen-tieth century fish catches had tripled; in fact, the average *annual* increase from 1950 to 1975 was five percent, much of it, however, being subjected to some form of processing. Following the World War II period, many nations, including Japan (whose citizens rely on fish for more than half their protein needs), the Soviet Union, and Europe, both East (let by Poland and East Germany) and West (led by Spain and France) took to the oceans—the "last of the continents"—with huge complexes equipped to handle and freeze thousands of pounds of fish daily,* on expeditions that fre-quently lasted for several months.

---

*Fish is also used in the production of fertilizer (often prepared on board factory ships), as well as for crude oils. In addition, about one-quarter of the world's production of fish is converted into fish meal to be fed to animals that eventually appear as meat on the table.

One of the frequent practices in the past of this vast industry and one that was to have far-reaching effects was the seizing of whole schools of fish, the younger ones being taken along with the full grown, thereby breaking up the life cycle. As a result of this and other undesirable practices, many species of fish were brought close to extinction—only time will tell the full extent of the loss. Cod and haddock which had been looked on as a mainstay in many a North American home, particularly during the lean years, were among those endangered. The yellowtail flounder suffered a similar fate, and mackerel stocks were among those hardest hit.

It became obvious that corrective measures had to be taken, and in time many countries established fishing zones off their borders.[†] However, it was not until January 1976, after years of controversy and opposition, that the United States passed a bill providing for federal control of all ocean fishing out to a 200-mile limit and beyond that in some areas (a 12-mile zone had been established in 1966). Jurisdictional rights, of course, had to be adjusted in certain areas to avoid conflicts with Canada, Cuba, and Mexico. Certain American fishermen were adversely affected by the law, among them southern California tuna fishermen (Americans consume more tuna than any other country in the world), who normally followed their migratory prey into South American waters, and Gulf shrimp fishermen whose interest conflicted in some measure with that of Mexican fishermen.

The intent of the new regulations, which went into effect in March 1977, was to cut back drastically on those species of fish that were threatened with extinction, as well as to replenish the stock of others that had been depleted by overfishing. The restrictions were particularly welcomed by small fishermen, many of whom invested in new boats for the first time in years. Consumers, too, were optimistic that over the long haul a greater quantity of top quality fresh fish might return to their shores, restoring—even if not completely— the abundance traditionally associated with America's harvests. However, while the new law with its many ramifications held out great promise (as did the Clean Water Law and the public's greater awareness of the need for pollution control), it was generally conceded that it would take three to five years for the fish to come back.

[†]Lobsters and some crabs—creatures of the continental shelf—had previously been protected from foreign fishermen.

PURCHASING FISH
AND SHELLFISH

With the exception of some testing in areas where contamination is a possibility, there are no compulsory grading and inspection standards for fish. A government grading and inspection system on a strictly voluntary basis is available for a fee to wholesale buyers and sellers. As a general rule, only the processed fish industry uses this service.

Fish may be purchased whole with the bone in and unskinned, in steak slices, or in fillets, that is, free of skin and bone. Shellfish may be purchased in or out of the shell. Frozen fish that is held for any length of time, particularly if not fast-frozen at extremely low temperatures, loses much of its flavor and nutrients, resulting in juice loss (drip) when thawed. This practice also results in dry meat that falls apart when cooked.

Whenever honest-to-goodness fresh fish is not available, fish should be purchased in its frozen state. Some retailers purchase frozen fish and defrost it before putting it up for sale. There is no justification for this practice, as fish defrosts in a relatively short period of time.

The low temperature of the natural environment of fish, that is, the cold waters in which they live, is thought to have a bearing on their rapid spoilage, having something to do with the high degree of activity of the enzymes.

Shrimp comes in several different sizes (jumbo, large, large-medium, medium, small) and can be coral, pink, grayish brown, or white. Unless the consumer is assured of their freshness, it is advisable to purchase shrimp in its frozen state. The relative size of shellfish is a general indication of their tenderness and flavor: Large fish will be tougher but will have more flavor, and vice versa.

How to Test for Freshness

The following signs will act as a guide when purchasing fish or shellfish:

1. Fresh fish will have no strong "fishy" or stale odor.

When fish is freshly caught, it has a pleasant, characteristic aroma.

2. If stale, it will have a slimy appearance, be flabby, and not hold its shape.
3. When fresh, the eyes will be bright and prominent.
4. The scales of stale fish will be loose.
5. Test fish for freshness by placing in a bowl of cold water: If fresh, it will lie at the bottom; if stale, it will float.
6. To check whether or not fish has been frozen and thawed, press fingers into the body: If they leave an indentation, fish has been frozen, otherwise it has not.
7. Before choosing a live lobster from a tank, observe the degree of activity for a while; if it is "slouched" in a corner and barely moving, look to one of its companions which appears to have more life.
8. If you are not familiar with the policies of a supplier, avoid purchasing precooked lobsters that are displayed in a showcase unless the following test is demonstrated: If the tail of a boiled lobster springs back when straightened out, it indicates the lobster was alive when cooked.

NUTRITIVE VALUE

The protein in fish is complete and is equal to that of meat. Most fish and shellfish contain vitamin B_6 and vitamin B_{12} (present in foods of animal origin only). The vitamin content of fish varies according to its fat content. Fish which have a higher fat content (salmon, trout, mackerel) are good sources of vitamin A. Vitamins A and D occur in high concentrations in such fish liver oils as cod liver oil.

Nearly all fish have a higher water content than other flesh foods, as well as a higher percentage of minerals such as calcium, phosphorus, copper, and iron. Shellfish, and shrimp in particular, have twice as many minerals as bone fish. Iodine is the most important element in saltwater fish and may be found there more abundantly than in any other food product.*

*All inland foods are dependent for their iodine content on the iodine in the water and soil in a given area; today, most table salt is iodized as a preventative against simple goiter.

Fish is extremely low in saturated fat—the fatty acids in fish and shellfish are more highly unsaturated that those found in most other foods. In flounder, sole, cod, and whiting, there is less than 1 percent. The saturated fat in fish which has a higher fat content, for example, salmon, trout, and mackerel, rarely exceeds 20 percent.

Because of its low fat content, fish is not classified as a high energy food. It is, therefore, frequently prepared using fat (butter, margarine, or oil), coated with breadcrumbs or cornmeal, or served with a sauce to add to the energy value.

Fish in the Diet

Some fish live in fresh water and some in the sea, while others boast a dual environment. Fish fall into two main categories: shellfish and bony fish, which are further subdivided into oily fish and nonoily fish. In oily fish, the fat is spread throughout and is responsible for the variations in flesh color. In nonoily fish, the fat is localized in the liver and the flesh is white.

In many countries, several kinds of raw fish are considered delicacies. In the U.S., creamed and smoked herring, smoked salmon, and raw oysters are exceedingly popular.

The flavor, texture, and aroma of fresh fish bears little resemblance to that which has been frozen or canned.

FREEZING FISH AND SHELLFISH

Thoroughly clean all fish before freezing. Fish may be frozen whole or cut into fillets or steaks, which should be placed between layers of heavy paper for easy separation. Pack all fish and shellfish for freezing in heat-sealed heavy plastic bags (pressing out as much air as possible) or in airtight containers.

Under normal home freezing conditions, it is advisable to keep fish and shellfish for relatively short periods—the length of time depends on how fresh the fish was to begin with. Owing to rapid freezing, lower temperatures, and more favorable conditions, commercially frozen fish and shellfish can be kept frozen for longer periods. It is advisable, however, to use commercially frozen fish or shellfish as quickly as possible after purchasing.

Under no circumstances, refreeze fish or shellfish that has been defrosted.

Oily fish (salmon, trout, mackerel) should be subjected to shorter freezing periods than nonoily kinds, such as sole and flounder, whose flesh is white in color.

Lobster and crab meat must both be cooked before freezing. Cooked shrimp, on the other hand, will turn tough and rubbery when defrosted. Remove cooked lobster and crab meat from the shell before freezing, but freeze uncooked shrimp with shells intact. To freeze scallops, clams, and oysters, remove from shells and freeze, uncooked, in enough lightly salted (1 teaspoon salt per quart or liter) liquid to cover. As all shellfish (whether cooked or uncooked) have a tendency to turn rubbery when frozen for any length of time, freezing periods should be limited to even shorter lengths than for other fish.

Cooking Frozen Fish and Shellfish

Thawed fish and shellfish are cooked according to the same procedures as for fresh fish.

Before cooking, thaw fish and shellfish at refrigerator temperature—never at room temperature or even cool room temperature.

Fish fillets may be broiled in their frozen state but they should be placed as far as possible from the source of heat to keep juice loss to a minimum.

Thaw all whole fish (particularly if thick) before steaming or baking.

Owing to their delicate nature, cook breaded fish sticks in their frozen state (baked, pan-fried, or deep-fried).

Frozen shrimp may be cooked with shells intact, following the same procedure as for thawed or fresh shrimp (see recipe for Poached Shrimp) with the exception that the cooking period is slightly longer. When cooked and drained, remove shells and cut along outside surface in order to remove intestinal tract (dark streak).

VARIOUS WAYS OF SERVING FISH

Fish may be prepared in a variety of ways. Their flavor is of a delicate and subtle nature and should be enhanced, not disguised. Aromatic vegetables such as carrots, celery, mushrooms, and onions will heighten the flavor when used in judicious amounts. They should be lightly fried before combining with the fish.

A light dusting of paprika on fried or broiled fillets lends color and gives a more attractive appearance. Parsley and dill are two herbs frequently used with fish dishes, and saffron is a favorite spice.

Flavored butters such as Maitre d' Butter, dill, tarragon, anchovy, shrimp, or curry may be lightly spread over either cooked or uncooked fish and shellfish. To prepare, combine softened butter with a small proportion of whatever herb, spice, or flavoring is being used, add salt and pepper to taste, and shape into blocks. Refrigerate and use as needed.

Cooked shellfish is frequently served au gratin. The fish is placed in shells or an ovenproof dish, topped with breadcrumbs, dotted with butter, and set under a preheated broiler until it is golden brown and crusty.

White Sauce, Hollandaise, and sauces enriched with dry white wine all combine well with fish preparations.

A highly spiced sauce, such as Creole, can act as a direct contrast to the bland flavor of fish or shellfish.

HELPFUL HINTS
FOR PREPARING FISH

ROLLING AND STUFFING Toothpicks, which are sometimes recommended to hold fish together, are not necessary, as the flesh will adhere to itself when exposed to heat. All that is necessary is to have edges touching one another. Of course, the backbone should always be removed before stuffing.

STEAMED OR POACHED Whole or large pieces of fish that are to be steamed or poached should be wrapped in cheesecloth so that they do not fall apart during cooking and can be easily removed for serving. When poaching fish such as salmon or shrimp, add 1 tablespoon vinegar or ¼ cup (60 ml) dry white wine per quart (l) of water. It will serve as both a sweetening agent and a tenderizer.

A thin slice of fresh ginger root added to the liquid in which fish is cooked will neutralize odors.

BROILING To prepare lobsters for broiling, split through the center from head to tail, and remove intestinal tract. When they are to be cooked in boiling water, live lobsters are dropped whole into the pot and the cover is replaced.

Shellfish may be cooked shelled or whole. Shells of shrimp are quickly removed by running the point of a sharp knife along the inside surface. The intestinal tract (a dark streak) on the outer surface is removed. This is done most easily when shrimp is raw.

When fish is to be broiled, softened or melted butter (a flavored butter may be used) may be brushed over the surface to prevent loss of juices, which is common with nonoily fish.

COOKING THEORY

Because of its very nature and tenderness, which is apparent even in its raw state, fish cooks in a relatively short period. The protein (albumin) in fish is quickly coagulated at low to medium temperatures, and there are no tough fibers or connective tissue to retard the cooking procedure. Overcooking will result in loss of juices in much less time than even the tenderest cut of meat of equal proportions.

While shellfish is firmer than bone fish and does not fall apart when overcooked, it does toughen and turn rubbery at the slightest degree of overcooking or if exposed to high temperatures.

As the protein in fish coagulates, the flesh takes on a definite firmness, much the same as it does with meat, and there is a certain amount of shrinkage. The juices in fish, however, are lost much more rapidly in the pan, leaving a dry, crumbly end-product.

Even greater care must be given to fish that has been frozen, as the freezing process results in considerable breakdown, and, consequently, juice loss, generally referred to as drip loss.

RECOMMENDED COOKING PROCEDURES

The procedures outlined in the table below for the various types of fish are described more thoroughly in the material that follows.

OUTLINE OF COOKING PROCEDURES FOR FISH AND SHELLFISH

Type	Procedure
Fillets	Pan-fried, broiled, coated and deep-fried, or poached
Steaks	Thick slices: Baked, broiled, poached, or steamed Thinner slices: Pan-fried, or coated and deep-fried
Whole Fish	Large or medium size: Baked or steamed Small size: Pan-fried, baked, or steamed
Shellfish	Pan-fried, broiled, coated and deep-fried, sautéed, poached, or steamed
	Lobsters: Split through center and broiled, or dropped whole into boiling water
	Hardshell Crabs: Broiled or boiled using same procedures as for lobsters
	Shrimp: Pan-fried, coated and deep-fried, broiled, or poached
	Oysters and Clams: Served raw, or simmered, as in stews and chowders
	Clams: Steamed in the shell
	Softshell Crabs: Broiled or pan-fried

Poaching

Arrange fish in a receptacle just large enough to contain it with enough liquid to barely cover, using water, fish stock, or dry white wine. When poaching fish of a texture similar to shrimp or salmon, add 1 tablespoon vinegar or ¼ cup (60 ml) dry white wine per quart (l) of water, to both sweeten and tenderize. Bring liquid to a boil and turn heat to low, or to a barely simmering point. Poach on top of stove, covered or uncovered, or in oven. If oven-poached, arrange a layer of buttered parchment paper over receptacle, cut to exact dimensions so as not to extend over sides.

Broiling

Spread softened or melted butter over fish to prevent juice loss. Because of its delicate nature, broil fish on a flat surface to avoid breaking when turning or serving. Broil fish several inches from source of heat; the more delicate the fish, the farther from the heat.

Baking

Arrange a rack, such as a roasting rack, in a shallow pan and lay fish on top. (There are fish racks especially designed for this purpose; however, any receptacle and make-shift rack may be used, so long as it provides for the circulation of heat.) Do not cover pan, as this traps heat and creates steam. Use a temperature setting between 300° F. (149° C.) and 325° F. (163° C.), depending on size and heaviness of fish.

Steaming

This procedure is especially suited to large and medium-size whole fish. A specially constructed receptacle for steaming fish gives the most satisfactory results. However, any other pan with a tight cover that will hold a rack of sorts may be substituted. Add enough boiling water to come to about one inch (2.5 cm) from pan bottom, or just up to rack. Water should not come in contact with fish during cooking. Check water from time to time for evaporation, and replenish when necessary. Water is kept at simmering point. If frozen fish is to be used, thaw fully before steaming, otherwise center will be raw when outside layers are cooked.

Before placing on rack, wrap fish in cheesecloth to prevent breaking and facilitate serving.

Pan-frying

Fish may be fried in butter or oil over medium low heat, either coated or uncoated. Cornmeal or breadcrumbs may be used as a coating. If no coating is used, fish may be given a light dusting of finely sifted flour. Fish is cooked and browned at the same time.

Deep-frying

Fish or shellfish is coated, using a Breadcrumb or Batter Coating, and is cooked in a thermostatically controlled deep-fat fryer set at 360° F. (182° C.) to 375° F. (190° C.), depending on thickness and nature of the fish. If the fryer is not overcrowded, fish will float to the surface when cooked. When keeping warm, do not cover or fish will lose its crispness.

Sautéing and Stir-frying

Bite size pieces of fish, or whole fish such as shrimp, are moved about and cooked quickly over medium to high heat in a small amount of oil, or a combination of butter and oil, using either a wok and a spatula, or a straight-sided frying pan with a long handle to flip the pieces from one hot area of the pan to another.

COOKING TESTS

More precaution should be taken with regard to overcooking fish than to undercooking. Fish cooked to the point is tender, flavorful, and has most of its nutrients intact.

In pan-frying or broiling, remove fish from source of heat when juice begins to appear on the surface. Fish will flake easily and take on an opaque appearance when cooked.

Lobster turns a bright red when cooked, and shrimp turns a pale pink.

Fish, as well as other foods, will retain a certain amount of heat after being removed from the source and will continue to cook for a time, depending on the size and thickness of the meat and the length of exposure to heat. However, generally speaking, keeping fish warm for serving presents more of a problem than heat retention.

FISH RECIPES

STEAMED FISH (SALMON, HALIBUT, BLUEFISH, TROUT, SHAD)

part or whole fish, cleaned	*lemon*
and head removed	*parsley*

Wash fish under cold running water. Wrap in cheesecloth to prevent breaking and for easy removal. If using frozen fish, defrost before cooking.

Place a rack in a covered roasting pan or other covered receptacle large enough to hold fish; or use a regular fish steamer with its own rack. Lay cheesecloth wrapped fish on top of rack and add water to just beneath rack (water should not come in contact with fish during cooking). Bring water to a boil over high heat and cover pan. Turn heat to low or to a temperature setting that will keep water at simmering point. Check water from time to time for evaporation, and replenish when necessary. Halfway through cooking, carefully reverse position of fish.

Steam fish until it takes on an opaque appearance, flakes easily when fork-tested, but is not too dry. Remove bones before serving. Garnish with lemon slices or wedges arranged on sprigs of fresh parsley.

Steamed Salmon with Sauce

Follow recipe for Steamed Fish. Remove skin and bones and pour on one of the following sauces or serve on the side: White Sauce, Mustard Sauce, Caper Sauce, or Lemon Sauce (see Sauce section).

POACHED SHRIMP

1½ to 2 pounds (675 to 900 g)   *vinegar or dry white wine*
   shrimp   *salt*

Remove shells from shrimp by running the point of a sharp knife along the inside surface. Remove intestinal tract (dark streak) from outside surface.

Bring a pot of water to a simmer (the water should be of sufficient capacity to allow shrimp to swim around during cooking). Add 1 teaspoon salt and 1 tablespoon vinegar (or ¼ cup [60 ml] dry white wine) per quart (l) of water. Drop shelled and deveined shrimp into simmering liquid and cook until tender and shrimp takes on a pale pink coloring and a slightly opaque appearance. Maintain temperature so that water barely simmers throughout. Be extremely careful not to overcook or fish will turn rubbery. To test, remove one shrimp, check appearance and test for tenderness using a fork or sharp knife. The length of cooking period largely depends on the size of the shrimp—jumbo shrimp will cook in approximately 4 to 5 minutes, while small to medium shrimp take 2 to 5 minutes, once water returns to a simmer. (Shrimp may be cooked covered or uncovered.)

Shrimp may also be poached by placing in cold water, adding 1 teaspoon salt and 1 tablespoon vinegar (or ¼ cup [60 ml] dry white wine) per quart (l) of water. Set over medium heat and partially cover. The procedure as to length of cooking time (once water returns to a simmer) and cooking test remains the same. Using this method, shrimp are less apt to curl during cooking.

When cooked, remove at once and drain.

When not serving immediately, reserve cooking liquid and cool by adding several ice cubes; use for storing shrimp in covered container in refrigerator.

SHRIMP COCKTAIL

1½ pounds (675 g) shrimp; or
5 or 6 medium shrimp per
serving

Seafood Cocktail Sauce (Hot)
lettuce
lemon wedges

Cook shrimp according to recipe for Poached Shrimp, and chill in refrigerator. To prepare sauce, follow recipe for Seafood Cocktail Sauce (Hot) on p. 222.

Arrange shrimp on a bed of lettuce, using a multi-service dish or individual cocktail glasses. Serve sauce in separate compartment in center or in a side dish. Garnish with lemon wedges and serve with fish cocktail forks.

SHRIMP CREOLE

1 pound (450 g) medium-size
shelled and de-veined
shrimp; or 4 or 5 shrimp
per serving
butter for frying
3 stalks celery, peeled and
sliced diagonally
1 green pepper, seeded and
sliced (julienne strips)
1 Spanish onion, peeled and
finely chopped
6 scallions (whites only),
sliced
1 clove garlic, peeled and
finely chopped
1 48-ounce (1340 g) can
tomatoes, pureed and
strained

1½ cups (360 ml) All-Purpose
Stock
3 tablespoons tomato paste
1 tablespoon fresh parsley,
finely chopped
1 tablespoon fresh tarragon;
or ¼ teaspoon dried
½ bay leaf (dried)
1 teaspoon salt
½ teaspoon pepper
1 teaspoon paprika
1 teaspoon chili powder
¼ teaspoon cayenne pepper
2 dashes Tabasco
juice of 1 large or 2 small
lemons

To cook shrimp, follow recipe for Poached Shrimp.

Fry vegetables (celery, green pepper, onion, scallions, garlic) one at a time in butter over medium low heat and set aside.

Place pureed and strained tomatoes, All-Purpose Stock, tomato paste, herbs and seasonings (parsley, tarragon, bay leaf, salt, pepper, paprika, chili powder, cayenne pepper, and Tabasco) in a saucepan and simmer over low heat for about 20 minutes. Remove bay leaf and add fried vegetables and lemon juice and cook long enough to blend. Add cooked shrimp and cook just long enough to heat through. Taste, and correct seasoning if necessary. Serve with rice.

DEEP-FRIED BREADED FISH CHUNKS

skinned and boned fish (halibut, flounder, sole, swordfish, or turbot)
salt and white pepper to taste
finely sifted flour
2 whole eggs
1 tablespoon vegetable oil } *lightly beaten*
¼ cup (60 ml) milk
breadcrumbs
oil for frying
parsley
lemon wedges

Cut skinned and boned fish into chunks and season with salt and white pepper. Roll in flour, shaking off excess. Dip in eggs, oil, and milk mixture and then in breadcrumbs.

Preheat oil to 375° F. (190° C.). Lower fish into fat, a few pieces at a time (do not overcrowd pan), using a long-handled slotted spoon or deep-frying basket. Cook until golden brown and fish floats to the surface. (Fish is cooked and browned at the same time). Drain on paper towels. Keep warm, uncovered (if covered, fish will overcook and lose its crispness), in a preheated 160° F. (71° C.) oven. Finish frying remainder of fish and serve with French Fried Potatoes (Chapter 8). Garnish with sprigs of parsley and lemon wedges.

Batter-Coated Deep-Fried Fish Chunks

Follow recipe for Deep-Fried Breaded Fish Chunks, substituting batter for breadcrumb coating. To prepare batter, follow recipe for Batter Coating on p. 80.

DEEP-FRIED BREADED SHRIMP

Follow recipe for Deep-Fried Breaded Fish Chunks, substituting shelled and de-veined shrimp (medium or jumbo) for fish chunks.

SHRIMP ORIENTAL NO. 1

1 to 1½ pounds (450 to 675 g)
medium-size shrimp
¾ pound (340 g) snow peas
3 or 4 stalks celery, peeled
4 or 5 scallions, peeled
vegetable oil (peanut)
soy sauce
thin slice ginger root
pinch of salt

dry sherry
Fish Stock, Chicken Broth, or
All-Purpose Stock
garlic clove, peeled
1 16-ounce (450 g) can bean
sprouts, drained
1 tablespoon cornstarch,
dissolved in sherry

Prepare all ingredients and arrange near cooking area.

Remove shells from shrimp by running the point of a sharp knife along the inside surface. Remove intestinal tract (dark streak) from outside surface.

Wash snow peas and trim ends. Cut peeled and washed celery across into 1" (2.5 cm) pieces, holding knife at an angle to produce a more attractive shape. Cut peeled scallions into ¼" (.5 cm) slices, including a portion of green tops.

Heat a small amount of oil in wok until just under smoking stage. Add shrimp (do not overcrowd pan) and stir-fry over high heat until tender and shrimp take on a pale pink coloring, being careful not to overcook. Remove to a heated dish.

Add additional oil to wok, a few drops soy sauce, a thin slice of ginger root, and 2 or 3 tablespoons Stock or Broth—pouring along inside rim of pan so it will be heated through before coming in contact with hot oil. Add garlic clove and stir-fry for a few seconds (or just long enough to extract flavor) and remove. Add snow peas and stir-fry until fairly tender and bright green in color. Remove to a heated dish. Add chopped celery and stir-fry until fairly crisp (do not overcook). Add scallions to wok and stir-fry until they take on a slightly translucent appearance. Return snow peas to pan along with drained bean sprouts. Gradually add

1 cup (240 ml) Stock or Broth in a circular motion along the inside rim. Add moistened cornstarch, stir-frying until sauce is slightly thick, smooth, and glossy. Add cooked shrimp and stir-fry just long enough to heat through (if overly exposed to heat, shrimp will turn rubbery). Serve with cooked rice.

SHRIMP ORIENTAL NO. 2

Oriental Sauce
1 to 1½ pounds (450 to 675 g)
  medium-size shrimp
3 or 4 stalks celery, peeled
¾ pound (340 g) snow peas;
  or 1 10-ounce (280 g)
  package frozen peas

vegetable oil
5 or 6 shallots or scallions,
  peeled and chopped
1 16-ounce (450 g) can bean
  sprouts, drained

To prepare sauce, follow recipe for Oriental Sauce (under Sauce section), deleting sugar. Chicken Broth may be substituted for All-Purpose Stock.

Remove shells from shrimp by running the point of a sharp knife along the inside surface, and remove intestinal tract (dark streak) from outside surface.

Cut washed and peeled celery into 1" (2.5 cm) lengths, holding knife at an angle so as to produce a more attractive shape. Wash snow peas and trim ends. Cook celery and snow peas in a large pot of lightly salted boiling water until celery is fairly crisp when tested and snow peas are bright green and fairly tender. Remove and drain. If using frozen peas, break up and cook in 1 teaspoon butter over medium low heat (do not add water) in a covered saucepan until heated through. (Do not overcook vegetables.)

Heat oil in frying pan and sauté shelled and de-veined shrimp over medium high heat until tender and pale pink in color. (Do not overcrowd pan and do not overcook or shrimp will turn rubbery.) Remove to a heated dish. (Shrimp may also be poached rather than sautéed; see recipe for Poached Shrimp.)

Add a small amount of oil to frying pan, and fry peeled and chopped shallots or scallions over low heat until they take on a slightly translucent appearance. Remove to heated dish.

Bring Oriental Sauce to a slow simmer over low heat, uncovered, and add cooked peas (snow peas or regular peas), along with celery, shallots or scallions, and drained bean sprouts. When sauce has returned to a simmer, add shrimp and cook for another few seconds, or just long enough to heat through. Serve with cooked rice.

SHRIMP WITH GARLIC SAUCE (SCAMPI)

1 pound (450 g) medium-size shrimp, shelled and de-veined; or 5 or 6 per serving
olive oil for frying
salt and white pepper to taste

fresh lemon juice
3 tablespoons fresh parsley, finely chopped
3 or 4 cloves garlic, peeled and very finely chopped

Sauté shelled and de-veined shrimp in a straight-sided frying pan in hot oil (about ¼" [.5 cm] in depth) over high heat, tossing and shaking pan until pink and tender (do not overcook). Transfer to a hot serving platter and season with salt and white pepper to taste. Squeeze two or three drops lemon juice over each shrimp. Set in a 160° F. (71° C.) oven to keep warm.

Place finely chopped parsley in a small strainer and scald with enough boiling water to moisten. Set aside.

Reduce heat to low, add finely chopped garlic, and cook, stirring, for about 1 minute. Add moistened parsley to pan, stir, and pour sauce over shrimp. Serve at once.

BUTTERFLY SHRIMP (TEMPURA)

jumbo shrimp, shelled and de-veined (approximately 4 per serving)

salt and white pepper to taste
Batter or Breadcrumb Coating

Split along back curve of shelled and de-veined shrimp, cutting close to inner edge, leaving tails intact if desired. Place between two sheets parchment or plastic wrap, and, using a mallet, lightly pound until flattened somewhat. Dip in Batter or Breadcrumb

Coating. (Chapter 3, under Coatings for Deep-Frying). Preheat fat to 375° F. (190° C.) and deep-fry until golden brown. Shrimp will float to surface when cooked.

SEAFOOD COCKTAIL SAUCE

¾ *cup (180 ml) ketchup*
¼ *cup (60 ml) chili sauce*
2 *tablespoons horseradish*
  sauce

juice of large lemon
½ *teaspoon salt*
¼ *teaspoon pepper*
dash of Tabasco

Combine all ingredients and taste. For a milder sauce, add additional ketchup and lemon juice; for a hotter sauce add additional Tabasco and horseradish.

POACHED FISH FILLETS (FLOUNDER, SOLE, TURBOT) NO. 1

Fish Stock or dry white wine
2 *pounds (900 g) fish fillets;*
  or 1 small whole fillet per
  serving
1 *tablespoon butter*

2 *tablespoons finely sifted*
  flour
1 *lemon*
salt and white pepper to taste
fresh parsley, finely chopped

To prepare stock, follow recipe for Fish Stock (Chapter 2, under Stocks).

Using a shallow, heat-proof dish, bring Fish Stock or dry white wine to a simmer and add fillets; liquid should just barely cover fish. Set in a preheated 325° F. (163° C.) oven for about 15 to 20 minutes (depending on thickness), or until fish takes on an opaque appearance and flakes easily when fork-tested, but is not too dry. Fish may also be poached on top of stove over low heat. In both methods, Stock or wine should just barely simmer throughout.

When cooked, transfer fish to a heated platter or individual serving plates, using a broad spatula, being careful not to break fish. Set pan containing liquid over high heat. Bring to a boil and reduce by about a third. Turn heat to low, so that Stock or wine just barely simmers. Blend 1 tablespoon butter with 2 tablespoons flour and stir into reduced liquid, using a wire whisk. Gently simmer until slightly thickened. Turn off heat and gradually stir in the juice of a whole lemon. Season to taste with salt and white pepper. Pour sauce over fillets and garnish with finely chopped parsley, or serve sauce on the side.

POACHED FISH FILLETS (FLOUNDER, SOLE, TURBOT) NO. 2

Follow recipe for Poached Fish Fillets No. 1, substituting water for Fish Stock or dry white wine. Add 1 tablespoon vinegar or ¼ cup (60 ml) dry white wine per quart (l) water. When cooked, remove fillets and serve plain, or with one of the following sauces: Lemon Sauce, White Sauce, Mustard Sauce, Parsley Sauce, Shellfish Sauce, or Mustard Sauce (under Sauce section). Fish Stock, Clam Broth, or Chicken Broth may be substituted for All-Purpose Stock, where indicated.

POACHED FISH FILLETS (FLOUNDER, ENGLISH OR LEMON SOLE, RED SNAPPER) NO. 3

butter for frying
½ pound (225 g) mushrooms, peeled and sliced
5 or 6 shallots, peeled and finely sliced
1 tablespoon fresh parsley, finely chopped
2 pounds (900 g) fish fillets, halved; or 1 small whole fillet per serving

salt and white pepper to taste
fresh lemon juice
1 cup (240 ml) dry white wine; or sufficient amount to cover fish
¾ cup (180 ml) light cream
1 egg yolk
¼ cup (60 ml) light cream

Melt butter to foaming; sauté mushrooms over medium high heat until lightly browned. Lower heat, add shallots, and fry until translucent. Transfer to a shallow ovenproof dish and add chopped parsley. Lay fillets over vegetables, side by side. Season lightly with salt and white pepper and sprinkle a few drops lemon juice over each fillet. Bring wine to a simmer and pour over fish. Wine should barely cover fish. Butter a piece of parchment paper cut to fit, and make a small hole in the center to allow steam to escape and prevent paper from bouncing. Lay over top of dish and set in a preheated 325° F. (163° C.) oven for about 15 minutes, or until fish appears opaque and flakes easily when tested with a fork. When cooked, transfer fish to a heated platter, using a broad spatula. Remove vegetables, using a slotted spoon and set aside. Set pan containing liquid over high heat and reduce by about a third. Return vegetables to pan and add ¾ cup light cream, boiling until slightly thickened. Beat egg yolk lightly with the remaining ¼ cup (60 ml) light cream, and add a little of the hot mixture before stirring in. Stir just long enough to blend and do not allow to boil, or sauce will curdle. Pour sauce over fish or serve on the side.

ROLLED FISH FILLETS (FLOUNDER, ENGLISH OR LEMON SOLE) NO. 1

Fish Stock, dry white wine, or milk
2 pounds (900 g) fish fillets*
Salt and white pepper to taste
lemon juice

1 tablespoon butter
2 tablespoons finely sifted flour
paprika

To prepare stock, follow recipe for Fish Stock (Chapter 2 under Stock section).

Cut fillets in half from end to end, that is, along connecting tissue running through center. Place between two sheets plastic wrap, parchment paper or wax paper, membrane side (dark skin side) down, and using a mallet, lightly pound, being careful not to break fish, until flattened somewhat. Remove top sheet and season to taste with salt and white pepper. Sprinkle a few drops lemon juice over each fillet and rub in. Reverse position of fillets so that skin side is facing up. Roll fillets from end to end, making certain white side is exposed. (Toothpicks are not necessary, as flesh will adhere to itself when exposed to heat.)

*Choose fillets that are more or less uniform in size and length.

Using a shallow, heat-proof dish, bring to a boil enough Fish Stock, dry white wine, or milk to barely cover fillets. Carefully lower rolled fillets into liquid. Poach on top of stove over low heat or in a preheated 325° F. (163° C.) oven. Using either method, liquid should just barely simmer throughout cooking period. Fish is cooked when it loses its translucency and flakes easily when fork-tested. (Do not overcook, or fish will be dry and fall apart.) Remove fillets to a heated platter or individual serving plates.

Place pan containing liquid over medium high heat and boil until reduced by about a third. Turn heat to low so that liquid is just barely simmering. Blend butter with flour and add to liquid, stirring with a wire whisk until lightly thickened. Pour sauce over fillets or serve on the side. Garnish with a light dusting of paprika. Serve 2 small or 1 large rolled fillet per serving.

ROLLED FISH FILLETS (FLOUNDER, ENGLISH OR LEMON SOLE) NO. 2

Follow recipe for Rolled Fish Fillets (Flounder, English or Lemon Sole) No. 1, substituting water for Stock, wine, or milk. Add 1 tablespoon vinegar or ¼ cup (60 ml) dry white wine for each quart (l) water.

When cooked, serve Rolled Fillets plain or with one of the following sauces: Lemon Sauce, Caper Sauce, Shellfish Sauce, Shrimp or Lobster Sauce, Parsley Sauce, White Sauce, or Mustard Sauce. Clam Broth or Chicken Broth may be substituted for All-Purpose Stock, where indicated.

ROLLED FISH FILLETS (PAUPIETTES) NO. 3

butter for frying
2 small carrots, peeled and
finely chopped
2 stalks celery, peeled and
finely chopped
1 onion, peeled and finely
chopped
2 tablespoons finely sifted
flour
1 tablespoon fresh parsley,
finely chopped
2 pounds (900 g) fish fillets
(flounder, English or lemon
sole); or 1 whole fillet per
serving

salt and white pepper to taste
fresh lemon juice
2 cups (480 ml) milk
2 tablespoons softened butter
2 tablespoons finely sifted
flour
¼ teaspoon dry English
mustard
¼ cup (60 ml) light cream

Fry finely chopped carrots, celery, and onion in butter over medium heat until slightly crisp. Add 2 tablespoons finely sifted flour and cook, stirring, over low heat for about 1 minute, adding more butter if necessary. Add finely chopped parsley, mix in, and remove from heat.

Place fillet halves, membrane side up (dark skin side), between two sheets parchment or plastic wrap, and, using a mallet, lightly pound until flattened somewhat. Remove top sheet and spread a thin layer of vegetable filling along center of fillets, leaving about 1½" (4 cm) on either end, and about ¾" (1.5 cm) along the sides. Season lightly with salt and white pepper and 2 or 3 drops fresh lemon juice on each fillet half. Roll fillets, making certain white side is exposed. Toothpicks are not necessary, as flesh will adhere to itself when exposed to heat.

Bring milk to a boil over medium high heat in a shallow ovenproof dish. Turn heat to low and add rolled fillets. There should be sufficient milk to barely cover the fish. Poach fish on top of stove over low heat, or set in a preheated 325° F. (163° C.) oven until fish loses its translucency or flakes easily when fork-tested. Do not overcook. Remove rolled fillets to a heated platter, using a broad spatula, and set in oven, adjusting temperature to 160° F. (71° C.) to keep warm. Transfer pan containing liquid to top of stove and add light cream. Blend softened butter, flour, and dry mustard, and add to liquid, stirring, using a wire whisk, over low heat, until lightly thickened. If too thick, add additional milk. Pour sauce over rolled fillets and serve.

ROLLED FISH FILLETS WITH SHRIMP

Substitute ½ pound (225 g) of finely chopped or shredded cooked shrimp for the vegetables in the Rolled Fish Fillet recipe.

POACHED SALMON

2-pound (900 g) piece salmon *salt*
vinegar *Hollandaise Sauce*

Wrap salmon in a piece of cheesecloth to prevent breaking apart. Bring water to a boil on top of stove and add 1 tablespoon vinegar for each quart (l) of water, along with a teaspoon salt. Add salmon and cook, covered, over low heat; water should just barely simmer. Salmon will take on an opaque appearance when cooked, and will flake easily with a fork. Drain and remove cheesecloth, skin, and bones. Serve with Hollandaise Sauce (Chapter 2, under Sauce section).

BROILED FISH FILLETS (FLOUNDER, SOLE, TURBOT, HADDOCK) NO. 1

milk *butter*
salt and white pepper to taste *paprika*
lemon juice

Dip fillets in cold milk and pat with paper towels to remove excess. Cover broiler pan with a layer of aluminum foil and lay fillets on top. Season with salt, pepper, and a few drops lemon juice. Dot with butter and dust lightly with paprika. Broil several inches from flame. It is not necessary to turn fish during cooking. Fillets take but a few minutes to cook and should be removed as soon as juice begins to appear on the surface, or when they flake easily when tested with a fork. Using a broad spatula, transfer to a warm plate, being careful not to break. Serve with lemon wedges.

BROILED FISH FILLETS (FLOUNDER, SOLE, TURBOT) NO. 2

2 pounds (900 g) fish fillets;   oil or melted butter
   or 1 small whole fillet per   salt and white pepper
   serving   sauce

Cover broiler pan with a layer of aluminum foil and lay fish fillets on top, skin side down. Brush lightly with oil or melted butter, using a pastry brush. Season to taste with salt and white pepper. Place under preheated broiler several inches from the flame. (It is not necessary to turn fish during cooking.) Remove when fish loses its translucent appearance or flakes easily when fork-tested. Do not overcook or fish will become dry and tasteless.

Pour over one of the following sauces, or serve sauce on the side: Lemon Sauce, Parsley Sauce, Mushroom Sauce, Shellfish Sauce, Shrimp or Lobster Sauce, White Sauce, Mustard Sauce, or Caper Sauce (Chapter 3, under Sauce section). Clam Broth or Chicken Broth may be substituted for All-Purpose Stock, where indicated.

Broiled Fish Fillets (Flounder, Sole, Turbot) with Flavored Butter

Follow recipe for Broiled Fish Fillets No. 2, substituting a flavored butter for sauce. To prepare flavored butter, blend 2 teaspoons fresh lemon juice with 3 tablespoons softened butter, salt and white pepper to taste and flavor with one of the following: ½ to 1 teaspoon dried mustard, or according to taste; 1 tablespoon finely chopped dill; 2 tablespoons anchovy paste; 2 tablespoons ground cooked shrimp; or 1 tablespoon finely chopped fresh parsley. Form into a block and refrigerate until firm. Before serving, place a slice of flavored butter on each fillet.

COQUILLES ST. JACQUES

White Sauce
butter
5 or 6 shallots, peeled and
  chopped
1½ pounds (675 g) scallops

lemon juice
⅓ cup (80 ml) dry white wine
salt and white pepper to taste
paprika

To prepare sauce, follow recipe for White Sauce (under Sauce section), substituting one cup (240 ml) Clam Broth for one cup White Stock.

Melt butter in frying pan; fry peeled and chopped shallots over low heat until they take on a slightly translucent appearance and set aside. Turn heat to medium high and sauté scallops until slightly opaque in appearance, adding more butter if necessary, and remove to a heated dish. Sprinkle fresh lemon juice over scallops.

Turn heat to high and de-glaze pan with dry white wine, scraping pan bottom using a rubber spatula or wooden spoon. Strain and add to barely simmering White Sauce, along with scallops and shallots. Gently simmer until heated through and well blended. Serve in shells and garnish with a sprinkling of paprika.

COQUILLES ST. JACQUES AU GRATIN

Follow recipe for Coquilles St. Jacques, omitting paprika garnish. When in shells, sprinkle grated Parmesan and Romano cheese over surface, dot with butter, and set under a preheated broiler until lightly browned.

BROILED SWORDFISH STEAKS
WITH MAITRE D' BUTTER

2 teaspoons lemon juice
1 tablespoon fresh parsley,
    finely chopped
3 tablespoons softened butter

salt and white pepper to taste
swordfish steaks
vegetable oil

To prepare Maitre d' Butter, add lemon juice and chopped parsley to softened butter and blend. Season to taste with salt and white pepper. Form into a block and store in refrigerator until firm.

Brush steaks on either side with oil and season with salt and white pepper. Place under a preheated broiler. (The proximity to the flame will depend on the thickness of steaks: The thicker the steaks, the farther from the flame.) Cook on either side until lightly browned and fish takes on a slightly opaque appearance, or flakes easily when fork-tested. Do not overcook or fish will become dry and lose its flavor. Remove to a heated platter or individual serving plates, using a broad spatula.

Remove Maitre d' Butter from refrigerator and place a slice on each steak.

BROILED SALMON STEAKS
WITH DILL BUTTER

Follow recipe for Broiled Swordfish Steaks with Maitre d' Butter, substituting salmon steaks for swordfish steaks. To prepare Dill Butter, substitute one tablespoon finely chopped fresh dill for parsley in Maitre d' Butter.

FRIED BROOK TROUT OR SMELTS

Brook trout or smelts, cleaned
milk

cornmeal or flour
butter and oil for frying

Dip cleaned fish in milk and then in cornmeal or flour. Melt butter and oil in frying pan and fry fish on either side over medium low heat until fish flakes easily when fork-tested, being careful not to overcook.

FRIED FISH FILLETS (FLOUNDER, SOLE, TURBOT)

fish fillets
finely sifted flour
2 whole eggs
1 tablespoon oil } *lightly beaten*
¼ cup (60 ml) milk }
breadcrumbs
butter and oil for frying
lemon wedges
fresh parsley, finely chopped

Roll fillets in finely sifted flour, shaking off excess. Dip in eggs, oil, and milk mixture and then in breadcrumbs.

Melt butter and oil in frying pan and fry fish on either side until golden brown. (Fish is cooked and browned at the same time.) Remove to a heated platter or individual serving plates, using a broad spatula, being careful not to break fish. Serve with lemon wedges and garnish with finely chopped parsley.

BOILED LOBSTER

live lobsters, weighing
    approximately 1 to 1¼
    pounds (450 to 560 g) each
salt

Bring a large pot of salted water (1 teaspoon per quart or liter) to a boil and add live lobsters, plunging in head first. Cook for approximately 15 to 20 minutes, once water returns to the boil. Length of cooking period will depend on size of lobsters. Lobster will turn bright red when cooked. When cooked, drain and place in cold water for a few seconds to stop cooking action.

Lobster may be served hot or chilled. Disjoint large claws and crack portion of shell using lobster shears. Split body from head to tail, using a sharp knife. Remove stomach which lies just back of the head, as well as the intestinal tract which runs the length of the body and tail.

Garnish with lemon wedges and serve a generous amount of drawn (melted) butter in a separate dish. Serve with fish cocktail forks.

When using lobster for separate preparations, remove all meat from shells and dispose of cartilage from large claws.

LOBSTER NEWBURG

White Sauce (Béchamel)   *melted butter*
⅓ cup (80 ml) dry white wine   *paprika*
cooked lobster meat, cut into
*   chunks*

To prepare sauce, follow recipe for White Sauce (Béchamel) under the Sauce section. Fish Stock or Clam Broth may be substituted for White Stock.

To cook lobster, follow recipe for Boiled Lobster.

Bring White Sauce to a slow simmer over low heat and add dry white wine. Gently simmer, uncovered, until slightly reduced. Reheat lobster chunks in melted butter over medium low heat before adding to sauce. Remove at once and serve on a bed of cooked rice, in patti shells, or with toast points. Garnish with a light dusting of paprika.

FISH QUENELLES NO. 1

Fish Stock or dry white wine
1 pound (450 g) skinned and
    de-boned fish (flounder,
    sole, pike, or salmon)
1 teaspoon salt
2 egg whites

1 cup (240 ml) light or heavy
    cream (optional)
1 tablespoon butter
2 tablespoons flour
finely chopped parsley or
    paprika

To prepare stock, follow recipe for Fish Stock (Chapter 2, under Stock section).

Put skinned and de-boned fish through grinder or food processor. Place in bowl of electric mixer, along with salt. Beat in egg whites one at a time at medium speed until absorbed. When using cream, add very gradually, beating until well blended. (The addition of cream will result in a lighter texture and richer flavor, but otherwise is not essential.) Cover (to prevent drying) and chill in refrigerator for an hour or so. When thoroughly chilled, shape into ovals about 2″ long and 1″ wide (1 cm x .5 cm). Place Fish Stock or dry white wine in a high-sided frying pan and bring to a boil. Reduce heat and carefully lower quenelles into simmering liquid. (There should be just enough liquid to cover fish.) Cover and poach over low heat—liquid should just barely simmer throughout. Cook until quenelles are firm and take on a slightly opaque appearance. Carefully remove to a heated dish, using a slotted spoon.

Bring liquid to a boil over high heat and reduce by about a third. Turn heat to low. Blend butter and flour and add to liquid, stirring using a wire whisk, until sauce is lightly thickened. Pour sauce over quenelles or serve on the side. Garnish with finely chopped parsley or a light dusting of paprika.

FISH QUENELLES NO. 2

Follow recipe for Fish Quenelles No. 1, substituting water for Fish Stock or dry white wine. Add 1 tablespoon vinegar or ¼ cup (60 ml) dry white wine per quart (l) of water. Serve with one of the following sauces: White Sauce, Mustard Sauce, Lemon Sauce, Shellfish Sauce, Parsley Sauce, Mushroom Sauce, or Caper Sauce (Chapter 3, under Sauce section). Clam Broth or Chicken Broth may be substituted for All-Purpose Stock, where indicated.

SHRIMP QUENELLES NO. 1

Follow recipe for Fish Quenelles No. 1, substituting 1 pound (450 g) of shelled and de-veined shrimp for skinned and de-boned fish.

SHRIMP QUENELLES NO. 2

Follow recipe for Fish Quenelles No. 2, substituting 1 pound (450 g) shelled and de-veined shrimp for skinned and de-boned fish.

SHRIMP WITH SHELLFISH SAUCE

Shellfish Sauce   *butter*
1½ (675 g) pounds shrimp *paprika*

To prepare sauce, follow recipe for Shellfish Sauce (under Sauce section).

Cook shrimp according to recipe for Poached Shrimp.

If necessary, reheat shrimp in melted butter over medium low heat. Bring Shellfish Sauce to a simmer and add shrimp. Remove at once, otherwise shrimp will overcook and turn rubbery. Serve with cooked rice. Garnish with a light dusting of paprika.

CLAMS ON THE HALF SHELL

Seafood Cocktail Sauce *lemon wedges*
5 or 6 clams per serving, live *parsley sprigs*

To prepare sauce, follow recipe for Seafood Cocktail Sauce on p. 222.

Check to make certain there are no dead clams, and wash under cold running water. Keep handling to a minimum as this causes clam to tighten up.

Open clams, using a clam knife, by placing the sharp edge of the knife between the outside edges of shells, exerting pressure against the dull side of blade. Force blade between shells and cut first muscle. Withdraw knife partway, holding handle downward so that blade rests against upper shell and not touching flesh of clam. Run knife clockwise around edge of shell to sever second muscle which is located opposite first muscle, being careful not to cut flesh of clam, otherwise it will lose its plumpness. Open clam and discard upper shell. Loosen clam from lower shell.

Arrange clams on individual serving plates and place small dish with Cocktail Sauce in the center. Garnish with lemon wedges and sprigs of parsley.

TUNA CASSEROLE AU GRATIN NO. 1

Mustard Sauce
1 10-ounce (280 g) package
  frozen peas
butter
1 8-ounce (225 g) package
  noodles

1 onion, peeled and chopped
grated Parmesan and Romano
  cheese
1 16-ounce (450 g) can of solid
  white tuna

To prepare sauce, follow recipe for Mustard Sauce (Chapter 2, under Sauce section).

Break up frozen peas by hitting package against a hard surface. Melt 1 teaspoon butter in a saucepan and add peas (do not add water). Cook over medium low heat, covered, until defrosted and heated through.

In the meantime cook noodles, according to package directions, in enough lightly salted boiling water so that the noodles can swim around while cooking. Remove and drain in a colander.

Fry peeled and chopped onions in a small amount of melted butter over low heat, until they take on a slightly translucent appearance and are fairly crisp. Remove and add to barely simmering Mustard Sauce, along with cooked peas. Break tuna into chunks and add to sauce. Cook over low heat, without stirring, just long enough to heat through.

Arrange noodles in a shallow buttered casserole dish and pour over sauce containing onions, peas, and tuna. Sprinkle grated cheese over surface, dot with butter, and place under a pre-heated broiler until slightly crisp and lightly browned.

TUNA CASSEROLE AU GRATIN NO. 2

Follow recipe for Tuna Casserole Au Gratin No. 1, substituting 3 or 4 baking potatoes for noodles. Peel potatoes, cut into bite-size cubes and cook in a large pot of lightly salted boiling water until fairly crisp when fork tested—potatoes should not be mushy. Arrange potatoes in casserole in place of noodles.

CREAMED TUNA

White Sauce
1 16-ounce (450 g) can solid
   white tuna

1 onion, peeled and chopped
butter

To prepare sauce, follow recipe for White Sauce (Chapter 3, under Sauce section).

Fry peeled and chopped onion in a small amount of butter over low heat until fairly crisp. Remove and add to barely simmering White Sauce. Break tuna into chunks and add to sauce. Cook over low heat, without stirring, just long enough to heat through, otherwise tuna will overcook and become stringy.

Remove and serve over cooked rice, noodles, with toast points, or in patti shells.

CRABMEAT AU GRATIN

White Sauce
pinch of cayenne pepper or
   dash of Tabasco
5 or 6 shallots, peeled and
   chopped
butter

¼ pound (115 g) mushrooms,
   peeled and sliced
⅓ cup (80 ml) dry white wine
grated Parmesan and Romano
   cheese
breadcrumbs

To prepare sauce, follow recipe for White Sauce (Chapter 3, under Sauce section). 1 cup Clam Broth or Chicken Broth may be substituted for White Stock. Add a pinch of cayenne pepper or a dash of Tabasco to sauce.

Fry peeled and chopped shallots in butter over low heat until they take on a slightly translucent appearance and remove. Add more butter to pan, if necessary, and sauté sliced mushrooms over medium high heat until golden brown and remove. Add dry white wine to pan, bring to a boil over high heat, and de-glaze pan, using a rubber spatula or wooden spoon. When slightly reduced, add to White Sauce, straining if necessary. Bring sauce to a slow simmer and add shallots, mushrooms, and crabmeat, cooking just long enough to blend flavors and heat through. Pour into shells or au gratin dishes and sprinkle a combination of grated cheese and breadcrumbs over surface. Dot with butter and place under a preheated broiler until lightly browned.

SALMON MOUSSE

1 pound (450 g) uncooked
   salmon, skinned and boned
2 egg whites, unbeaten
1 teaspoon salt
2 tablespoons fresh dill, finely
   chopped

½ pint (240 ml) light or
   heavy cream (optional)
melted butter or oil

Put skinned and boned salmon through grinder or place in food processor until finely ground. Place in bowl of electric mixer, along with salt, and beat in egg whites, one at a time. Mix in finely chopped dill. When using cream, add very gradually, beating until well blended. (The addition of cream will result in lighter texture and richer flavor, but otherwise is not essential.) Cover with plastic wrap (to prevent drying) and chill in refrigerator for about an hour.

When thoroughly chilled, remove and turn into a greased 1-quart (1-l) dish or circular mold. Brush surface with melted butter or oil to prevent drying. Set in a shallow pan containing enough hot (not boiling) water to come halfway up the sides and bake in a preheated 325° F. (163° C.) oven until mousse begins to shrink from sides of pan and is set. Remove and let stand for about 10 minutes.

Unmold onto a heated serving plate and serve plain or with one of the following sauces: White Sauce, Mustard Sauce, Lemon Sauce, or Caper Sauce (Chapter 2, under Sauce section).

SHRIMP MOUSSE

Follow recipe for Salmon Mousse, substituting 1 pound (450 g) of shelled and de-veined uncooked shrimp for the salmon. Serve with Lemon Sauce, Shellfish Sauce, Shrimp or Lobster Sauce, Caper Sauce, or White Sauce. Fish Stock, Clam Broth or Chicken Broth may be substituted for All-Purpose Stock, where indicated.

FILLET-WRAPPED SALMON MOUSSE

fish fillets (flounder, lemon or   salt and white pepper
    English sole)*   *lemon juice*
Salmon Mousse   *oil or melted butter*

To prepare filling, follow recipe for Salmon Mousse.

Place fillets between two sheets of parchment paper, wax paper, or plastic wrap, membrane side (skin side) down, and using a mallet, lightly pound until flattened somewhat, being careful not to break fish. Remove top sheet and reverse position of fillets. Season with salt and white pepper and sprinkle each fillet with a few drops fresh lemon juice.

Lay fillets, membrane side (skin side) up, across a greased circular 1-quart (1-l) mold with ends hanging over sides and one fillet slightly overlapping the other. (This will produce a rope effect when unmolded.) Fill cavity with ground Salmon Mousse (uncooked). Bring ends of fillets over so as to enclose filling and completely cover it. (Any gashes or holes in fillets resulting from pounding may be patched using bits and pieces of any remaining flesh.) Refrigerate for at least an hour before baking. When thoroughly chilled, remove from refrigerator, and to prevent drying, brush oil or melted butter over surface. Set mold in a shallow pan containing enough hot (not boiling) water to come halfway up

---

*The number of fillets will vary according to size; however, they should be long enough to fill cavity of mold and to envelop mousse.

the sides. Bake in a preheated 325° F. (163° C.) oven until mold begins to set and shrink from sides. Remove and let stand for about 10 minutes before unmolding. To unmold, center serving plate over top of mold, and balancing mold in left hand and holding plate securely in place with right hand, carefully turn upside down. (If pan has been greased with a vegetable oil spray, contents will unmold quite readily.)

Serve plain or with Lemon Sauce, Shellfish Sauce, Caper Sauce, White Sauce, or Mustard Sauce (Chapter 3, under Sauce section). Fish Stock, Clam Broth, or Chicken Broth may be substituted for All-Purpose Stock, where indicated.

FILLET-WRAPPED SHRIMP MOUSSE

Follow recipe for Fillet Wrapped Salmon Mousse, substituting Shrimp Mousse for Salmon Mousse.

Serve plain or with Lemon Sauce, Shellfish Sauce, Shrimp or Lobster Sauce, or Caper Sauce. Fish Stock, Clam Broth or Chicken Broth may be substituted for All-Purpose Stock, where indicated.

PRODUCE
OF THE LAND

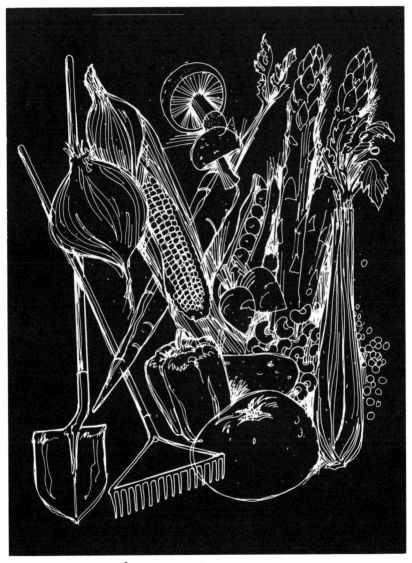

chapter seven

THE REAL THING

The American Indians' appreciation for the earth and the things that grew out of it came close to the point of worship. They revered and treated all plants with loving care. Their ability to cultivate the soil and their overall contribution to agriculture helped lay the groundwork for what was to become the world's most productive salad bowl and bread basket. Ships arriving in the New World from Africa introduced many new crops, and early settlers from England, Scandinavia, and other parts of Western Europe nurtured the new seeds and plants which they brought with them. These early horticulturists left a legacy almost impossible to estimate. Settlers arriving during the latter half of the nineteenth century were amazed at the ready availability and variety of fresh produce.

The variety remains and continues to expand, but the quality, shape, and form have undergone some changes. On the plus side, the greatest change has been in corn, the Indians' beloved legendary "lady with the long silk hair." Hybrid corn, developed by U.S. agriculturists and farmers and used as a mainstay in the diets of poultry and cattle, has affected agriculture more than any other single advance. On the other side of the coin, strains of vegetables have been developed which have a smooth and sleek appearance, are very hardy, and stand up to long periods of cold storage—but have little flavor. Agricultural experts theorize the greater quantities being made available justify the drastic changes in growing methods.

The food processing industry has played a major role in regulating certain overall changes. Peas have all but disappeared from the fresh vegetable section; when they are available, the consumer may come away with the impression of having bought pearls-in-a-pod. The quality of potatoes, which have the highest production rate of any vegetable in the country, especially in retail markets, frequently leaves something to be desired. Every year greater quantities of processed vegetables are being consumed, and, as already indicated, the largest share of the billion dollar food marketing bill goes to the processing industry. In one year, the total processing tonnage of eight major vegetables increased by 17 percent.

Initially, there was considerable resistance to canned foods based on many factors, including eating habits, possible health hazards, and an overall sense of distrust. This resistance was eventually suppressed. Label-wrapped cans illustrating bright and colorful vegetables played a part, and commercially processed produce was promoted as being superior to fresh, in that it was rushed from field to factory, preventing any but a minimal loss of nutrients.*

Processed frozen vegetables suffered their ups and downs for a time but eventually gained in popularity, so that Americans now consume them in greater quantities than do the citizens of any other country. Aside from the convenience factor, their eye appeal is one of their greatest assets. Their brightness of color is not always an indication of their full flavor and crisp texture, however. The practice of blanching vegetables and dousing them in cold water to stop the cooking action accentuates their natural color but at the same time detracts from both their flavor and texture. Further exposure to freezing temperatures for relatively long storage periods does not as a rule affect the color to any appreciable degree but it does result in breakdown and loss of flavor, texture, and nutrients. The relatively recent advance of distributing frozen vegetables in boilable, heat-sealed plastic pouches has brought considerable improvement.

Perhaps in response to some of the less desirable practices in growing and processing, vegetable gardens have been springing up in empty city lots, roof gardens, and in what were formerly groomed and preened lawns and backyards. The old delights of home-grown produce have been rediscovered. While the convenience and thrift of the home garden have not been negligible factors, the motivating force in this new development has been the harvesting of rich and flavorful vegetables and fruits cultivated with tender loving care.

NUTRITIVE VALUE

While vegetables contain many nutrients, they are especially valued for their vitamins and minerals. Most vitamins become co-

---

*By the time such produce reached the consumer it had been sitting in a can and more often than not soaking in liquid for weeks, months, and even a year or more, resulting in loss of natural flavor, texture, and nutrients. These aspects were frequently offset by the use of chemicals, coloring matter, or other artificial means.

enzymes in the body's complicated enzyme systems. This simply means that vitamins act as catalysts so that other food substances can be metabolized and serve their respective functions. Minerals (magnesium, calcium, iodine, phosphorus, and iron) regulate many vital body processes and are a necessary part of all cells and body fluids, as well as essential elements in bones and teeth.

The soil in which vegetables are grown, as well as the climate, affect their nutritive value.

A wide variety of vegetables contain ascorbic acid (vitamin C)—green and red peppers, broccoli, Brussels sprouts, cabbage, cauliflower, collard greens, tomatoes, and eggplant. The length and conditions of storage affect the vitamin C content, however.

The dark green leafy vegetables (spinach, broccoli, beet greens) and dried legumes (peas, beans, lentils) are important sources of iron and magnesium. Green leafy vegetables are also high in vitamin E.

This group, as well as the deep yellow and orange vegetables (carrots, turnips, sweet potatoes, winter squash) are valuable sources of carotene, which the body can convert to Vitamin A.

Most root vegetables (beets, turnips, carrots, parsnips) store their carbohydrate in the form of sugar and contain more carbohydrate than the fruit and flower vegetables (tomatoes, green and red peppers, eggplant, cauliflower).

A medium-size boiled white potato (a tuber) has only 65 calories and contains protein, calcium, phosphorus, potassium, and vitamin C. Its carbohydrate is mainly in the form of starch. The sweet potato, a root vegetable, has large amounts of both sugar and starch.

In addition to their valuable vitamin and mineral content, vegetables add bulk (fiber) to the diet and are a good source of water.

The Importance of Vitamins and Minerals, Fortified or Fresh

The importance of vitamins and minerals in basic metabolic processes, as well as their relationship to the maintenance of an overall state of good health, is well known and accepted. Fortified foods and manufactured vitamins and minerals have gone a long way in assuaging the guilt feelings of nutrition-conscious Americans confronted with innumerable bits of advice, charts, and warnings.

Claude Louis Berthollet (1748-1822), famous French chemist and private physician to Philip, Duke of Orleans, having given considerable thought to the problem of nutrition, made the following prediction:

> The problem of food is a chemical problem. . . . the day will come when each person will carry for his nourishment his little nitrogenous tablet, his pat of fatty matter, his package of starch or sugar, his vial of aromatic spices suited to his personal taste; all manufactured economically and in unlimited quantities, all independent of regular seasons, drought and rain, of the heat that withers the plant and the frost that blights the fruit; all free from pathogenic microbes, the origin of epidemics and the enemies of human life. At that time chemistry will have accomplished a world-wide revolution that cannot be estimated.

Monsieur Berthollet's prophecy makes no mention of such minerals as iodine, iron, and manganese, as they had not yet been accorded their proper place in the diet at the time of his death in 1822.

Fresh vegetables and fruits have always played a singular role in the human diet. The flavor, texture, and natural color of both cooked and uncooked produce is closely related to its nutritional value, and these qualities can serve as a reliable buying guide.

Most vegetables have a long history of cultivation and have been prepared in as many different ways as local cultures. Thanks to modern refrigeration and transportation, many vegetables are available in their fresh state all year round. Others, which are seasonal, can be served often and in great variety during their particular reign.

PURCHASING

Grading

The U.S. Department of Agriculture has established standards for grades of vegetables which are used to advantage by wholesalers and professionals. This system is not compulsory, however, and is not generally carried over into retail marketing. Such information would, of course, give the consumer a much better basis on which to make a selection. A posting in retail outlets showing a grade to be No. 1, or Grade A, is no guarantee that the produce is first quality, as the highest grades are U.S. Extra Fancy and U.S. Fancy, followed by No. 1 (Grade A) and No. 2. Grade standards are based upon ripeness, color, and uniformity of size and shape. Bruise spots and decay are also considered.

The next best thing to compulsory grading is to become familiar with what to look for and how to test for the best. Produce dealers can be questioned as to grade, quality, where grown, freshness, and ripeness. While better and higher grades may show a slight difference in price, they will prove to be more beneficial in terms of waste, quality, and nutrients.

The Produce Grab Bag

Although pre-packaged produce is more attractive in appearance and motivates the consumer to buy, it has many drawbacks. Generally, it is not of uniform size, thickness, or degree of ripeness. Damaged and spoiled produce is frequently disguised by having the bad area placed face-down in the container. The apparent freshness of the top layer of a box of berries is no guarantee the remainder will be the same, and the rubber-banded plastic coverings add to the difficulty of determining quality. A consumer has the right to examine produce before purchasing and to know what he or she is paying for.

SPRAYING AND WATER SOAKING VEGETABLES   Spraying and water soaking vegetables and greens, a practice frequently carried out by retail produce suppliers, perks them up temporarily but cuts down on their life in the long run. Cutting off outer leaves and roots also has a deleterious effect. One answer to this and similar problems is the obvious one of purchasing elsewhere, and making such reasons known.

PREPARATION FOR COOKING: PEELING, SLICING, CHOPPING

The outer skin of most vegetables is tough and often bitter, and should be removed before cooking. It acts as a protective coating for the plant but slows up cooking action when left on, giving poor results. One exception would be new, very young vegetables such as potatoes and baby carrots.

To achieve the best results, cut vegetables into relatively small pieces of uniform size and thickness. Both manual and electric slicing machines are readily available. Food processors and some electric mixers come equipped with slicing attachments. There are also hand slicers, which recall bygone days but still find a place on the shelves of most housewares outlets, as well as ruffle-shape cutters which are used to give vegetables such as turnips and carrots a more attractive appearance.

Using a good sharp knife, vegetables can be cut into varying shapes and combined. They can be sliced diagonally, cut into cubes and diamonds or julienne strips of different thicknesses, sculptured into miniature shapes, or scouped out into round balls. To assure that vegetables will be uniformly cooked, cut them into equal size pieces.

When cooking a number of different vegetables in the same pot, add the larger and coarser ones first.

Specific preparation of the various vegetables is dealt with on an individual basis.

VEGETABLE COOKING THEORY

1. Procedures which generally result in perfectly cooked vegetables have one outstanding feature in common: *relatively short cooking periods*. Both the large capacity boiling water procedure and stir-frying take about 3 to 5 minutes, as compared with the 15 or 20 minutes required for simmering vegetables in a small amount of water.

2. The structure of vegetables, in contrast to that of meats, quickly changes on exposure to heat. The temperature should be such that the heat travels to the center quickly and evenly. The correct degree of heat should be maintained so that the temperature is neither too high nor too low. For instance, the receptacle should be left uncovered during cooking, otherwise the steam created by the trapped heat would break down the constituents and the juices would escape into the pot, resulting in colorless, tasteless, and fiberless vegetables having little or no flavor.

3. One of the contributing factors to all successful cooking is a gradual, even exposure to heat, however fast or slow the particular procedure. In stir-frying, the vegetables are tossed about in the wok as they are cooked and not allowed to remain in one hot spot, and in the large capacity boiling water procedure they toss and swim about in the water with the same freedom as foods cooked in deep fat.

4. The high heat setting and the temperatures of the solutions used in both the stir-frying and the boiling water procedure make allowance for a drop in temperature when the uncooked vegetables are added. When properly carried out, both assure a drop in temperature not below the 150° F. (65° C.) mark.

5. With the exception of the liquid, which is generally a combination of oil, soy sauce, sherry, and stock added at a specified time and in that order, the Chinese method of cooking vegetables in a wok over high heat is based on the same theory as that of the boiling water method. Stir-frying, however, requires a much better understanding of the underlying theory, and is a good deal more difficult. While success in most areas and modes of cooking depends on knowing what you are doing and why, stir-frying is the prime example of a procedure that requires split-second responses, supported by good judgment and a firm knowledge of general cooking theory.

6. Poor results occur when vegetables are cooked in a small quantity of water in a covered pot, over medium to low heat, for a relatively long cooking period. This procedure is more satisfactorily applied to making stock, where the aim is to extract the vegetable juices and thereby enrich the water solution. The method came about more or less as a result of the discovery that high heat destroys vitamins; however, no consideration was given to the *length* of the cooking period nor to the other subtle changes that take place in the chemistry and nutritive values of vegetables.

7. The oil used in stir-frying, deep-fat frying, and sautéing contributes in that it coats the vegetables, thereby giving them some protection against loss of juices, but only, however, when used in conjunction with the other aspects of these particular procedures.

8. Water reaches the boiling point at 212° F. (100° C.), however fast or slow it is boiling. The bubbles and movement of the water is caused by escaping steam, which is lost heat. A pinch of salt or sugar added to the water increases the density,

and the temperature will rise to 224° F. (106° C.) before the steam escapes.

9. In the final analysis, the procedure that is best is the one that gives the best results. This can be determined more or less by the flavor, texture, color, and aroma of the cooked food.

COOKING TESTS

Vegetables should be cooked just long enough for the heat to reach the center. Any further exposure will result in a breakdown of the nutrients and juice loss.

Doneness is signalled by a slight resistance when fork-tested or a fairly crunchy texture when tasted. Vegetables should be carefully watched toward the end of the cooking period and removed immediately when cooked to the right degree. Consideration should be given to the fact that they will retain a certain amount of heat and continue to cook to a slight degree upon being removed, especially if they are enveloped by steam, such as when they are drained.

The fresher the vegetable, the shorter the cooking period. Freshly picked home-garden vegetables require one-third the cooking time of vegetables which have been exposed to long periods of cold storage. Older vegetables, as compared to younger and tenderer ones, also require longer cooking periods.

STOPPING THE COOKING ACTION If vegetables are to be served somewhat later, stop the cooking action and cool quickly by tossing in the air to remove trapped heat and steam. Vegetables may also be placed over a container of very cold water. However, do not plunge them into cold water, as this tends to diminish their flavor, despite heightening the color somewhat. If properly cooked and cooled as recommended, not only will vegetables be bright enough, but they will retain more of their natural coloring. The cold water bath has a particularly deleterious effect on certain vegetables. Green beans, for instance, will turn a much brighter green, but will also become rubbery and lose a good deal of their flavor.

KEEPING WARM Vegetables may be kept warm in a 160° F. (71° C.)

oven, *uncovered*, otherwise trapped heat and steam will result in further cooking and soggy, overcooked vegetables.

REHEATING One of the most satisfactory methods of reheating cooked vegetables is to use heat-sealed, boilable plastic pouches. Place in boiling water just long enough to heat through.

GARNISHES Use garnishes that are simple, fresh, and flavorful whenever possible. Turnips and carrots shaped into flowers and roses made from tomato skins are traditional garnishes. These decorations belong to a nineteenth-century approach characterized by the lavishness of such decorations but a relative lack of attention to the temperature and freshness of food. Today they are sometimes used to detract from an otherwise stale dish.

To add color, contrast, and design, use sprigs of fresh crisp greens such as watercress or parsley, yolks and whites of hard-boiled eggs, carrot curls, various shaped lemon slices, pimientos cut into julienne strips, or chopped fresh parsley.

Adding Precooked Vegetables to Sauces and Other Preparations

Preheat any sauce to which cooked vegetables are to be added, so that it will act as a coating and not, on the other hand, drain them of their nutrients while it slowly reheats. Allow vegetables to remain in sauce just long enough to heat through and blend flavors.

Whenever vegetables are to form part of such dishes as casseroles and vegetable-meat pies, they should be only partially cooked or blanched, since they will be subjected to further cooking. If vegetables are still fairly crisp, colorful, and succulent when a casserole or other preparation is cooked, they will add immeasurably to it; however, if they are dull, soggy, and lacking in flavor as a result of being overcooked, they will only serve to detract.

When vegetables are to form part of a cooked preparation which is to be frozen for later use, cook for approximately 1 or 2 minutes after water returns to boiling point, or until fairly crisp, as the exposure to freezing temperatures will result in a certain breakdown.

PRESERVING METHODS:
FREEZING VS. CANNING

FREEZING VEGETABLES Peel and uniformly slice vegetables, and rinse under cold running water. Bring a large pot of water to a full boil (2½ to 3½ quart [2.5-3.5 l] capacity for every 2 to 3 pounds [900 to 1350 g] of vegetables). Add a pinch of salt along with vegetables and bring water back to boiling point over high heat. Cook, uncovered, for approximately 1 or 2 minutes, depending on thickness. Vegetables will be fairly crisp when done. Remove and drain. Using a colander, toss in air to allow trapped heat and steam to escape, thus keeping further cooking to a minimum. Cool as quickly as possible but do not douse in cold water.

When completely cool, pack in plastic bags or containers as airtight and moisture-proof as possible. Heat-sealed plastic pouches work extremely well and may be taken directly from freezer and placed in boiling water for anywhere from 10 to 15 minutes, or until thawed and heated through.

Mark dates of freezing on bags or containers using a crayon-type pencil; limit storage period to 6 months.

Vegetables may be combined with lemon butter, sauces, herbs, or grated cheese. Chill all ingredients before sealing and freezing. Freeze combinations of vegetables using various colors and textures as a guide, or check for unusual and original vegetable combinations at the supermarket.

CANNING* This method of preserving vegetables is generally much more time-consuming. It requires extreme care with regard to temperature control and frequently results in flavor loss and unfavorable changes in texture and color, particularly if the vegetables are stored in water for any length of time.

STORING FRESH VEGETABLES
AND GREENS

Store fresh produce in any type of moisture-proof container, such as heat-sealed or "zipper-locked" plastic bags, in the produce bin of refrigerator. The insertion of a few paper towels will act as an absorbent for excess moisture.

*Publications on canning techniques may be obtained by writing the Superintendent of Documents, Government Printing Office, Washington, D.C. 20402.

If produce, particularly greens, has been washed under running water, dry thoroughly before storing. However, most vegetables purchased from the supermarket keep best when stored unwashed.

There are crispers especially designed for storing washed greens, as well as salad baskets which are whirled around to remove moisture. When thoroughly washed and dried, a variety of salad greens can be stored in the refrigerator for several days and used as needed.

To store greens such as broccoli, asparagus, and watercress, place in an open mouth receptacle, such as a pitcher, and add about an inch or so (2-3 cm) of cold water. Arrange a plastic bag loosely over tops and set in refrigerator. Stored in this manner, green vegetables will keep for several days.

COOKING PROCEDURES FOR VEGETABLES AND GREENS

BOILING   Vegetables will retain their flavor, color, and texture when cooked in an uncovered pot of lightly salted boiling water that is of sufficient capacity to bring the water temperature back to somewhere between 150° F. (65° C.) and 210° F. (99° C.) at the time the vegetables are added. Vegetables should also have enough room to swim around while cooking.

For every 2 to 3 pounds (900 to 1350 g) of vegetables, bring 3 to 4 quarts (3-4 l) of water to a full boil over high heat. Add a pinch of salt along with the peeled and uniformly sliced vegetables. Maintain a high temperature setting throughout the cooking period and leave the pot uncovered. Cook until slightly crisp when fork-tested.

All vegetables peeled and prepared in this manner will cook in a relatively short period. Peeled broccoli and asparagus, for example, will cook in approximately 2 to 4 minutes, depending on size and thickness. Most other vegetables, when peeled and cut into small pieces of a uniform size and thickness, rarely take longer than 5 or 6 minutes to cook, and some require even less time.

STIR-FRYING   Stir-frying requires a wok, or pan similar in shape, constructed of very thin metal—the thinner the metal, the faster it conducts the heat. A wok, which has a rounded rather than a flat bottom, usually comes accompanied by a separate metal rim for use over a regular gas burner.

Set wok over high heat until hot enough to make a drop of water sizzle. (Home ranges, of course, do not produce the intense heat of the commercial ones found in Chinese restaurants.) Add a small amount of oil, a few drops of soy sauce, and a pinch of salt. Oil is hot enough when it runs freely, is clear, and is not smoking. If oil shows signs of smoking, remove from heat for a few seconds. When oil is the correct temperature, add a proportionately small amount of sherry and stock, pouring it along the inside rim of pan so that it will be heated through before coming in contact with the hot oil.

Add vegetables in small amounts in order to maintain the high temperature of the oil and liquids. Keep a constant check on the heat to ensure that the correct temperature is maintained. *Vegetables must cook quickly, but not be scorched.* On the other hand, if cooked too slowly, their goodness will run into the pan and they will become soggy and limp and lose both flavor and color. Stir quickly but carefully. Coarse vegetables are cooked first, followed by the more tender ones. Some vegetables, such as scallions, take but a few seconds. Timing is of the utmost importance.

One kind of vegetable, or two or three of the same texture, may be cooked at a time. Remove vegetables as cooked and set aside. When all have been stir-fried, return to pan, along with any cooked meat or fish that is to form part of the dish.*

Add just enough stock to moisten the dish and blend flavors. Unless stock is hot, add in a circular motion along the inside of rim. The rule is that cold liquids toughen meats and draw out juices from vegetables.

Sauce may be thickened using cornstarch paste, prepared by mixing 2 tablespoons of stock, sherry, or water with 1 tablespoon cornstarch. This paste should be prepared in advance (as should all other ingredients) but will require last minute stirring, as it separates. Add gradually, stirring until vegetables glisten and sauce is slightly thick and smooth. A good, rich gelatinous stock will give sauce a velvety smooth appearance.

If not serving at once, set in a preheated 160° F. (71° C.) oven, *uncovered*.

BLANCHING   Blanching is identical to what has been termed the

---

*Note that during final steps, pan must still be kept at the correct temperature—hot but not smoking.

boiling water procedure except that the cooking period is considerably shorter. Vegetables peeled and cut into pieces approximately ⅛" (.3 cm) thick require about 60 seconds for blanching, once the water has returned to a boil. Vegetables which are left whole or quartered require anywhere from 3 to 7 minutes, depending on size and thickness.*

BRAISING   Prepare vegetable and blanch for 1 or 2 minutes. Drain and tie into bunches, or simply place in a braising pan containing melted butter. Cover pan and set in a preheated 300° F. (149° C.) oven for about 5 minutes, or long enough to exude some of the moisture. Remove and add enough heated stock to cover vegetables. Cover tightly and cook very gently until barely tender, or until some resistance is met at the point of a fork. Transfer to a warm serving dish and remove strings if these have been used. Set pan over high heat and reduce stock by two-thirds before pouring over vegetable.

STEAMING   Add boiling water to lower section of steamer or pot to a height of approximately 1 to 2 inches (3 to 5 cm). *Water should not come in contact with vegetables.* Place prepared vegetables in upper section, on a rack or in a colander or regular steamer basket. Cover and cook over medium heat (water should be boiling at all times) until vegetable has reached the proper degree of doneness. Check occasionally to see that water has not been depleted.

Steaming is a slower procedure than that of boiling. It is, however, especially suited to young vegetables such as small new potatoes, carrots, and cauliflower, all of which are generally left whole with their skins intact.

DEEP-FRYING   If the proper procedure is understood and followed, deep-frying can be a very satisfactory way to cook morsels of vegetables. They are cooked quickly at relatively high temperatures, based on the same theory as the boiling water procedure. Electric fryers, thermostatically controlled, have made this type of cooking fairly scientific.

Scrub vegetables clean before peeling, and dry thoroughly. Peel and cut up vegetables into bite size pieces, strips, or cubes. Preheat oil to 375° F. (190° C.). Dip vegetables in batter or use a Breadcrumb Coating (see Chapter 3, Coatings for Deep-Frying).

*This procedure is generally referred to as parboiling, the cooking period is slightly longer than in blanching. In both procedures the vegetables are only partially cooked.

When oil has reached the correct temperature, place vegetables in a frying basket and lower into fryer. Most vegetables will cook in less than 1 minute. Bear in mind that they will continue to cook and the heat will reach the center sometime after removal. If they are not overcrowded, vegetables will rise to the top and float when done.

To keep warm, set in a 160° F. (71° C.) oven, *uncovered*, otherwise trapped heat will result in soggy vegetables inside and out.

Dried Vegetables

Dried beans, peas, limas, and lentils can be put to a variety of uses. They make excellent soups, or they may be served as an accompanying vegetable, used in salads, or added to vegetable soups. They can stand on their own as a main dish, particularly when combined with lean salt pork, ham, ground beef, or rice.

To prepare, sort dried vegetables and remove any that are discolored or blemished. Place in a strainer and wash under cold running water. To allow for swelling, transfer to a pot of at least double the capacity of the dried vegetable. Cover with cold water and soak for several hours or overnight. Bring soaked vegetable to a slow simmer over low heat, adding more water if necessary. Vegetable may then be cooked in one of two ways: (1) Cover pot, add seasoning and flavorings and continue barely to simmer until tender. (This is a type of stove-top braising.) (2) Transfer vegetable and liquid to an ovenproof dish, such as a bean crock, add seasoning and flavorings, and braise in a 225° F. (107° C.) oven until tender.

In both procedures, vegetable should be fully covered with liquid throughout the cooking period to prevent drying and hardening.

Cooking time will vary depending on size of dried vegetable. Dried beans require about 5 or 6 hours, while smaller vegetables, such as peas, cook in approximately 3 to 4 hours.

When salt pork or ham is added to vegetable as a flavoring, salt is omitted.

Frozen Vegetables

When using commercially frozen and packaged vegetables, disregard package directions about cooking in a small amount of water. The flavor and texture of a packaged frozen vegetable are best retained when prepared as follows: Melt 1 teaspoon butter in a saucepan and add vegetable. Add no water. Season with salt and pepper and sprinkle with a few drops of fresh lemon juice. Herbs may be added to heighten flavor. Cover and set over medium low heat until defrosted and heated through. Remove and serve. A frozen vegetable is best if cooked just prior to serving.

To hasten cooking, remove package half an hour or so before serving, but do not totally defrost. Hitting an unopened package of certain frozen vegetables, such as peas, against a hard surface will break them up, and will not only shorten their cooking time, but will allow for more even cooking.

Boil-proof plastic pouches of vegetables are cooked by placing in boiling water in an uncovered saucepan for about 10 to 15 minutes, or until defrosted and heated through.

Canned Vegetables

To heat, drain off any liquid vegetable is packed in and reserve for stockpot. Melt a teaspoon of butter in a saucepan and add drained vegetable. Season to taste with salt and pepper and sprinkle on a few drops fresh lemon juice. Dried or fresh herbs may be used to heighten flavor. Cover and cook over medium low heat until heated through.

VARIOUS WAYS TO SERVE VEGETABLES

LEMON BUTTER   Melt 1 or 2 tablespoons of butter in a saucepan, add a pinch or two of sugar, a few drops of lemon juice, and salt and pepper to taste. Add to vegetables and toss.

SAUCES   Most sauces combine well with vegetables, either directly or served on the side. Lemon Sauce, White Sauce, tomato-based sauces, Cheese Sauce, and Hollandaise are particularly suitable (Chapter 2, under Sauce section).

HERBS AND SEASONINGS   Dried and fresh herbs and seasonings can be used to heighten the flavor of vegetables, particularly the bland ones. Parsley, dill, chervil, tarragon, basil, and mint are among those most commonly used. A few grains of garlic powder will give vegetables a lift, particularly when used in conjunction with a few drops of lemon juice.

MAITRE D'HOTEL BUTTER Add 1 tablespoon fresh lemon juice to 2 tablespoons finely chopped parsley. Blend with 6 tablespoons softened butter and season to taste with salt and white pepper. Form into a block and store in refrigerator, cutting off slices as needed. Other herbs or flavors, such as finely chopped tarragon, dill, garlic juice, onion juice, or dried mustard may be substituted for the parsley. The amounts used will be according to taste.

AU GRATIN Pour a thin layer of sauce, such as White Sauce or Cheese Sauce, over vegetable and sprinkle with grated cheese (Parmesan, Cheddar, or Swiss). Set under a preheated broiler or in a 500° F. (260° C.) oven until lightly browned.

MILANESE Sprinkle with grated Parmesan cheese and pour over nut-brown butter, or dot lightly with butter to prevent cheese from burning and drying out. Set under preheated broiler or in 500° F. (260° C.) oven until lightly browned.

ROMANO Sauté a crushed garlic clove in olive oil and add the juice of one small lemon. Strain and add to vegetable. Toss and garnish with finely chopped fresh parsley.

NUT-BROWN BUTTER Melt desired quantity of butter over medium heat until light brown in color. Add salt and pepper to taste, along with a few drops of fresh lemon juice.

POLONAISE Mix finely chopped fresh parsley with chopped hard-boiled egg yolk and spread over surface of vegetable. Lightly sprinkle breadcrumbs over parsley-egg yolk mixture. Lightly dot with butter and set under a preheated broiler until lightly browned.

NUTS AND SEEDS Fry nuts in butter for a few minutes over low heat, or set in a preheated 325° F. (163° C.) oven. Remove, add to vegetables, and toss. Seeds such as sesame and sunflower give vegetables a lift.

GLAZING Glaze vegetables using 1 or 2 tablespoons of flavored or plain melted butter. To heighten glaze, add a pinch of sugar, stirring until dissolved. Sweet vegetables, such as sweet potatoes, take nicely to honey, brown sugar, or one of the fruit glazes.

COMBINATIONS Various combinations of vegetables can result in an entirely new taste experience. Almost all vegetables combine well, but colors, textures, and the time when certain vegetables are in season are fairly reliable guidelines. Vegetables may be cut into contrasting shapes such as rounds, cubes, or julienne strips for variation. Check packages of commercially frozen vegetables for interesting combinations.

SOUR CREAM DRESSING Mix 1 tablespoon horseradish and a few drops of lemon juice with one pint (480 ml) of sour cream. Add a tablespoon finely chopped dill and blend in.

PURCHASING TIPS, PREPARATION, RECOMMENDED COOKING PROCEDURES, AND SERVING SUGGESTIONS

Artichokes

To check the quality of artichokes cut away darkened portion at end of stem to determine if remaining area is white and moist. The whole artichoke should be of a good color with unblemished leaves.

To prepare, trim top leaves straight across, leaving an opening. Cut out the inside, known as the choke. Round off leaves with scissors to give a more attractive appearance. Wash well in salted water and turn upside down to drain.

COOKING SUGGESTIONS Braise, or cook using boiling water procedure. Leaves will pull out easily when cooked and bottom of artichoke will be tender when fork-tested.

SERVING SUGGESTIONS Lemon Butter. Plain melted butter. Oil and Vinegar Dressing. Hollandaise Sauce.

Asparagus

Look for asparagus that are tightly folded near the top—if leaves have already formed, they have lost much of their flavor. For evenness in cooking select asparagus that are uniform in size.

To prepare, snap off tough bottom portion. Wash and drain. Remove outer skin, which is both tough and bitter, using a vegetable peeler. To facilitate serving, tie in small bunches using string, leaving one free for testing.

COOKING SUGGESTIONS Using boiling water procedure, vegetable will cook in from 2 to 4 minutes, depending on size and thickness. There should be considerable resistance when fork-tested. Be careful not to overcook. Drain at once.

SERVING SUGGESTIONS Lemon Butter. Polonaise. Au Gratin. White or Cheese Sauce. Lemon Hollandaise Sauce. Asparagus may be made into soups, creamed and molded, served cold in salads, or used in soufflés and omelets.

Green Beans and Wax Beans

Beans are fresh when they snap easily and are bright in color. Select beans that are small to medium in size, as large ones are tough and rubbery.

To prepare, trim off ends. For best results, cut into ½″ (1 cm) slices or cook whole.

COOKING SUGGESTIONS Using boiling water procedure, beans will cook in a matter of minutes. They should be bright in color and slightly crisp when fork-tested.

SERVING SUGGESTIONS Lemon Butter. Lemon, White, Cheese, or Tomato Sauce. Tossed with slivered almonds. Oil and Vinegar Dressing. Beans combine well with many other vegetables.

Beets

Select beets that are smooth skinned and have no blemishes—whenever possible with both leaves and stems attached. Leaves should be straight and not curled and bent.

To prepare, peel and cut into uniform size slices, strips, or cubes.

COOKING SUGGESTIONS   Boiling water procedure. Vegetable retains more of its flavor and texture if removed and drained when there is considerable resistance when fork-tested. Length of cooking period will depend on size and tenderness.

SERVING SUGGESTIONS   Plain melted butter. Sour Cream Dressing. Orange Sauce. Oil and Vinegar Dressing. Plain vinegar. Combined with onion rings in a salad.

Broccoli

This vegetable is freshest when buds are very tightly closed. It should be bright green in color and have no blemishes. Select ones with short stems.

To prepare, remove woody portion from stem and peel away tough outer fiber. Cut stems into uniform size lengths and thicknesses.

COOKING SUGGESTIONS   Broccoli will cook in from 2 to 5 minutes, using boiling water procedure, depending on size and tenderness. It may also be steamed. A careful watch should be kept on this vegetable, as it should be fairly firm and bright green in color when removed from heat.

SERVING SUGGESTIONS   Lemon Butter. Maitre d' Butter. Tossed with slivered almonds. Au Gratin. Lemon, Cheese, White or Tomato Sauce. Milanese. Romano.

Brussels Sprouts

Select firm, bright green sprouts with leaves tightly wrapped and not puffing out. If storage results in a withered and yellow appearance, they have lost most of their flavor and should be discarded.

To prepare, remove any outside leaves that are blemished and soak in cold salted water for about 30 seconds. Turn upside down and drain.

COOKING SUGGESTIONS   They may be steamed or cooked using the boiling water procedure. They should be removed from heat when they are bright green in color and not too soft.

SERVING SUGGESTIONS Plain melted butter. Nut-Brown Butter. White or Cheese Sauce. Milanese.

Cabbage

There are several varieties of cabbage; among the most common are white, savoy, and red cabbage. Young and tender cabbage has closely packed leaves and a faint aroma. Its leaves are unwithered. Beware of cabbage with too many outside leaves removed, and check for splits, as this usually indicates worms at the center.

To prepare, remove core and soak in cold salted water for about 30 seconds. Turn upside down and drain. Quarter, slice, or cut into uniform size pieces.

COOKING SUGGESTIONS Steam or cook using boiling water procedure, being careful not to overcook. Finely sliced cabbage requires 3 to 4 minutes to cook once water returns to boiling point. Properly cooked, cabbage will be slightly crisp and bright in color with a sweet aroma rather than a sour odor.

SERVING SUGGESTIONS Plain melted butter. Nut-Brown Butter. Au Gratin. Salads.

Carrots

Select firm skinned, brightly colored carrots with their tops attached whenever possible. Plastic wrapped carrots that have been exposed to long periods of cold storage have little or no flavor. If the green portion near the stem has spread, carrots are old and tough. Also, look for small or medium-size carrots rather than large ones which are sometimes tough.

To prepare, peel and cut carrots into slices, sticks or olive shapes of uniform size and thickness. Very attractive slices may be made using a fluted cutter designed for this purpose.

COOKING SUGGESTIONS Stir-fry, steam, or cook using boiling water procedure. Remove from heat while still bright in color and slightly crisp.

SERVING SUGGESTIONS Lemon or White Sauce. Lemon Butter. Maitre d' Butter. Au Gratin. Carrots combine well with many other vegetables lending color, flavor, and texture contrast.

Celery

Select celery that is firm, tightly packed, and without blemishes. Leaves should be bright in color and show no signs of wilting.

To prepare, trim tops from stalk—leaves and all—and reserve for stock pot. Pare off the tough outer fibers, using a sharp knife or vegetable peeler. Wash, and if being stored, dry thoroughly using paper towels. Cut stalks diagonally into uniform size pieces to give an attractive appearance, or cut in halves or quarters for braising.

COOKING SUGGESTIONS Stir-fry, braise, or cook using boiling water procedure. The texture of celery should be quite crisp when served, which does not necessarily preclude its being tender. Peeling this vegetable is important if you wish to have good results in cooking.

SERVING SUGGESTIONS White or Cheese Sauce. Au Gratin. Combines well with most other vegetables.

Cauliflower

This vegetable is best when it is young and creamy white and the heads are tightly packed. Leaves should be firm and green and show no sign of wilting. Check underside to see it shows no sign of spoilage.

To prepare, soak for 30 seconds in cold salted water. Remove and turn upside down to drain. Remove core and cut into small uniform size flowerets.

COOKING SUGGESTIONS Steam or cook using boiling water procedure. Cauliflower takes but a few minutes to cook, and care should be taken to remove from heat while it is fairly firm and not mushy. If properly cooked, there will be no strong odor.

SERVING SUGGESTIONS   Cheese or White Sauce. Hollandaise. Plain melted butter. Au Gratin. Nut-Brown Butter.

Corn

Leaves should be tightly wrapped around the husks and of a good color. The practice of drawing back the husks or removing them sometime before cooking is inadvisable, as this results in loss of flavor and texture. Select ears that are young and tender as opposed to overly mature ones, store them in a cool place until ready to use.

COOKING SUGGESTIONS   Steam or cook using boiling water procedure. Care should be taken not to overcook corn. Uncooked kernels may be stripped from the cob and gently fried in a little butter. Corn should have considerable texture when served and not be mushy.

SERVING SUGGESTIONS   Corn on the cob is served with plain melted butter. Corn kernels may be served with a White Sauce or Tomato Sauce or combined with other vegetables such as green peppers, tomatoes, onions, and mild red peppers.

Cucumbers

Fresh cucumbers are juicy and very crisp. They are best when slim and firm; if bulbous and soft, they will have an abundance of seeds and very little flavor.
   To prepare, peel and slice in half. Remove seeds and cut into ½" (1 cm) slices or strips of a uniform size and thickness.

COOKING SUGGESTIONS   Cucumbers are mostly eaten raw, but they may be blanched, lightly fried, and served hot as a vegetable. Watch carefully, as this vegetable should be served fairly crisp.

SERVING SUGGESTIONS   Cheese Sauce using Bleu or Roquefort cheese. Lemon Butter. Maitre d' Butter. Sour Cream Dressing. Oil and Vinegar Dressing. In all kinds of salads.

Eggplant

Select young eggplant with firm, smooth skins. Eggplant should be heavy for its size, and the stem and green segments should adhere tightly to the skin. If these parts are somewhat detached, seeds and pulp will have turned dark.

Preparation of eggplant will depend on the cooking procedure being used. If pan-frying or deep-frying, peel and cut into slices before coating with a mixture of breadcrumbs and grated cheese. If it is to be stuffed, cut eggplant in half lengthwise and trim peel around edges. Slice center of each portion criss-cross fashion in order to facilitate cooking. Blanch, drain, and remove pulp, being careful not to break skin. Puree pulp in a food processor or foodmill and season to taste. Carefully spoon this mixture back into skin, and top with a mixture of grated cheese and seasoned breadcrumbs. Dot with butter and set under broiler until lightly browned.

SERVING SUGGESTIONS   Tomato Sauce. Milanese. Au Gratin.

Endive

Select endive that are firm and have not begun to wilt.

To prepare, soak in cold salted water for about 30 seconds and turn upside down to drain.

COOKING SUGGESTIONS   Blanch for about a minute to remove bitterness and finish cooking by braising. Endive may also be blanched and then fried over low heat in melted butter.

SERVING SUGGESTIONS   Lemon Butter. White Sauce. Au Gratin.

Greens

Select greens that are deep green in color with tightly curled leaves. Avoid coarse and stringy greens or those with large curved leaves (an indication of overgrowth). Whenever possible, choose greens with their roots intact and ones that have not been doused in water.

To prepare such greens as spinach, beet tops, kale, collards, Swiss chard, and dandelion, wash just prior to cooking, removing all sediment. Lay greens flat in a pile and fold over stems. Wrap leaves over stems, envelope fashion, and proceed to cut across, using a sharp knife. Prepared in this manner, stems and leaves will cook evenly, particularly if stems are somewhat coarse.

COOKING SUGGESTIONS Steam or cook using boiling water procedure. Greens cook in a matter of a few minutes with the boiling water method. They should retain their deep green hue.

SERVING SUGGESTIONS White Sauce. Melted butter. Plain vinegar. Lemon Sauce. Raw in salads.

Lettuce

Heads should be crisp and of a good color. Some lettuce, such as iceberg, can be checked by weighing to determine its fullness. If lettuce has been doused in water, the inside will be soft and have lost some of its flavor. Select heads with the outer leaves intact, whenever possible. There are many different varieties—Romaine, Boston, chicory, iceberg.

To prepare, wash under cold running water. If using in a salad, dry thoroughly, otherwise dressing will run off and settle at the bottom and lettuce will tend to wilt.

COOKING SUGGESTIONS While lettuce is generally served uncooked, it may be blanched and served hot. It is best when cooked in its own moisture in a covered pot over medium to low heat. Lettuce may also be used to supply the moisture as a bed for cooking very young vegetables, such as new peas and baby carrots.

SERVING SUGGESTIONS Lemon Butter. Plain melted butter. Raw in salads.

Mushrooms

The flesh of mushrooms should be white when the skin is raised, and they should be firm. If cooking whole, select mushrooms which are uniform in size.

To prepare, remove peel from cap using fingers. Stems are peeled using a sharp knife. (Wash peelings and reserve for stockpot, soups, or sauces.) If done carefully, all dirt and grime will be removed with peel, making it unnecessary to wash mushrooms. Leaving the peel on and washing mushrooms has certain drawbacks. It is very difficult to remove all grime without thoroughly dousing them, and this detracts considerably from their flavor and texture. Washing is also more time-consuming, as it takes but a second or two to peel a fully ripe mushroom. Finally, a mushroom that has been watersoaked tends to stew rather than fry, and it will not brown. Unpeeled mushrooms require longer cooking periods, resulting in loss of flavor and texture.

Mushrooms may be left whole or sliced diagonally to the desired thickness. They may also be fluted, using a special knife, to give a more attractive appearance.

COOKING SUGGESTIONS Mushrooms may be fried, stir-fried, sautéed, or broiled. Remove from pan as soon as they are golden brown, otherwise they will turn grey. Mushrooms are very tender and require a relatively short cooking period.

SERVING SUGGESTIONS Romano. Au Gratin. White or Lemon Sauce. Maitre d' Butter. Mushrooms are frequently used as a flavoring additive, but should not be neglected as a vegetable in their own right. Mushrooms are indigenous to the United States and make an excellent substitute for truffles.

Onion Family

Some of the many different varieties of onions are ordinary white, Spanish, Bermuda, pearl, purple, garlic, scallions, shallots, and leeks. All are best when firm and unblemished.

The outer skin of most onions is removed before cooking. When garlic cloves are knocked against a hard surface, the outside peel is easily removed. With the exception of leeks, which must be cut through the center and held under cold running water to remove sandy particles, peeled onions are not washed before cooking.

COOKING SUGGESTIONS When chopped, gently fry over low heat until onions take on a translucent appearance. Cooked onions should be slightly crunchy—overcooked onions are soft and have lost most of their flavor. Do not overcrowd pan, or they will stew rather than fry. Whole onions, such as ordinary white or pearl onions, may be blanched and either braised in the oven or fried over low heat in a small amount of butter. Large onions, such as Bermuda or Spanish, may be sliced into rings, dipped in batter or coated with breadcrumbs, and deep-fried. Chives, which is a type of green stalk, are chopped and added at the last moment of cooking.

SERVING SUGGESTIONS   Glazed. Au Gratin. White or Cheese Sauce. Plain melted butter. Onions are used as a flavoring additive for a wide variety of preparations.

Parsnips

This vegetable is best when it is firm, light in color, and has no blemishes. If tip begins to turn brown and vegetable is easily bent, it should be discarded. Extra large parsnips may be tough and have a strong flavor. The parsnip has a distinctive flavor and warrants much greater attention than it is generally shown.

To prepare, peel and cut or slice into pieces of uniform size and thickness.

COOKING SUGGESTIONS   Cook using boiling water procedure. Vegetable should be removed from heat while there is some resistance when fork-tested.

SERVING SUGGESTIONS   Plain melted butter. Au Gratin. White Sauce. Maitre d' Butter.

Peas

When fresh, pod is crisp and bright green in color and will show signs of sap when punctured. Select peas that are more or less uniform in size, and discard those that are beginning to wither and turn yellow.

To prepare, break open pods and remove peas. When using snow peas, stem and strings are removed and pod is left whole.

COOKING SUGGESTIONS   Stir-fry, steam, or use boiling water procedure.

SERVING SUGGESTIONS Plain melted butter. White Sauce. Lemon Butter. Maitre d' Butter. Peas combine well with many different vegetables.

Peppers (Green and Red)

Sweet peppers can be either green or red, whereas hot peppers are always red. One of the best tests for freshness is the old nose test. They should give off the beautiful aroma typical of a fresh pepper. A comparison may be made with a dark, thick-skinned pepper that may have been in cold storage for a period. Peppers should be light in color and have no blemishes. Young and tender peppers are best for frying, whereas larger and more mature ones are suitable for stuffing.

To prepare, wash and dry thoroughly. Cut off top and remove inside pulp and seeds. Leave whole when used for stuffing, otherwise cut into julienne strips, cubes, or diamonds.

COOKING SUGGESTIONS Stuffed peppers are braised. Cut up peppers are fried, stir-fried, or sautéed. Overcooking leaves this vegetable limp, dull in color, and with a somewhat bitter flavor. Vegetable is properly cooked when it takes on a slightly translucent appearance.

SERVING SUGGESTIONS Peppers are used extensively as flavoring additives and in combination with other vegetables. Raw sweet peppers make an excellent salad, particularly when young and tender, or they may be combined with other raw vegetables and greens and served with a dressing.

Potatoes

Potatoes are, as everybody knows, part of the staple diet
of the English people, their taking in a way the same
place as the bread of the Frenchman, of which we eat so much,
and they are cultivated with great care in England.
The introduction en masse of this vegetable to the European
countries was the greatest service done to the industry
this century.

Antoine Careme (1784-1835)

It is difficult to judge a potato by its exterior, aside from the fact that it should be firm to the touch. For instance, the whitest potato with the smoothest skin does not necessarily have the best flavor and texture. The soil in which potatoes are grown and the area they come from have a definite bearing on their flavor and overall quality. There is such a variety of potatoes grown—in as many different areas—that grade is one of the best guides. Top grades are usually designated as Extra Fancy and Fancy. Grade A (No. 1) is next in line.

To prepare, peel, wash and cover with cold water until ready to cook to avoid discoloration. Cut into slices, strips, cubes, rounds, olive shapes, or leave whole. Sliced or cut up potatoes cook in a relatively short time and can be put to many uses. Baking potatoes and young new potatoes are scrubbed clean under running water, or wiped clean with a damp cloth.

COOKING SUGGESTIONS   Potatoes may be cooked in a variety of ways: Baked, steamed, pan-fried, deep-fried, blanched and braised, or cooked using the boiling water procedure. The degree to which potatoes are cooked will depend on how they are to be served. For instance, if potatoes are to be riced or mashed, they should be cooked until fairly tender—otherwise there should be a slight resistance when fork-tested. Upon removal from the heat source, potatoes will continue cooking longer than most other vegetables.

Baked potatoes will be mealier if pricked with a fork beforehand to allow some of the steam to escape. The length of time required to bake a potato depends on its size; however, a fairly large potato at refrigerator temperature requires about an hour in a preheated 375° F. (190° C.) oven.

When potatoes are to be mashed, combine with hot milk as soon as they are cooked in order to keep them white and to avoid discoloration.

Riced potatoes are fluffier and lighter than mashed potatoes and can be served quite simply with salt and white pepper to taste.

Deep-fried potatoes are cooked in two stages. The first may be done hours in advance of the second. First, peel and wipe potatoes with a damp cloth. *Do not* wash under running water. Electric slicing machines and food processors with a slicing attachment not only facilitate the slicing operation but yield pieces of uniform thickness. The initial frying is done at a temperature setting of 360° F. (182° C.) and potatoes are cooked until they begin to turn a light brown. They are removed and placed on paper towels to drain, uncovered. If cooked several hours in advance, place in a container when cool and refrigerate until needed. Immediately before serving, adjust temperature to 375° F. (190° C.) and cook potatoes until crisp and golden brown.

SERVING SUGGESTIONS   Au Gratin. Melted butter. Maitre d' Butter. White or Cheese Sauce. Potatoes combine well with almost every vegetable.

Sweet Potatoes

Select potatoes bright in color, with smooth skins and no blemishes. If potatoes have rootlets attached, they will be fibrous and have little flavor.

To prepare, peel and cut into slices of uniform size and thickness. When baking, scrub clean under cold running water, or wipe clean with a damp cloth.

COOKING SUGGESTIONS   Baked or blanched and pan-fried. Sweet potatoes require less time to bake than white potatoes. A fairly large sweet potato will bake in about 45 minutes in a 350° F. (177° C.) oven.

SERVING SUGGESTIONS   Plain melted butter. Orange Sauce. Glazing.

Summer Squash

This vegetable, also identified as zucchini, comes in yellow and green varieties. Both are cooked and served in the same manner. Select young, very firm, and undamaged ones. Soft squash is almost completely lacking in flavor.

To prepare, wash under running water and dry. Peel and slice in half. Unless very young, remove seeds and pulp along center. Cut into slices or sticks of a uniform size and thickness. Vegetable may also be kept boat-shape and stuffed.

COOKING SUGGESTIONS Using the boiling water procedure, this tender vegetable cooks in a matter of minutes. Doneness is signaled by a fairly crisp texture when fork-tested. Stuffed summer squash can be either baked or broiled. When cut up and sliced, it may be coated (using equal quantities of breadcrumbs and grated cheese) and deep-fried.

SERVING SUGGESTIONS Plain melted butter. Glazed and tossed with grated cheese. Lemon Butter. Mild flavored sauces.

Tomatoes

A fully ripe tomato is deep red in color, plump, and heavy. The degree of ripeness and freshness can be judged by the aroma given off when it is sliced, as well as by its firmness. As with all other vegetable-fruits, tomatoes are best when sun-ripened on the vine.

To remove skin of a tomato, blanch in boiling water for about 60 seconds, or until skins begin to loosen. Drain and set aside until cool enough to handle. Do not douse in cold water, as this detracts from the flavor and texture. Peel off skins. If tomato is a little on the unripe side, cut out stem and blossom end before blanching.

To prepare tomatoes for stuffing, blanch or set under broiler for about 1 minute. Cut out core and gently press out seeds. Remove skin and fill with desired stuffing.

To broil a tomato, cut out stem leaving a small opening. Cut a thin slice off bottom so tomato will lie flat. Season with salt and pepper and fill small cavity with grated cheese or breadcrumbs. Dot with butter and set under broiler until tender but still firm. Before serving, remove skin which will have loosened during broiling.

When tomatoes are to be used as a base for sauces or soups, place skinned tomatoes in blender for about 30 seconds and strain to remove seeds, which are bitter.

To remove the seeds from a ripe tomato, hold between hands, stem side down, and squeeze.

COOKING SUGGESTIONS Both green and red tomatoes may be sliced and fried in a small amount of butter over low heat. Whole tomatoes may be broiled or stewed.

SERVING SUGGESTIONS   Cheese Sauce. Oil and Vinegar Dressing. Sliced ripe tomatoes can stand on their own as a salad or may be combined with other raw vegetables and greens. They are used as a base for soups and sauces.

Truffles

This fungus grows underground and is not indigenous to the United States. It is imported in bottles and cans which are generally exorbitant in price. Few preserved foods can compete with the fresh variety. As a general rule, fresh mushrooms can be substituted whenever a recipe calls for truffles. However, the black truffle—termed the "fairy apple" by George Sand—makes an attractive contrast when used as a garnish. If truffles are not readily available, pitted black olives may be used instead to create a sculptured effect.

Turnips (Yellow and White)

The white turnip is much smaller in overall size and is milder in flavor than the yellow turnip, which has a distinctive flavoring when properly cooked. Both varieties should be smooth and without blemishes (particularly the yellow). Freshness may be determined by checking for firmness where the stalk was removed.

   To prepare, peel and cut into fairly thin, uniform size slices, strips, or cubes so that the vegetable may cook quickly.

COOKING SUGGESTIONS   Cook using boiling water procedure, adding a pinch of sugar to the water. Length of cooking time will depend on size, freshness, and tenderness. Vegetable should be slightly crispy when fork-tested, and, if not overcooked, will give off a pleasant aroma. Yellow turnips are frequently served riced or mashed.

SERVING SUGGESTIONS   Plain melted butter. Glazed. White Sauce.

Watercress

Leaves should be bright green and crisp with a varnished appearance. Avoid watercress which has been doused in water.

To prepare, wash under running water and, if using in a salad, dry thoroughly.

COOKING SUGGESTIONS When using as a soup base, finely chop and simmer over low heat.

SERVING SUGGESTIONS Serve as a salad or combine with other fresh greens. Watercress is frequently used as a garnish or as a bed on which aspics, cold mousses, and molded salads are served.

RECIPES FOR VEGETABLES AND GREENS

ASPARAGUS POLONAISE

2 pounds (900 g) asparagus
fresh lemon juice
salt and pepper to taste
3 tablespoons hardboiled egg
* yolk, chopped*

1 tablespoon fresh parsley,
* finely chopped*
breadcrumbs
grated Parmesan cheese
butter

Peel asparagus and cook in boiling salted water until bright in color and there is a slight resistance when fork-tested. Arrange drained asparagus on a heat-proof serving platter, placing tips at either end. Squeeze on a few drops of lemon juice and season to taste with salt and pepper. Sprinkle a mixture of egg yolk and parsley over tips only. Spread breadcrumbs and grated cheese over stalks in center of dish. Dot the whole with butter and set under broiler until lightly browned. (This dish may be prepared in advance and set under broiler just prior to serving.)

GREEN BEANS ALMONDINE

2 pounds (900 g) green beans   blanched almonds, slivered
2 tablespoons butter   butter for frying
salt and pepper to taste

Cook green beans in boiling salted water until bright green and fairly crisp when fork-tested. Melt 2 tablespoons butter in frying pan, add drained green beans, and toss. Season to taste with salt and pepper.

Gently fry slivered almonds in butter and add to green beans.

GLAZED CARROTS

2 pounds (900 g) carrots,   2 teaspoons sugar
  peeled and uniformly sliced   salt and white pepper to taste
2 tablespoons butter   fresh parsley, finely chopped

Cook peeled and uniformly sliced carrots in boiling salted water until fairly crisp. Melt butter in a high-sided frying pan over low heat and add drained carrots. Sprinkle sugar over carrots and toss. Season with salt and white pepper to taste. Transfer to a serving dish, sprinkle with finely chopped parsley and serve.

BROCCOLI WITH WHITE SAUCE

2 pounds (900 g) broccoli,   2 cups (480 ml) White Sauce
  peeled and chopped   salt and pepper to taste

Cook peeled and chopped broccoli in boiling salted water until bright green in color and fairly crisp and drain.

Prepare White Sauce (for recipe see Chapter 3 under Sauce section) according to recipe. Combine with broccoli and season to taste with salt and pepper.

SUMMER SQUASH AU GRATIN

2 pounds (900 g) summer
  squash, peeled and
  uniformly sliced

Cheese Sauce
grated Parmesan cheese
salt and white pepper

Cook peeled and uniformly sliced summer squash in boiling salted water until fairly crisp. Drain and combine with Cheese Sauce (for recipe see Chapter 2, under Sauce section), using an ovenproof serving dish. Sprinkle surface with grated Parmesan cheese, and set under broiler until lightly browned.

SUMMER SQUASH WITH CHEESE

2 pounds (900 g) green and
  yellow summer squash,
  peeled and uniformly sliced
1 tablespoon butter

lemon juice
salt and white pepper to taste
grated Parmesan cheese

Cook peeled and uniformly sliced green and yellow summer squash in boiling salted water until still fairly crisp. Drain and toss with butter, a few drops of lemon juice, and seasoning to taste. Sprinkle with grated Parmesan Cheese and toss once again.

ASPARAGUS WITH LEMON HOLLANDAISE SAUCE

2 pounds (900 g) asparagus,
  peeled

1 cup (240 ml) Lemon
  Hollandaise Sauce

Snap off tough bottom portion of asparagus and peel. Cook in boiling salted water until bright in color and there is a slight resistance when fork-tested. Arrange drained asparagus (hot or chilled) on a serving platter and serve Lemon Hollandaise Sauce (see Chapter 2, under Sauce section) on the side.

BROCCOLI WITH MAITRE D'HOTEL BUTTER

Maitre d'Hotel Butter　　　　　*2 pounds (900 g) broccoli, peeled*

Prepare Maitre d'Hotel Butter according to recipe on p. 258. Cook broccoli, either in sprigs or coarsely chopped, in boiling salted water until bright green and fairly crisp. Drain and arrange on serving platter, placing slices of Maitre d'Hotel butter on top or in a separate dish to the side.

CREAMED BROCCOLI

2 cups (480 ml) Cream Sauce　　*1 teaspoon English (dried)*
2 pounds (900 g) broccoli,　　　　*mustard, moistened in 1*
peeled　　　　　　　　　　　*tablespoon water*
　　　　　　　　　　　　　salt and white pepper to taste

Prepare Cream Sauce according to recipe in Chapter 2.

Cook peeled broccoli in boiling salted water until bright green and fairly crisp. Drain and finely chop. Add moistened English mustard and salt and white pepper to Cream Sauce and blend. Combine broccoli and Cream Sauce and serve.

GREEN BEANS WITH CHERVIL

2 pounds (900 g) green beans　　*fresh lemon juice*
1 tablespoon butter　　　　　　*½ teaspoon dried chervil*
salt and pepper to taste

Cook green beans in boiling salted water until bright green and fairly crisp and drain. Add butter, seasoning, few drops of lemon juice, chervil, and toss.

CAULIFLOWER AU GRATIN

1 large head cauliflower   salt and white pepper
2 cups (480 ml) Cheese Sauce   grated Parmesan cheese

Break up cauliflower into flowerets and soak in salted water for about 1 minute. Drain and cook in boiling salted water until tender, being careful not to overcook.

Prepare Cheese Sauce according to recipe in Chapter 2, and add salt and white pepper to taste.

Arrange cooked cauliflower on a serving platter and pour over Cheese Sauce. Sprinkle with grated Parmesan cheese and place under broiler until lightly browned.

PEAS WITH DILL

1 10-ounce (284 g) package   1½ teaspoons fresh dill, finely
    frozen peas, slightly   chopped
    defrosted   salt and pepper to taste
2 teaspoons butter

Break up frozen peas and cook in a covered saucepan over low heat in two teaspoons butter until defrosted and heated through. Add finely chopped fresh dill, seasoning to taste, and toss, adding more butter, if necessary.

PUREE OF PEAS

2 10-ounce (284 g) packages   salt and pepper to taste
    frozen peas, slightly   2 egg yolks, slightly beaten
    defrosted   butter
4 teaspoons butter

Break up slightly defrosted peas and cook in 4 teaspoons butter in a covered saucepan over low heat until heated through. Season to taste with salt and pepper. Puree peas using a food mill or electric food processor. Combine pureed peas with beaten egg yolks and turn into buttered dariole (plain individual metal molds about 2½″ to 3″ high [6.35 cm to 7.62 cm]) molds or custard cups and dot with butter. Set in a pan containing an inch or two (2.54 cm to 5.08 cm) of hot water and bake in a 325° F. (163° C.) oven until set.

Alternate method: Using a pastry bag with a star tube, pipe puree into a heat-proof serving dish, pour a little melted butter over surface, and place under a preheated broiler until lightly browned and heated through.

Pureed peas may also be used as a fancy border around prepared meat and fish dishes.

BEETS WITH SOUR CREAM DRESSING

6 or 7 beets, peeled and   sour cream dressing
  uniformly sliced

Cook uniformly sliced and peeled beets in boiling water until tender, and drain. Prepare Sour Cream Dressing according to recipe in Chapter 7, and serve with hot or chilled beets.

BAKED STUFFED POTATOES

8 baking potatoes   ¾ cup (85.05 g) grated
vegetable oil (sesame or   Parmesan cheese
  peanut)   butter
3 egg yolks, lightly beaten   salt and white pepper to taste
2 tablespoons butter

Scrub potato skins and dry with paper towels. Using a pastry brush, coat skins with vegetable oil and bake in a preheated 375° F. (190° C.) oven for about an hour, or until tender. Halfway through baking, prick with a fork to allow steam to escape. Remove and cut off a ½″ (1 cm) lengthwise slice from top. Scoop out inside of potato, and return shells to oven to dry and crisp. In the meantime, put scooped out portion of potatoes through a ricer and mix in egg yolks, 2 tablespoons butter, salt and white pepper to taste, and ½ cup grated Parmesan cheese. Using a pastry bag with a star tube, pipe back into shells and sprinkle remaining cheese over tops. Dot lightly with butter and bake or broil until lightly browned.

BAKED STUFFED POTATOES WITH SOUR CREAM

8 *baking potatoes*
vegetable oil (sesame or
  peanut
3 *egg yolks, lightly beaten*
2 *tablespoons butter*

2 *tablespoons fresh dill, finely*
  chopped
salt and white pepper to taste
butter
½ *pint (240 ml) sour cream*

Scrub potato skins and dry with paper towels. Using a pastry brush, coat skins with vegetable oil and bake in a preheated 375° F. (190° C.) oven for about an hour, or until tender. Halfway through baking, prick with a fork to allow steam to escape. Remove and cut off a ½" (1 cm) lengthwise slice from top. Scoop out inside of potato, and return shells to oven to dry and crisp. In the meantime, put scooped out portion of potatoes through a ricer and mix in egg yolks, 2 tablespoons butter, salt and white pepper, and finely chopped fresh dill. Using a pastry bag with a star tube, pipe back into shells. Dot lightly with butter and bake or broil until browned. Serve sour cream on the side.

FRENCH FRIED POTATOES

baking potatoes　　　　　*fat for frying*

Wipe potatoes with a damp towel—*do not* wash. Peel and uniformly slice into rounds (⅛" [.3 cm] thick) or into strips (¼" to ¾" [.5 to 1.5 cm] thick). Pat dry using clean linen or paper towels. Fry in two stages. Preheat fat to 360° F. (182° C.) and fry until light brown. Do not overcrowd pan. (This stage may be done hours in advance.) Drain on paper towels but do not cover. Increase temperature to 375° F. (190° C.) and fry potatoes until golden brown and crisp. Drain on paper towels and serve at once, or, keep warm in a 160° F. (71° C.) oven, *uncovered.*

DUCHESS POTATO MIXTURE

6 to 8 baking potatoes
2 tablespoons butter

4 egg yolks or 1 whole egg
plus 2 yolks, well beaten
salt and white pepper to taste

Peel potatoes, cut into halves or quarters, and cook in a large, uncovered pot of lightly salted boiling water until tender. Drain and put through a ricer while hot. Mix in two tablespoons butter with beaten eggs. Season to taste with salt and white pepper. Transfer to a greased ovenproof dish and bake in a preheated 375° F. (190° C.) oven until heated through, or prepare in any of the ways listed below. (Duchess Potatoes freeze well and can be cooked in frozen state.)

DUCHESS POTATOES WITH CHEESE

Duchess Potato Mixture

½ cup (56.70 g) grated
Parmesan or Swiss cheese

Prepare Duchess Potato Mixture according to recipe, and mix in grated Parmesan or Swiss cheese. Transfer to a greased ovenproof dish and bake in a preheated 375° F. (190° C.) oven until heated through. This mixture may also be used for Potato Croquettes or Potato Rings.

POTATO CROQUETTES

Duchess Potato Mixture
finely sifted flour
2 eggs
1 tablespoon oil   } *lightly beaten together*
¼ cup (60 ml) milk
breadcrumbs
fat for frying

Prepare Duchess Potato Mixture according to recipe and shape into croquettes. Roll in finely sifted flour, then in mixture of eggs, oil, and milk, and finally in breadcrumbs. Reshape if necessary. Fry in a deep-fat fryer, preheated to 375° F. (190° C.), until crisp and golden brown. Drain on paper towels. Keep warm in a 160° F. (71° C.) oven, uncovered. (Croquettes may be prepared in advance, frozen, and fried without defrosting.)

DUCHESS POTATO RINGS

Duchess Potato Mixture   *½ teaspoon sugar*
egg yolk   *light cream*

Prepare Duchess Potato Mixture according to recipe, and, using a pastry bag with a star tube, pipe 3″ (7.5 cm) rings on to a greased or nonstick baking sheet. Glaze with beaten egg yolk mixed with ½ teaspoon sugar and enough light cream to moisten, using a pastry brush. Bake in a preheated 400° F. (205° C.) oven until browned.

DUCHESS POTATOES MOT D'OR

Duchess Potato Mixture   *butter*
grated Parmesan or Swiss
  cheese

Prepare Duchess Potato Mixture according to recipe, and spoon two-thirds into a heat-proof serving dish. Pipe an attractive mound over top with remaining third, using a pastry bag with a star tube. Sprinkle with grated cheese, dot with butter, and brown under broiler.

POTATO PEARS

Duchess Potato Mixture
finely sifted flour
2 eggs
1 tablespoon oil $\Big\}$ *lightly beaten*
¼ cup (60 ml) milk
breadcrumbs
fat for frying
¾" (1.5 cm) pieces dried potato sticks

Prepare Duchess Potato Mixture according to recipe, and hand-shape into pieces representing pears. Roll in finely sifted flour, then in mixture of eggs, oil, and milk, and finally in bread-crumbs. Reshape, if necessary. Chill in refrigerator for about one-half hour before frying in deep fat, preheated to 375° F. (190° C.). Drain on paper towels, and insert ¾" (1.5 cm) pieces of dried potato sticks in top to represent stems. (Potato Pears may be prepared in advance and frozen. It is not necessary to defrost before frying.)

POTATO STUFFING

5 or 6 baking potatoes
2 tablespoons butter
1 large onion, finely chopped
butter for frying
1 cup breadcrumbs
  (unflavored)
1 teaspoon dried summer sa-
  voury
salt and freshly ground
  pepper
butter

Peel potatoes, cut into halves or quarters, and cook in a large pot of boiling salted water, uncovered, until tender. Drain and put through a ricer while hot. Mix in 2 tablespoons butter. Fry finely chopped onion in a generous amount of butter until translucent, and mix in, along with breadcrumbs and summer savoury. Season to taste with salt and freshly ground pepper. Transfer to a greased ovenproof dish, dot lightly with butter, and bake in a 325° F. (163° C.) oven for about 20 minutes, or until heated through. (Potato Stuffing may be prepared in advance and refrigerated. It may also be used to stuff cavities of chicken or turkey.)

SCALLOPED POTATOES

1 pint (480 ml) Cream Sauce
5 or 6 baking potatoes
1 onion, peeled and finely
  chopped

1 tablespoon fresh dill, finely
  chopped
salt and white pepper

Prepare Cream Sauce (Chapter 2, under Sauce section) according to recipe. Peel potatoes, cut into uniform size slices, and cook in lightly salted boiling water in an uncovered pan over high heat for about 5 or 6 minutes, or until fairly crisp. Remove and drain. Fry onion in 1 tablespoon butter until translucent and add to Cream Sauce, along with finely chopped dill and seasoning (salt and white pepper) to taste. Combine potatoes with Cream Sauce and transfer to a buttered ovenproof dish. Bake in a preheated 350° F. (177° C.) oven for about 20 minutes, or until potatoes are tender.

FLUFFY POTATOES

5 or 6 baking potatoes

salt and white pepper

Using good quality potatoes, peel, cut into halves or quarters, and cook in an uncovered pot of boiling salted water until tender. Remove and drain. Put through a ricer, dust lightly with salt and white pepper, and serve. Do not mix seasoning in or add butter.

PUREE OF TURNIPS AND POTATOES

1 onion, finely chopped
1 tablespoon butter
1 medium-size yellow turnip

3 or 4 baking potatoes
salt and white pepper

Fry finely chopped onion in melted butter over low heat until translucent. Remove and set aside.

Peel turnip and cut into uniformly small pieces. Cook in a large, uncovered pot of boiling salted water until tender. Remove and drain.

Peel potatoes, cut into halves or quarters, and cook in boiling salted water in an uncovered pot until tender. Remove and drain.

Put both potatoes and turnips through ricer while hot, and mix in fried onion, seasoning to taste. Add additional butter, if desired, and serve.

SUMMER SQUASH AND BROCCOLI WITH TOMATO SAUCE

Tomato Sauce
1 pound (450 g) broccoli
1 pound (450 g) green and
yellow summer squash

1 tablespoon butter
salt and pepper to taste

Prepare Tomato Sauce (Chapter 2, under Sauce section) according to recipe.

Remove tough, woody portions from stems of broccoli, peel, and chop.

Peel squash, cut in half, remove center seeds and pulp, and slice.

Cook both broccoli and squash in an uncovered pot of boiling salted water until fairly crisp. Drain, and toss in butter and seasoning to taste. Serve with Tomato Sauce.

SPINACH VINAIGRETTE

1 pound (450 g) fresh spinach   *Oil and Vinegar Dressing*
No. 1

Wash spinach under cold running water, removing all grit, and cook in a large pot of unsalted boiling water (there should be room for spinach to swim around) for about 2 or 3 minutes after water returns to the boil. Spinach should be tender but still retain most of its deep green color. Remove and drain, using a colander.

To prepare dressing, follow recipe for Oil and Vinegar Dressing No. 1 given in this chapter. Place about a third of a cup of dressing over low heat until warm. Remove and toss spinach in dressing or serve on the side.

GREENS VINAIGRETTE

Follow recipe for Spinach Vinaigrette, substituting collards, beet greens, or Swiss chard for spinach.

ASPARAGUS WITH LEMON SAUCE

Lemon Sauce   *pimiento*
2 pounds (900 g) asparagus,
  peeled

To prepare sauce, follow recipe for Lemon Sauce (Chapter 2, under Sauce section).

Cook peeled asparagus in a large pot of lightly salted boiling water (large enough so that asparagus can swim around) for about 3 or 4 minutes (depending on thickness of asparagus) or until just barely tender. Do not overcook. Remove and drain. Arrange asparagus on a heated platter or individual serving plates and pour over Lemon Sauce. Garnish with julienne strips of pimiento.

BROCCOLI WITH LEMON SAUCE

Lemon Sauce
1 pound (450 g) broccoli,
*   peeled*
hardboiled egg yolk

To prepare sauce, follow recipe for Lemon Sauce (Chapter 2, under Sauce section).

Cut peeled broccoli into sprigs, cutting through stems and leaving flowerets at the top (stems should be no more than ¼" (.5 cm) thick). Or coarsely chop ¼" thick stems, leaving flowerets whole.

Cook broccoli in a large pot of lightly salted boiling water, uncovered, for about 2 or 3 minutes once water returns to a boil. Vegetable should be fairly crisp when fork-tested and still maintain its deep green color. Remove and drain in a colander. Arrange on a heated platter or individual serving plates and pour on Lemon Sauce. Garnish with chopped egg yolk.

BROCCOLI WITH ORANGE SAUCE

Follow recipe for Broccoli with Lemon Sauce, substituting Orange Sauce No. 1 or Orange Sauce No. 2 (Chapter 2, under Sauce section) for Lemon Sauce. Omit chopped egg garnish.

TURNIPS AND PEAS

1 yellow turnip, peeled   *melted butter*
1 pound (450 g) peas, shelled   *salt and white pepper*

Cut peeled turnip into cubes approximately ½" (1 cm) in size. Cook shelled peas and turnips in a large pot of lightly salted boiling water (enough so that vegetables can swim around) until tender. Do not overcook. Remove and drain. Place in a heated serving dish, add melted butter, and toss. Season to taste with salt and white pepper.

Turnips and Peas with White Sauce

Prepare White Sauce according to recipe under Sauce section. Follow recipe for Turnips and Peas, and when drained, omit melted butter and add vegetables to heated sauce.

RICED YELLOW TURNIPS

1 yellow turnip, peeled *salt and white pepper*
melted butter

Cut peeled turnip into small uniform size pieces and cook in a large pot of lightly salted boiling water, uncovered, over high heat until fairly tender. Remove and drain. Put turnip pieces through ricer, a cupful or so at a time. Mix in melted butter and season to taste with salt and white pepper.

BRAISED CELERY

1 head of celery *All-Purpose Stock or chicken*
butter *broth*
pimiento

Remove tops from celery and reserve for stock pot. Cut off root end and peel stalks. Wash stalks under cold running water. Cut stalks through center from one end to the other before cutting into strips approximately 1½" (4 cm) in length. Blanch celery in a large pot of lightly salted boiling water for 1 or 2 minutes after water returns to a boil. Remove and drain. Melt a tablespoon or so of butter in braising pan and add celery. Cover and set in a preheated 250° F. (121° C.) oven for 5 to 10 minutes, or long enough to exude some of the moisture. Bring stock or broth to a boil and add enough to fully cover celery. Replace cover and braise in oven until barely tender when fork tested. Transfer celery to a heated serving dish. Set braising pan over high heat and bring stock to a full boil. Continue to cook until reduced by about two-thirds and pour over celery. Garnish with strips of pimiento and serve.

SHREDDED CABBAGE

1 head white cabbage   salt and white pepper
melted butter

Remove core from cabbage and soak in cold salted water for about 1 minute. Remove and turn upside down to drain. Cut cabbage into shred size pieces and cook in a large pot of lightly salted boiling water, uncovered, until fairly crisp and bright in color. This should take no longer than 4 or 5 minutes once water returns to a boil. Remove and drain. Place in a heated serving dish and toss in melted butter. Season to taste with salt and white pepper.

VEGETABLES ORIENTAL NO. 1

1 pound (450 g) carrots,
   peeled
4 or 5 stalks of celery, peeled
   and sliced
1 green pepper, seeded and
   chopped
4 or 5 scallions, peeled and
   sliced
1 16-ounce (450 g) can bean
   sprouts, drained
1 6-ounce (170 g) can water
   chestnuts, sliced

vegetable oil (peanut)
soy sauce
pinch of salt
dry sherry
½ cup (120 ml) chicken broth
   or All-Purpose Stock
1 tablespoon cornstarch,
   moistened in 2 tablespoons
   sherry

Cut peeled carrots into ¼" to ½" (.5 to 1 cm) thick slices (depending on thickness) using a fluted shape cutter. Blanch in a large pot of lightly salted boiling water, uncovered, over high heat for 2 to 3 minutes once water returns to a boil. Remove and drain.

Prepare all other ingredients and arrange near cooking area, along with blanched carrots. Heat a small amount of oil, a few drops of soy sauce, and a pinch of salt in wok until hot but not smoking. Add a proportionately small amount of dry sherry (about 1 tablespoon) and stock or broth (2 or 3 tablespoons), pouring along the inside of the rim, so that it will be heated before coming in contact with the hot oil. Stir-fry sliced celery, chopped green pepper, and sliced scallions until fairly crisp. Remove and keep warm. Add blanched carrots and stir-fry long enough to complete cooking. Return celery, green pepper and scallions to pan, along with drained bean sprouts and sliced water chestnuts. Gradually add remaining stock or broth, pouring in a circular motion along the inside rim. Add moistened cornstarch (stirring to dissolve) to pan, and cook, stirring, until sauce is smooth and glossy. Serve with cooked rice.

VEGETABLES ORIENTAL NO. 2

Oriental Sauce
1 pound (450 g) carrots,
*   peeled*
4 or 5 stalks of celery, peeled
1 green pepper, seeded and
*   chopped*

4 or 5 scallions, peeled and
*   sliced*
1 16-ounce (450 g) can bean
*   sprouts, drained*
1 6-ounce (170 g) can water
*   chestnuts, sliced*

To prepare sauce, follow recipe for Oriental Sauce (Chapter 2, under Sauce section).

Cut peeled carrots into ¼" to ½" (.5 to 1 cm) thick slices (depending on thickness of carrote) using a fluted shape cutter. Cut peeled celery stalks across at ½" (1 cm) intervals, holding knife at a slant so as to produce attractive shaped slices. Cook carrots and celery in a large pot of lightly salted boiling water, uncovered, over high heat until fairly crisp. Remove and drain. Fry chopped green pepper and sliced scallions over low heat in a small amount of oil until fairly crisp. Do not overcook.

Bring Oriental Sauce to a slow simmer and add cooked carrots, celery, green pepper and scallions, along with drained bean sprouts and sliced water chestnuts and cook just long enough to heat through. Serve with cooked rice. (Leftover roast pork may be cut into cubes and added to sauce to make a main dish.)

SUCCOTASH

3 *or 4 ears of fresh corn*   2 *tablespoons pimiento, diced*
butter   *salt and white pepper*
1 *onion, peeled and chopped*

Remove husks from corn, and using a sharp knife, cut off kernels. Melt butter over low heat and fry chopped onions until they take on a slightly translucent appearance. Add corn and fry, uncovered, until tender—stirring and tossing now and then. Do not overcook. Add chopped pimiento and cook just long enough to heat through. Season to taste with salt and white pepper. Remove and serve.

SUCCOTASH WITH RICE

Follow recipe for Succotash and combine with 1 cup cooked rice. Serve plain or with Tomato Sauce or White Sauce (Chapter 2, under Sauce section).

BROILED TOMATOES

fresh tomatoes, fully ripe   *breadcrumbs*
salt and pepper   *butter*
grated Parmesan cheese   *parsley*

Cut out stem end of tomatoes leaving a small opening. Cut a thin slice off bottom so tomatoes will lie flat. Season with salt and pepper and fill cavities with a mixture of grated cheese and breadcrumbs. Dot with butter and set under preheated broiler several inches from the flame. Broil until tender but still fairly firm. Remove and detach skin which will have loosened during broiling. Garnish with a small sprig of parsley and serve.

SAUTÉED MUSHROOMS

1 pound (450 g) button size   *butter*
    mushrooms, peeled   *fresh parsley, finely chopped*
olive oil

Brush peeled mushrooms lightly with olive oil, using a pastry brush. Melt a small amount of butter and oil in frying pan and sauté mushrooms over medium high heat until golden brown. Remove to a heated serving dish and garnish with finely chopped parsley.

Sautéed Mushrooms in White Sauce

White Sauce   *butter and oil for frying*
1 pound (450 g) mushrooms,
    peeled and sliced

To prepare sauce, follow recipe for White Sauce (Chapter 2, under Sauce section), using 1 cup stock and 1 cup milk. Heat butter and oil in frying pan and sauté peeled and sliced mushrooms over medium high heat until golden brown. Add to White Sauce and serve.

Sautéed Mushrooms in Lemon Sauce

Follow recipe for Sautéed Mushrooms in White Sauce, substituting Lemon Sauce for White Sauce.

MIXED VEGETABLES WITH LEMON SAUCE

1 small green summer squash, peeled
1 small yellow summer squash, peeled
½ pound (225 g) broccoli, peeled

1 pound (450 g) carrots, peeled
Lemon Sauce

Cut peeled squash across into ¼" (.5 cm) thick slices. Cut peeled broccoli into sprigs, cutting through stems and leaving flowerets at the top—stems should be about ¼" (.5 cm) thick. Coarsely chop stems leaving flowerets whole. Cut peeled carrots into ⅛" (.3 cm) thick slices.

Bring a large pot of lightly salted water to a boil. Add carrots and cook, uncovered, over high heat for 2 or 3 minutes after water returns to a boil before adding chopped broccoli and squash. After water returns to a boil, cook for 1 or 2 minutes longer. Remove and drain.

Prepare Lemon Sauce according to recipe under Sauce section. Bring sauce to a slow simmer and add cooked vegetables, or serve sauce on the side.

MIXED VEGETABLES AU GRATIN

Cheese Sauce
1 small green summer squash, peeled
1 small yellow summer squash, peeled

½ pound (225 g) broccoli, peeled
2 tomatoes, peeled and sliced
grated Parmesan cheese
butter

Prepare sauce according to recipe for Cheese Sauce (Chapter 2, under Sauce section).

Cut peeled summer squash across into ¼" (.5 cm) thick slices. Cut peeled broccoli into sprigs, cutting through stems and leaving flowerets whole. Stems should be about ¼" (.5 cm) thick and about ¾" (1.5 cm) long. Bring a large pot of lightly salted water to a boil, and cook vegetables, uncovered, over high heat for 2 or 3 minutes (once water returns to the boil), or until fairly crisp when fork-tested. (Do not overcook.) Remove and drain. Place vegetables in a shallow, ovenproof serving dish, and pour Cheese Sauce over vegetables. Arrange fresh tomato slices on top. Sprinkle grated cheese over the whole surface, dot with butter, and place under a preheated broiler until lightly browned and the tomatoes are slightly cooked. Remove and serve.

CARROTS WITH LEMON SAUCE

Lemon Sauce　　　　　　　　　*fresh parsley, finely chopped*
2 pounds (900 g) carrots,
　peeled

Prepare Lemon Sauce according to recipe under Sauce section. Cut peeled carrots into strips approximately 1″ (2.5 cm) in length and ½″ (1 cm) wide, and cook in a large pot of lightly salted boiling water, uncovered, over high heat for about 4 or 5 minutes after water returns to a boil, or until fairly crisp when fork-tested. (Do not overcook.) Remove and drain. Place in a heated serving dish or on individual serving plates and pour over sauce. Garnish with finely chopped parsley.

ASPARAGUS AND CARROTS WITH LEMON SAUCE

Lemon Sauce　　　　　　　　*1 pound (450 g) asparagus,*
1 pound (450 g) carrots,　　　　*peeled*
　peeled

Prepare Lemon Sauce according to recipe under Sauce section. Cut peeled carrots into strips approximately 1″ (2.5 cm) in length and ½″ (1 cm) wide, and cook in a large pot of lightly salted boiling water, uncoverd, over high heat for about 4 or 5 minutes after water returns to a boil, or until fairly crisp when fork-tested.

Cut peeled asparagus into ½″ (1 cm) lengths, leaving buds whole, and cook in a large pot of lightly salted boiling water, uncovered, over high heat for 2 or 3 minutes after water returns to the boil, depending on the thickness of asparagus. (Do not overcook.) Combine carrots and asparagus and place in a heated serving dish. Pour Lemon Sauce over or serve on the side.

CARROTS WITH ORANGE SAUCE

Follow recipe for Carrots with Lemon Sauce, substituting Orange Sauce No. 1 or Orange Sauce No. 2 (Chapter 2, under Sauce section) for Lemon Sauce.

CARROTS AND ASPARAGUS WITH ORANGE SAUCE

Follow recipe for Asparagus and Carrots with Lemon Sauce, substituting Orange Sauce No. 1 or Orange Sauce No. 2 for Lemon Sauce.

BUTTERNUT SQUASH

1 butternut squash, peeled   *salt and white pepper*
melted butter

Cut peeled squash in half and remove seeds and inner pulp. Cut into uniform size pieces and cook in a large pot of lightly salted boiling water, uncovered, over high heat until tender. Remove and drain. Puree squash by putting through a ricer, or whip using an electric mixer or hand beater. Mix in melted butter and season to taste with salt and white pepper.

BAKED ACORN SQUASH

acorn squash   salt and white pepper
butter

Cut squash in half (in the direction of the ribbing). Remove seeds and pulp. Brush inside surface with butter. Arrange on a baking sheet or shallow heat-proof pan, cut side down, and bake in a preheated 350° F. (177° C.) oven for about 45 minutes (depending on size) or until tender. Remove and season with salt and white pepper. Each serving consists of half a squash.

BUTTERED PARSNIPS

2 pounds (900 g) parsnips,   melted butter
  peeled   salt and white pepper

Cut peeled parsnips into strips approximately 1½″ (4 cm) in length and ½″ (1 cm) wide, or into slices ⅛″ (.3 cm) thick.

Cook in a large pot of lightly salted boiling water, uncovered, over high heat until fairly crisp when fork-tested. (Do not overcook.) Remove and drain. Transfer to a heated serving dish and toss in melted butter. Season to taste with salt and white pepper.

PEARL ONIONS

1½ pounds (675 g) small pearl   melted butter
  onions, peeled   salt and white pepper

Cook peeled onions in a large pot of lightly salted boiling water, uncovered, over high heat until tender but still fairly firm when fork-tested. Remove and drain. Transfer to a heated serving dish. Pour melted butter over and toss until thoroughly coated. Season with salt and white pepper.

Pearl Onions in White Sauce

To prepare sauce, follow recipe for White Sauce (Chapter 2, under Sauce section). Follow recipe for Pearl Onions, but do not toss in melted butter. Bring sauce to a simmer and add cooked onions.

Glazed Onions

Follow recipe for Pearl Onions, dissolving a teaspoon or so of sugar in melted butter before tossing with onions.

SPINACH MOUNDS WITH SAUCE

2 pounds (900 g) fresh
   spinach; or 2 10-ounce
   (280 g) packages frozen
   chopped spinach
2 teaspoons butter
1 onion, peeled and finely
   chopped

salt and freshly ground
   pepper
pinch of nutmeg
Sauce

Wash fresh spinach, removing all grit, and cook in a large pot of unsalted boiling water for about 3 or 4 minutes, or until tender but still maintaining most of its deep green color. Drain and finely chop.

If using frozen spinach, cook one package at a time in order to exude as much of the water content as possible. Cook in a covered saucepan in a teaspoon of butter, over medium low heat. (Do not add water to pan.) Remove from heat as soon as spinach has defrosted and is heated through. Drain off excess liquid, using a wire strainer.

Fry onion in a small amount of butter over low heat until translucent, and add to chopped spinach along with salt and freshly ground pepper and nutmeg. Shape into well-rounded mounds and arrange in a buttered, heat-proof serving dish. Spoon the following Sauce over each and place under a broiler until lightly browned and heated through.

Sauce

2 tablespoons butter
3 tablespoons finely sifted
flour
½ teaspoon dry mustard
1 teaspoon prepared mustard
(Dijon)
1½ cups (360 ml) milk or light
cream, scalded

¼ cup (60 ml) light or heavy
cream
salt and white pepper
4 tablespoons grated Parmesan
cheese

Melt butter over low heat, add flour and cook, stirring, for about 1 minute. Blend in mustards and gradually add scalded milk or light cream. Cook over medium low heat, stirring, until mixture begins to bubble. Add light or heavy cream, stirring until heated through. Remove from heat and mix in grated cheese.

CREAMED SPINACH

Follow recipes for Spinach Mounds and Sauce. Combine Sauce with spinach mixture and turn into a lightly buttered ovenproof dish. Bake in a preheated 350° F. (177° C.) oven for about 20 minutes, or until heated through.

SALADS

Salads may be comprised of greens and other vegetables, fruits, meats, fish, or dairy products, served singly or in combination. They may be served as a main course or as a side dish. Salads may also be molded using gelatin. Fruit salads are frequently served as desserts.

Preparing Salads

Freshness is the key to a good salad—both in terms of ingredients and the time interval between preparation and serving. Appearance runs a close second: Whatever the shape or form,

pile higher toward the center (always in a very neat fashion), contrast textures and colors (even varying shades of green), and let simplicity be the guide. Keep garnishes relatively small and simple and give some consideration to their appropriateness. For example, a sprig of mint would be more suitable as a garnish for a fruit-based salad than would a sprig of parsley, and finely chopped parsley would make a sliced tomato salad more appealing than would strips of pimiento. Strips of pimiento, on the other hand, would be more in keeping with a green bean salad than would a sprig of parsley.

It is extremely important to wash thoroughly any fresh greens, vegetables, or fruits to be used in salads. Dry greens using paper towels, clean linen, or a salad basket which can be whirled around to remove moisture. Dressing will not cling to greens that are moist, but will run off and settle at the bottom of salad bowl or plate.

Because tomatoes have a high water content, they should be combined with greens just prior to serving, otherwise they tend to wilt the greens (whole cherry tomatoes would be an exception). As a general rule, it is best to place cut-up tomatoes on the salad as a garnish in the center, to one side, or around the outside edges.

The core of iceberg lettuce may be removed by holding the head in the palm of one hand, core side up, and exerting slight pressure against the core with the other. Smashing the core with force against a hard surface frequently results in bruising the whole head.

NUTRITIVE VALUE

The green leafy vegetables, as well as the other vegetables and fruits used in salads, are extremely valuable sources of vitamins and minerals. For the most part, they are low in calories. Since they are generally eaten raw, one of their most important functions is to provide fiber in the diet. No longer are salads thought of as "rabbit food"—their nutritive benefits run high and form a very necessary part of a well-balanced diet.

Members of the lettuce family contain vitamin A, calcium, vitamin C, and iron. Raw spinach is a good source of vitamin A, ascorbic acid, potassium, calcium, riboflavin, niacin, thiamine, and phosphorus. Radishes are high in potassium and contain vitamin C, phosphorus, and calcium. Celery is high in potassium and vitamin A, as well as containing phosphorus, calcium, and ascorbic acid.

Nearly all raw fruits and many raw vegetables (cabbage, green and red peppers, tomatoes) are especially valued for their vitamin C content.

Salad dressings are beneficial in that they are a source of energy.

GARNISHES FOR VEGETABLE, MEAT, AND FISH SALADS

◇ Parsley, sprigs or finely chopped
◇ Watercress, sprigs
◇ Pimiento, julienne strips or cubes
◇ Carrots, curls or sticks
◇ Radishes, sliced or rose-shaped
◇ Cucumbers, slices
◇ Tomatoes, wedges
◇ Peppers, julienne strips or rings
◇ Stuffed green olives, slices
◇ Hardboiled eggs, wedges, slices
◇ Hardboiled egg yolks, finely chopped

GARNISHES FOR FRUIT SALADS

◇ Watercress, sprigs
◇ Nuts, coarsely chopped
◇ Mint, sprigs
◇ Strawberries, whole or sliced
◇ Cherries
◇ Grapes

◇ Blueberries
◇ Kumquats
◇ Pineapple, slices
◇ Melon balls
◇ Apple, slices (peel intact)
◇ Orange and grapefruit sections
◇ Shredded cocoanut
◇ Rosettes of whipped cream or whipped cream cheese

PURCHASING, PREPARATION, AND STORAGE OF SALAD INGREDIENTS

Refer to the Purchasing Tips section in Chapter 6 for procedures for the various greens, lettuce, and specific vegetables. For fruits refer to the preparation section of Chapter 8.

Gelatin Molds

Any shape container or mold, as well as individual molds, may be used.

For easy unmolding, grease interior of molds or containers with a thin layer of a canned vegetable oil spray.

When set, gelatin should have a soft and shiny appearance.

The longer gelatin sets, the stiffer it becomes; therefore, it is advisable not to prepare gelatin molds too far in advance.

An excess amount of gelatin results in a stiff, rubbery mold, and too little, produces one that is soft and watery.

As a general rule, a ¼-ounce (7 g) package unflavored gelatin or a 3-ounce (90 g) package flavored gelatin requires 2 cups fluid (water, fruit or vegetable juice, gingerale, consommé, or combinations thereof). However, vinegar and high acid fruits cut down on the action of the gel and adjustments should be made accordingly, either by increasing the amount of gelatin powder or decreasing the amount of liquid. (Fresh or frozen pineapple is one fruit that will almost completely inhibit the action of the gel.)

To prepare unflavored gelatin, sprinkle gelatin powder over a small amount of cold liquid (i.e., ¼ to ½ cup [60-120 ml] in a 2-cup [480 ml] liquid recipe), using a small heat-proof container, and set over hot (not boiling) water over low heat, stirring until dissolved. (This takes approximately 3 to 5 minutes.) Remove and set aside to cool slightly before combining with remaining liquid or other preparation. To ensure even distribution, ingredients may be placed in electric blender for about 1 minute. Place in greased mold(s) and chill in refrigerator until set.*

To prepare packaged flavored gelatin, add a small amount of hot liquid (about ½ to 1 cup [120-240 ml] in a 2-cup [480 ml] liquid recipe), stirring to dissolve, before combining with remaining cold liquid. Place in greased mold(s) and chill in refrigerator until set.†

When combining with fruits, vegetables, or other ingredients, chill in refrigerator until gelatin begins to set or takes on the consistency of an uncooked egg white. Remove and fold in filler ingredients before placing in greased mold(s). Filler ingredients may also be arranged in layers for a more attractive appearance, allowing each layer to chill and become fairly firm before adding another layer. (Bear in mind that the bottom layer will be the top layer when unmolded.) Use approximately 1½ cups (127 g) filler ingredients to 2 cups (472 ml) gelatin.

Mixed Salad (Greens and Vegetables)

Wash greens and dry thoroughly, otherwise they will be limp and dressing will lie at bottom of salad bowl. Cut or break up greens into bite-size pieces.

Use any one or all of the following greens (amounts will vary according to taste and size of salad):

◇ Romaine lettuce
◇ Iceberg lettuce
◇ Bibb lettuce
◇ Escarole

*Use 4 or 5 leaves of gelatin to 1 tablespoon (15 mi) powdered unflavored gelatin.

†Liquid used to dissolve gelatin need not necessarily be boiling. Also, the correct measure of cold water, juice, or consommé may be frozen in ice-cube trays in advance and used to decrease the time gelatin will take to cool and set.

◇ Watercress
◇ Spinach
◇ Endive
◇ Chicory (curly endive)
◇ Chinese cabbage
◇ Boston lettuce

Combine greens with any of the following uncooked fresh vegetables:

◇ Tomatoes, sliced, quartered, or coarsely chopped
◇ Cherry tomatoes, whole or halved
◇ Cucumbers, sliced
◇ Radishes, whole or sliced
◇ Onion family—red or white onions, scallions, chives, shallots—sliced
◇ Garlic, peeled and finely chopped
◇ Celery, sliced or chopped
◇ Carrots, grated, sliced, chopped, or in sticks
◇ Cabbage—red or white—shredded, sliced, or chopped
◇ Olives—green or black—whole and pitted, sliced, or chopped
◇ Pimiento, sliced or cut into julienne strips

Finely chopped fresh herbs, such as parsley, dill, tarragon, basil, and mint, may be added for additional flavoring.

Toss with Oil and Vinegar or other salad dressing, or serve dressing on the side.

SALAD RECIPES

CAESAR SALAD

1 large head romaine lettuce
4 slices crisp bacon, crumbled
½ cup (42.52 g) croutons
1 tablespoon fresh parsley,
   finely chopped
Oil and Vinegar Dressing
   No. 2

2 tablespoons grated Romano
   or Parmesan cheese
2 hardboiled eggs, quartered
8 anchovy fillets

Separate lettuce leaves, wash, and dry thoroughly. Break into bite-size pieces and place in salad bowl. Add bacon, along with croutons and chopped parsley. Toss with Oil and Vinegar Dressing No. 2 (see p. 316). Add grated cheese and toss again. Pile greens slightly higher toward the center. Garnish quartered eggs with anchovy fillets, and arrange near inside edge of salad bowl. Ingredients may also be arranged on a tray and salad prepared at table.

SPINACH SALAD

½ pound (225 g) raw spinach,
   coarsely chopped
Oil and Vinegar Dressing
   No. 1

2 hardboiled egg yolks, finely
   chopped

Wash spinach and dry thoroughly. Break into bite-size pieces or coarsely chop. Toss with Oil and Vinegar Dressing (see p. 316) and garnish with finely chopped egg yolk. Or serve dressing on the side.

SPINACH SALAD WITH BACON

4 slices crisp bacon, crumbled

Follow recipe for Spinach Salad, substituting crisp bacon for chopped egg yolk.

CUCUMBER SALAD WITH SOUR CREAM

2 cucumbers
salt
1 pint (480 ml) sour cream
1 tablespoon horseradish

1 tablespoon fresh dill, finely chopped
salt and white pepper

Peel and slice cucumbers in half. Remove center pulp containing seeds.

Cut into thin slices and place in a colander. Dust lightly with salt and toss. Set colander on a plate and refrigerate for 1 or 2 hours. Remove from refrigerator and discard water which cucumbers will have exuded. (Cucumbers will now be fairly crisp.) Combine cucumbers, sour cream, horseradish, and dill and mix. Season to taste with salt and white pepper. Refrigerate for several hours or overnight to blend flavors (cucumbers will remain crisp).

CUCUMBER AND CHIVE SALAD

2 cucumbers
Oil and Vinegar Dressing
*   No. 1*

1 tablespoon fresh lemon juice
2 tablespoons fresh chives,
*   finely chopped*

Prepare cucumbers as in Cucumber Salad with Sour Cream.

Combine crisp cucumbers with Oil and Vinegar Dressing No. 1. Add lemon juice and chives and toss. Marinate in refrigerator for about an hour to blend flavors.

TOMATO ASPIC

1 28-ounce (780 g) can
tomatoes; or 3 cups (720
ml) tomato juice
2 ¼-ounce packages (total of
15 g) unflavored gelatin

¼ cup (60 ml) water
4 tablespoons lemon juice
1 dried clove
1 tablespoon sugar
pinch of salt

Place canned tomatoes in blender for about 1 minute and strain, or use 3 cups tomato juice. The former will give more body and flavor to aspic. Dissolve gelatin in water and lemon juice over hot (not boiling) water, and stir over low heat until dissolved.

Combine pureed tomatoes or tomato juice, clove, sugar, and salt in a saucepan and set over low heat. Cook, uncovered, at a slow simmer for about 10 minutes. Remove clove and stir dissolved gelatin into mixture, or blend using electric blender.

Pour into a greased 1-quart (1 l) ring mold or individual molds and refrigerate for 6 to 8 hours or overnight. Remove and unmold.

CUCUMBER ASPIC

2 to 3 cucumbers, or 3 cups
(720 ml) pureed cucumbers
1 tablespoon freshly grated
onion
2 teaspoons prepared
horseradish
2 ¼-ounce packages (total 15
g) unflavored gelatin

¼ cup (60 ml) water
2 tablespoons fresh lemon
juice
1 tablespoon fresh dill, finely
chopped

Peel and slice cucumbers in half. Remove center pulp containing seeds. Cook in boiling water, uncovered, for about 3 minutes, or until fork tender. Puree in blender, food processor, or food mill. (There should be approximately 3 cups.) Add onion, horseradish, and dill and blend. Dissolve gelatin in ¼ cup (60 ml) water and 2 tablespoons lemon juice over hot (not boiling) water, and stir over low heat until dissolved. Add to cucumber mixture, stirring until well blended (or use electric blender). Pour into greased 1-quart mold or individual molds and refrigerate for 6 to 8 hours or overnight, before unmolding.

CUCUMBER MOUSSE

Prepare recipe for Cucumber Aspic and refrigerate until aspic has begun to set. Remove and fold in one-half pint (240 ml) of heavy cream, whipped. Pour into greased mold or individual molds and refrigerate for 6 to 8 hours or overnight, before unmolding.

SPRING SALAD

½ *recipe for Tomato Aspic*   *watercress*
½ *recipe for cucumber mousse*

Arrange Tomato Aspic and Cucumber Mousse, in alternate layers, on a bed of watercress.

FRUIT AND COTTAGE CHEESE SALAD NO. 1

lettuce   *fresh mint or watercress*
pineapple slices   *Fruit Salad Dressing*
cottage cheese   *   (optional)*
orange and grapefruit sections

Separate lettuce leaves, shape into cups, and arrange on salad plates. Place a slice of pineapple in the center of each and top with a scoop of cottage cheese. Lay orange and grapefruit sections on lettuce in alternating layers (2 of orange to 1 of grapefruit). Garnish with a small sprig of fresh mint or watercress. Serve with or without fruit Salad Dressing (p. 318).

FRUIT AND COTTAGE CHEESE SALAD NO. 2

lettuce
pear halves
cottage cheese

mint jelly
Fruit Salad Dressing
(optional)

Separate lettuce leaves, shape into cups, and arrange on salad plates. Lay pear halves cut-side up in center and top with a scoop of cottage cheese. Garnish with mint jelly, using small end of melon ball scoop. Serve with or without Fruit Salad Dressing (p. 318). (Canned pear juice may be substituted for orange and grapefruit juice in the dressing.)

FRUIT AND COTTAGE CHEESE SALAD NO. 3

lettuce
peach halves
cottage cheese

cherries
Fruit Salad Dressing
(optional)

Prepare as in Fruit and Cottage Cheese Salad No. 2, substituting peach-halves for pear-halves and cherries for mint jelly. (Canned peach juice may be substituted for orange and grapefruit juice in the dressing.)

ORIENTAL SALAD

Chinese cabbage
Oil and Vinegar Dressing No.
  1; or Italian Dressing

fresh parsley, finely chopped

Cut through center of cabbage and wash under cold running water. Dry thoroughly, using paper towels or a salad basket. Slice across at about ¼" (.5 cm) intervals. Toss with Oil and Vinegar Dressing No. 1 or Italian Dressing and arrange on salad plates. Garnish with finely chopped parsley.

GREEN BEAN SALAD

green beans, whole or sliced   lettuce
Oil and Vinegar Dressing   pimiento strips
  No. 1

Cut stems off green beans and cook whole or sliced in an uncovered pot with enough lightly salted boiling water so that the
beans can swim around while cooking. They should be bright
green and fairly crisp when fork-tested. Remove and drain using
a colander. Cool quickly but do not douse in cold water, otherwise beans will turn rubbery and will lose some of their flavor.
Marinate beans in Oil and Vinegar Dressing No. 1 for several
hours or overnight. Drain and arrange on a bed of lettuce.
Garnish with pimiento strips.

AVOCADO SALAD

1 grapefruit   cherries
1 ripe avocado   Fruit Salad Dressing
lettuce

Peel grapefruit and cut into sections, reserving a portion of juice.
Peel avocado, cut in half, and remove pit.* Cut across into thin
slices and dip in reserved grapefruit juice. Using individual salad
plates, arrange avocado and grapefruit sections on lettuce leaves
in alternate layers (2 of avocado to 1 grapefruit), piling slightly
higher toward the center. Garnish with cherries (1 per salad) and
serve Fruit Salad Dressing on the side.

*When storing avocado, leave pit intact to prevent discoloration.

GELATIN FRUIT MOLD NO. 1

¼ cup (60 ml) cold water
1 ¼-ounce (7 g) package
   unflavored gelatin
1½ cups (360 ml) less 1
   tablespoon fruit juice
1 tablespoon fresh lemon juice
1 to 2 tablespoons sugar,
   according to sweetness of
   fruit juice

pinch of salt
1½ cups cut-up fresh fruit
   (except fresh or frozen
   pineapple)
4 tablespoons unsweetened
   cocoanut (optional)

Place cold water in a small heat-proof dish or pan and sprinkle over gelatin. Set over hot (not boiling) water over low heat, stirring until dissolved. Set aside to cool slightly before combining with fruit juice, lemon juice, sugar, and salt. (To ensure even distribution, blend in electric blender for about 1 minute.) Chill in refrigerator until gelatin begins to set or takes on the consistency of uncooked egg white. Remove and fold in cut-up fruit and cocoanut. Turn into 1-quart (1 l) mold or individual molds which have been lightly greased with a vegetable oil spray (for easy unmolding). Set in refrigerator and chill until firm. When set, unmold onto individual serving plates or platter.

GELATIN FRUIT MOLD NO. 2

½ cup (120 ml) boiling water
1 3-ounce (80 g) package
   flavored gelatin (orange,
   strawberry, lemon,
   raspberry)

1¼ cups (300 ml) fruit juice
   or cold water, less 1
   tablespoon
1 tablespoon fresh lemon juice
1½ cups cut-up fresh fruit

Gradually add boiling water to flavored gelatin, stirring to dissolve. Stir in fruit juice or water, along with lemon juice. Chill in refrigerator until gelatin begins to set or takes on the consistency of uncooked egg white. Remove and fold in fruit. Turn into a 1-quart (1 l) mold or individual molds which have been lightly greased with a vegetable oil spray (for easy unmolding). Set in refrigerator and chill until firm. When set, unmold onto platter or individual serving plates.

GELATIN VEGETABLE MOLD NO. 1

1 ¼-ounce (7 g) package
  unflavored gelatin
¼ cup (60 ml) cold water
1½ cups (360 ml) vegetable
  juice or consommé, less 1
  tablespoon
1 tablespoon lemon juice
1 teaspoon cider vinegar

pinch of salt
1¼ cups fresh cut-up
  vegetables (cucumbers,
  celery, green pepper,
  tomato)
¼ cup cooked corn kernels
watercress

Sprinkle gelatin over cold water in a small heat-proof container and set over hot (not boiling) water over low heat, stirring to dissolve. Set aside to cool slightly before combining with vegetable juice or consommé, lemon juice, vinegar, and salt. (To ensure even distribution, blend in electric blender for about 1 minute.) Chill in refrigerator until gelatin begins to set or takes on the consistency of uncooked egg white. Remove and fold in vegetables. Turn into 1-quart (1 l) mold or individual molds which have been lightly greased with a vegetable oil spray, and chill until firm. (Vegetables may also be arranged in layers for a more attractive appearance; allow each layer to chill in refrigerator and become fairly firm before adding another.) When set, unmold onto platter or individual salad plates and garnish with watercress.

GELATIN VEGETABLE MOLD NO. 2

½ cup (120 ml) boiling water
1 3-ounce (80 g) package
  flavored gelatin (lemon or
  lime)
1¼ cups (300 ml) vegetable
  juice or cold water, less 1
  tablespoon

1 tablespoon lemon juice
1 teaspoon vinegar
pinch of salt
1½ cups cut-up fresh
  vegetables
watercress

Gradually add boiling water to flavored gelatin, stirring to dissolve. Stir in vegetable juice or water, lemon juice, vinegar, and salt. Chill in refrigerator until gelatin begins to set or takes on the consistency of an uncooked egg white. Remove and fold in cut-up vegetables. Turn into a 1-quart (1 l) mold or individual molds that have been lightly greased with a vegetable oil spray, and refrigerate until firm. When set, unmold onto platter or individual serving plates and garnish with watercress.

TOMATO SALAD

fully ripe tomatoes   *fresh parsley, finely chopped*

Carefully peel tomatoes and remove stem section (skin should peel off easily if fully ripe). Cut into ⅛″ (.3 cm) thick slices and arrange on salad plates, piling slightly higher toward the center. Garnish with finely chopped parsley.

CHICKEN, SHRIMP, OR LOBSTER SALAD

*1 pound (450 g) cooked
  chicken, shrimp, or lobster,
  diced
4 stalks celery, peeled and
  finely chopped
4 shallots or 1 small onion,
  finely chopped
salt and white pepper to taste*

*1 tablespoon fresh parsley,
  finely chopped
mayonnaise, according to
  desired consistency
lettuce
tomato wedges
cucumber slices*

Combine diced chicken, shrimp, or lobster with celery, shallots or onion, salt and white pepper, and chopped parsley and toss. Carefully mix in mayonnaise according to desired consistency. Using a scoop, serve on a bed of lettuce and garnish with tomato wedges and cucumber slices.

CRABMEAT OR TUNA SALAD

Follow recipe for Chicken, Shrimp, or Lobster Salad, substituting shredded crabmeat or tuna for diced chicken, shrimp, or lobster.

BEET SALAD

1 16-ounce (450 g) can sliced
  beets
1 onion
1 teaspoon mixed pickling
  spices

2 tablespoons cider vinegar
lettuce

Drain and reserve liquid from beets. Peel and cut onion into thin slices. Place pickling spices on a double layer piece of cheesecloth and tie to form a small bag. Add vinegar to beet juice along with bag of spices, sliced onions, and beets. Marinate in refrigerator for several hours or overnight. (It may be necessary to add water, as beets should be fully covered.) Drain and serve on a bed of lettuce on individual salad plates. Garnish with 2 or 3 onion rings.

POTATO SALAD NO. 1

7 or 8 potatoes, unpeeled
1 onion, peeled and finely
  chopped
2 tablespoons chives, finely
  chopped
4 stalks celery, peeled and
  finely chopped
salt and white pepper to taste

mayonnaise, according to
  desired consistency
lettuce
parsley
hardboiled eggs, quartered
tomato wedges
cucumber slices

Scrub potatoes clean and cook in lightly salted boiling water until fairly crisp when fork-tested. Drain, cool, peel, and uniformly slice or dice. Combine with chopped onions, chives, and celery. Season to taste with salt and white pepper. Mix in mayonnaise according to desired consistency. Using a scoop, serve on a bed of lettuce neatly arranged on individual salad plates. Top with a sprig of parsley, and garnish with quartered hardboiled eggs, tomato wedges, and cucumber slices.

POTATO SALAD NO. 2

Prepare according to recipe for Potato Salad No. 1, substituting Oil and Vinegar Dressing No. 1 or Italian Dressing for Mayonnaise.

WALDORF SALAD

4 celery stalks, peeled
4 or 5 apples
mayonnaise, according to
   desired consistency

walnuts, coarsely chopped
lettuce

Wash peeled celery stalks under cold running water and dry thoroughly. Cut from end to end into long ½″ (1 cm) wide strips. Collect several strips and cut across at ½″ (1 cm) intervals. Wash apples and peel, leaving a portion of red skin. Quarter and core using an apple-corer slicer. Cut into ½″ (1 cm) cubes and toss in lemon juice to prevent discoloration. Combine apples and celery and stir in mayonnaise. Using individual salad plates, neatly arrange on lettuce leaves and garnish with chopped walnuts.

CHEF'S SALAD

carrot curls
mixed greens
radishes
cherry tomatoes
pitted black olives
breast of cooked turkey slices,
   ¼″ (.5 cm) thick

cooked ham slices, ¼″ (.5 cm)
   thick
Swiss cheese slices, ⅛″ (.3 cm)
   thick
dressing

Peel carrots, wash under running water and cut into thin ribbons, using a vegetable peeler. Cover with ice-cold water and refrigerate. (A medium-size carrot will make approximately 7 or 8 carrot curls.)

Wash greens and dry thoroughly with paper towels or in a salad basket. Break up or cut into bite-size pieces. Wash radishes and tomatoes. Cut radishes into thin slices. Place greens in salad bowl or individual salad bowls, along with radishes, tomatoes, and black olives and toss. Cut turkey, ham and cheese slices into julienne strips and place across salad. Remove carrot curls from refrigerator, drain, and use as a garnish. Serve salad dressing on the side.

SALAD DRESSINGS

Oil and Vinegar Dressings

As a general rule, use three parts oil to one part vinegar.

While olive oil suits this type of dressing best, other oils, such as sesame, safflower, or salad oil may be substituted. Certain oils are lighter and milder than others, for example, French olive oil, and require a slightly higher proportion of vinegar to oil. Some vinegars are also milder than others—tarragon vinegar, for instance, is generally milder than cider vinegar.

Lemon juice may be substituted for all or part of vinegar content.

OIL AND VINEGAR DRESSING NO. 1

1½ cups (360 ml) vegetable oil
½ cup (120 ml) vinegar
½ teaspoon salt
¼ teaspoon pepper

½ teaspoon dry mustard, dissolved in water
1 clove garlic, peeled and left whole

Place ingredients, with the exception of garlic clove, in a cruet or bottle and shake well, or blend in an electric blender. Add garlic clove and store until ready to use. Remove garlic clove before serving. (The flavor of the dressing will largely depend on the quality of the oil and vinegar.)

OIL AND VINEGAR DRESSING NO. 2

1½ cups (360 ml) vegetable oil
½ cup (120 ml) vinegar, less 2 tablespoons
2 tablespoons fresh lemon juice
1 teaspoon granulated sugar
½ teaspoon dry mustard, dissolved in water
2 teaspoons prepared mustard (Dijon)

½ teaspoon salt
¼ teaspoon prepared mustard (Dijon)
½ teaspoon salt
¼ teaspoon pepper
1 whole egg plus 1 yolk
1 clove garlic, peeled and left whole

Place ingredients, with the exception of garlic, in electric blender for about 1 minute, or until thoroughly blended. Add garlic clove and store in airtight container in refrigerator for several hours. (Dressing will thicken somewhat upon refrigeration.) Remove garlic clove before serving.

CHEESE DRESSING

Follow recipe for Oil and Vinegar Dressing No. 2 and add three ounces (80 g) of crumbled Roquefort or Blue cheese.

CREAMY FRENCH DRESSING

Follow recipe for Oil and Vinegar Dressing No. 2 and add 1 cup (240 ml) tomato juice and 1 additional egg yolk.

ITALIAN DRESSING

Follow recipe for Oil and Vinegar Dressing No. 1 or No. 2 and add 1 0.6 ounce (17 g) package of Italian seasonings.

HERB DRESSING

1 tablespoon fresh parsley, finely chopped

1 tablespoon fresh basil, finely chopped

Follow recipe for Oil and Vinegar Dressing No. 1 and add finely chopped parsley and basil.

LOW CALORIE FRENCH DRESSING

¼ cup olive oil (vegetable oil)

1½ tablespoons vinegar, mildly flavored

2 tablespoons fresh lemon juice

1½ teaspoons Worcestershire sauce

dash of Tabasco

2 cups (480 ml) tomato juice

pinch of salt

2 tablespoons beaten whole egg

1 garlic clove, peeled

Place ingredients, with the exception of garlic, in electric blender for about 1 minute, or until thoroughly blended. Add garlic clove and refrigerate for several hours. (Dressing will thicken somewhat upon refrigeration.) Remove garlic clove before serving.

SOUR CREAM DRESSING

1 pint (480 ml) sour cream

1 tablespoon fresh onion juice

1 tablespoon prepared horseradish, or according to taste

1 tablespoon fresh dill, finely chopped

Blend ingredients and refrigerate in airtight container (or cover with plastic wrap) until ready to use. About 1 to 2 hours is required in order for flavors to blend properly. For a thinner dressing, add 2 or 3 tablespoons light cream and mix in.

FRUIT SALAD DRESSING

½ cup (120 ml) vegetable oil (olive)

½ cup (120 ml) fresh orange or grapefruit juice; or a combination

1 tablespoon fresh lemon juice

1 tablespoon sugar

pinch of salt

Place ingredients in electric blender for about 1 minute, or until thoroughly blended; or use a cruet, shaking until well blended.

MAYONNAISE

2 egg yolks or 1 whole egg
½ teaspoon salt
¼ teaspoon paprika
dash of cayenne pepper
pinch of white pepper

2 tablespoons vinegar or fresh
  lemon juice
1 cup (240 ml) olive or sesame
  oil

Blend egg yolks or egg with seasonings, using electric blender. Add one tablespoon vinegar or lemon juice and blend. Add oil a teaspoon at a time, blending after each addition. When ½ cup of oil has been used, add remaining vinegar or lemon juice. Blend in remaining oil.

Mustard Mayonnaise

Follow recipe for Mayonnaise and add 1 teaspoon prepared mustard, along with seasonings.

Roquefort Mayonnaise

Combine ½ cup finely crumbled Roquefort cheese with ½ cup (120 ml) sour cream and fold into finished Mayonnaise.

Horseradish Mayonnaise

Follow recipe for Mayonnaise and add 1 tablespoon well-drained horseradish along with seasonings.

Extra Light Mayonnaise

Follow recipe for Mayonnaise and fold ½ cup (120 ml) whipped cream into finished Mayonnaise.

FRUITS
FOR ALL SEASONS

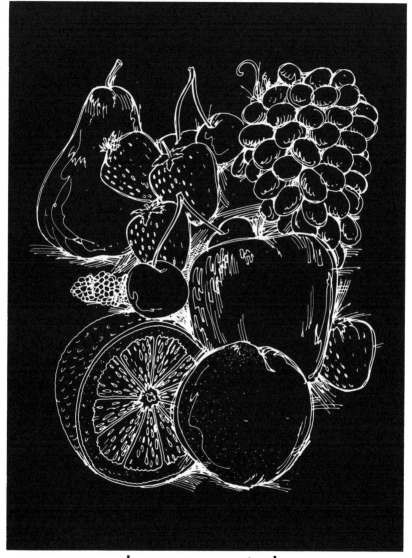

chapter eight

FRUITS

Rare, exotic, and *bountiful* are just a few of the descriptive words that come to mind when one dwells, if only momentarily, on the rather unique status given fruit in the annals of recorded history. Even the origin of its name holds out the promise of something special, for it stems (through the French) from the Latin, *fructus — frui,* meaning "to enjoy."

Its status is further shown in its wide use as a symbol. The New Testament tells us, "By their fruits ye shall know them." The Old Testament offers, "He kept him as the apple of his eye." Shakespeare's works are replete with such sayings as, " . . . the weakest kind of fruit drops earliest to the ground" and "For one sweet grape who will the vine destroy?" In Julia Ward Howe's "Battle Hymn of the Republic"—

> He is tramping out the vintage
> Where the grapes of wrath are stored.

And in Robert Browning's "A Woman's Last Word":

> Where the apple reddens
> Never pry—
> Lest we lose our Edens,
> Eve and I.

And almost everyone has heard of the forbidden fruit, the olive branch, the fruit of the womb, the grapevine, and a real plum.

It was no accident that so many great and famous desserts created by the incomparable nineteenth-century chefs have one or another fruit as a base. Take, for instance, Peach Melba, Cherries Jubilee, Strawberries Romanoff, Pears Helene, or Apple Charlotte. These delectable creations were made from only the choicest fruit, sun-ripened, and at the peak of perfection. It was, in fact, the superb quality of the fruit that earned the desserts their reputation.

In the past fruits, for the most part, were enjoyed in season. Their arrival was celebrated with strawberry festivals, apple festivals, and grape harvesting celebrations. Spring brought forth one family of fruit, summer another, and autumn still another. The fully ripe fruit was prepared in any number of ingenious and creative ways, and what was left over was dried, canned, or preserved in some way to be enjoyed in its own particular fashion during the long winter ahead.

When fruit is fully ripe it has developed to its full size, the color has changed, and it is succulent and tender. In addition, the starch content has changed to sugar, causing it to be sweet and to give off its full, characteristic, delectable aroma. When fruit is left to mature naturally, these changes are brought about in nature's own inimitable fashion.

The introduction of cold storage systems around 1800 marked the beginnings of a whole new approach in the distribution of fruit and led, among other things, to harvesting the greater percentage of fruit while it was still green, that is, underripe. Then the fruit was ripened artificially—as opposed to sun-ripening. Ethylene gas was and is used to destroy the green color pigment, chlorophyll. Artificial color is then added to the skins of such fruit as oranges and tomatoes to give them a fully ripe appearance. (Many vegetables are given similar treatment.) The fruit is then shipped, or it is stored in warehouses where both temperature and humidity are controlled according to the nature of the fruit. These practices have led to fresh fruits being available all year long. They have also moderated fluctuations in the supply of fruit and, consequently, its price. Regarding price, it should be noted that the storage of fruit adds to its overall cost.

The great variations of climate in America make it possible to grow a wide variety of fruit in great quantity, probably more so than in any other country in the world. The fruit is shipped from and to all points, as well as to many other parts of the globe. This abundance is truly a blessing, but it is to be regretted that we have little opportunity to experience the true flavor of fruit in its perfectly ripe state.

NUTRITIVE VALUE

Fresh fruits provide a host of vitamins, minerals, and enzymes. Their greatest single attraction is their high percentage of natural sugars, which the body can use to advantage, as opposed to other sugars. The enzymes in fresh fruit facilitate the rapid assimilation by the body of the nutrients in all fruits.

Most fresh fruits contain large amounts of vitamin C. The yellow fruits (bananas, peaches, cantaloupe, apricots) contain vitamin A. A generous proportion of phosphorus and iron, as well as smaller amounts of calcium, are found in most fruits. Dried fruits such as raisins, apricots, prunes, peaches, and dates are good sources of iron. A ½ cup serving provides at least one-sixth of the recommended daily requirement of iron (for normal healthy individuals).

In addition, fresh fruits add needed fiber to the diet.

With the exception of avocados and ripe olives, fruits do not contain any appreciable amount of fat. Sweetened processed (frozen and canned) fruits in sugar syrup are considerably higher in calories than fresh fruit.

GUIDE TO PURCHASING
AND STORING FRESH FRUITS

The U.S. Department of Agriculture has set up a grading system for the purchase and sale of fruit which applies, however, only to the wholesale trade. The grades are Extra Fancy, Fancy, Extra No. 1. The lower grades, U.S. No. 1 and No. 2, are those generally made available to the consumer. The overall quality of these two categories, combined with a high degree of waste, frequently leaves much to be desired.

It is best to purchase fruits in amounts which can be used within a short period. For the most part, overripe and underripe fruits have little value. When at the peak of perfection, the starch content in fruit will have changed to sugar, resulting in full sweet flavor and characteristic aroma and color. The liquid content of some fruits increases as they ripen; thus citrus fruits, peaches, pineapple, and all kinds of melons can be judged to a degree by their relative heaviness.

It is the enzymes in fruit which bring about the changes that improve its quality. These changes, however, continue working after the fruit has reached maturity, resulting in loss of flavor, brown spots, and overall deterioration.

It is advisable not to purchase fruit that is green or underripe, unless it is to be cooked, as it is difficult to ripen most fruits without the proper temperature and humidity controls. However, when only unripened fruits are available, store at room temperature rather than in the refrigerator. Some fruits, such as citrus, ripen more easily at cool-room temperature. Strawberries, blueberries, and other berries should be refrigerated and kept dry.

Deterioration of fully ripe fruits may be retarded to a degree by refrigerating. However, they should be eaten as soon as possible.

HOW TO RETAIN FLAVOR, COLOR, AND FRESHNESS

The most important rule when preparing fully ripe fresh fruit is to add no sugar, or a minimal amount. It draws out the natural juices and detracts from the fruit's own flavor.

Certain fruits turn brown or discolor when they are cut up in advance of serving. This can be prevented to a degree by combining these fruits with one or more citrus fruit and adding a small proportion of dried unsweetened cocoanut, which is available in most health food and specialty stores. (Most supermarket cocoanut is the sweetened variety and has no value as a preservative.) Sliced fruit prepared in this manner will maintain its freshness and color under refrigeration. Other substances which act as preservatives are fresh lemon juice and powdered ascorbic acid (vitamin C). One caution, however. If lemon juice is added in too large a quantity, it will overpower the sweet flavor of the fruit. A mixture of powdered ascorbic acid and sugar, available at most drugstores under a trade name, is also useful in retaining the flavor of fresh fruit. Dissolved in a teaspoon or so of lemon juice and tossed with fresh fruit, it lends both color and freshness. It can also be added to frozen and canned fruit juices to enhance their flavor and nutrition.

PREPARATION OF FRESH FRUITS

CITRUS FRUIT   Peel, using a stainless steel sawtooth knife, cutting around the fruit with a sawing motion, removing all skin and white pulp. Divide fruit into sections by cutting along each dividing membrane, or cut into thin, uniform size slices. Sections of fruit may also be served without removing membrane.

Citrus fruit may also be grated, using a ceramic or stainless steel hand grater. (Tin will discolor and rust.) Remove extreme outer layer of peel with a vegetable peeler or sharp, thin-bladed knife.

STONE FRUITS Remove skin (peaches, plums, nectarines) by blanching in boiling water for about 60 seconds, or until skin has loosened. Drain, and when cool enough to handle, remove skins. (Do not douse in cold water.) Slice fruit in half and remove stone. Serve fruit halved, quartered or uniformly sliced.

SEEDED FRUITS Remove skin from such fruits as apples and pears, using a vegetable peeler or a sharp knife. (There are automatic peelers on the market but they are not readily available to consumers.) Use a corer-slicer, which may be purchased at most housewares outlets, to remove core and produce uniform size slices.

MELONS Slice melons (cantaloupe, honeydew) in half and remove pulp containing seeds. Cut into halves, quarters, or eighths, depending on size and use. Before serving, carefully cut pulp away from outside rind, but do not remove.

Remove rind from watermelon and serve in slices, accompanied by a dessert knife and fork.

BANANAS Bananas are more appealing when peeled and sliced across diagonally, rather than straight across. Sliced bananas to be served sometime later will not discolor if they are tossed in unsweetened, shredded cocoanut.

PROCEDURES:
COOKED AND UNCOOKED FRUITS

FRYING Fry fruit slices from apples, pears, bananas, peaches, or pineapple in a small amount of butter over low heat until heated through and barely tender. (Do not overcook.) Fried fruit may be put to the following uses:

◇ With a sauce
◇ As a filling for pancakes (crêpes)
◇ With waffles
◇ As a filling for dessert omelettes
◇ With French toast
◇ Over sherbet or ice cream
◇ With puddings and custards
◇ Folded into whipped cream
◇ With meats (apple, pear, pineapple, peach, or orange slices combine well with duck, poultry, ham, pork)

POACHING   Poaching is suitable to both fully ripe and slightly underripe fruit. Poach in water, wine, or a light sugar syrup if fruit is fairly green. Add lemon juice, diced citrus peel, fruit extract, liqueurs, or seeds from vanilla pod to poaching liquid to enhance flavor.

Bring liquid to a slow simmer, lower heat, and add prepared fruit (peeled and cored, whole, halved, or sliced). Cook over low heat until barely tender. Regulate heat so as to keep liquid just about at simmering point.

When wine has been used as a poaching liquid, remove fruit, and reduce over high heat until alcohol content has evaporated. Lightly thicken with fruit jelly, or use a thickening agent such as arrowroot or cornstarch dissolved in wine or water, and serve with fruit.

STEWING   This cooking procedure is particularly suited to green and underripe fruit, as well as to fully ripe fruit which is not going to be put to immediate use. Green fruit will require the addition of some type of sweetener (honey, brown sugar, maple syrup, or white sugar); however, a minimum amount should be added.

Remove peel, core, seeds, and stones from fruit and cut into halves, quarters, or slices. Add sweetener, if necessary, and enough water to create steam. Cover and set over low heat just long enough to soften fruit. Remove and add a few drops of lemon juice.

Strawberries, blueberries, or raspberries may be stewed in their own juices in an uncovered saucepan over low heat. A small amount of sugar may be added, depending on degree of ripeness. However, if fully ripe and filled with juice, no other sweetener is necessary.

MARINADES   Wines, champagne, sherry, and liqueurs can be used as a marinade for fresh fruit. Their flavor and overall quality should be equal in stature to that of the fruit, otherwise they will serve only to detract.

LEMON JUICE   The addition of a small proportion of fresh lemon juice will both draw out and enhance the flavor of many foods. (It can also be used as a substitute for salt.) In order to retain its natural flavor and high vitamin C content, add lemon juice to cooked preparations *after* they have been removed from the heat, unless otherwise specified.

While most foods will benefit from the addition of fresh lemon juice, cooked greens is one exception. A good flavor substitute that will not discolor greens is vinegar. Keep in mind, however, that cooked greens served with lemon sauce (thickened with flour or other starch) make an excellent entree or side dish.

Add fresh lemon juice to any of the following:

◇ Fresh fruit sauces
◇ Stewed fruit
◇ Cooked vegetables
◇ Raw salad vegetables
◇ Both hot and cold fish and shellfish dishes
◇ Cut up fresh fruit
◇ Boiled water or very weak tea as a substitute for strong tea or coffee
◇ White meats (chicken, veal, pork)
◇ To deglaze pan in which meats or fish were cooked
◇ Soups and sauces
◇ Salad dressings
◇ Flavoring for baked goods
◇ Gelatin desserts and salads

GELATIN DESSERTS AND VEGETABLE SALADS   Substitute fresh fruit juice for water in the preparation of gelatin desserts, and omit sugar. (Use one ¼-ounce [7 g] package unflavored gelatin for every 2 cups [480 ml] liquid.) Use fresh vegetable juice in the preparation of gelatin vegetable salads.

FRUITS AND NUTS.   Use grated and chopped nuts to garnish fruits and to provide a contrasting flavor and texture as well as added nutrition.

FRUIT RECIPES

PEACHES MELBA

Raspberry Sauce   *sherbet or ice cream*
4 fresh peaches (fully ripe)

Prepare sauce according to recipe for Raspberry Sauce (p. 335).

Blanch peaches in boiling water for about 1 minute, or until skins become loosened. (Peaches should be fully ripe and tender.) Drain and remove skins. Cut peaches in half and remove stones.

Arrange peach halves in sherbet glasses and top with a scoop of sherbet or ice cream. Spoon over 2 or 3 tablespoons Raspberry Sauce and serve.

STRAWBERRY FOOL

1 quart (1 l) fresh   *½ pint (240 ml) heavy cream*
  strawberries   *2 tablespoons powdered sugar*
2-inch (5 cm) piece vanilla
  pod

Hull and wash strawberries and drain on paper towels. Cut into slices.

Add seeds from vanilla pod to heavy cream and whip, gradually adding powdered sugar. Reserve several strawberry slices for garnishing and fold remainder into whipped cream. Serve in champagne glasses and garnish with two or three slices of strawberry.

RASPBERRY FOOL

Follow recipe for Strawberry Fool, substituting whole raspberries for sliced strawberries.

MEDLEY OF FRESH FRUIT

1 grapefruit, peeled	*2 tablespoons powdered sugar*
2 oranges, peeled	*(optional)*
2 apples, peeled	*2 bananas*
unsweetened cocoanut	*kirsch*
½ pint (480 ml) heavy cream	
(optional)	

Divide peeled grapefruit and oranges into sections by cutting along dividing membrane. Core and uniformly slice peeled apples, using a corer-slicer. Cut apple slices into cubes. Sprinkle fruit (with exception of bananas) with unsweetened cocoanut, and toss. (Do *not* add sugar.) Refrigerate until ready to serve.

Whip heavy cream, gradually adding powdered sugar, and refrigerate.

When ready to serve, slice bananas across diagonally and fold into prepared fruit. Spoon into dessert dishes and sprinkle with a few drops of kirsch. Ladle a tablespoon or two of whipped cream over each, or serve cream on the side.

PEARS HELENE

Chocolate Sauce	*sherbet or ice cream*
fresh pears, fully ripe	*finely chopped hazelnuts*

Prepare sauce according to recipe for Chocolate Sauce (p. 334).

Peel pears, slice in half, and remove seed portion. Cut into uniform size slices and poach until barely tender. Remove and drain.

Arrange a scoop of sherbet or ice cream in dessert dishes and top with pear slices. Spoon on Chocolate Sauce and garnish with finely chopped nuts.

APPLE SNOW

7 or 8 apples, peeled
Juice of ½ lemon
½ to ¾ cup (120-180 ml)
   boiling water

½ pint (240 ml) heavy cream
2 tablespoons powdered sugar
mint jelly

Core and uniformly slice peeled apples, using a corer-slicer. Cook apple slices in lemon juice and boiling water (there should be just enough water to create steam) in a covered pan over high heat until slightly softened. This should take but a few minutes. Puree cooked apples in blender.

Whip cream, gradually adding powdered sugar, and fold into warm apple puree. Serve warm or chilled. Top with mint jelly, or serve on the side.

MELONS

cantaloupe or honeydew
   melons

cinnamon sugar

Slice through center of melons and scoop out pulp and seeds. Serve halved or quartered, depending on size. Using a sharp knife, carefully cut melon away from outside skin, but do not remove. Combine powdered cinnamon and finely granulated sugar (according to taste) and sprinkle over melons.

FRESH PEARS GRACIENNE

8 fresh pears, fully ripe
Custard Sauce
pinch of cream of tartar
5 egg whites   *meringue*
½ cup (99 g) powdered sugar
8 stem-size pieces angelique
slivered almonds

Peel *fully ripe* pears and remove cores through bottom end, using a fruit corer, leaving stem end whole. Poach until tender and drain. Pat dry and set aside.

Prepare sauce according to recipe in Chapter 5 for Custard Sauce, and set aside.

Add cream of tartar to egg whites and beat until they begin to foam. Gradually add powdered sugar, beating until meringue can be shaped into soft peaks and takes on a glossy appearance. Place two-thirds meringue in pastry bag with a plain tube, and remaining one-third in pastry bag with a star tube.

Carefully cut out stems from pears and set on baking sheet, several inches apart, stem side up. Using pastry bag with plain tube, pipe meringue around pears until completely encased. Using pastry bag with star tube, pipe a rosette on top of each pear, finishing off with a peak. Place stem-size pieces of angelique near peak to represent stems. Arrange a border of slivered almonds around bottom of meringue-encased pears. Bake in a preheated 450° F. (232° C.) oven until lightly browned. Remove and set in a draft-free area. (Pears may be baked in advance and stored in refrigerator when cool.)

Assemble by ladling Custard Sauce at room temperature into wide-mouth, shallow dessert dishes about ½″ (1 cm) up from bottom. Using a broad spatula, carefully arrange pears in center, and serve.

SYRUP AND SWEET SAUCES

SUGAR SYRUP (LIGHT)

5 tablespoons sugar
pinch of cream of tartar
juice of 1 lemon

grated lemon rind
4 cups (960 ml) water

Add sugar, cream of tartar, lemon juice and rind to water and set over low heat, stirring until sugar is dissolved. Bring to a slow simmer and cook until slightly thickened. Use for poaching fresh fruit which is not fully ripe.

CHOCOLATE SAUCE

2 squares (2 oz. or 60 g)
   unsweetened baking
   chocolate
5 tablespoons sugar
¼ cup (60 ml) light corn
   syrup

pinch of cream of tartar
pinch of salt
¾ cup (180 ml) water
2 tablespoons chocolate
   liqueur
1 to 2 tablespoons butter

Pour enough boiling water over chocolate to cover, and set aside to melt.

Combine sugar, corn syrup, cream of tartar, salt, water, and liqueur and set over low heat, stirring until sugar has dissolved. Turn heat to medium and simmer for 2 or 3 minutes. Carefullly drain water from chocolate; add melted chocolate to sugar mixture, cooking just long enough to blend. Remove from heat and stir in 1 or 2 tablespoons butter. For a thinner sauce, add 1 or 2 tablespoons boiling water.

SERVING SUGGESTIONS Serve with fruit, ice cream, brownies, cakes, and other desserts.

RASPBERRY SAUCE

1½ cups (360 ml) fresh orange
    juice, strained
1 tablespoon fresh lemon juice
3 tablespoons seedless
    raspberry jam, unsweetened

1 tablespoon cornstarch
2 tablespoons kirsch

Bring strained orange juice, lemon juice, and raspberry jam to a slow simmer over low heat. Dissolve cornstarch in 2 tablespoons kirsch and add, stirring until lightly thickened.

SERVING SUGGESTIONS   Serve with fresh fruit, sherbet, ice cream, puddings, and other desserts.

GRAINS: BROWN IS BEAUTIFUL

ENDOSPERM
(used to make
white flour)

BRAN
(outer layers
of kernel)

GERM
(sprouting section
of seed)

WHEAT KERNEL

chapter nine

THE STAFF OF LIFE

I made a study of the ancient and indispensable art
of bread-making, consulting such authorities as offered,
going back to the primitive days, and first invention
of the unleavened kind, when from the wildness of nuts
and meats men first reached the mildness and refinement of
this diet, and travelling gradually down in my studies through
the accidental souring of the dough which it is supposed,
taught the leavening process and through the various fermentation
thereafter, till I came to "good sweet wholesome bread,"
the staff of life.

Henry David Thoreau (1817-1862)

During his two-year experiment in living with nature in the Massachusetts woods, Thoreau, American philosopher and naturalist, pondered and researched what he termed "the grossest groceries" with which humans have sustained themselves throughout the ages. He recorded his thoughts and findings in *Walden*, published some nine years later.

Whether or not Thoreau raised his own grains is uncertain. During the eight-month period from July 4, 1845 to March 1, 1846, he spent a total of 99¾ cents for Indian corn and 88 cents for rye flour. He later recorded, "I saw that I could easily raise my bushel or two of rye and Indian corn, for the former will grow on the poorest land, and the latter does not require the best, and grind them in a hand-mill, and so do without rice and pork. . . ."

For thousands of years, all that was needed to produce grain was a few seeds, a pointed stick, a pair of oxen, and some kind of sickle. From the very beginning, the major civilizations of the world rested on grain culture. It was to the abundance of the grain harvests of one season that people looked to meet the needs of the next. Grains stored well, satisfied even the most hearty appetite and, in economic terms, were the foodstuff par excellence. Of greater significance culturally was both the inherent love (and need) peoples around the world have had for one or the other grain food, be it bread, tortillas, or bowls of rice.

The discovery of these "flowers" of the grasses as foodstuffs is shrouded in the dawn of civilization. It is known that one of the first flours was made from wheat and "flour" still designates that particular grain. Its overall importance was expressed in the garlands of wheat used to symbolize plentitude and power, both in the ancient shrines erected to pay it homage and in celebrated festivals, old and new.

With the exception of rye, which contains a very limited amount, wheat is the only grain that has embedded in it a protein called gluten. Gluten is defined as a "tenacious elastic protein substance especially of wheat flour that gives cohesiveness to dough." When flour is combined with liquid and yeast, the gluten content gives elasticity to the dough, allows it to expand, and when exposed to heat, results in a fine-textured, flavorful product called bread.

The story of sour dough and of the first leavened bread dates back to early Egyptian civilization. In those days grain had to be toasted before it could be parted from its chaff and ground. However, once the gluten-forming property of wheat is exposed to heat, it hardens, making raised bread an impossibility. Thanks to the ancient Egyptians, a variety of wheat was eventually produced that parted easily and could be ground without the application of heat. Before too long, leavened bread was created— supposedly through the accidental souring of the dough. When it was realized that fermentation was at work, a fermenting agent was introduced into the dough. (For a long time, however, a piece of sour dough was kept and used as a starter whenever and wherever yeast was not readily available.) The leavened bread did not immediately appeal to all, and today many peoples cling to their traditional unleavened cakes.

These early Egyptians crushed their grain between stones and then pounded it by hand, a method still used in many parts of the world. Later, grains were ground between two huge wheels, made to rotate by means of either wind or water power, and milling—the world's oldest industry—came into being. Fine, medium, and coarse grains could be produced by adjusting the stones. The whole nutritious grain was used.

Many refinements were developed to make milling easier and to produce a finer grade, but no drastic changes were made until about the beginning of the 1800s. At this time purifiers were introduced, making it possible to remove all bran particles. The far-reaching significance of this development, and of those that were to follow, can best be illustrated by a description of the make-up of whole grains, whether wheat, rice, oats, or rye:

◇ A grain is a single seed, kernel, or nut-like fruit and each seed or kernel has three distinct portions:

◇ The *bran* layer is the outer coat.

◇ The *endosperm* consists of an inner portion made up largely of starch grains and an outer portion (lying next to the bran) which contains valuable nutrients.

◇ The *germ*, located at one end or side, is the portion from which new grain develops, and, nutritionally, is the richest component.

Since the different parts of the kernel serve different functions, the nutrients are not distributed evenly throughout the grain. It is the nutritionally rich components that are largely responsible for any spoilage during long, extended periods of storage; when these are removed, the remaining 70 percent (the starch portion) can be kept almost indefinitely—if further dried and chemically treated.

The new aim in flour milling was thus not only to remove the bran by means of purifiers, but to separate the inner portion (made up largely of starch grains) and thereby obtain a whiter flour that would stand up to longer periods of storage. Products made from this flour (cake mixes, bread, pasta) would automatically have a longer shelf life. This major development was made possible by the invention of roller mills in Hungary in the latter part of the nineteenth century. Now the various components of wheat could be separated to produce a very fine white flour—milled from the part of the grain with the lowest nutritive value.*

The grinder and the wheel were harnessed to so many units of horsepower at about the same time that purifiers were first introduced. As farm machinery improved, the production of wheat also increased. Towns and cities grew and bakeries sprung up in quick succession. Bakers did everything to sell their new product—among other things, they loaded it with alum to improve its appearance. It was a highly profitable business as no more than a penny's worth of flour went into a loaf of bread. (Today, it is still not much more than a few pennies worth.) In England and Eu-

*Concern for nutrition had not reached the plateau it has today, particularly with regard to the effects of consuming over a long period of time a food source made up mainly of starch grains. The switch to white flour without the benefit is the more startling when one considers that the natural nutrients of the whole grain had played such a major role in the human diet for so many thousands of years. Of course, a century or more ago, the benefit of analysis and research using today's advanced methods and equipment was entirely lacking.

rope, the "white" bread produced from the newly milled flour sold for much higher prices than its "brown" counterpart, and thus became associated with the rich and the affluent.

In the middle of the nineteenth century, most families in rural America were making their own bread. All in all, bread making was part of a long tradition and a labor of love. Before Thoreau completed the structure that was to be his shelter during his stay at Walden, he baked his bread (made from rye and Indian corn) over an open fire in the out-of-doors. Later he used his fireplace. His bread and butter not only sustained him on many an occasion but was something which held great fascination for him:

> How could youth better learn to live than by at once trying the experiment of living? Methinks this would exercise their minds as much as mathematics. If I wished a boy to know something about the arts and sciences, for instance, I would not pursue the common course, which is merely to send him into the neighborhood of some professor, where anything is professed and practised but the art of life; (—to survey the world through a telescope or a microscope, and never with his natural eye; to study chemistry and not learn how his bread is made. . .).*

By the turn of the century, new agricultural methods were producing yields from the "amber fields" that filled both the coppers and cupboards of America. The end products of this burgeoning commercial enterprise, however, were not always recognizable in terms of past expectations. The bread, for instance, bore little resemblance to the flavorful, textured, golden "brown" bread that had been made with loving care from whole grain flour. Incidentally, much of the flour that went into this bread derived from the hard red winter wheat introduced into America in the 1870s and later known as the "gold of the Great Plains."

Commercially produced "white" bread was more or less the order of the day. Immigrants landing in the New World were impressed with its abundance, surely a symbol of richness. They

---

*Concern for nutrition had not reached the plateau it has today, particularly with regard to the effects of consuming over a long period of time a food source made up mainly of starch grains. The switch to white flour is the more startling when one considers that the natural nutrients of the whole grain had played such a major role in the human diet for so many thousands of years. Of course, a century or more ago, the benefit of analysis and research using today's advanced methods and equipment was entirely lacking.

were unaware that it was made from the portion of the grain with the lowest common denominator; and despite industry's attempts to "fortify" its protégé with vitamins and 6 percent powdered milk, white bread retained its light (and sometimes clammy) texture. The lion's share of the valuable nutrients (the bran and germ) now went into the feed bags and buckets of cattle and other animals (except for a small percentage that was sold as separate products) to be converted into high priced meats and animal products. The one step forward began to appear like two steps backwards. Consumer awareness grew as the true ingredients of the staff of life were widely publicized; some felt a more fitting appellation might be the "dough of the grain foods industry."

Running hand in hand with improvements in machinery was a more sophisticated knowledge of the use of chemicals. Chemicals were first used to bleach flour about 1900, and chemical maturing agents were introduced some 20 years later. Nitrogen peroxide was the first chemical used as a flour bleach. It was promoted as giving flour a more attractive appearance. By 1920, nitrogen trichloride was considered a much more effective bleaching and improving agent. Its use was discontinued about 30 years later when it was shown that it might cause canine hysteria. Benzoyl peroxide was then introduced as a bleaching agent, but it did not improve baking quality. Eventually chlorine dioxide gas replaced nitrogen trichloride as the most widely used agent for both bleaching and maturing, and had the industrial advantage of acting instantaneously. It was used chiefly on bread flour. Chlorine gas was used in the treatment of cake flours, especially those to be used with large amounts of sugar, such as in commercial cake mixes—which frequently contain more sugar than flour.

The baking qualities effected by the use of one chemical or another largely concerned commercial bakers.

As a result of the addition of one or another chemical, commercial bakers found they had to combat new, unwanted qualities in their doughs. For example, special conditioning of the dough used to make commercial white bread is required to preserve its elasticity and strength during high-speed molding and rounding. This is achieved through the use of fungal enzymes. Needless to say, today's commercial process bears little resemblance to the ancient art of bread making. Furthermore, automatic ovens are used for both proving and baking.

By the 1960s, America's annual consumption of grains per capita had gone from 216 pounds to 116 pounds—in the short span of 50 years. During this period, more and more emphasis had been placed on meat, particularly beef, and its consumption had almost doubled. In many parts of the world, grains still accounted for 75 percent of the diet, with the remaining 25 percent being comprised of flesh foods and other products. In America, these percentages had practically reversed, with flesh foods and animal products now making up 75 percent of the diet.

The switch away from whole grains is significant in that it resulted in the depletion of a food source that formerly provided proteins, carbohydrates, fats, important vitamins and minerals, and a significant portion of the bulk necessary in the human diet. Americans were left with breads, pasta, pastries, and cereals produced from the milled portion of the grain with the lowest nutritive value (rolled oats and one or two other cereals being the exception). These products are fortified, for the most part, with synthetically manufactured vitamins and minerals that often give the impression on package labels of being an integral part of the product. Of course, manufacturers and processors play their part in overemphasizing the value of fortified products.

Thoreau, who lived mainly on fruits, vegetables, fish, dairy foods, and whole grains had visions of a trend away from meat:

> True, he [man] can and does live, in a great measure, by preying on other animals; but this is a miserable way,—as any one who will go to snaring rabbits, or slaughtering lambs, may learn,—and he will be regarded as a benefactor of his race who shall teach him to confine himself to a more innocent and wholesome diet. Whatever my own practice may be, I have no doubt that it is a part of the destiny of the human race, in its gradual improvement, to leave off eating animals, as surely as the savage tribes have left off eating each other when they came in contact with the more civilized.

America was the world's second largest producer of wheat with about 2.3 billion bushels harvested in one year during the 1970s, and approximately 6 billion bushels of corn. (Three man-hours were needed to handle an acre of wheat as compared to 50 manhours a century ago.) Americans consumed about 700 million bushels of wheat for food, feed, and seed—or about 30 percent of the harvest. As a result of the high yields, grain prices dropped 47 percent, but bread prices remained up. The continued trend toward a high consumption of meat was reflected in the increased production of corn, barley, sorghum, oats, soybeans, and other grains used primarily for animal feed.

Dried breakfast cereals (Ceres was the ancient Roman goddess of agriculture), challenged for their poor nutrient content, have steadily gained in popularity and continue to replace wholesome bread, especially in the diets of young Americans. Most have the advantage of an extended shelf life for which, however, the consumer must pay dearly. There is in actuality no relationship between the price of cereal and the wholesale market price of whole grains. One popular cereal made from milled corn, sugar, corn syrup, molasses, salt, and artificial coloring sold at $1.10 a pound, while the wholesale market price of corn was 6½¢ a pound.

Dried breakfast cereals, or R-T-E (Ready to Eat) as they are known in the industry, have been cloaked in mystery from the beginning. Pre-packaged food marks its beginning with the introduction of graham crackers in 1829 by Sylvester Graham, a lecturer on food and temperance, who preached that the way to lead souls to heaven was through their stomachs—it eventually did lead to a multi-million dollar industry!

Others were quick to follow in Graham's footsteps. Tranula (the forerunner of Grape-Nuts) was marketed by James Jackson in 1863, and Shredded Wheat by Henry Perky in 1893. The Western Health Reform Institute was formed in Battle Creek, Michigan, in 1866 by the Seventh-Day Adventists. Ten years later, it became the Battle Creek Sanitarium, under the direction of John Harvey Kellogg, physician, inventor, and writer. It became world famous, along with Dr. Kellogg's cereals.

Those were the days of the much-feared tuberculous disease, which eventually took Thoreau's life. He showed signs of the disease from a very early age. The fact that fresh air and healthful living were beneficial in fighting the disease might have prompted his experiment in living with nature, as well as the concern and interest he took in his food and diet.

It was during his recuperation that C. W. Post had eaten "health foods." Perceiving their possibilities, he began promoting what he called "Postum," which eventually led in 1897 to the formation of the Postum Cereal Company, the parent company of General Foods. W. K. Kellogg, who had worked with his brother, left the sanatarium in 1906 and formed his own cereal company.

The flakes, puffs, nuts, shreds, and what-have-you were created and patented. The process which shapes, cooks, and toasts remains a closely guarded one. From the beginning, advertising and promotion played a major role.

Early man's dream of "bounteous stores of grain" became a reality in the twentieth century. The form they took, however, became open to question. While nutritive values were recognized, economy and convenience received top priority in the minds of producers and marketers of processed grains. Nutrition came in a poor fifth to color, appearance, consistency, and freedom from defects.

While mountains of commercial white bread were still being consumed, grocers' shelves showed a trend back toward a more wholesome and nutritious type of bread. On the homefront, there was the promise of a return to the ancient and satisfying art involving the mixing, kneading, proving, shaping, and baking of the dough, using flour milled from the whole grain . . . filling the air with the incomparable and unmistakable aroma of freshly baked bread.

Thoreau, who cherished his daily bread, wrote:

> Bread may not always nourish us, but it always does us good, it even takes stiffness out of our joints, and makes us supple and buoyant, when we knew not what ailed us, to recognize any generosity in man or Nature, to share any unmixed and heroic joy.

NUTRITIVE VALUE

All unmilled grains* contain significant amounts of minerals and are highly valued for their B vitamins. They also contain vitamin E (wheat germ oil is probably the richest natural source of vitamin E). Calcium, phosphorus, magnesium, and iron are the minerals present in the largest amounts.

Corn, unlike the other grains, contains carotenes which are convertible in the body to vitamin A.

The germ portion of grains contains proteins, minerals, vitamins, and fat. The mineral (ash) content of a sample of grain is indicative of its bran content (bran is a source of ash) and also correlates directly with its protein content. The following is a list of the approximate percentages of protein in the unmilled grains:

---

*The nutrient content of grains is, of course, greatly reduced by the milling process to which they are subjected.

Grain	Percentage
barley	12.8
wheat	11.7
rye	11.2
rice	7.5
oats	14.2
corn	10.0
buckwheat	12.4

With the exception of soybeans, grains belong to the incomplete protein group. However, when they are mixed with other proteins (dairy products, meats, fish, dried legumes), they serve to bolster the total protein effect. The following is a list of a few of the many possible combinations:

◇ rice, pasta, wheat germ : ground meats, ground fish, and shellfish
◇ pasta, rice, wheat germ : meat and fish casserole-type preparations
◇ pasta, rice : dried beans
◇ flours (whole wheat, rye, cornmeal) : milk and eggs in breads, cakes, crêpes

Because of their starch and fat, all grains are excellent sources of energy; wheat, for example, contains slightly under 1500 calories per pound. The fat content of grains is located chiefly in the germ. Because of the instability of the fat, the major processing methods have been designed to discard the germ. This practice reduces deterioration during storage but is extremely wasteful of nutritive value, for the germ portion contains proteins and valuable vitamins and minerals as well as fat.

Whole grains which are not overly processed provide bulk (fiber) to the diet.

WHOLE GRAINS

The most important factor to remember in purchasing and using grains is that the various nutrients are not distributed throughout the grain structure. Recall that processed flours contain only the inner portion of the endosperm, which is largely a storage place for starch grains.

Unmilled grains are available at health food and specialty stores. Dried corn kernels can be purchased at most super-markets (generally merchandized as corn for popping). These can then be milled or ground, using an electrically operated home mill or food processor, to a fine, medium, or coarse consistency, as desired. Home grinding not only has the advantage of preserving the nutrients, but it makes it possible to provide the fiber necessary in the diet. A percentage of such grains can also be combined with commercially milled flours, particularly those from the whole grain.

THE MOST IMPORTANT GRAINS

The most important grains are wheat, rye, rice, corn, oats, and buckwheat. Flour, meal, starch, breakfast cereals, and dried paste (used in products such as spaghetti, macaroni, and noodles) are prepared from these grains.

In recent years, agriculturists have been working on the development of a new grain, triticale. It is a cross between rye and wheat, and is becoming a food crop in several isolated areas of the U.S.

Definitions and Standards for Wheat Flour

The federal government has established definitions and standards for wheat flour, but they are of little direct use to the consumer. The professional has a wide range of wheat flours to choose from, whereas the consumer is comparatively limited. The two main categories generally available are all-purpose white and all-purpose whole wheat flour. Rye flour is available to a more limited degree. Highly processed white flour contains the part of the grain with the lowest nutritive value.

Composition of Flour

The chemical composition of flour varies according to the variety. For instance, soft wheats are lower in protein and mineral content than hard wheats. Hard red winter wheat is nutritionally the most valuable and the most flavorful. Soft wheats are used to produce family flours for home baking, cakes, crackers, and pastry. Among the varieties are hard red winter wheat, hard red spring wheat, soft wheat, and white wheat.

◇ *Enriched flour* contains no more than 5 percent wheat germ or de-fatted wheat germ by weight.

◇ *Pastry flours* are made from soft wheat, are finely ground, and have a low gluten content.

◇ *Cake flours* are made from soft wheat, finely pulverized, to which various agents have been added to soften and whiten their proteins.

◇ *Hard wheat flour* has a high gluten content, feels velvety to the touch, and is the color of rich cream. It is used in the preparation of pizza dough, high-grade pasta products, and special breads, such as French bread. High gluten flour is available in health food and specialty food stores and departments.

◇ *Graham flour* is a broad classification given to whole wheat flours.

The Gluten Content of Flour

It is the gluten content of wheat that gives elasticity to the dough and allows it to expand when combined with liquid and yeast. The second most desirable flour in the preparation of bread and bread products is rye, which imparts its own distinctive flavor. However, because of its much lower gluten content, it makes a soggy, heavy bread, unless combined with a portion of wheat flour. Rye is milled from a gradual process, which differs from wheat milling in many respects. Commercial rye bread often contains flour milled from whole rye grains.

Wheat Germ

Wheat germ may be purchased toasted or uncooked. The latter is more readily available in health food and specialty stores. Some form of sweetener is sometimes added to toasted wheat germ—the variety and amount may be checked on the package label.

Flour Containing 85 Percent of the Grain

During the World War II period, Canada introduced a wheat flour known as "Canada Approved Flour," which contained about 85 percent of the grain. Great Britain later manufactured a similar flour. It is considered superior to common white flour in vitamin and mineral content and in the quality of its proteins. (American All-Purpose Flour contains about 70 percent of the grain.)

Other Forms of Grain Products

CORNMEAL Look for cornmeal that has not had the bran and germ removed in processing, or purchase dried corn kernels and grind them yourself, using an electric grain mill or food processor.

OATS Rolled oats are prepared by first removing the hull and then cutting, steaming, and rolling the whole inside kernel. Oatmeal is made by grinding the rolled oats. Either preparation thus represents practically a whole grain food that is highly nutritious.

BREAKFAST CEREALS A quick perusal of the listed ingredients on the individual boxes will serve to indicate how much nutrition you are getting for your dollar, particularly as compared with whole grain products or bread made from flour milled from the whole grain. Pound for pound and dollar for dollar, packaged ready-to-eat cereals are far from being the best buy, with the possible exception of rolled oats and one or two others.

Pasta

A good pasta product is made from a special Durum wheat flour and is deep yellow in color. Many pasta products are made from Semolina flour (the purified middlings* of Durum) and Farina (a fine meal made of vegetable matter or any of various powdery substances).A good, flavorful, and nutritious pasta product (macaroni, spaghetti, noodles) is made from a flour with a high gluten content.

*Middlings are a by-product of flour milling which consists of several grades of granular particles generally used as animal feed.

Noodles are pasta products to which eggs have been added. Frozen and dried eggs are used more often than fresh, and usually only the egg yolk is added to give the product a better color. The egg ingredients in noodles cost almost as much as the flour, even though they usually represent only 5.5 percent of the total solids. Egg noodles cost more per pound than other pasta products.

PROCEDURE FOR COOKING PASTA Bring a pot of lightly salted water to a full boil. (Pot should be large enough for pasta to swim about during cooking.) Add a small amount of oil to prevent pasta from sticking together during cooking.

Add pasta and cook, uncovered, over high heat, until it takes on a firm, chewy texture. Be careful not to overcook. Remove and drain, using a colander. If the product contains excess starch, rinse under cold running water.

To reheat: Heat 1 or 2 tablespoons olive oil and add enough water to come to approximately ¼″ (.5 cm) of pan bottom. Bring to a boil and add cooked pasta. Stir long enough to thoroughly coat. Turn heat to low and cover pot. Cook just long enough to heat through.

Bread—the Staff of Life

In the Middle Ages, bakers guilds were regulated by very strict ordinances, from which practices came the expression, "the baker's dozen." Bakers took an oath just as certain public officials do today, and severe punishment was meted out to those who didn't abide by the rules. Those who gave short-weight bread were beheaded in England. In Germany, they were subjected to a public ducking. As dough throws off alcohol content during baking, it invariably weighs less upon removal. Taking no chances, bakers threw in an extra bun. Bakers were also obliged to produce a certain amount of bread each day, and, being without refrigeration and present-day sophisticated use of chemicals, this, too, influenced their generosity at times.

A good bread can be recognized by its natural flavor, texture, and color. In an effort to compensate for the lack of nutrients, many commercial breads are fortified with manufactured or other vitamins, as well as 6 percent nonfat milk solids.

Bread made from flour milled from the whole grain, along with certain other ingredients, can come very close to representing a complete food.

Rice

Rice is known to have been under cultivation for at least five thousand years, and is the staff of life for nearly half the world's population. It ranks next to wheat, both in the amount produced and the acreage used for planting.

PROCESSED RICE   Like most other grains for human consumption, the greater part of the rice consumed in America is highly processed. It is polished to remove the bran coating and germ, making long periods of storage possible but removing a large percentage of the protein, fat, minerals, and vitamins. Many of the natural nutrients of white rice having been removed, manufacturers proceed to fortify it with synthetic vitamins and minerals. An interesting side note is that the substitution of polished rice for the whole grain can lead to the disease beriberi.

BROWN RICE   Brown rice, so called because of its natural coloring, has the hull removed, but most of the bran coating and germ are retained, making it highly nutritious. Its flavor is quite distinctive and pleasantly different from that of white rice.

COATED RICE   As the name indicates, this rice has been treated with some form of sugar, as well as talc, in order to improve its keeping qualities and give it a white appearance. It should be washed before cooking, to remove coating.

CONVERTED RICE   Treated according to a special process that, supposedly, retains some of its natural vitamins, this rice is also fortified. How much of the germ and bran are retained is not stated by the manufacturer on the label. It is parboiled, prior to packaging, to facilitate easier cooking.

COOKED RICE   Cooked rice has been precooked, rinsed, and dried by a patented process.

WILD RICE   This is not a true rice, but could be classified as a grain. It derives its name from the fact that it grows wild in the western section of North America. This natural product is more nutritious than cultivated rice and is considered a delicacy. Attempts are now being made to cultivate it.

VARIETIES OF RICE   While there are many varieties of rice, broadly speaking, rice falls into three categories—long, medium, and oval grained. Long-grained rice calls for a greater quantity of liquid in the cooking, as it is more absorbent. It cooks into a firmer rice, but has less flavor than the oval. (The two can be combined to produce a more satisfactory texture and flavor.) Medium-grained rice falls between long and oval.

Cooking Perfect Rice

Cooking Schedule*

Long-grained and wild rice:	1 cup (226 g) raw rice to 3 cups (720 ml) water or stock
Medium-grained rice:	1 cup (226 g) raw rice to 2½ cups (600 ml) water or stock
Oval-grained rice:	1 cup (226 g) raw rice to 2 cups (480 ml) water or stock
Brown rice (long, medium, or oval):	Use same proportions as above

*One cup (226 g) of uncooked rice makes approximately 3 to 4 cups (670 g to 907 g) cooked rice, depending on amount of liquid used and absorbency of rice.

Wash rice under cold running water, using a wire strainer. Place rice and specified amount of liquid in a flame- and ovenproof pan, such as a straight-sided frying pan with an ovenproof handle. Season to taste with salt and white pepper. Do not cover. Cook over low heat until liquid is absorbed. *Do not* stir—if necessary, shake rice about, using handle. Liquid should be just under simmering point throughout. If liquid begins to bubble, remove from heat for a minute or so, and lower heat.

When liquid has been absorbed, turn rice into a wire strainer, using a rubber spatula.

Brush a small amount of butter or oil over bottom layer of pan (to prevent sticking) and return rice. Cover rice with a sheet of aluminum foil, folding securely around edges. Place pan cover over foil, being careful not to break foil. Set in a preheated 325° F. (163° C.) oven for 20 minutes. If you do not plan to use the rice at once, adjust heat to 160° F. (71° C.), or turn off oven altogether. When ready to serve, remove, uncover, and turn into a preheated receptacle at once (rice should not remain in the same dish it was cooked in).

TO STORE Large portions of rice may be cooked in advance and kept in the refrigerator for up to 5 or 6 days.

Properly cooked rice (so that each grain is separate) may also be frozen, in containers, airtight plastic bags, or heat-sealed boilable plastic bags. Boilable plastic bags are the most satisfactory and convenient way of storing rice, whether frozen or refrigerated, as they can be quickly defrosted or reheated in boiling water with a minimum loss of flavor and nutrients.

Stored rice may also be reheated in a covered frying pan over low heat, adding a few sprinkles of water, or just enough to create steam. Cook just long enough to heat through.

A steamer may also be used to reheat rice.

FRIED RICE Fried rice is made by tossing cooked rice in a few drops of condensed liquid gravy additive until it is of the desired color. Soy sauce may also be used, but will not give the same flavor.

Almost any kind or combination of food may be added to fried rice. All vegetables, meat, and seafood are cooked and cut into bite-size pieces before adding to rice. Vegetables should be cooked to the crisp stage so that they retain most of their natural coloring. Lightly fry flavorings such as mushrooms, onions, scallions, and peppers before combining with rice.

RICE AND PASTA RECIPES

FRIED RICE A LA GRECQUE

1 10-ounce (280 g) package
frozen peas
2 teaspoons butter
butter and oil for frying
3 stalks celery, peeled and
finely chopped
½ pound (225 g) button-size
mushrooms, peeled
1 small clove garlic, peeled
and finely chopped
½ Bermuda onion, peeled and
chopped

4 scallions, peeled and
chopped
1 green pepper, seeded and
uniformly chopped
1 Polish style sausage, mildly
spiced
3 to 4 cups (670 g to 907 g)
cooked rice
3 tablespoons pimiento, cut
into julienne strips
salt and white pepper to taste

Remove peas from freezer and set in refrigerator until slightly defrosted. Cook in 2 teaspoons butter in a covered saucepan over low heat. Remove as soon as defrosted and heated through.

Heat butter and oil in frying pan and cook peeled and chopped vegetables (celery, mushrooms, garlic, onion, scallions, green pepper) one at a time. Remove vegetables (with the exception of mushrooms) when they take on a slightly translucent appearance and while still retaining their full color. Fry mushrooms until golden brown and remove at once.

Set vegetables in a 160° F. (71° C.) oven, uncovered, to keep warm.

Place sausage in boiling water, and cook over low heat, until simmering point is reached. Cook for 4 or 5 minutes longer, or until fully cooked. Remove skin and chop into shred size pieces.

Melt a small amount of butter in pan, add rice and 2 tablespoons hot water. Cover and cook over low heat just long enough to heat through. Add sausage, fried vegetables, peas, julienne strips of pimiento and mix in. Season to taste with salt and white pepper.

DARIOLES OF NOODLES

1 pound (450 g) noodles
4 whole eggs
⅓ cup (80 ml) light cream or milk

salt and white pepper to taste
grated Parmesan cheese
butter

Cook noodles in boiling salted water until tender. Drain and rinse off excess starch under cold running water.

Beat cream or milk into eggs, using a wire whisk, and add seasoning to taste. Add noodles and mix in. Butter individual dariole or custard molds, or use 1-quart (1 l) ring mold, and fill with noodle mixture. Sprinkle grated Parmesan cheese over tops and lightly dot with butter.

Set molds or mold in a pan of hot water and bake in a preheated 350° F. (177° C.) oven until set, or noodles begin to shrink from sides. Remove and unmold. Serve cheese side up.

RICE PILAF

2 cups (453 g) long-grained converted rice
6 cups (1440 ml) White Stock or chicken broth

1 onion, peeled and finely chopped
4 tablespoons butter

Wash rice under cold running water, using a wire strainer, until water runs clear. Bring White Stock or chicken broth to a boil and remove from heat. Fry onion in a small amount of butter over low heat until translucent, using a high-sided frying pan with ovenproof handle. Melt remaining butter and add rice, stirring until thoroughly coated. Add heated stock or broth. Cook, uncovered, over low heat until liquid has been absorbed. (Liquid should remain just under simmering point throughout.) Remove from heat and strain off any remaining liquid. Butter surface of pan and return rice. Shake pan, if necessary, but do not stir. Cover loosely with a layer of aluminum foil, pinching around edges of pan. Set lid of pan over foil, being careful not to break foil. Bake in a preheated 325° F. (163° C.) oven for 20 minutes. Remove and turn into a warm serving dish. (Do not allow rice to remain in pan it was cooked in.)

Portions of rice may be frozen in heat-sealed plastic pouches to be used as needed. When ready to serve, drop pouch in boiling water for about 15 minutes, or until defrosted and heated through.

RICE RING MOLD

5 or 6 scallions, peeled and
   finely chopped
butter and oil for frying
⅓ pound (150 g) mushrooms,
   peeled
⅓ cup (80 ml) milk or light
   cream

3 eggs, separated
3 cups (670 g) cooked rice
2 tablespoons butter, melted
1 tablespoon fresh parsley,
   finely chopped

Fry finely chopped scallions in a small amount of butter and oil over low heat until translucent. Remove and set aside. Turn heat to medium high and sauté peeled mushrooms. Remove and finely chop.

Beat scalded milk or light cream into egg yolks, using a wire whisk, and add to cooked rice along with melted butter, scallions, mushrooms, and chopped parsley. Beat egg whites until they form soft peaks and fold in. Turn into a greased or nonstick ring mold and cover with a layer of buttered parchment paper. Set mold in a pan containing enough hot water to come halfway up sides and bake in a preheated 325° F. (163° C.) oven until set, or a knife inserted in center comes out clean. Remove and unmold *as soon as baked* onto a warm serving platter. (Do not overcook or mold will become dry.)

SPAGHETTI WITH SAUCE

1 pound (450 g) spaghetti

Spaghetti Sauce

Cook spaghetti in lightly salted boiling water to which a small amount of oil has been added, until tender. Remove excess starch, if necessary, under cold running water. Reheat spaghetti and serve with Spaghetti Sauce (Chapter 2, under Sauce section).

MACARONI AND CHEESE

2 cups (480 ml) Cheese Sauce   grated Cheddar cheese
½ pound (225 g) elbow   butter
    macaroni

Prepare Cheese sauce (Chapter 2) using Cheddar cheese.

Cook macaroni in lightly salted boiling water until tender. Drain and turn into an ovenproof dish. Pour over Cheese Sauce and sprinkle grated Cheddar cheese over surface. Dot lightly with butter and place under broiler until lightly browned.

SPAGHETTI CASSEROLE

1 pound (450 g) linguini
    spaghetti
1 28-ounce (980 g) can
    tomatoes, pureed and
    strained
2 onions, peeled and finely
    chopped
1 green pepper, seeded and
    chopped
butter and olive oil for frying
1 15-ounce (420 g) can tomato
    sauce
1 10-ounce (280 g) can chicken
    broth

2 tablespoons finely sifted
    flour
½ teaspoon dried oregano
dash of garlic powder
salt and pepper to taste
½ pound (225 g) Cheddar
    cheese, grated
6 ounces (170 g) coldpack
    sharp Cheddar cheese
grated Parmesan cheese
butter

Cook linguini in boiling salted water to which a small amount of oil has been added, until barely tender, and drain using a colander. If necessary remove excess starch under cold running water.

Puree tomatoes in blender and remove seeds using a wire strainer.

Fry onions and green pepper in a small amount of butter and olive oil until translucent and fairly crisp.

Bring strained tomatoes, tomato sauce, and chicken broth to a slow simmer over medium low heat. Reduce heat to low and stir in two tablespoons finely sifted flour, using a wire whisk. Add fried onions, green pepper, oregano, garlic powder, and salt and pepper to taste. Gradually add grated Cheddar and coldpack Cheddar, stirring over low heat until well blended. Transfer to a casserole dish and fold in cooked spaghetti, coating with sauce. Sprinkle Parmesan cheese over surface and dot lightly with butter. Set in a pan of hot water and bake in a preheated 325° F. (163° C.) oven until heated through. Or, set under broiler until lightly browned.

LASAGNA

Spaghetti Sauce
1 pound (450 g) lasagna
   noodles (1½" wide noodles)
1 pound (450 g) Ricotta cheese

grated Parmesan and Romano
   cheese
Mozzarella cheese

To prepare sauce, follow recipe for Spaghetti Sauce (Chapter 2, under Sauce section).

Cook noodles in a large pot of lightly salted boiling water until al dente (fairly firm). Remove and drain, using a colander. If noodles contain excess starch, rinse under cold running water.

Using a shallow ovenproof pan, spoon a layer of Spaghetti Sauce over bottom and top with a criss-cross layer of noodles. Spread a layer of Ricotta cheese on top and sprinkle grated Parmesan and Romano cheese over that. Repeat, finishing off with a layer of noodles. Spread sauce over top layer of noodles, and cover with slices of Mozzarella cheese. Bake in a preheated 325° F. (163° C.) oven until heated through and cheese has melted somewhat.

SPAGHETTI WITH MEATBALLS

Spaghetti Sauce
meatballs

1 pound (450 g) spaghetti
grated Parmesan cheese

Follow recipe for Spaghetti Sauce (Chapter 2, under Sauce section), omitting ground beef and sausage.

Prepare meatballs according to recipe in Chapter 3.

Cook spaghetti in a large pot of lightly salted boiling water until tender. Remove and drain, using a colander. Rinse under cold running water to remove any excess starch; however, if made from whole wheat flour, do not rinse.

Bring Spaghetti Sauce to a slow simmer over low heat and add Meatballs. Cook just long enough to heat through—do not expose to high heat or overcooking, otherwise, meatballs will dry out and harden.

Arrange spaghetti* on a heated platter or individual serving plates and top with Sauce and Meatballs. Serve grated Parmesan cheese on the side.

NOODLE PUDDING

1 pound (450 g) noodles
½ cup (120 ml) milk or light
 cream
¼ to ¾ cup (49.6 g to 148.8
 g) sugar, according to
 desired degree of sweetness

pinch of salt
4 whole eggs
butter

Cook noodles in a large pot of lightly salted boiling water and drain.

Bring milk or light cream to a boil over low heat and remove.

Add sugar, along with a pinch of salt, to eggs and beat until light and slightly foamy. Gradually add milk or light cream, beating at low speed. Add noodles and fold in. Turn into a greased or nonstick ovenproof dish. Dot surface with butter. Set dish in a shallow pan containing enough hot (not boiling) water to come about half-way up the sides and bake in a preheated 325° F. (163° C.) oven until set, or pudding begins to shrink from sides of pan.

---

*If spaghetti must be reheated, follow directions on p. 351.

RICE PUDDING

2 cups (480 ml) milk or light
cream
¼ to ¾ cup (49.6 g to 148.8
g) sugar, according to
desired degree of sweetness
3 whole eggs plus 2 yolks
seeds from 2-inch (5 cm) piece
vanilla pod; or 1 teaspoon
vanilla extract

1 to 1½ cups cooked rice
nutmeg
butter
½ cup raisins (optional)

Bring milk or light cream to a boil over low heat and remove (watch carefully to prevent liquid from boiling over).

Using an electric mixer, gradually add sugar to whole eggs and yolks, beating until pale yellow and slightly creamy. Add vanilla seeds or vanilla extract and mix in at low speed. Gradually add scalded milk or light cream, beating at low speed or using a wire whisk. Fold cooked rice and raisins (if desired) into mixture and turn into a greased ovenproof dish or individual dishes. Dust nutmeg very lightly over surface and dot with butter. Set dish(es) in a shallow pan containing enough hot (not boiling) water to come halfway up the sides and bake in a preheated 325° F. (163° C.) oven. To test for doneness, insert a knife halfway into pudding when it appears to be set. If knife comes out clean, pudding is cooked. Serve warm or chilled.

Note: To prevent rice from settling on the bottom and custard from rising to the top, gently stir ingredients as soon as custard begins to set, that is, about halfway through cooking period.

BREAD MAKING

FLOUR The natural properties of wheat make it the most desirable for making leavened bread. Its gluten content gives elasticity to the dough and allows it to expand. The richer the flour (nutritionally), the more liquid it will absorb. (Flour milled from the whole grain—100% whole wheat flour—will absorb more liquid than all-purpose flour). Rye flour may be combined with wheat to add a distinctive flavor, but, owing to its low gluten content, should not be used by itself, otherwise bread will be heavy. Small proportions of corn meal, soy flour, oatmeal, and other flours may be combined with wheat flour to produce a richer bread, as well as a variety of flavors.

YEAST Yeast is a plant that requires food and thrives at temperatures which are neither too hot nor too cold. It is for this reason that the remaining ingredients for bread making are to be at barely warm (tepid) temperatures, and that the mixed dough is placed in a draft-free area, when proving.

Fermentation is commenced and carbon dioxide gas is formed (characterized by the bubbles in the dough) when yeast and the natural sugar content of the flour are combined through mixing and kneading. Enzymes in the yeast convert the starch content of the flour into maltose, continuing the fermentation process. This chemical process is complete when the dough has about doubled in bulk, or when two fingers inserted about 1 to 2″ (2.5-5 cm) into the dough leave a definite indentation. Dough should be punched down at once, otherwise it will sour.

Dry yeast may be substituted for fresh compressed yeast, but does not give as good results.

LIQUIDS All liquids should be tepid, that is, barely warm. They are added to flour at the same time as activated yeast.

SALT Salt and yeast are incompatible when they come in direct contact. It is therefore distributed throughout the flour and thoroughly blended before adding yeast and liquids.

Salt brings out the natural flavor of the flour and retards the fermentation process to a slight degree. It also acts as a preservative.

SUGAR The small amount of sugar added to yeast (1 teaspoon to 1 ounce [28 g] yeast), as well as to flour (2 teaspoons per 12 cups flour) aids in the fermentation process. Honey may be substituted for sugar.

FATS The addition of a fat, such as oil or melted butter, softens the dough and adds both to the flavoring and the nutrition content. It also aids the leavening process to a slight degree.

KNEADING Kneading stretches the gluten content of the flour and thoroughly blends all ingredients, most importantly, the yeast. In chemical terms, it sets off a chain reaction.

The best procedure for kneading is to cup the dough in the hand and bring a small portion over bottom layer, stretching and kneading the two layers together with the heel of the palm. This action is continued until the whole is kneaded back into a single mass. The position of the dough is then reversed and the kneading continues, in all 5 to 6 minutes, or until the dough begins to feel soft and silky, and two or three bubbles appear.

MOLDING AND SHAPING Well-made dough is easily handled and will almost shape itself. Dough may be cut and weighed on a scale before shaping; rolled dough may be cut to shape using the baking pan as a guide. Shape dough by holding in both hands and folding under, using fingers. Shaped loaves should no more than half fill baking pans, as they will rise and double in bulk.

Dough may also be molded and shaped into rolls or loaves of all sizes and shapes and baked on a cookie sheet. Shapes may be round, plaited, mushroom, brioche, or any other shape one might fancy.

GLAZING To produce crusts of various textures, glaze dough with a pastry brush before baking.

◇ Soft crust: Milk or cream
◇ Soft crust: Beaten egg yolk and milk
◇ Soft and shiny crust: Melted butter
◇ Dark brown crust: ½ teaspoon sugar beaten into 1 egg-yolk
◇ Crisp crust: Ice cold water
◇ Crisp and shiny crust: Beaten egg white and ice cold water

Glaze dough with a mixture of egg and milk before sprinkling with poppy or sesame seeds, otherwise seeds will not adhere to dough.

BAKING Dough will increase in size to a slight degree when first placed in oven. Within about 10 or 15 minutes, dough will become firm and lose its elasticity.

A one-pound (450 g) loaf of bread generally takes about an

hour to bake in a 350° F. (177° C.) to 400° F. (205° C.) oven. Rolls bake in about 40 minutes, depending on size.

The higher the initial temperature setting, the browner and crisper the crust. (Too high a temperature will, of course, harden the crust without penetrating to the center.) Bread and rolls baked at a constant temperature of 325° F. (163° C.) to 350° F. (177° C.) will have a softer and lighter crust and a more even texture throughout.

As a general rule, the smaller the bread product, the higher the initial temperature.

Do not open oven door during the first 10 or 15 minutes of baking, that is, until dough has set. Once this has occurred, check color and texture of crust from time to time, and be guided accordingly. If crust is browning too quickly, lower heat.

To test whether or not a bread product is baked, knock on the underside near the center, using the knuckles of the hand. There will be a definite hollow sound when baked. It also will have shrunk from the sides of the pan and can be removed quite easily.

It is as important not to overbake bread products as it is not to underbake them, as this will result in a dry product.

STORING BREADS

When baked, turn out onto racks, and do not cover.

Do not store until completely cool. Wrap in foil or opaque paper, and store in airtight plastic bags or containers.

Bread will keep for 5 or 6 days, when stored in a cool, dry place.

Frozen bread products keep extremely well for extended periods and take a relatively short time to defrost. Frozen bread can be cut with a sawtooth knife or a slicing appliance.

BASIC BREAD-MAKING FORMULA

12 cups flour
1 tablespoon salt
3 teaspoons sugar
1 1-ounce (28 g) cake
compressed yeast, dissolved
in ¼ cup (60 ml) tepid
water; or, ¼ oz. (7 g) pkg.
dry yeast

4 cups (960 ml) liquid (water
or milk) at room
temperature

The basic formula for bread making is a simple one, but must be followed precisely:

1. Place flour in mixing pan, sifting if necessary. Distribute 1 tablespoon salt and 2 teaspoons sugar throughout flour by sifting together, using hands. Make a well in the center by pushing flour to the sides.

2. Dissolve remaining teaspoon sugar in ¼ cup (60 ml) tepid water, using a mug-size cup, and add yeast. Stir until completely smooth. Set aside to activate (rise and foam) in a draft-free area. (This takes but a minute or so.)

3. When yeast is activated, add it at once, along with the remainder of the tepid liquid (water or milk) to the flour mixture. Using a wooden spoon or a mixer with a bread dough hook, mix until liquid has been absorbed. Turn out onto a well-floured board and let rest for a few minutes.

4. Knead for about 5 or 6 minutes, or until one or two bubbles begin to form.

5. Shape kneaded dough into a round ball, and set in a greased pan or bowl. Cover with a clean cloth and prove (let it rise to doubled bulk) at room temperature in a draft-free area. The first proving should take approximately 1 hour. If you are not sure the dough is ready, test it by pressing two fingers into the dough about an inch; if they leave an indentation, dough is ready to be kneaded a second time. The size of the dough, however, is the easiest and quickest guide. (Dough should be checked from time to time, as once it is fully risen and doubled in bulk, it will quickly sour.)

6. Turn dough out onto floured board without delay, and commence kneading a second time for another 5 or 6 minutes, or until bubbly. Shape dough into a ball, and return to greased pan or bowl. Cover, and set in a draft-free area to rise a second time. The second proving requires slightly less time than the first.

7. Turn risen dough out onto board, and roll out to an even thickness, using a rolling pin. (Do not knead dough after second proving.) Cut dough into sections of the desired size. Shape sections into loaves, using both hands to tuck the edges under. (Well-worked dough is easy to handle and shape.)

8. Place in greased or nonstick coated breadpans. Loaves should no more than half fill pans, as dough will rise again and double in bulk. Set pans in a draft-free area at room temperature, and cover with a cloth. Loaves will be doubled in bulk and ready for the oven in slightly less time than was required for second proving, that is, in approximately 40 .ninutes. Oven should be preheated to 350° F. (177° C.) so that it will be hot when bread is ready to be baked.

9. Set risen loaves in preheated 350° F. (177° C.) oven, and bake for approximately 1 hour, depending on size.

10. When done, bread will have shrunk from sides and will practically fall out of the inverted pan. However, the best and easiest test is to knock with the knuckles on the bottom near the center of the loaf. Properly baked, bread will have a definite hollow sound. Turn baked bread out onto racks away from drafts, but do not cover. Store when completely cool.

BREAD RECIPES

ENRICHED BUTTER AND EGG BREAD

12 cups (1.36 kg) flour
1 tablespoon salt
3 teaspoons sugar
1 1-ounce (28 g) cake
* compressed yeast, dissolved*
* in ¼ cup (60 ml) tepid*
* water; or, ¼ oz. (7 g) pkg.*
* dry yeast*

4 cups (960 ml) milk at room
* temperature*
4 eggs, well beaten
1 stick (¼ pound or 115 g)
* butter, melted*

Follow steps as outlined in Basic Bread-Making Formula, adding beaten eggs and melted butter along with milk and activated yeast, as stipulated in Step 3.

BREAKFAST BREAD

6 cups (0.68 kg) whole wheat
* flour*
1 cup (113 g) wheat germ,
* untoasted*
3 cups (340 g) high-gluten
* flour*
1 cup (113 g) soy flour
1 cup (113 g) corn meal
1 tablespoon salt
3 teaspoons sugar
1 1-ounce (28 g) cake
* compressed yeast, dissolved*
* in ¼ cup (60 ml) tepid*
* water; or, ¼ oz. (7 g) pkg.*
* dry yeast*

4 cups (960 ml) milk at room
* temperature*
2 eggs, well beaten
1 stick (¼ pound or 115 g)
* butter, melted*
¼ cup (60 ml) honey or
* molasses*

Follow steps as outlined in Basic Bread-Making Formula, substituting various flours listed above (quantity remains the same, i.e., 12 cups). Add beaten eggs, melted butter, honey or molasses along with milk and activated yeast, as stipulated in Step 3.

RYE BREAD

5 cups (567 g) rye flour
2 cups (227 g) high-gluten
  flour
5 cups (567 g) whole wheat
  flour
1 tablespoon salt
3 teaspoons sugar

1 1-ounce (28 g) cake
  compressed yeast, dissolved
  in ¼ cup (60 ml) tepid
  water; or, ¼ oz. (7 g) pkg.
  dry yeast
4 cups (960 ml) water at
  room temperature

Follow steps as outlined in Basic Bread-Making Formula, substituting various flours listed above (quantity remains the same, i.e., 12 cups).

FRENCH BREAD

12 cups (1.36 kg) high-gluten
  flour
1 tablespoon salt
3 teaspoons sugar
1 1-ounce (28 g) cake
  compressed yeast, dissolved
  in ¼ cup tepid water

4 cups (960 ml) water or
  milk–at room temperature
  (barely tepid)

Follow steps as outlined in Basic Bread-Making Formula, using high-gluten flour. (The quality of the flour will greatly affect the finished product.) To improve flavor, allow dough to rise and prove three times.

In Step 7, shape and mold dough into long rolls (cylinder shapes) with slightly pointed ends.

In Step 8, place shaped loaves in specially designed baking tins for French bread; or place on greased or nonstick cookie sheets, several inches apart. Make 3 or 4 curved slashes about ½″ (1 cm) deep in top of loaves, using a razor blade or knife with a fine, sharp blade. For a browner and crisper crust, preheat oven to 400° F. (205° C.) for first 15 minutes of baking, and then reduce to 375° F. (190° C.). Immediately before baking, glaze loaves with ice cold water, using a pastry brush.

After first 5 minutes, open oven door and sprinkle ice cold water over surface of oven. Bake another few minutes and repeat.

Because of its shape, size, and higher oven temperature, French Bread takes slightly less time to bake than regular bread. Use the same test for doneness as described in Step 10.

CHALLAH

4 cups (0.45 kg) high-gluten
   flour
8 cups (0.90 kg) whole wheat
   flour
1 tablespoon salt
3 teaspoons sugar
1 1-ounce (28 g) cake
   compressed yeast, dissolved
   in ¼ cup (60 ml) tepid
   water; or, ¼ oz. (7 g) pkg.
   dry yeast
4 cups (960 ml) milk at room
   temperature

2 whole eggs plus 2 egg yolks,
   well beaten
2 sticks (½ pound or 225 g)
   butter, melted
few strands saffron, dissolved
   in 2 tablespoons hot water
egg yolk
milk
melted butter   }   for glazing
sugar

Follow steps as outlined in Basic Bread-Making Formula, using high-gluten and whole wheat flour. Add beaten eggs, yolks, melted butter, and dissolved saffron along with milk and activated yeast, as stipulated in Step 3. (Saffron will impart a characteristic faint yellow coloring and distinctive flavor to bread.)

Allow dough to rise and prove three times. When dough has fully risen for the last time and has been rolled out, as outlined in Step 7, divide into sections about 6″ (15 cm) wide and 12 to 14″ (30-35 cm) long, using a sharp knife. Cut each section into 3 lengths and braid together, bringing to a slight point at either end. Beat egg yolk into 1 or 2 teaspoons milk and glaze loaves, using pastry brush. Allow glaze to dry and glaze a second time.

In Step 8, place on greased or nonstick baking tins, allowing enough space between loaves for each to rise and double in bulk. Continue as outlined in Steps 9 and 10.

When baked, glaze with melted butter in which ½ teaspoon or so of sugar has been dissolved. This will soften and enrich flavor of crust.

BRIOCHE

6 cups (0.68 kg) whole wheat
   flour
6 cups (0.68 kg) high-gluten
   flour
1 tablespoon salt
3 teaspoons sugar
1 1-ounce (28 g) cake
   compressed yeast, dissolved
   in ¼ cup (60 ml) tepid
   water; or, ¼ oz. (7 g) pkg.
   dry yeast

4 cups (960 ml) milk at room
   temperature
4 whole eggs, well beaten
2 sticks (½ pound or 225 g)
   butter, melted
sugar   ⎫
egg yolk ⎬ for glazing
      ⎭

Follow steps as outlined in Basic Bread-Making Formula, using whole wheat and high-gluten flour. Add beaten eggs and melted butter along with milk and activated yeast, as stipulated in Step 3.

Allow dough to rise and prove three times. When dough has fully risen for last time and has been rolled out, as outlined in Step 7, divide into sections according to the size of the brioche pans (or individual brioche pans) being used. Reserve a portion of the dough for small balls to be set on top of loaves. Shape sections into round balls using both hands, folding under with fingers, and set in greased brioche pans. Cut smaller sections, about 1 or 2″ (2.5-5 cm) in diameter (depending on size of brioche pans), and shape into smaller balls. Make an opening in larger ball by pressing two fingers down into center of dough, and insert small ball by pulling one end into a tear shape. (If necessary, moisten dough with a little cold water.) Beat about ½ teaspoon (2.5 mi) sugar into egg yolk and glaze loaves, using a pastry brush. Let dry and glaze a second time. Continue as outlined in remainder of Bread-Making Formula.

COOKING THEORY:
THE CHEMICAL CHANGES IN
DOUGHS AND BATTERS

FLOUR It is the gluten property that enables flour and liquid to form a dough. As mentioned previously, the richer the flour, nutritionally, the more liquid it absorbs. Flour milled from the whole grain will absorb more liquid than highly processed white flour.* Flours that lack gluten strength, such as corn meal and rye, are usually combined with a larger proportion of wheat flour.

LIQUIDS Liquids serve to dissolve solid ingredients, as well as to bring about the physical and chemical changes that take place upon mixing and baking. The amount of liquid used depends on the consistency desired, as well as the absorbency of the flour. When water is used in place of milk, a slightly smaller amount is added. The fat content of milk contributes to browning. (As a rule of thumb, 1 cup (240 mi) of liquid is required for every 2 cups (226 g) flour.)

FAT The flavor of the fat (butter, margarine, vegetable oil, shortening) will affect the flavor of the finished product. Fats are interchangeable, that is, melted butter may be substituted for vegetable oil, margarine for butter, and so on. Fats also aid in softening and tenderizing the product. Creaming the fat mixes air into it and assists slightly in leavening, but with the development of refined flours, electric mixers, and controlled oven temperatures, this is no longer as necessary as it once was. (The average amount of fat for a 2-cup (226 g) flour, 1-cup (240 mi) liquid recipe is 4 to 6 tablespoons.)

EGGS Eggs aid in leavening and provide color, flavor, and nutritive value. When the dough is exposed to heat, the albumin content of the egg coagulates and assists in maintaining the texture as the dough rises. Egg yolks act as an emulsifier and help

*In the recipes that follow, when using whole wheat flour, as opposed to cake flour or all-purpose flour, either reduce quantity of flour or add additional liquid; for example, in a 2-cup (226 g) flour recipe, reduce flour by 2 tablespoons or add 1 tablespoon liquid.

distribute the fat evenly throughout the mixture. (Two to three eggs is the average number used in a recipe calling for 2 cups (226 g) flour and one cup (240 mi) liquid.)

LEAVENING AGENTS   Mixtures such as cakes, muffins, drop cookies, and biscuits depend on air, steam, and/or a chemical agent, such as baking powder or baking soda and sour milk, to make them light and porous. Beer can be used as a leavening agent in pancakes and batters. A thinner batter requires slightly more baking powder than a thicker one. (As a general rule, 1 teaspoon baking powder is used per cup (114 g) of flour.)

SUGAR   Sugar is primarily a flavoring or sweetening agent. Anywhere from ¼ cup (0.49 g) to 1 cup (198 g) sugar may be used in a 2-cup (226 g) flour recipe. Sugar also acts as a tenderizer. Too much sugar (particularly in a cookie recipe) can result in a poor, crumbly texture.

FLAVORINGS   Cocoa, chocolate, vanilla seeds, extracts, spices, grated citrus rind, liqueurs, and fruit juices may be used as flavorings. Liquid flavorings are added to moistened ingredients, and dry flavorings are mixed in with dry ingredients.

BASIC CAKE-MAKING FORMULA (WITH SELF-RISING FLOUR)

Dry ingredients

2 cups (226 g) self-rising flour
⅓ to 1 cup (65-198 g) sugar, according to desired degree of sweetness

Moist ingredients

5 ⅓ tablespoons melted butter or oil
¾ cup plus 2 tablespoons (210 ml) milk
2 eggs

Flavoring

Dry: 5 to 8 tablespoons cocoa; 1¼ to 1¾ teaspoons mixed spices

Moist: 2 tablespoons fresh orange juice or 1 tablespoon fresh lemon juice; grated rind from 1 orange or 1 lemon; 1 teaspoon flavor extracts; seeds from 2" (5 cm) piece vanilla pod; 1 to 2 tablespoons rum or liqueur; 2 ounces (60 g) melted chocolate

Sift dry ingredients twice (including any dry flavoring) and place in bowl of electric mixer.

Add moist ingredients (including any moist flavoring) and blend in at low speed. When moistened, turn mixer to medium and beat for about 2 minutes, or until thoroughly blended. Turn batter into greased or nonstick 8" (22.5 cm) tubular pan, layer cake pans, square, round, or oblong cake pans. Fill no more than one-half to two-thirds full.

Bake in a preheated 350° F. (177° C.) oven for 40 to 60 minutes, depending on thickness of cake. Cake will begin to shrink from sides of pan when baked. Or test by inserting a cake tester into center; if it comes out clean, cake is done. (*Do not* open oven door during first 20 minutes or so of baking.)

Remove from oven and let stand in a draft-free area for about 5 minutes before turning out onto cake rack. Serve as is or use any one of the glazes, frostings, or fillings listed under Icings, Frostings and Fillings.

BASIC CAKE-MAKING FORMULA (WITH WHOLE WHEAT FLOUR)

Dry ingredients

2 cups (226 g) whole wheat flour

⅓ to 1 cup (65 g to 198 g) sugar, according to desired degree of sweetness

3 teaspoons baking powder

pinch of salt

Moist ingredients

5 ⅓ tablespoons melted butter or oil

1 cup plus 2 tablespoons (270 ml) milk

2 eggs

Flavoring

Dry: 5 to 8 tablespoons cocoa; 1¼ to 1¾ teaspoons mixed spices

Moist: 2 tablespoons fresh orange juice or 1 tablespoon fresh lemon juice; grated rind from 1 orange or 1 lemon; 1 teaspoon flavor extracts; seeds from 2" (5 cm) piece vanilla pod; 1 to 2 tablespoons rum or liqueur; 2 ounces (60 g) melted chocolate

Proceed as in Basic Cake-Making Formula (with Self-Rising Flour), substituting above ingredients and measurements.

CAKE RECIPES

SPICE CAKE

½ to ¾ teaspoon ginger

½ to ¾ teaspoon cinnamon

¼ teaspoon ground cloves

Follow Basic Cake-Making Formula for either self-rising or whole wheat flour, adding the above-listed spices as flavoring to the dry ingredients.

ORANGE CAKE

grated rind of 1 orange

2 tablespoons fresh orange juice

Follow Basic Cake-Making Formula for either self-rising or whole wheat flour, adding grated orange rind and juice as flavoring to the other moist ingredients.

COCOANUT ORANGE CAKE

grated rind of 1 orange
2 tablespoons fresh orange juice

½ cup (56 g) grated unsweetened cocoanut

Follow Basic Cake-Making Formula for either self-rising or whole wheat flour, adding grated orange rind and juice as flavoring to the other moist ingredients. *Increase baking powder to 4 teaspoons in the formula using whole wheat flour.* Fold cocoanut into finished batter and turn into cake pan(s).

CHOCOLATE CAKE

5 to 8 tablespoons cocoa; or 2 ounces (60 g) baking chocolate, melted

Follow Basic Cake-Making Formula for either self-rising or whole wheat flour, using cocoa or chocolate as flavoring. Add cocoa to dry ingredients and chocolate to moist ingredients. To melt chocolate, pour over enough boiling water to cover and let stand until soft. Carefully pour off water and add to batter. *Increase baking powder to 4 teaspoons in formula using whole wheat flour.*

VANILLA FLAVORED CAKE

seeds from 2" (5 cm) piece
  vanilla pod; or 1 teaspoon
  vanilla extract

Follow Basic Cake-Making Formula for either self-rising or whole wheat flour, adding vanilla along with other moist ingredients. When using vanilla pod, cut in half from end to end, and scrape out seeds using the point of a sharp knife. Add seeds to mixture and discard pod.

RAISIN CAKE

½ teaspoon ginger
½ teaspoon cinnamon

¼ teaspoon ground cloves
⅓ to ½ cup raisins, moistened

Follow Basic Cake-Making Formula for either self-rising or whole wheat flour, adding spices as flavoring to other dry ingredients. To moisten raisins, add enough boiling water or hot orange juice to fully cover and let stand until absorbed. *Increase baking powder to 4 teaspoons in formula using whole wheat flour.*

Drain off excess liquid from moistened raisins and fold into batter, using a rubber spatula.

BANANA CAKE

1 cup (170 g) mashed ripe
  bananas

Follow Basic Cake-Making Formula for either self-rising or whole wheat flour, using bananas as flavoring. *Increase baking powder to 4 teaspoons in formula using whole wheat flour and decrease milk by 2 tablespoons in formula using self-rising flour.* Mix mashed bananas into finished batter.

CORN CAKE

1 cup (113 g) cornmeal   1 cup (113 g) white or whole
                                wheat flour

Follow Basic Cake-Making Formula (with whole wheat flour), substituting 1 cup (113 g) cornmeal and 1 cup (113 g) white or whole wheat flour for 2 cups (226 g) whole wheat flour. *Increase baking powder to 4 teaspoons.* To obtain a crisper crust, bake in a preheated 375° F. (190° C.) oven.

CUPCAKES

Follow basic Cake-Making Formula for either self-rising or whole wheat flour, using either vanilla or chocolate as flavoring. Replace cake pan or pans with greased or nonstick cupcake pans. (Pans may be lined with individual paper cups especially designed for this purpose.) Bake in a preheated 375° F. (190° C.) oven for approximately 30 to 35 minutes, depending on thickness. Test using a cake tester.

MUFFINS (PLAIN)

Follow Basic Cake-Making Formula for either self-rising or whole wheat flour, omitting flavoring and using a minimum amount of sugar (4 to 5 tablespoons). Substitute greased or nonstick muffin pans for cake pan, and bake in a preheated 375° F. (190° C.) oven for approximately 30 to 35 minutes, depending on thickness. Test using a cake tester.

BLUEBERRY MUFFINS

Prepare batter as for Muffins (Plain) and fold in ½ (118 mi) to 1 cup (236 mi) fresh blueberries.

CORN MUFFINS

Prepare batter as for Corn Cake, using a minimum amount of sugar (4 to 5 tablespoons). Substitute greased or nonstick muffin pans for cake pan. Bake in a 375° F. (190° C.) oven for approximately 30 to 35 minutes, depending on thickness. Test using a cake tester.

GUGELHUPF

blanched almonds
½ cup white raisins
fresh orange juice
1 stick (¼ pound or 115 g)
butter
½ to 1 cup (99 g to 198 g)
granulated sugar,
depending on desired
degree of sweetness
4 whole eggs

seeds from 2" (5 cm) piece
vanilla pod
2 cups (226 g) cake flour
pinch of salt
4 teaspoons baking powder
1 cup (236 mi) milk
rind of 1 lemon, finely grated
finely sifted flour
powdered sugar

Place almonds in a well-buttered Gugelhupf cake pan and dust lightly with flour (one whole almond in each indentation).

Soak raisins in a sufficient amount of fresh orange juice to fully cover and set aside.

Cream butter and sugar, using electric mixer, beating until light and fluffy. Add eggs one at a time, beating after each addition. Using a sharp knife, split vanilla pod in half and scrape seeds into mixture, blending in.

Combine flour, salt, and baking powder and put through two siftings. Add flour and milk alternately, beginning and ending with flour, beating well after each addition. Mix in finely grated lemon rind.

Strain raisins if necessary, but do not squeeze, and toss lightly in finely sifted flour before folding into batter, using a rubber spatula.

Turn into Gugelhupf tin, being careful not to disturb almonds, and bake in a 350° F. (177° C.) oven for about 50 minutes, or until cake tester comes out clean or cake begins to shrink from sides of pan. Allow cake to rest for about 10 minutes before turning out onto cake rack in draft-free area.

Dust lightly with powdered sugar.

GLAZED CHOCOLATE CAKE

2 1-ounce packages (total of 60 g) unsweetened baking chocolate
2 cups (226 g) flour
pinch of salt
5 teaspoons baking powder
1 stick (½ cup or 225 g) butter, softened
½ to ¾ cup (99 g to 148 g) granulated sugar
3 whole eggs, separated
1 tablespoon chocolate liqueur (crème de cacao)
1¼ cups (300 ml) milk
¼ cup (49 g) powdered sugar

Pour boiling water over chocolate and set aside to melt.

Combine flour, salt, and baking powder and put through two siftings.

Cream butter, using electric mixer, and gradually add granulated sugar, beating until light and creamy. Add egg yolks one at a time, beating well after each addition.

Add sifted flour and milk alternately, beginning and ending with flour, beating well after each addition. Carefully drain water off chocolate and mix in, along with chocolate liqueur.

Gradually add powdered sugar to egg whites, beating until they are glossy and can be shaped into soft peaks. Fold beaten egg whites into batter, using a spatula, and turn into a greased or nonstick tubular cake pan—or use a brioche or other metal pan having a fancy shape. Bake in a 350° F. (177° C.) oven for about an hour, or until cake tester comes out clean (cake begins to shrink from sides of pan). Remove and rest for about 10 minutes before turning out onto cake rack in draft-free area.

Prepare glaze according to recipe for Chocolate Glaze (p. 399).

When cool, set cake on plate and glaze by placing layers of wax paper under outside edges to catch drippings. If Chocolate Glaze is too thick, add 1 or 2 tablespoons hot water at a time until it is of the desired consistency.

SPONGE CAKES (PETIT FOURS, LAYER CAKES, RUM CAKES)

1 stick plus 1 tablespoon (9 tablespoons or 130 g) sweet butter, clarified
6 whole eggs

1 cup (198 g) powdered sugar
seeds from one dried vanilla pod
2 cups (226 g) flour

To clarify, set butter over low heat until melted. Remove and set aside to cool slightly. Carefully draw off top portion, discarding any sediment which has collected on bottom. Set drawn portion aside.

Combine eggs and sugar in top of double boiler and set over low heat (water in lower portion should be just under boiling point). Beat with an electric beater until smooth and thick, or until mixture draws out in a ribbon-like shape. Using a sharp knife, split vanilla pod and stir seeds into mixture. Transfer to a warm mixing bowl.

Sift flour three times. Alternately fold flour and clarified butter into beaten egg mixture, beginning and ending with flour. Turn batter into one of the following: (1) petit four molds lightly greased with a canned vegetable oil spray; (2) a rectangular baking pan, if cutting into small cakes; or (3) two round cake pans, if using for a filled, rum, or liqueur-soaked cake.

Bake in a preheated 350° F. (177° C.) oven until lightly browned and sponge comes back after pressing lightly with fingers (or until cake begins to shrink from sides of pan). Turn off heat and let stand in oven for a few minutes with oven door open. Transfer to cake racks and set in a draft-free area.

Layer cakes may be sprinkled with rum or a fruit-based liqueur, such as Grand Marnier, and iced with Butter Cream. Chill before serving.

Small cakes may be (1) dipped in Plain or Chocolate Fondant; (2) glazed with a thin coating of Apricot Glaze and dipped in Fondant; or (3) iced with Plain or Tinted Butter Cream and chilled before serving. (See section on Icings, Frostings, and Fillings at end of this chapter.)

MINIATURE CHOCOLATE SWEETS (MIGNONETTES AU CHOCOLATE)

6 1-ounce squares (total of 170 g) semi-sweet baking chocolate

2 ounces chocolate liqueur (crème de cacao)

1 stick (½ cup or 115 g) sweet butter

5 eggs, separated

½ to ¾ cup (99 g to 148 g) extra fine granulated sugar

6 level tablespoons flour

Melt chocolate, liqueur, and butter over low heat, stirring to form a smooth cream. Remove from heat and stir in egg yolks one at a time. Gradually add sugar, beating well after each addition. Sift flour three times and fold in a little at a time. Beat egg whites until they can be shaped into soft, glossy peaks and gradually, but thoroughly, fold into mixture.

Using a pastry bag with a plain tube, half fill greased (using a canned vegetable oil spray) and lightly floured petit four molds. Set molds on baking sheets and bake in a preheated 350° F. (177° C.) oven for about 15 or 20 minutes, or until cakes begin to shrink from sides of pans.

Miniature Sweets may be treated in any of the following ways: (1) dust lightly with powdered sugar; (2) dip in Plain or Chocolate Fondant; (3) decorate with liqueur-flavored Butter Cream (tinted in pastel shades), using a pastry bag with various shaped tubes (star, rosette, plain).

Mignonettes may be served with fresh fruit and other desserts. Since they are quite rich, one or two per serving is adequate.

BROWNIES (WITH WHOLE WHEAT FLOUR)

2 squares (2 ounces or 60 g)
  semi-sweetened or
  unsweetened baking
  chocolate
¾ cup (85 g) whole wheat
  flour
1 teaspoon baking powder
pinch of salt

⅓ to 1 cup (65 g to 198 g)
  sugar, according to desired
  degree of sweetness
8 tablespoons (½ cup or
  115 g) butter, softened
2 eggs
1 cup walnuts, chopped
powdered sugar

To melt chocolate, pour over enough boiling water to cover and let stand until soft.

Put flour, baking powder, and salt through two siftings.

Using an electric mixer, gradually add sugar to butter, beating until light and creamy. Beat in eggs, one at a time. Carefully pour water off chocolate and add chocolate to mixture, beating at low speed until well blended.

Gradually add sifted flour, mixing in at medium speed. Fold chopped nuts into mixture, using a rubber spatula. Turn into a greased or nonstick 8″ × 8″ × 2″ (20 × 20 × 5 cm) square baking pan. Bake in a preheated 350° F. (177° C.) oven for about 30 to 40 minutes, or until cake tester comes out clean. Remove from oven and sprinkle powdered sugar over surface. Cool slightly (in pan) before cutting into squares.

BROWNIES (WITH SELF-RISING CAKE FLOUR)

Follow recipe for Brownies (with whole wheat flour), substituting ¾ cup (85 g) self-rising cake flour for ¾ cup (85 g) whole wheat flour. Omit the teaspoon of baking powder and pinch of salt.

FUDGE BROWNIES

These are a heavier, more chewy version of either of the two Brownie recipes already given. To make Fudge Brownies with whole wheat flour, reduce flour to ½ cup (56 g) and baking powder to ¾ teaspoon. If you wish to use self-rising cake flour, add only ½ cup (56 g) and omit both the baking powder and the salt.

BASIC FORMULA FOR REFRIGERATED COOKIES

2 sticks (½ pound or 225 g)
  butter
½ to 1 cup (99 g to 198 g)
  sugar
seeds from one whole vanilla
  pod

2 whole eggs
½ teaspoon baking soda
4 tablespoons heavy cream
3½ cups (396 g) flour

Cream butter and sugar until light and fluffy, using electric mixer. Split vanilla pod through center and add seeds to mixture, blending in. Add eggs one at a time, beating after each addition. Dissolve baking soda in heavy cream. Sift flour and add, along with cream-soda mixture, beginning and ending with flour, blending well after each addition.

Divide mixture into three sections, and shape into rolls about 2″ (5 cm) in diameter. Transfer to sheets of wax paper (dusted lightly with flour) and wrap. Cover with a second wrapping of aluminum foil and set on refrigerator shelf for several hours, or overnight. (Cookies may also be frozen and baked as needed).

Remove rolls from refrigerator and cut into uniform-size slices about ¼″ (.6 cm) thick, using a sharp knife or slicer. Bake on greased or nonstick cookie sheets in a preheated 350° F. (177° C.) oven for 10 or 15 minutes, or until lightly brown around edges. Remove from cookie sheet, using a spatula. (Do not pile cookies on top of one another, until completely cool.)

To decorate, press pieces of walnuts, hazelnuts, slivers of almonds, cherry slices, or fruit peel into center of uncooked dough. Or, dust lightly with plain or colored granulated sugar, or finely chopped nuts.

For sandwich-type cookies, spread with Quick Creamy Chocolate Frosting (recipe in this chapter) or fruit jam, and top with another layer.

BASIC FORMULA FOR ROLLED COOKIES

The dough for Rolled Cookies is prepared the same way as for Basic Formula for Refrigerated Cookies, with the exception that it is not shaped into rolls nor is it refrigerated. Additional flour may be added until dough is of the right consistency for easy handling; however, do not add too much flour, otherwise cookies will not be tender.

Roll dough out on lightly floured board to ⅛" to ¼" (.3-.6 cm) thickness and cut to desired shapes, using cookie cutters. Bake on greased or nonstick cookie sheets in a preheated 350° F. (177° C.) oven for about 10 minutes, or until lightly brown around the edges.

CHOCOLATE COOKIES

2 1-ounce squares (a total of
60 g) semi-sweet baking
chocolate

Follow Basic Formula for either Refrigerated or Rolled Cookies and mix melted chocolate into beaten butter, sugar, and egg mixture, omitting vanilla flavoring. (To melt chocolate, place in small bowl or container and pour over enough boiling water to cover. Set aside to soften. This takes but a minute or so. Carefully pour off water and add to mixture).

COCOANUT COOKIES

1 cup (113 g) unsweetened
cocoanut

Follow Basic Formula for either Rolled or Refrigerated Cookies and blend unsweetened cocoanut (may be purchased in specialty or health food store) into finished mixture. (Do not omit vanilla flavoring.)

LEMON WAFERS

rind of 1 lemon, finely grated   juice of 1 lemon, strained

Follow Basic Formula for Refrigerated Cookies and add grated rind and lemon juice to beaten butter, sugar, and egg mixture. Mix until well blended. (Omit vanilla flavoring.)

Refrigerate rolls of dough for several hours or overnight.

When ready to bake, slice rolls into very thin wafers about ⅛″ (.3 cm) thick. Bake in a preheated 350° F. (177° C.) oven and remove as soon as wafers begin to turn slightly brown around edges. Wafers will be crisp and may be served with fresh fruit, sherbets, ice cream, and similar desserts.

ALMOND WAFERS

¾ cup (113 g) almonds, finely   slivered almonds (blanched)
chopped
2 tablespoons Amaretto
Liqueur

Follow Basic Formula for Refrigerated Cookies, substituting Amaretto, or other almond-based liqueur, for vanilla. Blend finely chopped almonds into finished mixture. Refrigerate rolls of dough for several hours or overnight.

When ready to bake, slice rolls of dough into wafers about ⅛″ (.3 cm) thick and press a slivered almond into center of each. Bake in a preheated 350° F. (177° C.) oven and remove as soon as wafers begin to turn slightly brown around edges.

BASIC FORMULA FOR DROP COOKIES

1 stick (¼ pound or 115 g)
  butter
½ to ¾ cup (99 g to 148 g)
  sugar
seeds from 2" (5 cm) piece
  vanilla pod

2 eggs
3 teaspoons baking powder
pinch of salt
2 cups (226 g) flour
1 cup (236 mi) milk

Cream butter and sugar until light and fluffy, using electric mixer. Split vanilla pod through center and add seeds to mixture, blending in. Add eggs one at a time, beating after each addition. Sift baking powder, salt, and flour. Alternately mix in flour and milk, beginning and ending with flour, blending well after each addition. Drop onto greased or nonstick cookie sheets, two or three inches (5-7.5 cm) apart (depending on size), using two teaspoons moistened in water or pastry bag with a plain tube.

Bake in a 375° F. (190° C.) oven until fully risen and lightly browned. For a softer crust, bake in a 350° F. (177° C.) oven.

CHOCOLATE CHIP COOKIES

1 8-ounce (225 g) package real
  chocolate chips

Follow Basic Formula for Drop Cookies and fold chocolate chips into finished mixture. (Two tablespoons of a chocolate liqueur may be substituted for vanilla).

RAISIN COOKIES

½ cup (113 g) white raisins

Follow Basic Formula for Drop Cookies and fold raisins into finished mixture. (Do not omit vanilla flavoring.)

NUT COOKIES

*½ cup (113 g) walnuts,
  almonds, or hazelnuts,
  finely chopped*

Follow Basic Formula for Drop Cookies and stir finely chopped nuts into finished mixture. (Two tablespoons of a chocolate liqueur may be substituted for vanilla).

BRANDIED GINGER ROLLS

*3 sticks (1½ cups or 340 g)
  butter
1½ cups (297 g) finely
  granulated sugar
1 cup (240 ml) molasses*

*3 teaspoons powdered ginger
⅓ cup (80 ml) brandy
2¾ cups (311 g) finely sifted
  flour*

Melt butter in saucepan over medium heat. Add sugar, molasses, and ginger, stirring until sugar has dissolved. Add brandy and continue to cook for another 2 or 3 minutes. Remove from heat, and, using an electric mixer, gradually add flour, beating until well-blended.

Using a small spoon (demitasse size) drop onto a lightly greased cookie sheet a few inches apart. Bake in a preheated 300° F. (149° C.) oven for about 15 minutes, or, until lightly browned. Using a spatula, turn out one at a time onto board or counter, and, working quickly, roll over a wooden spoon handle (or use special tin rolls designed for this purpose). Rolls will be crisp and have a lacy pattern.

ORDINARY PASTRY

*5 cups (0.56 kg) flour
½ teaspoon salt
1 cup (½ pound or 225 g)
  vegetable shortening*

*1 cup (½ pound or 225 g)
  butter
1 egg, lightly beaten
ice cold water*

Blend flour and salt. Cut butter and shortening into flour mixture, using a pastry cutter or food processor. Place lightly beaten egg in a 1-cup measurement and fill remainder with ice cold water. Turn into flour mixture and quickly mix the whole together, using a fork, or, mix in food processor. Do not overmix.

Shape into a solid mass using hands, and let stand for an hour or so before using; or wrap in plastic or wax paper and set in refrigerator for several hours or overnight. Bring to cool-room temperature before rolling out. Pastry can be kept refrigerated for several days, or it can be frozen. Pies, tarts, and so on are normally baked in a 425° F. (218° C.) oven until lightly browned. If browning occurs too quickly, reduce heat to 400° F. (205° C.).

QUICK ENRICHED PASTRY

1 10-ounce (283 g) package pie   1½ tablespoons butter,
  crust mix   softened

Add softened butter to pie crust mix and prepare according to package directions; or combine ingredients and place in electric food processor for a few seconds or until well blended.

For a tenderer crust, set rolled out crust in refrigerator for an hour or two before filling.

FINE PASTRY

3½ cups (396 g) pastry flour   ½ teaspoon salt
1 whole egg plus one egg   4 tablespoons powdered sugar
  white, lightly beaten   2 sticks (½ pound or 225 g)
½ cup (120 ml) ice cold water   sweet butter, softened
1 tablespoon fresh lemon juice

Sift flour and set aside.

Blend lightly beaten egg, egg white, water, lemon juice, salt, and sugar. In a separate bowl, cut butter into flour, using a pastry cutter or food processor. Make a well in center and add combined liquid ingredients, and mix, using tips of thumb and fingers, or blend in food processor. Let stand for a few minutes before shaping into ball. If food processor has not been used, knead until smooth.

Wrap and chill in refrigerator for several hours or overnight. Remove an hour or so before rolling out. (Uncooked dough may be frozen.)

FRUIT FILLED PIES

Ordinary Pastry or Quick Enriched Pastry
6 or 7 cups fresh fruit (apples, pears, or peaches), peeled and uniformly sliced
½ cup (53 g) unsweetened cocoanut

1 tablespoon fresh lemon juice
grated rind of 1 lemon
pinch of salt
¾ teaspoon cinnamon
1 tablespoon butter

Prepare pastry, divide in half, and roll out. Line 9″ (22.5 cm) pie plate with one-half and refrigerate.

Combine peeled and uniformly sliced fruit (combinations of fruit may also be used), cocoanut, lemon juice, grated lemon rind, salt, cinnamon and toss. (If fruit is fully ripe, sugar should not be necessary.) Remove pie plate from refrigerator and fill with fruit mixture. Dot with butter and cover with remaining pastry. Trim overhang even with edge of pie plate. Fold upper crust under slightly and pinch edges together, using thumb and index finger. Lightly glaze with cold milk using a pastry brush. Refrigerate for at least an hour before baking.

When ready to bake, make holes at intervals, using a fork, to allow steam to escape. Bake in a 425° F. (218° C.) oven for about 30 minutes, or until lightly browned.

Pie may be frozen unbaked, since cocoanut acts as a preservative for fruit. When ready to serve, bake in frozen state in a pre-heated 425° F. (218° C.) oven until lightly browned. It will take slightly longer to bake than when unfrozen.

BASIC FORMULA FOR CHOU PASTE*

1 cup (240 ml) water
1 stick (¼ pound or 115 g)
  butter
½ teaspoon salt
2 tablespoons finely
  granulated sugar

1¾ cups (198 g) finely sifted
  flour
4 large whole eggs plus 2
  yolks
2 egg whites, beaten
1 tablespoon powdered sugar

Combine water, butter, salt, and granulated sugar in a saucepan and bring to a brisk boil over medium high heat. Remove and mix in flour all at once. Return to heat and cook over medium low heat, stirring, until butter begins to ooze slightly, or, mixture no longer sticks to sides of pan. (This should take but a few minutes.) Remove from heat and set aside to cool. When slightly cool, using an electric hand beater or wire whisk, add eggs plus yolks one at a time, beating after each addition. However, do not overbeat, as this reduces the volume and consistency. Add a tablespoon of powdered sugar to remaining two egg whites and beat until they form soft peaks. Fold into mixture, using a rubber spatula.

Drop by spoonfuls onto a greased or nonstick baking sheet about 1½" (4 cm) apart. Or, using a pastry bag with a plain tube, pipe in any of the following ways:

◇ 3" (7.5 cm) long fingershape for eclairs
◇ 2" (5 cm) rounds for creampuffs
◇ 1" to 1½" (2.5-4 cm) rounds for profiterolles (miniature cream puffs) or hors d'oeuvres

Bake in a preheated 425° F. (218° C.) oven for about 10 minutes. Lower heat to 400° F. (205° C.) and bake for approximately 10 minutes longer. Pastry should puff up and be slightly browned. *Do not open oven door during first 10 minutes.*

Remove and set on oven door, pricking with a cake tester or the point of a sharp knife to allow steam to escape and cooked pastry to dry. Set in a draft-free area to cool.

---

*This dough is the basis for Cream Puffs, Eclairs, Beignets, Profiterolles, and Cheese Puffs.

CREAM PUFFS

Cut open baked and cooled pastry and fill with Chantilly Cream or Sweetened Whipped Cream (Chapter 5). For a more attractive appearance, pipe in using a pastry bag with a star tube.

Puffs may also be filled with ice cream, pastry cream or with various cream puddings.

Dust powdered sugar over top layer of puffs before serving.

ECLAIRS

Cut open Chou Pastry shaped for Eclairs and fill center with chilled Pastry Cream (Chapter 5) or with Sweetened Whipped Cream (Chapter 5). Brush tops with the following chocolate glaze:

Chocolate Glaze for Eclairs

3 squares (3 ounces or 85 g)   *1½ tablespoons water*
  semi-sweet baking   *1½ tablespoons butter*
  chocolate; or 3 packages   *1 tablespoon crème de cacao*
  pre-melted chocolate   *(optional)*
2 tablespoons corn syrup

If using chocolate squares, pour over enough boiling water to cover and set aside to melt.

Combine syrup, water, and butter and bring to a slow simmer over medium low heat. Carefully drain water from melted chocolate, or use pre-melted chocolate, and add to mixture along with liqueur. Stir long enough to blend, and brush over tops of Eclairs.

CHEESE PUFFS

Follow Basic Formula for Chou Paste and add one part grated Swiss, Cheddar, or Parmesan cheese to three parts finished, but unbaked, paste (1 cup or 170 g grated cheese to 3 cups (approximately 680 g) of paste). If using for hors d'oeuvres, shape into 1″

or 1½″ (2.5-4 cm) rounds. Bake, following the same procedure as for regular Chou Paste.

BEIGNETS (DEEP-FRIED ROUND AND FILLED DOUGHNUTS)

1 cup (240 ml) milk　　　　　　*½ cup (99 g) finely granulated sugar*

Follow Basic Formula for Chou Paste, substituting 1 cup milk for 1 cup water and ½ cup granulated sugar for 2 tablespoons sugar.

When ready to cook, shape into rounds, using two spoons moistened in water or a pastry bag with a plain tube, and drop into hot fat, preheated to 365° F. (185° C.). Beignets will float to surface when done, providing pan is not overcrowded. Drain on paper towels and roll in sugar. When cool, split open and fill with fruit jam, preserves, or Pastry Cream (Chapter 5).

FILLINGS FOR PROFITEROLLES (MINIATURE PUFFS) OR HORS D'OEUVRES*

1. Grind or finely chop 8 to 10 cooked shrimp and combine with 2 tablespoons softened butter. Add a few drops of lemon juice, salt and white pepper to taste. One or two dashes of Tabasco or a pinch of cayenne pepper may be added, if desired.

2. Combine 2 cups ground or finely chopped cooked ham or tongue with 2 tablespoons softened butter or mayonnaise, along with 1 tablespoon chopped chives or finely chopped dill.

3. Combine 1 tablespoon prepared mustard with 2 tablespoons softened butter or mayonnaise and blend with 2 cups ground or finely minced cooked ham.

*Fillings may also be spread over bread slices, cut into various shapes (rounds, squares, diamonds) and served as canapes, or used as fillings for sandwiches.

4. Mix 2 tablespoons softened butter or mayonnaise with ½ pound (225 g) of finely chopped cooked mushrooms and combine with 2 cups ground or finely minced cooked ham or chicken.

5. Put the yolks of 5 or 6 hardboiled eggs through a sieve and add 1 tablespoon softened butter and enough heavy cream or mayonnaise to form a smooth paste. Add one or two drops fresh lemon juice and season to taste with salt, white pepper, and curry powder.

6. Combine 3 or 4 finely chopped hardboiled eggs with enough butter or mayonnaise and finely chopped scallions or chives to form a smooth paste. Season to taste with salt and white pepper.

7. Add enough softened butter to grated Cheddar or Swiss cheese to form a smooth paste. Season to taste with cayenne pepper. Spread over lower half of puffs and place under broiler for a few seconds, or until melted. Top with remaining half and serve hot.

8. Combine ground or finely chopped cooked breast of chicken with enough softened butter or mayonnaise to form a smooth paste. Add one or two drops of Tabasco, and season to taste with salt and white pepper.

THIN DESSERT PANCAKES (CRÊPES)

8 tablespoons flour
pinch of salt
1 tablespoon powdered sugar
2 tablespoons oil (sesame or
    olive) or melted butter

6 whole eggs
4 tablespoons light cream
3 tablespoons flat beer

Sift flour, salt, and sugar and cut in oil or melted butter, using a pastry cutter. Mix in eggs, one at a time, until completely absorbed. Gradually add cream, followed by flat beer. (Ingredients may also be placed in electric blender until well blended.) To ensure a tender crêpe, refrigerate batter for several hours, or overnight.

Fry on both sides in a lightly greased crêpe-size (7-8″ or 17.5-20 cm) pan or a nonstick coated pan until lightly browned. Pan should be hot but not smoking. Pancakes will take but a few seconds to cook on either side and should be flexible and very tender when done.

Serve with fried fresh fruit slices, fruit preserves, ice cream, fruit sauces (apple or pear), or with fresh berries (strawberries, blueberries, raspberries) folded into whipped cream. Crêpes may also be used with flambéed preparations.

Batter will keep for several days, when refrigerated. To freeze crêpes, pack between layers of parchment or wax paper, before wrapping.

TO RE-HEAT. Brush a thin layer of melted butter over crêpes (to prevent them from drying out) and set in a 300° F. (149° C.) oven for a few minutes, or just long enough to heat through.

MAIN DISH PANCAKES (CRÊPES)

4 tablespoons (½ stick or 60 g) butter
1¼ cups (300 ml) milk
½ teaspoon salt
1¾ cups (198 g) flour

2 tablespoons oil (sesame or olive)
5 whole eggs
¼ cup (60 ml) flat beer

Melt butter in milk over low heat and set aside. Add salt to flour and cut in oil, using a pastry cutter. Mix in eggs, one at a time, until completely absorbed, using a wire whisk. Gradually add milk containing melted butter, followed by flat beer. (Ingredients may also be placed in an electric blender until well blended.) To ensure a tender crêpe, set batter in refrigerator for several hours, or overnight.

Fry on both sides in a lightly greased pancake or crêpe-size pan, or use a nonstick coated pan. Pan should be hot but not smoking. Pancakes will take but a few seconds to cook on either side.

Batter will keep for several days, when refrigerated, and used as needed.

Serve as a breakfast, luncheon, or supper dish with a filling, as is, or with eggs, sausage, ham or baked beans.

SPINACH-FILLED CRÊPES

2 pounds (900 g) fresh
   spinach; or 2 10-ounce
   packages (total of 560 g)
   frozen chopped spinach
butter
½ pound (225 g) mushrooms,
   peeled
olive oil
½ cup finely chopped ham or
   cooked bacon pieces

2 tablespoons light cream
salt and freshly ground
   pepper
dash of cayenne pepper
crêpes
½ cup freshly grated Swiss
   cheese

Wash fresh spinach, removing all grit, and cook in a large, uncovered pot of unsalted boiling water for about 3 to 4 minutes, or until tender. (Spinach cooked in this way should retain its deep green coloring.) Drain and finely chop.

If using frozen spinach, cook one package at a time (in order to exude as much of the water content as possible). Cook in a covered saucepan in a small amount of butter, over medium low heat. (Do not add water to pan.) Remove from heat as soon as spinach has defrosted and is heated through. Drain off excess liquid, using a wire strainer.

Peel mushroom tops and stems and brush lightly with olive oil. Sauté in a small amount of butter and oil over medium high heat until golden brown. Remove and chop.

Combine chopped spinach, ham or bacon pieces, mushrooms, 2 tablespoons light cream, seasoning to taste, and a dash of cayenne pepper. Spread mixture over a third of each crêpe and roll up. Lay crêpes in a greased or nonstick, shallow, heat-proof pan and sprinkle lightly with grated cheese. Dot with butter and place under broiler until lightly browned.

RECIPES FOR ICINGS, FROSTINGS, AND FILLINGS

QUICK CREAMY CHOCOLATE FROSTING AND FILLING

1 teaspoon instant coffee
2 tablespoons boiling water
1 14 oz. (397 g) can sweetened
  condensed milk

2 ounces (60 g) unsweetened
  baking chocolate
1 tablespoon chocolate liqueur
  (crème de cacao)

Dissolve coffee in boiling water and place in top of double boiler along with remaining ingredients. Set over medium low heat, stirring until chocolate has dissolved. Turn heat to medium high and beat, using an electric hand beater, until frosting forms soft peaks. (This should take about 5 minutes.) Add boiling water or cream, a tablespoon at a time, until of desired consistency. (Frosting will not harden upon standing.)

CHESTNUT BUTTER CREAM

1 pound (450 g) can
  unsweetened chestnut puree
  (imported French)
3 sticks (¾ pound or 340 g)
  butter, softened

8 to 12 tablespoons powdered
  sugar, (according to desired
  degree of sweetness)
3 tablespoons chocolate
  liqueur (crème de cacao)

Drain off any water that may have accumulated in can and place contents in bowl of electric mixer. Gradually beat in softened butter until thoroughly blended. Add sugar a few tablespoons at a time and taste, adding more or less according to desired degree of sweetness. Blend in chocolate liqueur.

SEVEN-MINUTE ICING

2 egg whites, unbeaten
pinch of cream of tartar
2 cups (396 g) finely
    granulated sugar; or 1 cup
    (198 g) white and 1 cup
    (198 g) brown sugar

pinch of salt
⅔ cup (160 ml) boiling water
1 teaspoon vanilla or lemon
    extract

Combine all ingredients in top of double boiler and set over medium high heat. (Water in lower section of boiler should simmer throughout.) Using an electric hand beater, beat mixture until stiff enough to form soft peaks. In about 7 minutes, icing should be light and fluffy. Icing is best when spread immediately. However, if it is not to be used immediately, place a damp cloth over pan to prevent crust from forming.

APRICOT GLAZE AND FILLING

dried apricots

powdered sugar, according to
    degree of sweetness

Pour a sufficient amount of boiling water over dried apricots to cover and soak for several hours, or until most of the water has been absorbed and apricots are soft. Purée in blender, food processor, or hand food mill; if necessary, thin out with hot water until of desired consistency.

For a sweeter flavor, set purée over low heat and add powdered sugar a tablespoon or two at a time, stirring to dissolve, until desired degree of sweetness has been reached.

Use as a filling for cakes or as a glaze for cakes, tarts, petit fours. It is also suitable as a glaze for ham, pork, duck, or chicken.

CHOCOLATE BUTTER CREAM

3 *ounces (85 g) sweet baking*   2 *teaspoons instant coffee*
   chocolate   1 *tablespoon boiling water*

Follow recipe in Chapter 5 for Butter Cream No. 2.

Pour a sufficient amount of boiling water to cover over chocolate and set aside to melt (takes but a minute or so). Dissolve instant coffee in 1 tablespoon boiling water. Carefully drain water off chocolate, and add dissolved coffee, stirring to blend. When cool, blend with finished Butter Cream No. 2.

FLAVORED AND TINTED BUTTER CREAM

liqueurs   *vegetable coloring matter*

Follow recipe in Chapter 5 for Butter Cream No. 2.

Add 1 tablespoon liqueur (maraschino, crème de cacao, kirsch, amaretto, crème de menthe) to finished Butter Cream No. 2 and blend in. Divide Butter Cream into equal portions and tint according to flavor base (green for mint, pink for cherry), blending in 1 or 2 drops of vegetable coloring at a time. Colors should be light and delicate, rather than deep in tone.

QUICK BUTTER CREAM

2 *sticks (½ pound or 225 g)*   *flavoring*
  butter, softened
2 *cups (396 g) powdered*
  sugar

Gradually add sugar to softened butter, beating until smooth and creamy. Add additional sugar until of desired consistency.

Flavor with any one of the following:

     ◇ 2 tablespoons liqueur (fruit based, chocolate, or almond)
     ◇ 1 teaspoon vanilla or lemon extract

◇ 1 tablespoon fresh lemon juice plus 1 teaspoon finely grated lemon peel
◇ 2 tablespoons fresh orange juice plus 1 teaspoon grated orange peel
◇ 2 tablespoons cocoa dissolved in 1 tablespoon boiling water
◇ 2 teaspoons instant coffee plus 1 tablespoon cocoa dissolved in 1½ tablespoons boiling water

ROYAL ICING

3 egg whites
pinch of cream of tartar
2 cups (396 g) powdered
  sugar

blue vegetable coloring
fresh lemon juice

Beat egg whites and cream of tartar until they form soft peaks. Mix in powdered sugar a little at a time, using a wire whisk or electric mixer set at low speed. If necessary, add additional sugar until mixture is smooth and creamy. Mix in a drop of blue vegetable coloring to make icing whiter, and a few drops of fresh lemon juice for flavoring. To decorate cakes, use a pastry bag with decorative tubes, or use plain tubes for signature writing. Icing may be tinted various colors using one or two drops of vegetable coloring.

CHOCOLATE GLAZE FOR CAKES

3 ounces (85 g) sweet baking
  chocolate
3 ounces (85 g) semi-sweet
  baking chocolate

4 tablespoons light corn syrup
⅔ cup (160 ml) water
2 tablespoons butter

Cover chocolate with sufficient boiling water to cover and set aside to melt. Do not stir.

Combine corn syrup, water, and butter in a saucepan and bring to a boil over low heat. Remove as soon as liquid reaches a full boil. Carefully drain water off chocolate and stir into syrup. If too thick, add boiling water a tablespoon at a time until of desired consistency. Place layers of wax or parchment paper under edges of cake before glazing.

FONDANT (ICING FOR PETIT FOURS AND CAKES)

6 cups (.73 kg) extra fine
  granulated sugar
1½ cups (360 ml) distilled
  water

pinch of cream of tartar
3 tablespoons light corn syrup
lemon juice

Combine all ingredients in stainless steel or porcelain lined pot (*do not* use aluminum, otherwise mixture will turn grey and discolor). Set over low heat and stir until sugar is dissolved. Remove any crystals that may form on sides of pot with a pastry brush dipped in hot water. Turn heat to medium high and boil syrup until temperature reaches 230° F. (110° C.) on candy thermometer. Remove from heat and pour syrup onto a marble or plastic slab. Cool slightly. Work syrup by scraping and moving back and forth in all directions, using a metal spatula or stiff rubber one. Make certain syrup is uniformly worked, otherwise it will harden and form lumps. Work syrup until it has become opaque and has taken on the appearance of a white, granulated paste. Shape into a mound, cover with a damp cloth, and let stand for about 10 minutes.

Taking small amounts at a time, knead with the heel of the palm until smooth. When kneaded, set in a container and place a well-dampened cloth over surface. Cover securely and set in a cool area to ripen for a minimum of 24 hours. (Fondant will keep in refrigerator almost indefinitely and will take on an entirely different flavor after ripening for a day or two.)

When ready to use, place desired amount in top of double boiler over hot (not boiling) water, and set over low heat. For a tinted fondant, add 1 or 2 drops vegetable coloring matter, choosing one to suggest flavoring used. A drop or two of blue coloring will give a whiter appearance to fondant.

To flavor, add 1 tablespoon liqueur or 1 teaspoon vanilla or lemon extract, for every 2 cups fondant.

Stir fondant until melted and just barely warm to the touch. If overheated, fondant will lose its gloss.

If fondant appears too thick, add 2 teaspoons beaten egg white per cup fondant. This will also result in a smoother and more easily handled fondant.

Dip Petit Fours and small cakes in warm fondant and set on a rack, using parchment paper or freezer paper to catch drippings, which may be re-heated and used. Fondant may also be used to ice cakes.

Chocolate Fondant

For every 2 cups fondant, add 2 ounces (60 g) of melted sweet baking chocolate. Blend into melted fondant before removing from heat.

Coffee Fondant

For every 2 cups fondant, dissolve 1 tablespoon instant coffee in 1½ tablespoons boiling water, and blend into melted fondant before removing from heat.

Marzipan

Blend an equal amount of finely ground almonds into softened fondant and knead together on marble slab. Marzipan may be colored using 1 or 2 drops of vegetable coloring matter, and may be hand molded into various shapes) oranges, apples, pumpkins, strawberries and so on). A toothpick may be used to make indentations and whole cloves for stems.

COOKING WITH SPIRITS

chapter ten

HENRI CHARPENTIER AND CRÊPES SUZETTE

Henri Charpentier left his small country home at the tender age of ten to begin his career as a page in the Hotel Cap Martin on the Riviera—catering to such notables as King Leopold of Belgium, Queen Victoria, and Franz Josef. He was, in a sense, paving the way for his later acceptance into an arduous apprenticeship that would one day allow him to fulfill his dream of becoming a great chef. Even at that, he was more fortunate than most, because his much older foster brother, Jean Camous (who had trained under Escoffier), was the esteemed chef in charge. Not that he would extend to Petit Henri any favorable treatment—his code, like that of others in a similar position, was both strict and uncompromising.

Three years later, following a series of mishaps, adventures, and misadventures, Henri set out for London to master the Queen's English, having already learned to make his way in Spanish and German. Being proficient in languages was a must for those who would climb the ladder in the field of the culinary arts. He became a cook in one of London's large houses, but, after some time in service, was summarily dismissed, a not unusual circumstance in the 1890s, as there were other anxious Henri's standing in line, ever ready to step into the shoes of their predecessors. This oversupply of an expendable source of labor frequently led to gross and unfair treatment of both boys and girls. Completely dependent on their "benefactors," these young people often worked for no more than their bread and bacon.

A few weeks after "being given the sack," as the English were wont to put it, his savings ran out and he could no longer pay for his lodging, whereupon he was forced to live on the banks of the Thames with the Waterloo Bridge his only shelter. He was not alone, for the "gay nineties" also had a gloomier side. He was close to death from exposure and starvation when rescued by a small dog and a London bobby. (For the rest of his life he greatly concerned himself with those in need of food).

It was the year following this episode and his return to France, that he created his now famous Crêpes Suzette for Edward, Prince of Wales, at the Café de Paris in Monte Carlo. He was fourteen at the time but had already lived through four years of fighting to be first in line, of being hired and fired, and had made the rounds from France to Spain, to Germany, to England, and back to France, where he, and many others like him, followed the seasons catering to the whims of a very small, select group of people accustomed to the best of everything. Competition was keen on many fronts. One way to be recognized was to create something new. The society to which the great chefs catered was frequently bored and always on the alert for some novel twist.

Henri's Mama Camous, as he called his foster mother, whom he dearly loved, had, of course, made thin pancakes, but out of necessity had used no more than one or two eggs in her batter. Having been an extremely resourceful cook, she had concocted a sugar syrup using orange peel, which she mixed in with the batter. Henri remembered them with relish, and felt that, with the aid of the hotel's larder and supply of fine French liqueurs, he could improve on them. He experimented many times and was waiting for the opportunity to show his new creation off to advantage.

As an assistant waiter, he had helped serve the Prince of Wales on several occasions, but on this particular day, it fell to his lot to be fully responsible for him and his party of seven gentlemen and a little girl, the young daughter of one of the gentlemen. When the Prince wanted to know what would be served for lunch, Henri informed him it was to be a special sweet, a surprise. He then proceeded to prepare his sauce before the Prince and his party, using a chafing dish. To the melted butter and orange and lemon peel, he nervously added a blend of cordials, whereupon the sauce accidentally began to flame. He was convinced he was ruined, but, on the sheer instinct of one schooled in the culinary arts, he tasted the concoction, and his mood quickly changed to one of exhilaration upon finding the flavor almost heaven sent. With added confidence, he laid his folded crêpes (which he had previously fried in the kitchen) in the sauce, and poured in two more ponies (jiggers) of the blended cordials. Given the great interest that prevailed among the privileged classes in the culinary arts, and as everyone had relished the surprise, the Prince asked what the new dish was to be called. Henri, always on the alert with a quick reply, proudly announced they were to be called Crêpes Princesse in his honor. In a gallant spirit, Prince Edward, deferring to the young lady at the table, requested they be given her name instead, and so Crêpes

Princesse became Crêpes Suzette. The following day, Henri was to receive a jewelled ring, a panama hat, and a cane—a gracious custom put into practice by many of the gentry to honor those who had served them well.

Monsieur Charpentier's career had yet to undergo many ups and downs, but wherever he went his Crêpes Suzette went with him. He continued to work on the sauce until he had perfected it, experimenting with a number of liqueurs. His favorite became five ponies of blended maraschino, curacao, and kirschwasser. Like so many French chefs, he too came to America in the early 1900s to find fame and fortune. He became a highly successful restaurateur, serving his crêpes and other creations to such patrons as Diamond Jim Brady, the Vanderbilts, Theodore Roosevelt, Sarah Bernhardt, and many others.

NUTRITIVE VALUE

Alcoholic beverages contain traces of carbohydrate but consist mainly of calories. This is why they are often referred to as being empty calories. The number of calories may be roughly assessed by the alcohol proof: One ounce of a 100-proof gin, vodka, or whiskey is equal to about 100 calories, and one ounce of 80-proof is equal to about 80 calories.

A 3½ fluid ounce serving of wine (about 1 glass) is equal to about 141 calories. Wine contains some potassium.

HAVING FUN WITH FLAMBÉING

Wines, sherry, liqueurs, brandy, and champagne are used in cooking to develop and enhance the flavor of foods. They also act as tenderizing agents. In certain preparations beer acts as a leavening agent.

All alcoholic beverages contain a characteristic percentage of alcohol which, in itself, has an unpleasant and somewhat bitter taste. The alcohol content is volatized and vanishes quickly when exposed to heat. What remains is the flavor. The flame also causes a certain amount of the moisture to evaporate, further contributing to the intensity of the flavor.

Alcohol Content

Foods are flambéed by adding alcoholic beverages and igniting, either with a match or by tilting the pan toward the flame. To assure that the alcohol content has been evaporated, the beverage can be set over heat until the liquid is slightly reduced. (A simple taste test will indicate whether or not this has occurred.)

When to Add

In order to capture the full flavor of the somewhat delicate oils and essences that have been preserved by the alcohol, add beverage as near as possible to the close of the cooking period, and cook just long enough to blend flavors and allow alcohol and a certain amount of moisture content to evaporate. However, when alcoholic beverages are to be used in pot roasting, braising, or similar procedures, combine the chosen beverage with other ingredients at the beginning of the cooking process, thereby contributing to both tenderizing and flavoring.

What to Use

Wines and brandy are frequently used together for the reason that properly made brandy is a distillate of wine, that is, the very essence, and so is used to enforce the flavor of wine or sherry.

Liqueurs are heavy, sweet-flavored alcoholic beverages. They are useful with dessert dishes and come in a variety of flavors. They may be blended to achieve any number of distinct flavors.

As with most flavorings, excessive amounts are not recommended. While a small amount will serve to enhance a dish, the opposite may overpower it.

Purchasing Alcoholic Beverages for Flambéing

When selecting beverages for flambéing, check the "proof" on the label—a high proof alcohol will give more satisfactory results.

The overall quality of the wines, liqueurs, brandy, and other alcoholic beverages is just as important as the quality of other ingredients in cooking.

The Brazier versus the Chafing Dish

Flambéing not only improves and blends flavors, but it can add drama and interest. It is particularly effective when done directly over the flame in a brazier rather than in a chafing dish, which is a pan set over another containing hot water. The chafing dish should be confined primarily to reheating foods and keeping them hot.

A LIST OF PRECAUTIONS

There are a few simple precautions worth following when flambéing:

1. Before proceeding, have all ingredients fully prepared and laid out in an organized fashion; try also to make the tray look as appealing as possible.

2. It is advisable not to preheat bottle of beverage in hot water prior to use (sometimes recommended as a means of ensuring that it will ignite). If the alcohol content is high enough and a sufficient amount is used, there will be no trouble producing a flame. On the other hand, a preheated bottle containing an alcoholic beverage could easily result in an explosion.

3. When adding beverages, use a long narrow-necked bottle rather than an open-mouth receptacle such as a pitcher, which could easily ignite when coming in contact with the heat or in close proximity to the flame. Bottles containing beverages should be re-corked and removed from the source of heat when not in immediate use.

4. Further precaution may be taken by placing brazier on a heatproof surface or metal tray as added insurance against fire.

5. If too great a quantity of beverage is used, the alcohol will burn for an extended period and may quite possibly overcook and/or overpower the preparation. On the other hand, an insufficient quantity will result in little or no flame, as well as very little flavor. The exact amount used depends on the quantity and nature of the dish, as well as on the alcoholic beverage itself.

RECIPES USING LIQUEURS

BASIC FORMULA FOR FLAMBÉED DESSERTS

1 stick (½ cup or 115 g)
   butter
5 ounces (140 g) liqueur

2 teaspoons Flavored Sugar

Melt butter, using a brazier, chafing dish, or high-sided frying pan, and set over direct heat. (Do not use a nonstick coated pan.) When butter foams, add 3 ounces (85 g) of liqueur (or blend of liqueurs), and ignite by tipping pan toward flame, or by using a match. When flame has subsided, add Flavored Sugar (recipe follows), stirring to dissolve.

Add sliced fruit (pears, apples, bananas, oranges) berries (strawberries, raspberries, blackberries), or folded crêpes and cook just long enough to heat through, turning or tossing where necessary. Add remaining 2 ounces (55 g) of liqueur (or blend of liqueurs) and re-ignite. Serve as soon as flame has subsided.

When serving simply as a sauce with ice cream, fruit, or other dessert, add the 5 ounces of liqueur at once and ignite. When flame has subsided, spoon sauce over dessert.

Flavored Sugar

seeds from dried vanilla pod
2 cups (396 g) finely
   granulated sugar
thin slivers of orange rind,
   diced

thin slivers of lemon rind,
   diced

Split open vanilla pod and scrape seeds into sugar. Peel thin slivers of rind from orange and lemon, dice, and add to sugar. Distribute ingredients evenly throughout sugar, and store in an airtight container in a dry area. Sugar will keep almost indefinitely.

Use Flavored Sugar with flambéd desserts, as well as to flavor sauces, cakes, cookies, and other sweet preparations.

PEACHES SUPREME

2 teaspoons Flavored Sugar
4 peaches, skinned and sliced
1 stick (½ cup or 115 g) butter
5 ounces (140 g) Grand Marnier

8 scoops French vanilla ice cream
whipped cream (optional)

Prepare Flavored Sugar according to foregoing recipe.

Blanch peaches in boiling water for about 1 minute, or until skins are loosened. Drain and remove skins. Split in half, remove pits, and cut into uniform size slices.

Melt butter over a brazier, and, when foaming, add 3 ounces (85 g) of Grand Marnier. Ignite by tipping pan slightly toward flame, or use a match. When flame has subsided, add 2 teaspoons Flavored Sugar, stirring to dissolve. Add sliced peaches and cook just long enough to heat through. Add remaining 2 ounces (55 g) of liqueur and re-ignite. When flame has subsided, ladle peaches and sauce over ice cream.

If desired, garnish with rosettes of whipped cream, using a pastry bag with a star tube.

CRÊPES SUZETTE

16 Dessert Crêpes
2 teaspoons Flavored Sugar
2 ounces maraschino liqueur ⎫
2 ounces kirsch   ⎬ blended
1 ounce crème de cacao   ⎭
1 stick (½ cup or 115 g) butter

To prepare crêpes, follow recipe for Thin Dessert Pancakes (Crêpes) in Chapter 9. Prepare Flavored Sugar according to the recipe in this chapter. Blend maraschino, kirsch, and crème de cacao in a long-necked bottle or a decanter.

Fold crêpes in half, and fold once again to form a triangle. Melt butter in a brazier pan; when it begins to foam add 3 ounces (85 g) of blended liqueurs. Ignite by tipping pan toward flame, or by use of a match. When flame has subsided, add Flavored Sugar, stirring to dissolve. Plunge folded pancakes into sauce, turning once. When heated through, add remaining 2 ounces (55 g) of liqueurs and re-ignite. When flame has subsided, serve crêpes, two per serving, on a warmed dessert plate, spooning a little sauce over each.

CRÊPES NORMANDE

8 *Dessert Crêpes*	1 *stick (½ cup or 115 g)*
2 *teaspoons Flavored Sugar*	*butter*
4 *McIntosh apples, peeled,*	3 *ounces (85 g) apple*
cored, and sliced	*brandy (Calvados)* ⎱ *blended*
butter for frying and melting	2 *ounces (55 g)* ⎰
fresh lemon juice	*crème de cacao*
powdered cinnamon	

To prepare crêpes, follow recipe in Chapter 9 for Thin Dessert Pancakes (Crêpes).

Prepare Flavored Sugar according to recipe in this chapter.

Peel, core, and cut apples into uniform size slices, using an apple corer-slicer. Fry apple slices in a small amount of butter until just barely tender. Sprinkle with a few drops lemon juice and dust lightly with powdered cinnamon. Spread apple slices over one-third of crepes and fold over either side, envelope fashion. Lay in a buttered, ovenproof dish and pour a small amount of melted butter over each (to prevent drying out). Bake in a preheated 325° F. (163° C.) oven about 10 minutes, or just long enough to heat through. In the meantime, melt butter in a brazier pan; to foaming butter add 3 ounces (85 g) of blended brandy and crème de cacao. Tip pan toward flame to ignite, or use a match. When flame has subsided, add 2 teaspoons Flavored Sugar, stirring to dissolve. Add remaining 2 ounces of brandy-liqueur mixture and re-ignite. When flame has subsided, spoon over apple-filled crêpes, and serve on warmed dessert plates.

BANANAS FLAMBÉ

2 teaspoons Flavored Sugar
8 slices French Toast
4 bananas, firm but not
   underripe
unsweetened cocoanut
1 stick (½ cup or 115 g)
   butter

3 ounces (85 g)
   rum (Barbados,
   light)
2 ounces (55 g)
   banana liqueur
   or Grand
   Marnier

} blended

Prepare sugar according to recipe in this chapter, for Flavored Sugar.

Follow recipe for French Toast in Chapter 5, using slices of Brioche or Enriched Butter and Egg Bread cut into rounds or squares with crusts removed. Fry on both sides until golden brown and set in a 160° F. (71° C.) oven to keep warm. (Do not pile one slice on top of another or they will lose their crispness.)

Peel and slice bananas across diagonally and toss in unsweetened cocoanut.

Melt butter in brazier or high-sided frying pan until foaming, and add 3 ounces (85 g) blended rum and liqueur. Ignite by tilting pan toward flame, or use a match. When flame has subsided, add 2 teaspoons Flavored Sugar, stirring to dissolve. Add bananas and cook just long enough to heat through, turning once. Add remaining 2 ounces (55 g) of blended rum and liqueur and ignite. When flame has subsided, spoon a portion over French Toast and serve on warm dessert plates.

CHERRIES JUBILEE MAURA ANNE

1 cup (240 ml) fresh orange
   juice
2 ounces (55 g) dried
   cherries*

1½ cups (360 ml) fresh orange
   juice
¼ cup (60 ml) sherry
2 tablespoons raspberry syrup
2 tablespoons black currant
   jelly
¼ teaspoon powdered ginger
2 tablespoons cornstarch
2 tablespoons sherry
juice of ½ lemon

vanilla, cherry, and butter
   pecan ice cream
sugar rose petals*
3 ½" (1 cm) sticks angelique*
sugar green leaves*

2 teaspoons Flavored Sugar
1 stick (½ cup or 115 g)
   butter
3 ounces (85 g)
   kirsch   ⎫
2 ounces (55 g)   ⎬ blended
   Grand Marnier ⎭

Bring 1 cup (240 ml) orange juice and dried cherries to a simmer over low heat. Remove at once, cover, and set aside until cherries have absorbed most of the liquid and have softened.

Bring 1½ cups (360 ml) orange juice, ¼ cup (60 ml) sherry, raspberry syrup, currant jelly, and ginger to a slow simmer over low heat. Blend cornstarch with 2 tablespoons sherry and add, stirring until thickened. Add cherries and simmer long enough to blend. Remove from heat and stir in juice of ½ lemon.

Form ice cream balls of equal proportions out of vanilla, cherry, and butter pecan ice cream (or substitute sherbet), using a small scoop (Italian size). On a round serving platter, make a "croc-quembouche" mound by placing balls in graduated layers; alternate ice cream flavors, and top with a scoop of cherry ice cream. Shape a rose out of sugar rose petals, using angelique sticks for leaves, and arrange in center of top layer. Arrange additional rose petals tastefully between scoops of ice cream. Lay sugar green leaves at various points around bottom of mound, as though

*These items are available at specialty stores.

growing out of it. (The crocquembouche may be prepared in advance and placed in freezer until ready to use. At serving time, allow ice cream balls to soften but not to melt before continuing procedure.)

Prepare sugar according to recipe in this chapter, for Flavored Sugar.

Using a brazier, melt butter in pan until foaming, and add blended kirsch and Grand Marnier. Ignite by tilting pan toward flame, or use a match. When flame has subsided, add Flavored Sugar, stirring to dissolve. Add sauce containing cherries and blend in. Cook, stirring, just long enough to heat through.

Using dessert dishes, serve two or three ice cream balls per serving, and ladle a portion of hot sauce over each.

MEAL
PLANNING

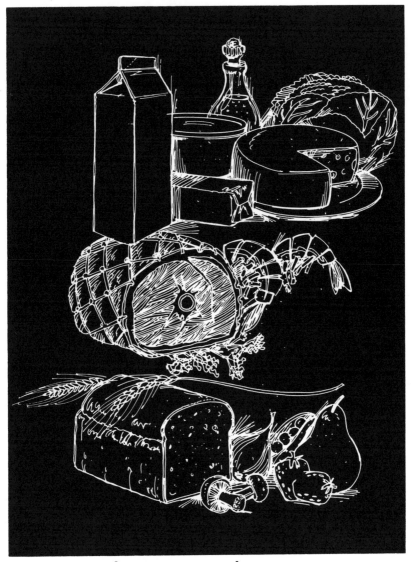

chapter eleven

Every year new food products appear on grocers' shelves. They originate from all corners of the globe. There are now close to 2500 items available. Furthermore, nutritionists have identified more than 60 nutrients—all distinct chemical compounds. They include proteins, carbohydrates, fats, minerals, and vitamins. Each plays one of several roles within the body: They serve as a source for heat and energy; provide for growth, maintenance and repair; or help regulate body processes. Some are present in a wide variety of foods in varying amounts, others are present in a restricted number of foods in smaller amounts. The National Research Council, U. S. Department of Agriculture, and other government agencies have established a list of Recommended Daily Allowances (US RDA) to help define the key nutrients.*

Many products now display nutritional information on their labels, which should help in maintaining a balanced diet. Such information may include: (1) number of calories per portion size (slice, cup, ounces), as well as amounts of protein, fats, and carbohydrates; (2) the percentage of U.S. Recommended Daily Allowance (US RDA) for protein, vitamin A, vitamin C, three of the B vitamins (thiamin, riboflavin, and niacin), calcium, and iron furnished by a serving of food as it comes from the container; (3) the amounts of polyunsaturated fat, saturated fat, and cholesterol furnished by a serving of a specified size; and (4) the amount of sodium per serving (particularly useful to those on low salt diets).

The minimum amounts of specific nutrients that are presently used as a basis for computing how much of the US RDA a product satisfies are as follows:

◇ Protein   65 grams

45 grams for foods with high quality protein, generally those of animal origin (meat, fish, poultry, eggs, milk)

◇ Vitmin A   5000 International Units†

◇ Vitamin C   60 milligrams

◇ Thiamin   1.5 milligrams

*The U.S. Recommended Daily Allowances (US RDA's) are the amounts of protein, vitamins, and minerals used as standards in nutrition labeling. These allowances are derived from the Recommended Dietary Allowances (RDA's) set by the Food and Nutrition Board of the National Research Council. The RDA's are judged by the National Research Conucil to be adequate for nearly all healthy persons and generous for most persons.

†The International System of units is an extension and refinement of the Metric System.

◇ Riboflavin   1.7 milligrams
◇ Niacin   20 milligrams
◇ Calcium   1.0 milligrams
◇ Iron   18 milligrams

THE FOUR FOOD GROUPS

The following four food groups may be used as a guide in planning well-balanced meals on a daily basis:

Grain Foods

Bread, bread products, cereals, and pasta, *whole grain and enriched*, furnish worthwhile amounts of iron, thiamin, riboflavin, and niacin, and are important for the protein and energy they provide. Products prepared from whole grains which have not been overly processed add bulk to the diet.

Vegetables and Fruits

The produce group supplies important vitamins and minerals. Most fruits contain some vitamin C; dark green leafy vegetables are an important source of iron and vitamin A. The yellow and orange vegetables and fruits are also a source of vitamin A. Dried fruits are a valuable source of iron. Vegetables (particularly when prepared from the fresh state) and fruits are important sources of bulk (fiber).

Meat, Poultry, Fish, Eggs, Dried Legumes, and Nuts

All of these are valued for their protein, as well as providing iron, thiamin, riboflavin, niacin, and other nutrients. Pork is important for its thiamine content and liver is an especially good source of iron. Fish is valued as a protein source, and its fat content is both low and unsaturated.

Milk and Milk Products

They provide protein, riboflavin, vitamin A, calcium, and other nutrients. Cheese, sherbet, and yoghurt are included in this group.

Other Foods

To make meals more interesting—as well as to provide energy and additional nutrients—butter, margarine, other fats and oils, salad dressings, and dessert-type foods (low in sugar) may be added.

ENRICHED FOODS

As the average American diet was found to be deficient in certain essential nutrients, the federal government set standards for the nutritional improvement of those foods found lacking. "Enriched," "restored," and "fortified" were the terms used to identify them.

Enriched was chosen to describe the addition of three B-vitamins and iron to white flour, pasta products, cornmeal, and rice.

Restored was defined as the total replacement of certain nutrients which had been lost in refining or processing of a food.

Fortified was used to designate the addition of one or more nutrients normally not present in that food (Vitamin D concentrate added to milk and vitamin A to margarine, for example).

BASIC GUIDE TO MEAL PLANNING

Nutritionists on the whole still recommend the time-honored practice of eating a wide variety of foods. Eating small portions of many different foods rather than large portions of a limited number assures one of obtaining all or almost all the necessary nu trients.

Serve foods that are in season—when they are freshest an at their best.

Serve foods of contrasting colors and textures. Serve bot hot and cold foods.

Make foods as appealing and appetizing as possible.

FATS & OILS

chapter twelve

MARGARINE VERSUS BUTTER

As recently as the early 1800s, animal and vegetable fats were used for light, and sometimes for heat, although their use was not as extensive as it had been in earlier times. About this time the sperm oil lamp, using whale oil as a fuel, came into wide use. As the population increased and new industries became ever more greedy for fuel, whalers found themselves hard pressed to keep up with demands. The answer to these unprecedented requirements came in 1847 when James H. Young took out a patent for extracting oil from oil shales. Close upon this discovery followed the more revolutionary development of the petroleum oil industry. Both of these fuels more or less eliminated traditional use of animal and vegetable fats in most parts of the world. They were, however, to be salvaged very shortly in a remarkable way. In the 1860s, what is now known as margarine (then termed oleo-margarine) was introduced by the French chemist Hippolyte Mege-Mouries. Not only was this substance envisioned as a cheap substitute for butter—it would also serve to stimulate the flagging use of animal fats.* Although Monsieur Mege-Mouries received wide recognition for his contribution, margarine had a long uphill climb before it could compete economically with "the real thing." Its status—and price—today is on a par with that of butter.

By the 1930s, imported oils, such as cocoanut and palm, were replacing to some extent the animal fats originally used in the manufacture of margarine. U.S. manufacturers did considerable research before coming up with a satisfactory product that could make use of domestic oils—cottonseed and soybean were the eventual choices. By this time, margarine was being made from animal fats, vegetable oils, or a combination of both.

The war between margarine and butter began just a little over a hundred years ago when margarine was first introduced. Dairy industry protests were registered by the considerable legislation to which margarine became subjected. In some areas, artificial coloring (to give it the appearance of butter) had to be deleted altogether or, at best, included in a separate package to be worked in by the consumer. Later, high taxes and other restrictions were imposed on the yellow-colored substitute. The margarine industry also had to contend with "tradition," which

---

*Vegetable oils were used only some time later in the manufacture of margarine. Of course, both substances were later put to a variety of uses.

has always played a major role in the consumer's choice of food products.

However, in America at least, concern over one's health runs a close second—to inherited practices. The wide publicity given to the relationship of cholesterol to many of the major health problems of the twentieth century (elevated blood pressure, heart attacks, arteriosclerosis) pretty well coincided with the development of hybrid corn in the 1950s. Before too long large quantities of margarine were being produced using corn oil (containing no cholesterol). No expense was spared in promotion and advertising and *saturated*, *polyunsaturated*, and *cholesterol* became household words. As a result, the consumption of butter went down.

The dairy industry was not to be outdone. Cheese—also made from milk—was widely promoted. Leaflets were distributed, connoisseurs began to make themselves known, and cheese and wine parties became a popular way to entertain. Cheeses of all varieties (sometimes costing two, three or four times the price of butter) steadily increased in consumption.

VARIOUS KINDS OF FATS AND OILS

Fats, known chemically as triglycerides, are extracted from both plant and animal products. A fat that is liquid at room temperature is referred to as an oil; one that is solid is properly termed a fat. However, all oils solidify when sufficiently cooled, and all fats liquefy at higher temperatures. The temperature at which a fat changes to an oil is referred to as its melting point. Some fats can withstand higher temperatures than others.

BUTTER Federal regulations require that butter contain at least 80% butterfat. Salt, coloring matter, and water are added. A minimum of salt is added to sweet butter.

MARGARINE Margarine contains milk solids, liquid fats (animal and/or vegetable fats), and salt. The ingredients are thoroughly blended and chilled before being kneaded to form a mass. Additional additives may include diacetyl as a flavoring agent, sodium benzoate or benzoic acid as a preservative, lecithin as an emulsifier, and yellow coloring matter. A concentrate of vitamin A is usually added to replace that found naturally in butter. The label must state the fats and other ingredients used. *Imitation margarine* contains about half the fat normally found in regular margarine.

LOW FAT SPREADS   These are similar to butter but contain only between 30 and 80 percent milk fat. They also contain an emulsifier, salt, and coloring matter.

VEGETABLE OILS   Such oils are designated either by the vegetables, seeds, or nuts from which they are made (corn, sesame, peanut) or by trade names. *Vegetable shortenings* are manufactured from refined, bleached vegetable oils.

LARD   Lard is made from the fat adhering to the organs of a hog, as well as the fat from other parts of the carcass.

FAT COMPOUNDS   These are made by combining animal fats (20 percent) and vegetable oils (80 percent).

SHORTENINGS   Shortening agents are fats characterized by their plasticity, which enables them to combine readily with the ingredients in pastry and other flour mixtures. The purpose in using shortening in such mixtures is to produce a tender product or, alternately, a flaky one. The flavor of shortening is as important as that of the other fats used in baking.

Shortening and butter, or another fat, are frequently combined to ensure a tenderizing effect and to enhance the flavor of the product.

PEANUT BUTTER   This product is made by grinding roasted blanched peanuts. Salt and a stabilizer (to prevent oils from separating) are added.

SMOKE POINT

When fat begins to smoke, its chemical breakdown begins. A fat that is suitable for deep-frying has a fairly high smoke point.

Cooking oils (with the exception of olive oil) and compound fats (mixtures of hard and soft fats made up of approximately 20 percent animal fats and 80 percent vegetable oils) decompose at higher temperatures than butter, margarine, and lard. Shortenings that contain emulsifiers (used to improve baking quality) have a lower smoking point than those that contain no emulsifiers.

SMOKE POINTS OF FATS AND OILS

Type	° F.	° C.
Corn, peanut, cottonseed oil	450° F.	232° C.
Shortenings (containing no emulsifiers)	450° F.	232° C.
Lard	360° - 400° F.	182° - 205° C.
Shortenings (containing emulsifiers)	300° - 350° F.	149° - 177° C.

NUTRITIVE VALUE

Fat is the most concentrated source of food energy, supplying nine calories per gram, or 252 calories per ounce. Proteins and carbohydrates (the other two high-energy nutrients) supply four calories per gram.

Americans have increased their consumption of fats and are getting more of their calories from meat and animal products and fewer from carbohydrates (grains, dried legumes) than they did at the turn of the century or even 50 years ago.

On the positive side, the vegetable and grain oils used more frequently today contain vitamin E. Butter and fortified margarine contain good amounts of vitamin A.

Saturated and Unsaturated Fats

The higher the proportion of unsaturated fatty acids, the softer the fat, and the higher the proportion of saturated acids, the harder the fat. Unsaturated is defined as "capable of dissolving more of something," and saturated as "being a compound that does not tend to unite directly with another compound." *Poly* as in *poly-unsaturated* means excessive.

Saturated fats are usually hard at room temperature. They occur chiefly in animal fats.

Nearly all fats from plant sources are unsaturated. (Cocoanut oil is one exception.) Polyunsaturated fats, typically oils, are most abundant in plant seeds and fish oils. The most common polyunsaturated fatty acid is *linoleic acid*. In general, the degree of unsaturation of a food fat depends on how much linoleic acid it contains. Linoleic acid is an essential nutrient that must be supplied from a food source because the body cannot manufacture it. *The fat in grains has a relatively high proportion of this essential fatty acid that plays a major role in the metabolism of cholesterol.*

Oleic acid is the most common monounsaturated fatty acid.

It has been suggested that for normal, healthy persons, saturated, monounsaturated, and polyunsaturated fats should each supply about one-third of the total amount of fat in the diet.

Cholesterol and Plant Sterols

Sterols are defined as "any of the various solid cyclic alcohols (as cholesterol) widely distributed in animal and plant lipids (fats)."

The oils from plants—vegetables, grains, fruits, legumes, nuts—contain *plant sterols*, originally referred to as phytosterol. *They contain no cholesterol.*

Cholesterol (from the Greek *chole* for bile and *steros* for solid) occurs in products of animal origin—muscle (meat), blood, bone marrow, and organ meats.

Cholesterol is a normal constituent of blood and tissues and is found in every animal cell. A certain amount is synthesized by the human body itself and some is supplied by the diet. There are, however, differences of opinion as to what constitutes a desirable amount. That portion supplied by the diet depends on the kinds and amounts of foods ingested.* Foods of plant origin (fruits, vegetables, whole grains, legumes, and nuts) which contain only plant sterols have been shown to reduce blood cholesterol levels.

*The amount of cholesterol in the blood varies directly with the amount of cholesterol in the diet.

CHOLESTEROL CONTENT OF FOODS

Item*	Amount of Cholesterol in 100 Grams (about 3½ ounces), Edible Portion	1 Pound (454 g.), Edible Portion
	milligrams†	milligrams
Beef, raw (without bone)	70	320
Brains, raw	2,000	9,000
Butter	250	1,135
Caviar or fish roe	300	1,300
Cheese		
Cheddar	100	455
Cottage	15	70
Cream	120	545
Other (25% to 30% fat)	85	385
Cheese spread	65	295
Chicken, flesh only, raw	60	274
Crab, meat only	125	565
Egg, whole	550	2,200
Egg white	0	0
Egg yolk		
Fresh	1,500	6,800
Frozen	1,280	5,800
Dried	2,950	13,380
Fish§		
Steak (16% non-edible)	70	265
Fillet	70	320
Heart, raw	150	680
Ice cream	45	205
Kidney, raw	375	1,700
Lamb, raw (without bone)	70	320
Lard and other animal fat	95	430
Liver, raw	300	1,360
Lobster, meat only	200	900
Margarine		
All vegetable fat	0	0
66% animal fat, 33% vegetable fat	65	295
Milk		
Fluid, whole	11	50
Dried, whole	85	385
Fluid, skim	3	15
Mutton (without bone)	65	295
Oysters, meat only	200	900
Pork (without bone)	70	320
Shrimp, flesh only	125	565

CHOLESTEROL CONTENT OF FOODS (Continued)

Item*	Amount of Cholesterol in	
	100 Grams (about 3½ ounces), Edible Portion	1 Pound (454 g.), Edible Portion
	milligrams†	milligrams
Sweetbreads (thymus)	250	1,135
Veal (without bone)	90	410

*As cholesterol does not occur in plants, none would be present in grains, fruits, nuts, vegetables, or in the oils and various products prepared from them.

†A milligram is one-thousandth of a gram.

§The oil, liver, and skin of fish have a higher content of cholesterol than does the muscle. Little information is available on the cholesterol content of meats and poultry.

THE KITCHEN LABORATORY

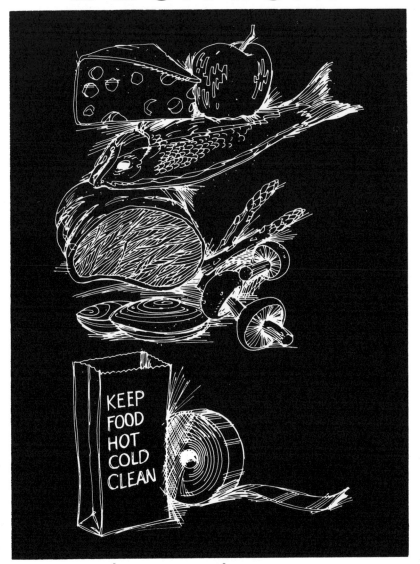

KEEP
FOOD
HOT
COLD
CLEAN

chapter thirteen

FOOD PRESERVATION

Food preservation has always been one of the major human concerns. Until chemists were able to analyze the reasons for decomposition, all attempts were necessarily empirical—that is, the methods used were arrived at through observation and trial and error. Salt is the oldest known chemical preservative. Smoking was a very common means of treating meats and fish, and the drying of many different kinds of food (meats, fish, vegetables, fruits, grains) has been practiced for centuries. Today the design of food drying equipment is a highly specialized branch of engineering. As the world began to open up, explorers in the Far North soon observed that foods left in the frozen state kept extremely well for long periods—Arctic Eskimos had long made use of nature's vast outdoor icebox. In areas where the temperature fluctuated and did not remain frigid for such extended periods, structures were built and insulated (icehouses) so that the winter ice from lakes and streams could be stored and used as needed. The icebox was a common sight in many households until as late as the World War II period. It was the precursor to the modern home refrigerator. On a commercial scale, refrigeration had been in use for some time. The first cargo of frozen meat (to arrive in sound condition) was shipped from the U.S. to Great Britain in 1875-76.

Refrigeration affected the economics of food preservation more than any other method to date, primarily because it was the most successful from many points of view. It was put into commercial use at a time when America was being urbanized at a whirlwind pace (following industrialization), and when the development of a more efficient means of preservation was a matter of vital necessity. Feeding the growing masses that were congregating in towns and cities presented challenges that had never before arisen on such a scale. Control over the environment—and the market—was of course the primary objective, one that refrigeration, as a satisfactory long-term means of preservation, eminently fulfilled. The introduction of the home freezer expanded the benefits to the food processing industry. Consumers, educated on the advantages of frozen foods and the convenience of buying in bulk, fell easily into the promotional gimmicks of weekly sales.

Refrigeration was not the only method of food preservation

that was being studied, tested, and applied. The use of chemicals by commercial processors and manufacturers took root in the early nineteenth century and stealthily and steadily increased. Today chemical preservatives far outstrip any other method. However, the aim is no longer merely to retard the spoilage of food—economy, convenience, and appearance are very important factors—nor is it necessarily to retain a food's natural flavor, color, texture, and aroma insofar as possible. Along with the chemical preservatives, there is a long list of other chemicals that are introduced into foods as firming agents, stabilizers, neutralizers, bleaching agents, antioxidants, and acidulants. Artificial coloring is used on a grand scale. Natural flavors are frequently chemically removed and used in the preparation of processed food and drinks which, in themselves, have little or no nutritive value.

A wide variety of chemicals have been in use for more than a hundred and fifty years. (Salt had been used for generations but had the distinct advantages of being noninjurious at ordinary doses and of betraying itself in taste when used in excess.) Individuals, consumer groups, and governments around the world have become increasingly concerned with the number of chemicals being ingested on a daily basis. Attempts are being made to enforce regulations against the use of those that may prove harmful. There is, however, generally a considerable time lapse before such proof is all-conclusive. The situation is further complicated by the conflicting opinions of the heads of various groups whose interests are sometimes as far apart as the poles. All in all, the use and control of chemicals is an extremely complex problem.

More and more individuals are checking labels for the use of artificial coloring, flavoring, and other chemicals, and also purchasing foods in their fresh state, or as close to their natural state as possible. Others are seeking foods which are both grown and handled without the aid of chemicals.

LOUIS PASTEUR

About the time that chemicals were coming into wider use, Louis Pasteur, a young chemist, was at work in France on a discovery that would revolutionize chemical as well as biological science. He proved to the world that the various changes occurring in the several processes of fermentation (as in beer, wine, or leavened bread) could be explained by the presence and growth of minute organisms (called ferments) and that if every trace of these organisms were excluded no change would occur.* Pasteur studied both "sick" and "healthy" beer under a microscope and saw that the globules from the former were elongated, while those of the sound and healthy beer were nearly spherical. He further proved that these invisible germs are always present in the atmosphere and that when the atmospheric microbes (germs) are absolutely excluded no changes take place. Later it was shown that each kind of fermentation occurs because of a specific ferment just as each disease is dependent on the presence of a distinct microbe.

The application of Pasteur's discoveries not only revolutionized surgical and medical practices through treatment by antiseptic methods, but, directly and indirectly, was influential in making cleanliness a byword in many fields of endeavor, not the least being those associated with food and sustenance. Chefs in the great hotel kitchens began to enforce new regulations and standards, both as to dress and the handling of foods and food preparation; new government regulations were passed (although not always enforced); and more and more emphasis was placed on sanitary conditions in the home.

Pasteur went on to do other invaluable work, including inoculation against various infectious diseases affecting plants, animals, and humans, and as is well known, his discoveries led to the "pasteurization" of milk against the tubercular germ (so widespread at the time) with which the cow might be infected.

Louis Pasteur died in 1895 at the age of 73, having left the world a better place than he found it. Of scientific discoveries, Pasteur wrote, " . . . science, in obeying the law of humanity, will always labor to enlarge the frontiers of life."

---

*Up to that time the phenomenon of fermentation was considered strange and obscure; explanations had been given but they lacked experimental foundation.

COMBATING THE PROBLEM OF FOOD SPOILAGE

Most foods carry or eventually acquire bacteria, molds, or yeasts, microorganisms that are one of the major causes of food spoilage. Enzymes which are naturally present in some foods also lead to deterioration. However, one would not wish unequivocally to ban all microorganisms; in fact some are quite indispensable, for example, in wine, molds in cheeses, and the bacteria introduced into milk to make it turn sour.

The problem of food preservation is a matter of keeping out or killing off those living organisms that might feed upon it and thus alter it. These living things may come from the air, the soil, or from animals or humans. Whenever foods come in contact with any one of these sources, they become infected with living cells, which, if allowed to develop, lead to their decomposition and destruction. These organisms may be killed by heat or by chemicals, or their development may be arrested by lower temperatures (refrigeration), water removal (dehydration), or the presence of agents that inhibit bacterial growth but do not destroy the microorganisms.

Bacteria require nutrients, moisture, and favorable temperatures to survive. Some grow best at one temperature and others thrive at another. Certain bacteria grow in low-acid food, others in acid food, and some in food that is neutral. Any food or food material containing high concentrates of sugar or salt will not support bacterial growth, although molds may grow in it. (Molds have a fuzzy appearance and are generally unfit to eat. They may be white, gray, blue, green or orange).

One of the most important functions of cooking is temporarily to kill off all organisms (until a new crop appears). Civilized man revolts against the consumption of food that is not sterile—few foods of animal origin are eaten raw and vegetables and fruits are peeled or they are given a thorough washing. At the boiling point of water, all living cells perish—few fully developed bacteria can survive in water which has reached 212° F. (100° C.). At or below the freezing point of water, few organisms are capable of growth and multiplication. Yet, while many perish in the frozen state, the vast majority simply remain dormant. *Dry heat* kills with certainty only at about 284° F. (140° C.).

TEMPERATURE GUIDE TO CONTROLLING BACTERIAL GROWTH

Temperature		Effect on Bacterial Growth
° F.	° C.	
212° F.	100° C.	Boiling point of water (at sea level). Most resistant bacteria killed within 2 minutes.
180° F.	82° C.	Recommended water temperature for dishwashers. Temperature will have reduced by about 10 degrees by the time water comes in contact with dishes, i.e., 170° F. (77° C.), still a very effective temperature for sanitizing.
170° F.	77° C.	Practically all common disease-producing bacteria killed at this temperature.
140° F.	60° C.	Bacterial *growth* practically stopped; some may be killed.
98.6° F.	36.5° C.	Body temperature—bacteria's most rapid growth.
70° F.	21° C.	Room temperature—bacteria grow fast.
50° F.	10° C.	Bacterial growth slowed greatly and almost stopped below this point.
45° F.	7° C.	Cool-room temperature—bacterial growth practically stopped.
38° F.	4° C.	Near freezing temperature.
32° F.	0° C.	Freezing point of water—practically no bacterial growth.
10° F.	−12° C.	Recommended temperature for frozen foods.

Delayed Cooking

The practice of holding foods several hours in advance of cooking, such as in automatic ovens, may afford a good opportunity for bacterial growth, particularly if they are held at room temperature. This practice has become increasingly common as many of the more recent models of regular ovens as well as microwave ovens, come equipped with automatic timers. In many instances the food is held for as long as 7 or 8 hours. Preparations based on ground meats are particularly susceptible and should be carefully watched.

Food Storage

The temperature of hot foods which are to be refrigerated should be lowered in the shortest possible time. Divide large quantities of cooked food into smaller amounts for rapid cooling. An area or room with a temperature approximating 45° F. (7° C.), that is, cool-room temperature is safe for relatively short periods. For rapid cooling, prepared foods may be placed in shallow pans and set over ice cold water or cracked ice.

When warm foods are placed in the refrigerator they interfere with the proper cooling of the other food.

Food Poisoning

"Ptomaine" poisoning (from the Greek *ptōma* meaning corpse) was coined by Francesco Selmi, an Italian toxicologist, in 1870— the smell of food that had gone bad was associated with that of decomposing corpses. The term *food poisoning* refers to the condition caused by the ingestion of foods contaminated by harmful bacteria or their toxins (poisons).

The bacteria that cause food poisoning include Staphylococcus and Botulinum. Their growth in food prior to its consumption produces certain toxins, among them the toxin formed by botulinum in inadequately processed canned foods. This type of food poisoning is fatal. The main food associated with such outbreaks are meats; it is therefore recommended that meats be cooked to a temperature above 140° F. (60° C.).

Staphylococcus food intoxications are initiated by careless handling of foods, such as when those preparing food have a cold, open cuts, or similar infections. Heating may destroy the growth of the organism but not the toxin, which is heat resistant. This type of food poisoning causes nausea, diarrhea, and cramps but is not fatal. Symptoms usually occur within 3 to 6 hours after the ingestion of the poisoned food.

Food infection differs from food poisoning in that it is caused by species of Salmonella bacteria that are able to grow in food and infect the persons who ingest it. Salmonella are able to grow in a large range of foods, including dairy products, meat and meat products, and fish. The disease is contracted from raw foods (for example, raw meats), improperly cooked foods, and by foods left unrefrigerated, giving the organism enough time to grow.

Foods may also be contaminated by careless handling. Body waste (both human and animal) is highly contaminated and is a direct or indirect source of the contamination of foods with Salmonella. The symptoms of food infection are similar to those of Staphylococcus infection.

FOOD SAFETY GUIDELINES

1. The rule is that if there is any doubt whatsoever about the safeness of a food, do not use it.
2. Never let foods stand for any length of time at room temperature.
3. Avoid long periods of storage during which bacteria can grow.
4. Prepare foods as near serving time as possible.
5. Keep food under such conditions that the bacteria which do get in or are already present do not have an opportunity to grow or multiply.
6. Avoid dented cans.
7. Discard cracked eggs.
8. Use federally inspected foods whenever possible.
9. Wash all fruits, vegetables, and greens.
10. Divide all foods into small portions for quick cooling.
11. Treat all leftovers with great care—discard any about which there is any doubt as to safety.
12. Avoid heating and reheating foods.

SANITARY GUIDELINES

The human body can eliminate and destroy an infinite number of bacteria without harm, but there is a point at which it can no longer cope. For this reason, sanitary measures are taken to prevent the bacteria that may be present from growing and multiplying to the danger point.

1. Scrubbing up: The number one rule is to scrub hands

often using a brush, hot water and soap, as and when indicated.

2. Keep all surfaces, floors, and other areas scrupulously clean, as well as crevices and corners where dust, grease, crumbs, and other food particles may collect.

3. Finger lickin' good? Manipulate food with fingers and hands as little as possible—use spoons, forks, tongs, or other appropriate tools.

4. Avoid soiled towels when handling utensils. Do not bring food in contact with soiled or dirty surfaces.

5. Dispose of garbage as quickly as possible (at least once a day) and keep covered at all times.

6. Cover and protect all food, particularly at night.

7. Place all opened cartons, boxes, or containers in sealable plastic bags.

8. Wash all can surfaces before opening.

9. Use a can opener that can be disassembled for cleaning, or a manual can opener that can be cleaned in a dishwasher.

10. When using an electric dishwasher, set water temperature at 180° F. (82° C.), otherwise wash dishes with hot water and soap and rinse with boiling water.

11. Scrub all wooden surfaces and cutting boards with boiling water and baking soda.

12. Wash all wooden utensils in electric dishwasher or scrub clean using boiling water and baking soda.

13. As many bacteria are spread by coughing and sneezing, cover nose and mouth, using disposable tissues, and scrub hands at once.

14. Open cuts and similar conditions are highly contaminated and cause a large percentage of food poisoning— take necessary precautions.

15. Poor sanitation attracts insects and animals that transmit food-spoilage organisms from one source to another (one of the major causes of food poisoning).

16. Refrain from allowing domestic pets to come in contact with any utensil used in the preparation or service of foods. Avoid physical contact with pets when preparing or serving foods.

SAFETY FIRST

1. Keep a fire extinguisher close at hand and learn how to use it. (Table salt or baking soda may be used as a substitute in an emergency).
2. To avoid having utensils brushed off stove, keep all handles pointed away from front of cooking area.
3. If oven has no pilot, open oven door several minutes before lighting.
4. Keep paper towels, dishcloths, matches, or other objects which may easily catch fire well away from source of heat.
5. Dry wet foods before deep-fat frying.
6. Lower foods into hot fat using a long-handled wire basket or slotted spoon. (Remove in the same manner.)
7. Do not attempt to strain or clarify fat used in deep-fat frying until completely cool.
8. Wipe up spilled liquids or grease off floor at once and dry thoroughly.
9. Lift pot covers away from face and body to avoid a blast of steam.
10. Keep pot handles pointed away from open flame or heated burners.
11. Assume that handles of all pots and pans are hot and handle accordingly.
12. Avoid distraction and give full attention to any operation involving removal or placement of dishes or utensils in or out of a hot oven, broiler, or other heated area.
13. Use heavy potholders rather than a towel grasped between two hands (this can prove dangerous). Make certain potholders are completely dry and have no holes or worn spots.
14. Keep oven, broiler, and top of stove free of grease (both for sanitary reasons and to prevent fires).
15. Warn family members and guests when plates and service dishes are hot.
16. Use a safety stool or ladder for reaching high places—do not overreach.
17. Store heavy materials on bottom shelves.

18. When lifting heavy objects, keep back straight and lift using leg muscles—do not carry boxes or objects large enough to block view.
19. When opening or closing drawers or doors, use handles or knobs.
20. When chopping, slicing or carving, use a cutting board—do not cut against metal.
21. When using a sharp knife, cut away from body and those in the immediate area.
22. When drying knife, have sharp edge pointed away from body.
23. If a knife or sharp utensil slips and falls, move out of the way and do not attempt to catch it.
24. Do not leave knives in places where they can't be seen easily—such as in the sink covered with water.
25. Store all knives in proper place when not in use. (Keep out of the reach of children.)
26. A sharp knife cuts easier, takes less pressure, and is less apt to slip than a dull one.
27. Read instructions carefully before attempting to operate an electric appliance with which you are not familiar.
28. Check switches of electric appliances (they should be in the off position) before plugging into outlet.
29. Keep fingers and hands away from moving parts of electric appliances. Turn to off position before attempting to make any adjustment, other than when turning to higher or lower speeds.
30. Start mixers and processors at low speed to avoid splattering and other accidents. Have bowl or container locked into position where indicated.
31. Use the proper tool with food processor and for forcing food through grinder (a wooden or metal mallet)—do not use knives or other instruments.
32. Do not tamper with toaster using a metal object such as a knife or fork *without first making certain it is unplugged.*
33. Discard all glassware and china that is chipped and cracked.
34. Use a broom and dustpan to sweep up large pieces of broken glass and china, and pick up slivers with dampened paper towels.
35. If there is a possibility that soapy water contains broken glass or china, drain first and remove carefully.

36. Read all warning labels on cleaning agents before using. (Do not combine bleach and ammonia—breathing in the fumes can be dangerous.)

APPENDIX

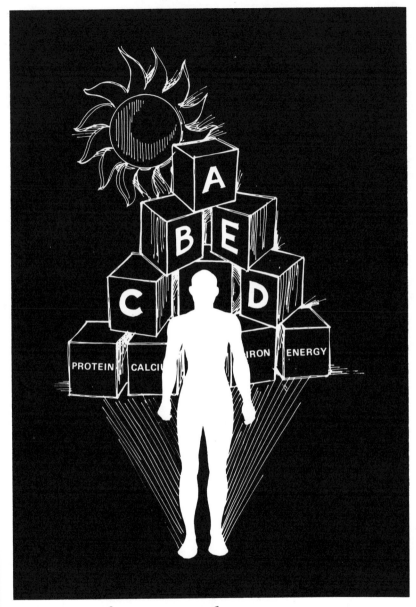

chapter fourteen

LIST OF FOODS THAT ARE IMPORTANT SOURCES OF NUTRIENTS

Vitamin A

Liver
Sweet potatoes
Carrots
Greens:
  collards
  spinach
  dandelion
  turnip
  watercress
  Swiss chard
  kale
Peas
Mango
Cantaloupe
Winter squash
Apricots
Cabbage
Brocccoli
Red peppers
Peaches
Tomatoes
Watermelon
Pumpkin
Plums

Vitamin C

Broccoli
Red and green peppers
Greens:
  collards
  kale
  turnip
  watercress
  mustard
  spinach
Brussels sprouts
Strawberries
Oranges
Peaches
Grapefruit
Cantaloupe
Papaya
Mango
Caulifower
Tangerines
Tomatoes
Raspberries
Cabbage
Lemons
Asparagus
Okra
Peas
Sweet potatoes
Turnips
Honeydew melon
Watermelon
Potatoes
Blackberries
Pineapple
Liver

Thiamin

Sunflower seeds
Pork
Nuts:
  cashews
  filberts
  peanuts
  almonds
  walnuts
  brazil nuts
  pecans
Kidneys (beef, hog, lamb)
Soybeans
Whole grains
Dried beans
Dried peas
Bacon

Lamb
Liver
Heart
Pork sausage
Dried limas
Crab
Lobster
Peas
Asparagus
Greens
Okra
Oranges
Pineapple
Potatoes

Riboflavin

Cheese
Milk
Buttermilk
Yogurt
Beef kidney
Liver
Heart
Almonds
Lamb

Pork
Veal
Whole grains
Beef
Turkey (dark meat)
Broccoli
Greens
Avocado
Oysters

Niacin

Peanuts
Liver
Chicken or turkey
  (light and dark meat)
Veal
Tuna
Lamb
Beef kidney

Beef
Heart (beef)
Halibut
Mackerel
Shad
Sardines
Whole grains
Lobster

Pork
Swordfish
Goose
Salmon
Sunflower seeds

Crab
Dates
Dried peaches
Peas

Calcium

Cheese
Milk
Buttermilk
Yogurt
Ice cream or ice milk
Sardines (canned)
Potatoes

Whole grains
Greens:
  spinach
  kale
  collards
  turnip
  mustard
Cabbage

Iron

Liver
Kidney
Sunflower seeds
Nuts:
  walnuts
  almonds
  cashews
  peanuts
Clams
Dried lima beans
Heart
Beef
Pork
Dried white or navy beans
Veal
Dried red kidney beans
Chicken or turkey
Dried lentils
Dried soybeans
Whole grains
Dried peas
Lamb

Crab
Canned sardines
Shrimp
Lobster
Tuna
Dried peaches
Dates
Raisins
Dried apricots
Greens:
  beet greens
  Swiss chard
  mustard
  spinach
Dried prunes
Asparagus
Peas
Boysenberries
Plums
Oysters
Molasses (blackstrap)

Vitamin B$_6$

Bananas
Whole grains
Chicken
Dried legumes
Egg yolk
Most dark green
  leafy vegetables
Most fish and shellfish
Muscle meats, liver,
  and kidney

Nuts:
  peanuts
  walnuts
  filberts
  peanut butter
Potatoes
Sweet potatoes
Prunes
Raisins
Yeast

Folacin

Liver
Dark green vegetables
Dried beans
Lentils

Nuts:
  peanuts
  walnuts
  filberts

Vitamin E

Whole grains
Vegetable oils
Peanuts

Salad dressing
Margarine

Magnesium

Bananas
Whole grains
Dried beans
Milk

Most dark green
  leafy vegetables
Nuts
Peanuts and peanut butter

Vitamin B$_{12}$*

Kidney
Liver
Meat
Milk

Most cheeses
Most fish
Shellfish
Whole egg and egg yolk

Vitamin D

Egg yolk
Saltwater fish

Vitamin D milks
Liver

Phosphorus

Whole grains
Cheese
Dried beans
Eggs

Meat
Milk
Peanuts and peanut butter

Iodine

Seafood

Iodized salt

*Present in foods of animal origin only.

WEIGHT AND VOLUME EQUIVALENTS

Common Units of Weight

1 gram	=	0.035 ounces
1 kilogram	=	2.21 pounds
1 ounce	=	28.35 grams
1 pound	=	453.59 grams

Common Units of Volume

1 bushel	=	4 pecks
1 peck	=	8 quarts
1 gallon	=	4 quarts
1 quart	=	2 pints
	=	946.4 milliliters
1 pint	=	2 cups
1 cup	=	16 tablespoons
	=	2 gills
	=	8 fluid ounces
	=	236.6 milliliters
1 tablespoon	=	3 teaspoons
	=	½ fluid ounce
	=	14.8 milliliters
1 teaspoon	=	4.9 milliliters
1 liter	=	1000 milliliters
	=	1.06 quarts

SCOOP SIZES

Number	Measure
30	2 tablespoons
24	2⅔ tablespoons
20	3 tablespoons
16	4 tablespoons
12	5 tablespoons
10	6 tablespoons
6	10 tablespoons

GUIDE FOR BAKING AT HIGH ALTITUDES

Adjustment	3,000 Feet	5,000 Feet	7,000 Feet
Decrease amount of baking powder: for each teaspoon reduce by	⅛ tsp.	⅛ to ¼ tsp.	¼ tsp.
Increase amount of liquid: for each cup add	1 to 2 tbsp.	2 to 4 tbsp.	3 to 4 tbsp.
Decrease amount of sugar: for each ½ cup reduce by	—	0 to 1 tbsp.	1 to 2 tbsp.

INDEX